TEACHING WORKING CLASS

TEACHING WORKING CLASS

EDITED BY
SHERRY LEE LINKON

UNIVERSITY OF MASSACHUSETTS PRESS

AMHERST

Copyright © 1999 by
The University of Massachusetts Press
All rights reserved
Printed in the United States of America
LC 98-32258
ISBN 1-55849-187-2(cloth); 188-0(pbk.)
Designed by Milenda Nan Ok Lee
Printed and bound by BookCrafters, Inc.
Library of Congress Cataloging-in-Publication Data
Linkon, Sherry Lee, 1959–
Teaching working class / edited by Sherry Lee Linkon.
p.   cm.
Includes bibliographical references and index.
ISBN 1-55849-187-2 (cloth : alk. paper). — ISBN 1-55849-188-0
(pbk. : alk. paper)
1. Working class — Education (Higher) — United States.
2. Multicultural education — United States.   I. Title.
LC5051.L494   1999
378.1'9826'23 — dc21   98-32258
                                                            CIP

British Library Cataloguing in Publication data are available.

This book is published with the support and cooperation of
the University of Massachusetts Boston.

This book is dedicated to Constance Coiner and to our students.

CONTENTS

Contents

Contents

ACKNOWLEDGMENTS

This book has been influenced by many people, starting with my working-class students at Metropolitan State College of Denver and Youngstown State University. They have taught me important lessons about education and about myself, and I am grateful for their energy and spirit. Constance Coiner inspired many teachers and students, myself among them, and although I will always be sorry that I did not have the opportunity to know her better, I also appreciate our conversations and her work, as well as her commitment to good teaching and working-class studies. In June 1995, at the second Youngstown working-class studies conference, I talked with many teachers of working-class students, most memorably Gerri McNenny. Those conversations convinced me that I should become involved in the Center for Working-Class Studies, and I am grateful for the unintentional persuasion of those who attended that conference.

Since then, I have been taught and encouraged by many friends and colleagues. My colleagues at the Center for Working-Class Studies — John Russo, Susan Russo, Beverly Gray, Linda Strom, Brian Corbin, and Donna DeBlasio — have encouraged me through their own commitment to working-class studies. Janet Zandy and Ira Shor encouraged me to organize this book and offered helpful suggestions on the initial proposal. The contributors were reliably friendly, cooperative, and supportive. Their good work made this book possible, and I have learned much from them. Karen Ford provided editing help as well as humor. My friends and family supplied distractions and support — intangible but essential elements of editing. Linda Adler-Kassner and John Russo listened to my complaints but kept reminding me to trust myself and not take myself too seriously. Frank and Roscoe made sure I went out to play regularly. My thanks to all.

TEACHING WORKING CLASS

INTRODUCTION:
TEACHING WORKING CLASS
SHERRY LEE LINKON

I have been teaching working-class students for most of my career, but it is only in the past few years that I have really considered how class might affect my students' lives or their educations, much less how class might affect me as a teacher. Race and gender were subjects of regular discussion with colleagues, but class rarely came up. And when I finally decided to look more closely at class issues in education, the materials I found were both helpful and frustrating. Most of the writing on working-class pedagogy took the form of autobiography, as working-class academics told their own eloquent, sometimes wrenching stories of feeling like outsiders when they first arrived at college and, after they completed Ph.D.'s, remaining outside of both the academy and their homes.[1] These stories were moving, and they offered some valuable lessons. As I read, I began to understand better why my working-class students might not resist grades that the middle-class students I had taught elsewhere would have challenged vociferously. I understood why they sometimes simply refused to discuss an especially obtuse text. I became more conscious of my students' use of language, and I was more understanding of requests for extensions on papers because someone's work shift had been changed or a car had broken down. Nonetheless, I found all this autobiography frustrating. Yes, the experiences of working-class academics are important and instructive, but what about the students? What about my students?

The majority of working-class students are not interested in becoming academics, and though they may share a cultural background with academics of working-class origin, they also differ in some important ways. Youngstown State University students are, I think, typical of many working-class students. Most of the "scholarship boys" — to use Richard Hoggart's familiar phrase for the bright kids who get opportunities to "improve" themselves through academic scholarships[2] — from this area go somewhere away from Youngstown, to the larger, better-known state schools or the private colleges that dot the Ohio and Pennsylvania state maps. My students come to college because, for some in this economically depressed town, there is nothing better to do or because they want to somehow improve their lives; and Youngstown State University is where they go because it is close and affordable. College is supposed to help them get the elusive and only vaguely imagined "better job." But they are often uninterested in what they find here, and though they are generally cheerful and willing, and I have been consistently impressed with how hard they work, many value the diploma more than any of the actual content of their education. They go on to become retail managers, high school teachers, and police officers, jobs that take them just a small step up the imaginary social class ladder from where their auto-worker fathers and clerical-staff mothers have been. My goal as a teacher is to engage them, to push them, to help them become more critical, committed readers, writers, thinkers, and actors. Understanding the experiences of working-class academics was a good starting place to help me learn how to do this well, but it wasn't quite enough. I was looking for ideas about methods and materials that would work best to engage and challenge my students; I wanted more concrete, practical information.

Working-class pedagogy is not just about the students. The title *Teaching Working Class* is meant to suggest a double sense of class as a subject: both a subject position and a subject for study. Studying class is not new, but working-class studies is experiencing a renewal. One sign of this renewal has been the successful series of conferences on working-class studies at Youngstown State University, starting in 1992 with a conference on the 1930s and now continuing every two years. The university's Center for Working-Class Studies (of which I am a founding member) is developing courses, community outreach programs, and an international network of scholars, teachers, artists, and activists whose work focuses on working-class culture. Youngstown State University is the only university in the country to institutionalize this kind of class-focused effort, but we are not the only people who are taking working-class culture seriously.

In spite of the growing interest in working-class studies, the principles of inclusion and recognition that have been so important in creating spaces for gender studies, black studies, queer studies, and ethnic studies in colleges and universities have not generally been extended to class. But if it is valuable for women to study women writers as a source of critical self-understanding, why wouldn't it be valuable for working-class people to read working-class writing? And if including black studies in the curriculum is important as a way of resisting racism, why wouldn't including working-class studies be valued as a way of resisting classism? Bringing class into the classroom is an important step both to benefit our working-class students and to expand our institutions' recognition of diversity. My interest in and commitment to these two categories — working-class students and working-class studies — led to the preparation of this book. *Teaching Working Class* examines both kinds of working-class subjects — the people and the culture, the students and the content of the course.

A significant portion of college and university instructors teach working-class students. As Ira Shor noted in his 1980 book *Critical Teaching and Everyday Life,* the working class has been coming to college in steadily increasing numbers since the 1950s, to community colleges and state schools designed especially for them as well as to more elite institutions that have admitted more "scholarship boys" — and girls — in response to increased competition for the college-age population in the 1980s and 1990s.[3] Indeed, it is probably true today that more college students attend "working-class institutions" (schools that serve largely commuter populations, schools with students who are among the first in their families to attend college and who work at least part-time if not full-time in jobs such as retail clerk, factory laborer, or waitress; many of those students have spouses and children) than attend "regular" colleges. Even in elite schools, more students seem to be working more hours in order to be able to afford to go to college, and so-called nontraditional students are becoming more common. Such students may not be from working-class backgrounds, but they may well share some qualities associated with working-class students. Thus, more and more college teachers have at least some working-class students.

But, as people ask me constantly, what do I mean by *working-class?* Defining this term has always been difficult in the United States, where our cultural faith in upward mobility and an idealized version of equality have led us to insist that class does not really matter here. For Hoggart and other British writers, working-class needs no definition. Carolyn Steedman can make a casual reference in her *Landscape for a Good Woman* to different British class categories ("social class III," for example)[4] without the slightest pause for explanation. In the United States our definitions have become muddled not only by ideology but also by economics. Polling data shows great disparity in terms of self-identification. The most recent data from the General Social Survey indicates that less than half (46 percent) of Americans identify themselves as middle-class (versus 45 percent who claim working-class status), but a 1992 *Christian Science Monitor* article states that 90 percent of Americans identify themselves as middle-class. Meanwhile, economists base their portraits of the class structure on income, defining the working class as those with incomes below fifteen thousand dollars, whereas other analysts base their definitions of the working class on whether one's income is wage-based or salary-based.[5]

Reading the scholarship on class offers no more conclusive definition, but it does clarify the issues involved. Economic structure, individual status, and discursive practices related to work and class all contribute to the meaning of working-class in our culture. The easiest definition of working-class is derived from the basic Marxist division between those who own the means of production and those who own only their bodies, who must sell their labor to support themselves. But this is complicated by a long-standing division between those whose labor is productive and those who work in service or managerial positions. A Weberian model of status based on a combination of education, occupation, and income would lead us to factor in the fairly high wages garnered by blue-collar workers since the 1950s, which have enabled them to buy homes, new cars, and all the consumer goods associated with a middle-class lifestyle. This model clarifies why so many Americans consider themselves middle-class, but its emphasis on individual status does not account effectively for class consciousness nor for the power relations inherent in class hierarchies. Discursive theories suggest the importance of images of class, suggesting that the language and images available in the culture construct people's experiences of and attitudes about class as much as (if not more so than) their work or lifestyle; yet this approach pays insufficient attention to economic structure, the production process, and other elements of material experience. Elements of all three of these theories are useful in understanding class, but their differences also highlight how difficult a task it is to define working-class clearly and concretely.

I am not convinced that it is necessary to settle on one fixed definition. Rather, I think we need to be aware of all three basic approaches and consider how they fit together. The division between owners and workers is a useful starting place, but the difference between the working class and the middle class — who also sell their labor and are often not in positions of power within the workplace — lies in the nature of the job as well as in some lifestyle elements. The working class has jobs, not careers. Their work is not geared to moving up through the ranks or to a model of progression. They tend to be paid hourly wages rather than a salary, and they do work that, for the most part, is left at the workplace when they leave at the end of the day. They have little power in their workplaces: someone else decides on their work schedules, determines production quotas and changes in procedures, handles long-term planning and development. They may have opportunities to make suggestions, but in most cases their work is directed by someone else who makes the decisions. Traditionally — though this is changing — working-class jobs do not require college education, though they may require some form of special training. Such work is not highly valued in the culture, even though it is essential to the day-to-day functioning of most of the society. The working class and its work are either denigrated or deliberately made invisible.

But the working class is not at all monolithic. Class is also a matter of local culture, for example. What it means to be working-class is different in different places. In some places, as in Youngstown, a central industry created a working class with a strong sense of shared history, but it also reinforced ethnic and racial divisions within the working class, since jobs within the steel mills were clearly divided along these lines. Rural working-class life differs markedly from urban, industrial working-class life. The working class in New York City may be very multicultural, including many immigrants and people of color, but the working class of rural Minnesota is almost exclusively white, Northern European, and Protestant. Indeed, what it means to be working-class differs according to a number of other factors, including race, gender, sexuality, age, and so on.

Yet, even with all these differences, the basic circumstances of the working class — the lack of power, the economic vulnerability, the level of education — form the groundwork for some basic attitudes and experiences that strongly influence our working-class students. A number of educators have sketched their versions of this profile, drawing on their own experiences as working-class academics and as teachers of working-class students. Larry Smith collaborated with his students at Firelands College, a branch of Bowling Green State University, to create a list of "general values of working-class culture," including direct, functional communication that is full of stories and humor, strong commitment to family and the sacrifice of the individual to the needs of the family or the community, a belief in fairness and cooperation, and respect for hard work.[6] Ira Shor similarly describes working-class students as hardworking and fair-minded. His description also highlights their combination of resistance to authority, their desire for and belief in respect, and their sometimes sentimental belief in "social harmony" and justice. He notes with appreciation their "seriousness" and their lack of arrogance — "They don't act spoiled," he writes. "When they want to learn, they learn *fast*."[7] He expresses admiration for their persistence and their positive attitudes in the face of a culture that doesn't value them, doesn't recognize their language or skills, and doesn't always offer them real opportunities.

They are not, Shor acknowledges, always well prepared in the traditional academic sense; they may have "weak literacy, low bases of information, and unevolved conceptual skills."[8] Part of the difficulty some working-class students have with traditional academic work stems from the relative quality of their high school education, which suffers from poorly funded schools, tracking of working-class students into nonacademic course work, or family and local cultures that do not emphasize traditional academic achievement. Yet, what seems on the surface to be simply lack of academic preparedness or even, in some educators' eyes, low ability, is rooted in working-class culture. Some of the most useful writing about working-class students identifies patterns of difference between working-class culture and the styles of communication and thinking developed in working-class communities, on the one hand, and the middle-class culture, on which most higher education has been based, on the other. Irvin Peckham draws on the work of British sociolinguist Basil Bernstein to explain some of the most important challenges facing working-class students and their teachers. Citing Bernstein's analysis of the working-class family as "position-oriented," Peckham suggests that working-class students are likely to be less comfortable than their middle-class peers with academic discourse, questioning authority, or independent critical thinking. The difference is not one of academic preparation or ability but of culture. As Peckham notes, "the authoritarian environment of the working-class students discourages them from questioning," and "because of the infrequent dialectical discourse in the home, working-class students do not learn how to qualify and substantiate assertions."[9] Although these patterns may not apply to all working-class students, the arguments that working-class students are likely not to fit comfortably in traditional college classrooms and that faculty may mistakenly read students' difficulties as "signs of stupidity"[10] suggest the importance of developing both awareness of working-class culture and an effective working-class pedagogy.

The more we can recognize and understand working-class culture, the more clearly we can recognize the strengths of our working-class students and, more important, the better our chances of engaging and inspiring them. Smith offers a useful, though rather sketchy, list of recommendations for "reaching and welcoming" working-class students, a list that emphasizes not how we should change working-class students so they will better fit into our schools and our classes but how we should adjust our behavior as teachers. First, we must identify working-class students, and I would add that it is not enough merely to tag certain students as working-class. We must also recognize differences within the working class. A student who commutes from an outlying farm on an old motorcycle is different from the one who appears for an eight o'clock class having just finished an overnight shift in the auto plant. We cannot identify these students by asking them, since they may not define themselves as working-class or be willing to claim that identity publicly even if they embrace it privately. To fully identify our working-class students, we must listen to them. Make time for stories in class, find ways to encourage people who may doubt the value of a rambling class discussion to join in, find out where they work and how they live.

I often begin a course with an individual questionnaire, asking about students' jobs and their work schedules, along with the usual questions about their major or why they are taking the course. This helps me understand their individual situations, and several times it has helped me identify students whose workplace expertise can be helpful in class. In a course on technology, for example, I have almost always had at least one student who works in the local GM plant, where the introduction of robotics contributed to the loss of almost 8000 jobs. These students have valuable insights into the course materials that I don't have, and their experience helps everyone in the class learn. They can tell us firsthand what it is like to work in a plant with robots, and their comments on the dilemma of balancing increased productivity against job losses include personal experiences as well as abstract ideas. As this example shows, recognizing the individual as well as being aware of the general characteristics of working-class students allows us to complete the stages of Smith's recommendations: including working-class students in college life, engaging their experiences and abilities in the classroom, and, perhaps most important of all, learning from them.[11] Many of the essays in this book offer lessons from the students; stories of how they respond when we begin to listen and insights gained from respectful, attentive classroom experiences.

As the essays here suggest, one of the most useful of Smith's recommendations is that we should include working-class students in college life. One central way of accomplishing that is by teaching about social class, especially about working-class culture. The easiest way to teach about social class is to include students' experiences in the classroom. Several writers here recommend the use of autobiography, positional responses to readings, family histories, and other personal work. Yet, this may not be enough to bring the working class into the college classroom, for one very simple reason: most students don't (or won't) identify themselves as working-class. They do not even have a clear idea of what working-class means, and much less have they any positive feeling about the category. We cannot assume that our students will respond if we begin by labeling them as working-class. Just as we need to learn to recognize working-class culture, our students need to learn about it, too.

I learned the value of this in a recent American studies course titled "Class and Work in American Identity." When I asked students at the beginning of the term to identify their own class status, some said they did not know, but most listed themselves as middle-class. When we began discussing the various class categories, their definitions of working-class focused on negatives: poverty, lack of education and intelligence, struggle, and low status. Working-class, it seemed, represented all the things one would want not to be. We then spent significant time discussing the various models of social stratification, ideas about status and power, and the way work influenced cultural patterns (including education, divisions of labor, where and how people lived, ideas about identity, and so on). We read the autobiographical essays by working-class cultural workers in Janet Zandy's *Liberating Memory*, poetry about industrial work in Nicholas Coles and Peter Oresick's anthology *Working Classics*, and a novel about a society divided very sharply into classes according to work (and the lack of work), Kurt Vonnegut's *Player Piano*.[12] Students also wrote family work histories and essays about their own work experiences. Within just a few weeks, as we were discussing the essays in *Liberating Memory* and students were starting their family histories, I began to hear phrases like "My family is working-class" and "I used to think I was middle-class, but now I think maybe I'm working-class." It was, I believe, the combination of creating space for their own stories and introducing them to other stories and to ideas about class that made it possible for them to view working-class culture not as something to hide or reject but as something that, as Zandy suggests in her introduction to *Liberating Memory*, is "an ambiguous gift," a "[tool] to shape culture."[13]

It's important to note that this increased understanding of working-class culture is valuable not only for working-class students but for all students. Americans have always been confused about class, unsure how to define class divisions in a society that values the ideals of upward mobility and equality, where we pride ourselves on being different from — and presumably better and fairer than — the class-oriented Europeans. For Americans, race, gender, and ethnicity appear to have had more significance in determining our social history and our cultural identities. The histories of slavery and civil rights have been read as significant only in terms of race, while the women's movement and changes in the family have been seen as issues of gender. But as many scholars have argued, most recently Gerda Lerner in "Rethinking the Paradigm," class, race, gender, ethnicity, and other hierarchical categories of identity form an interlocking system of oppression, each reinforcing the other.[14] If we are to understand our culture, we must understand all of these elements and the ways they work together. Yet class is the part of that system that has received the least focused attention in the United States, especially in the past two decades as attention has been fixed on race and gender. Class is often mentioned — in American Studies circles, especially, it has been invoked in a sort of academic mantra: "race, class, and gender" — but focused study of the working class has only recently begun to gain prominence and respect. Working-class literature is being published and reprinted, and critical attention to it has expanded significantly in the past decade. Studies in composition and communication have given class new attention, and although scores of readers focusing on issues of race, gender, and ethnicity have long been available, Benjamin DeMott's 1996 collection, *Created Equal,* is the first and only reader to focus on class. Tom Zaniello's book *Working Stiffs* has helped us become aware of working-class representations in film, while George Lipsitz's work in *Time Passages* and *A Rainbow at Midnight* highlights the role of class in other areas of popular culture. Labor history has long focused its attention on working-class people through examinations of the history of unions and work, but recent scholarship has expanded to include much more than the history of organized labor; and it has, along with scholarship in literature and popular culture, placed new emphasis on the way class intersects with race and gender.[15]

Clearly, working-class studies as a field has much to offer our students, regardless of their class backgrounds. And in a period when class stability seems less reliable, when downsizing, part-time employment, independent contracting, and regular career shifts define the landscape of the work world, understanding how class and work affect individual identity and social patterns is important for all of us. One of the goals of education is to give people tools and insights to help them make choices. Understanding class can help individuals recognize their own position within society and, perhaps, give them tools with which to act in and on society.

That vision of education as a tool for social change permeates this book. It can be seen most easily in the repeated invocation of the work of Paulo Freire, whose critique of the "banking model" of education and recommendations for a liberatory pedagogy are cited by nearly every contributor to this collection. Three aspects of Freire's work form the foundation of working-class pedagogy. First, Freire's belief that education can be transformative, personally and politically, inspires many of us to approach the work of education as a form of activism. Teaching is not, as Shor cautions us, sufficient in itself to change society, but the classroom can be a site of cultural challenge through which social change can begin.[16] Second, Freire suggests the importance of a pedagogical model that does not position the teacher as sole authority but rather sees students' interests and culture as the most important focus of study and as a starting place for the learning process. This paradigm is in itself liberatory, because it upsets the existing cultural hierarchies that reinforce oppression for both teachers and students. Yet, it also suggests a pedagogy that makes possible not only social change but also effective learning and the development of critical literacy skills for individual students. The final element of Freire's work, perhaps the most important one, is that he offers a clear, usable model for implementing liberatory pedagogy. That is, his work provides not simply a rationale for critical teaching but also specific ideas about how to do it. In this combination, he emphasizes the link between politics and action, the desire for change and taking steps to create it.

Closely tied with the theme of education as politically and socially powerful is a strong link between issues of class and other aspects of multiculturalism. Many of the essays here explicitly examine how ideas about class as well as students' working-class identities intersect with issues of race, ethnicity, and gender, as well as with place, age, and other issues of difference.[17] Several argue that awareness of class, especially of our students' working-class backgrounds, provides an opportunity to generate productive discussions of race and gender differences. Adding class to discussions of cultural diversity can help students recognize how complex identity and difference are, and several of the authors here suggest that class can also create a bridge for students (both white and black) who might otherwise see race as an uncrossable barrier. Still others, however, remind us that we must not expect too much; class is a useful, powerful concept in discussions of difference, but it is not a panacea.

One reason is that students and teachers alike enter the classroom from somewhere else, with a positionality based not only on class but also on race, gender, sexuality, personal history, political affiliation, and so on. The essays in this volume remind us that we must, as teachers, fully recognize that positionality in all its complexity. Working-class students bring a wide variety of specific influences with them, as Joseph Heathcott's description of his class's mix of urban and rural working class and Caroline Pari's discussion of the difference between her African immigrant students and the African Americans in her class highlight in different ways. The teacher's identity also matters, as Anthony Esposito suggests in discussing his role as a white working-class teacher at a historically black college and as Terry Easton and Jennifer Lutzenberger note in their examination of their experiences teaching working-class literature. Who we are and who our students are make a difference.

These essays come from several fields that have recently given considerable attention to class and critical analysis of pedagogy: composition, communication, literature, film, labor studies, and history. I have chosen quite deliberately to include pieces from a range of fields, because I want to emphasize that discussion of class should not be segregated, occurring only in special courses. Working-class students show up in all kinds of courses, and the curriculum should include them everywhere on campus. In addition, the fields represented here overlap and connect in many ways, especially as the academy moves to embrace more interdisciplinary approaches to scholarship and teaching. It's not surprising to find novels identified as useful texts by teachers of history and writing, or to find that a teacher of speech communication suggests that film and music provide good opportunities for practicing analysis. Regardless of the discipline in which the ideas originate, the strategies and suggestions here will be helpful for teachers in many departments.

Most of these essays discuss teaching in fairly typical college classrooms —

classrooms located on the campus of a state college or, in a few cases, a large research institution—but two essays deal with classrooms that are located away from the main campus, in union halls. Robert Bruno and Lisa Jordan describe their multimedia, interactive theatrical production *Illinois Labor Works,* which they have used as an educational tool in training union members. Kelly Belanger, Linda Strom, and John Russo discuss their experiences teaching college courses to union members at a United Steelworkers local. Both essays emphasize active learning and alternative ways of presenting information that invite students to see themselves in the subject matter and to get involved. Although most college teachers do not encounter their students in the union hall, we have much to learn from these nontraditional examples.

The essays are divided roughly between those that emphasize working-class students and those that focus on teaching about class, but the division is not absolute. Most of the essays in the first section suggest the value of class as a concept in engaging working-class students; those in the second half generally assume that any given course will include at least some working-class students. Moreover, both sections emphasize the importance of class as a concept and of working-class experience as a source of knowledge and identity. Thus, Ann E. Green and Eileen Ferretti both emphasize the benefit but also the challenge of asking working-class students to write autobiographically, a point echoed by Colette Hyman and Charles Johanningsmeier in their discussions of assignments drawing on students' and students' families' experiences in courses about the working class and immigrant history. Similarly, while several essays in the first section call for greater awareness of and attention to working-class culture as a way of meeting the needs of working-class students, in the second section Robert Bruno and Lisa Jordan, Laura Hapke, and Terry Easton and Jennifer Lutzenberger also suggest ways of doing this effectively. The two sides thus mirror each other, with the working class as the subject as well as the object of attention.

Not surprisingly, given Freire's powerful influence on so many of the contributors to this collection, the essays here move beyond arguments that we *should* develop effective methods for teaching working-class students or that we *should* teach about class to offering specific, practical ideas for doing so. *Teaching Working Class* emphasizes practical classroom application. The authors suggest useful texts for working-class studies courses, including literature, films, music, and historical documents. They offer strategies for course design, for interactions with students, and for evaluating students' work. They recount both successes and failures, inviting us to think critically about how well our best-laid plans play out. In this practical emphasis, they make an eloquent case for the value and possibility of teaching working class.

WORKING-CLASS
STUDENTS

WRITING THE PERSONAL:

NARRATIVE, SOCIAL CLASS, AND FEMINIST PEDAGOGY

ANN E. GREEN

It is August and I am home with my parents and sisters two years after graduating from Sarah Lawrence, just before starting an M.A. program at Penn State. We are sitting around an old yellow table in a cabin (no running water, bare electric light bulbs) that we rent by a lake a mile from our house. We don't go on vacations far way because my father hates to leave the farm, and we don't have time. We've just eaten salty, vinegary barbecued chicken (the sauce is called Reuben's receipt) and corn on the cob with our hands. We drink Budweiser from cans. My current boyfriend, Harvard-educated, Jewish, from New York City, is eating with us. We are talking about talking. We tell stories. The boyfriend watches and listens. My mother says, "Annie, Mrs. Davis is always talking about how articulate you are . . . how well you speak. You always sound like a Sarah Lawrence girl." One of my sisters says, "But, God, Ann, sometimes you can sound really country." And I reply, "Well, shit. What the hell is that supposed to mean? That I ain't had no fetching up?" We laugh. I wonder what it means that I sound like a Sarah Lawrence girl. I wonder what it means that I deliberately use dialect, fall into local grammar mistakes, when I am home.

This is a story about teaching and a story about learning. It is also a story about how to teach working-class students, about how to theorize a pedagogy that "reaches" those who have been excluded from the academy and from the language of academic discourse. What I suggest in this essay are the ways in which narratives, autobiographical stories, and lived experiences as constructed in writing can empower students in literature or writing classrooms and how theorizing those experiences through experimental writing and "diverse discourse" provides new ways of learning that can critique the dominant culture and teach students about the links between oppressions.

But I have to problematize the notion that teaching working-class students is different from teaching other kinds of students. Since class is not — necessarily — a visible marker on the bodies of the students when we teach, how does one know, initially, who among our students is working-class and who is not? And if we are teaching at "places of privilege," exclusive or expensive private colleges, class can become even further masked, further muted under the "right" clothes and the "right" attitude. If, as Janet Zandy writes in *Liberating Memory: Our Work and Our Working-Class Consciousness,*[1] working-class studies is majority studies, not minority studies, how does one define the kind of student who comes from a working-class background? It does not seem as important or necessary to me to define a working-class pedagogy as to acknowledge the erasure of class from most North American pedagogies and to try, with good faith, to teach with all the complexity and reflexiveness that we can muster, to hope that our teaching methods work against multiple and intersecting oppressions and reach as many students as possible.

It is also important to consider what we hope to achieve by this counter-hegemonic teaching endeavor. Do we want our working-class students to become bourgeois? Do we want our "bourgeois" students to drop out of school and experience a less privileged life? As Nancy Mack and James Thomas Zebroski write, "Is it to help working-class students transcend their world or to transform it? Do we simply want them to move on up into the academic world and then into the business world?"[2] In attempting to articulate a pedagogy of the working-class, we must consider the danger of reinscribing the same classes and categories that ultimately undermine a liberatory, critical-thinking, revolutionary pedagogy. In her essay "Confronting Class in the Classroom," bell hooks describes empowerment for teachers from working-class backgrounds and what happens when "those of us in the academy from working-class backgrounds . . . recognize our own agency, our capacity to be active participants in the pedagogical process . . . embrac[ing] a vision of wholeness of being that does not reinforce the capitalist version that suggests that one must always give something up to gain another."[3] This seems like my biggest challenge and responsibility in the classroom: to insist that "wholeness is possible," that it is possible for working-class students or African American students or Latina students to maintain connections with their home cultures and languages while still learning the skills that will bring them success in the academic world. As a teacher from a "working-class background," for me, wholeness means the ability to perform a feminist pedagogy that critiques classism and racism and sexism and homophobia and accounts for class, race, gender, and sexual preference, without denying either me or the students subject positions, without reducing or losing anyone's multiple and varied subjectivities.

Incorporating narratives into more "traditional" forms of writing has helped me think differently about the practices that my classroom replicates in its relationship to the dominant culture. These teaching practices have helped some of the students, part of the time; but sometimes teaching in this way leaves me unsure about what effect these teaching strategies are having or whether they are having any impact at all. Dorothy Allison writes that "class, race, sexuality, gender — and all the other categories by which we categorize and dismiss each other — need to be excavated from the inside," and this is a strategy that begins to do just that.[4] Maybe, maybe, this pedagogy is most useful in empowering students from marginalized groups, but it is sometimes useful for "mainstream" and "privileged" students as well. On the local level, in my classrooms at Penn State or the State University of New York at Albany or Skidmore, sometimes the approaches that are the most "liberating" or "critical" are most easily embraced by students who have enough confidence in their own positions in the world to grapple with the unknown and not fear for their own success in the academy — sometimes these students are "marginal" and sometimes they are not. What I hope is that this pedagogy will begin to change the academy in the same ways that open admissions changed the field of composition, that academics from various class backgrounds will be able to shift the kinds of languages that are used in the academy, and that "diverse discourse" will transform student writing. At the moment I am interested in smaller, perhaps attainable goals, which will begin transforming some small part of the university. This "diverse discourse" creates room for multivoiced responses and different kinds of language.[5] I first used it in a course called "Introduction to Women Writers" at the State University of New York at Albany.

My own experience of learning to write at an expensive, exclusive, private school of mostly white women was contradictory. I was learning to use two very different voices in my writing — an academic voice and a fiction-writing voice — and eventually neither voice could be as close to the "working-class voice" that I valued, the voice that connected me to home and home language, as I wanted it to be. The first literature class that I took was a Renaissance literature course. We read obscure Renaissance poetry and plays, and I had read only Shakespeare in high school. The kinds of sentence-level errors I made in writing papers and the lack of experience that I had with closely reading literature were detrimental, but the worst part was that I felt incompetent in the reading of this work from another place and time. I did not have ways of connecting with the text. I couldn't call home and talk about what I was reading or writing. I couldn't explain *The Faerie Queen* as an allegory about Queen Elizabeth to people who would have no frame of reference for such a text.

At the same time I was writing about home in "Freshman Studies in Fiction Writing." When I came back after the first semester, I showed my family the story that I wrote about my grandmother's death the year before, and everyone cried. That kept me going, kept me in school, and kept me in conversation with the community that I had come from. The creative writing connected me to home, to place, so that I did not feel as though I was completely abandoning my place and my people for this new language of symbol and metaphor and metaphysical conceit.

The memories that I wrote about began to tell multiple stories. Not only were they a way to keep me connected to the people that I was leaving behind, but they were also a way to create new communities through the stories told. It was, in a way, never as much about "my" experiences as it was about "our" experiences, our place, however troubled that was. Janet Zandy describes this connection to home in *Liberating Memory*. She characterizes home as a place of other knowledges for working-class people, a place outside the traditional educational establishment. She writes that the consciousness developed from these home places is "not just about family lore. It is a larger inheritance. These are historic, not narcissistic memories. That is why they are dangerous. They insist that reality is not merely a text."[6] The more I teach, and the more diverse the students are when I teach, the more I need to remind myself of that: reality is not a text.

When I teach, I attempt to differentiate between (in hooks's words) "a shallow emphasis on coming to voice, which wrongly suggests there can be some democratization of voice wherein everyone's words will be given equal time and be seen as equally valuable . . . and the more complex recognition of the uniqueness of each voice and a willingness to create spaces in the classroom where all voices can be heard because all students are free to speak, knowing their presence will be recognized and valued."[7] But what does it mean to recognize and value each voice? In a course on gender, does it mean that I, explicitly or implicitly, devalue male voices? In a course that focuses on representations of race from the nineteenth century to the present, do I value the African American voices over the white or do I appropriate the African Americans' voices to fit my agenda? And where is class in this classroom? As a teacher, I have become less and less concerned about issues of "nurturing" different voices; students who take my classes should understand that they will not always be "comfortable" in my classroom, that if we are to deal with difficult issues, sometimes we will all be uncomfortable. In other words, my classroom is not group therapy; there are specific functions for the personal, for the writing of "experience."

In designing "Introduction to Women Writers," I tried to create assignments that moved away from standard, audience-less, literary critical analysis papers. Since I wanted to focus on issues of marginalization, it made sense that students should be able to have more control over their texts than general analysis or report-writing assignments give. The first assignment was supposed to be in the form of a letter to me, because I hoped that a sense of audience would produce what I vaguely called "some engagement with the texts." Instead, the papers that came in were standard literary critical comparison-contrast papers, with "Dear Ann" at the top. Despite the fact that the assignment sheet asked "how your own inscription in a particular culture, race, class, and gender affects your reading of these texts," the papers did not engage this issue.

Since the first paper assignment had failed, I decided we would try some more explicit, personal, autobiographical writing, to encourage the use of an "I," or some kind of personal voice, in their next papers. The idea to include the personal in their next writing assignments came from reflecting on my own experience of the "literature" class as opposed to the creative writing class. Perhaps explicit personal writing, or what Hephzibah Roskelly calls "the story as a tool for teaching," would facilitate greater engagement with the texts and give us space to talk about race and class as well as gender.[8] During an in-class writing assignment, we wrote about experiences of being "othered." I hoped this autobiographical writing would get students thinking about "otherness" and oppression in their own lives and help them to understand the relationships between oppressions by writing about their experiences. For these students and for me, then, experience became an important category of analysis, an important place from which to theorize. It is, as Elspeth Stuckey writes, important to "remember who we really are. We are not just private individuals in whose private minds the printed word works powerful deeds. We are, to be sure, natural individuals, but we are social before we are born, and the commerce we do with literacy is always, fundamentally, social."[9] Writing about the personal reminds us that texts are social constructs, as we ourselves are. We are not disembodied minds encountering texts, but different people composed of differing experiences and different, sometimes contradictory, positionings. This assignment was a reminder that reality is not a text.

One woman wrote about the experience of immigrating from Nigeria to the United States and her first encounter with U.S. racism. She performed her free writing in front of the class. This is an excerpt from that text:

> Somebody called me a "nigger" today.
> NIGGER!
> Mama said it's cause o' the color of my skin
>   and the place I was born
> Somebody called me a "nigger" today.
> NIGGER!
> I didn't even know what to say,
> Mama say just hold your head up high
> Somebody called me a "nigger" today.
> NIGGER!

Jessica was one of two African American women in this small class, and her performance of this text surprised, encouraged, and shocked the rest of the class and me. I had not seen this level of engagement — with writing or with the texts — before, and it was hard to know how to respond without either reinscribing racism or essentializing Jessica's experience. We sat in silence for a few seconds afterward, considering what Jessica had written. At this point the class dynamic changed; writing about the personal gave the class a new way to talk to each other, connections with one another that were missing before.[10] Others wrote about being a white minority in an inner-city school or of experiencing blatant sexism. No one, not surprisingly given the erasure of class in this culture, wrote directly about an experience of alienation that highlighted class. I wondered how to incorporate these autobiographical texts into more "formal" writings, how to move beyond the personal into more analytic and critical engagement with texts, and how to interrogate the personal and complicate experience through expanding our definition of academic discourse. My next question was how to deal with the absence of class from their texts. Was this a problem of course design? The students? The assignment?

For the next paper, I asked the class to incorporate their autobiographical writings into their papers: to use their experiences of alienation to read a text. I was deliberately vague about what I meant about this "diverse discourse," writing that crosses boundaries and allows both writer and text more complexity, partly because I did not know what the outcome would look like.[11] I suggested a kind of dialogue between their experiences and the experiences of some of the characters in the stories. Students played with language, moving between the stories and experiences through page breaks, columns, and different type faces, and encountered a new way of argument. The papers looked different and were more interesting to me than others I had seen; the papers did take on issues of race, class, and gender, and students were interested in writing them. Students' writing in these papers was fragmented and engaged, as opposed to writing that simply fulfills an assignment. It seemed to me that this writing truly was "writing to learn" rather than writing as a performance for a teacher. The personal, for many of the students, was enabling, and moving back and forth between the personal and the analytic created space for experimentation, for new ways of seeing. Students expanded on their personal experiences and found ways of comparing them with other texts that revealed connections and junctures, as well as fissures and gaps. Many women in the class wrote about how aspects of their lives were both similar and dissimilar to what Dorothy Allison describes in her short story "Mama," from the collection *Trash:* "I do not enjoy being one step away. One step away from the labels of physical abuse and molestation, one step away from becoming a victim to all like him [her stepfather] that I will come across in life, hiding in excuses that I have made for myself. . . . I do not enjoy being one step away. — Melissa."[12]

Many of the students used Michelle Cliff's "If I Could Write This in Fire, I Would Write This in Fire" as a model and grappled with the issues of intersecting oppressions — race and class and gender — in their pieces, as Cliff does.[13] Jessica combined bell hooks, Dorothy Allison, and her own writing in a exploration of speech and silence that included class and race.

> To speak then when one was not spoken to was a courageous act — an act of risk and daring. And yet it was hard not to speak. mama says push it down. don't show it. don't tell anybody what is really going on[. . . .] and yet it was hard not to speak . . . voices . . . heated . . . at the crack of dawn . . . language so rich, so poetic, that it felt to me like being shut off from life smothered to death if no one were allowed to participate.
>
> And so I write. — Jessica

But although many of the students seemed happy with the assignment, at least one student was not happy; he expressed his anger. As a postscript to Dan's paper written in "diverse discourse," I received this response:

> Ann — I just want to take this opportunity to express my grievance about this project. First off, I think it was highly insensitive that you assigned something that a MAN in the class was very limited in choosing. While all the woman had a great deal of stories to choose from, I was limited to one, TWO tops, and they weren't even applicable. . . . Don't get me wrong, I am not the ideal student, but I do think that you could have been more sensitive to the fact that a MALE would have a harder time relating to one of the stories. Look the paper is done, and I will accept whatever you give me, but whatever it is, I have the knowledge that at least this class does not reflect my capability, and under a fair system I would have been able to prove that. — Dan.

The alternative ground rules for communication that produced Dan's anger came from an assignment that was designed to allow students more freedom in their creation of texts, not less. Why then Dan's anger? What about this assignment alienated him from his own work, and what did social class have to do with this project? The assignment created an "unfair system" where Dan was unable to perform up to his ability. When Dan said, "I was limited to one, TWO [stories] tops, and they weren't even applicable," what exactly did he mean? Yes, most of the women writers that we had read had written female protagonists, but why couldn't Dan "relate" to them? Certainly experiences of alienation, while not equivalent, could be discussed in the same texts and problematized. I asked Dan why he could not "relate" to a story with a female protagonist. (Later, he told me that he now understood what it must be like to experience patriarchy from a woman's perspective, to have your experience be "othered.") The two stories that Dan did feel he could work with both featured black male protagonists. Could this be what Dan meant when he said that they "weren't even applicable"? Was gender an insurmountable barrier and race almost insurmountable (except when it was assigned)?

Dan wrote about social class in relation to the black protagonist, Edwards, from Alice Dunbar Nelson's story "Hope Deferred." The other character that "didn't even apply" was the black, male, working-class protagonist of Ann Petry's story "Winding Sheet," who, after a frustrating day on the job, comes home to beat his wife. Dan could "relate" to protagonists, characters, across racial lines through social class, but not across gender lines; he could write himself (or a version of himself) into a story only if he could "relate" to it. He connected with Edwards through social class because they were both outside of mainstream, "middle class" culture. Dan described his attempts to fit in through buying the "right" clothes, by attempting to mask his class of origin, and compared this with Edwards's struggle to achieve a middle-class life. Although the struggles were different, the character Edwards was locked out of the middle class through both his race and his class; Dan did not oversimplify or essentialize the similarities and differences as some of his classmates did.

In a very unusual move for most of the undergraduates that I have taught, Dan identified himself as working-class. He described being called "the best dressed white trash in school" and wrote about his and Edwards's struggles, similarly difficult, toward the American dream. Dan wrote,

> I always looked at my father's store as being beneath me, and I guess in essence I thought I was better than my dad. I always looked at other people'[s] cars, houses, yards etc. as being better than my own and I dreamed of the day when I can go away to college and leave my house for a better life. . . .
>
> In the story, I see myself and Edwards as kinda going through the same

things. When Edwards has to lower his standards and go to work as a waiter because no one wants to hire a black engineer, I see that as how the RICHIES would not accept me because I didn't have money.

Dan's class position is complicated because he is not traditionally working-class. His father owns a store, but Dan is the first in his family to attend college. He worked at Ben & Jerry's part-time to obtain the clothes that would help him to "pass" as upper-middle-class. The paper also incorporated poetic, nonlinear sections into its narrative. As I read and reread the paper, I am struck by its deeply personal content, by how much it reveals about Dan. In one of the poetic sections, Dan wrote:

> It's kinda funny
> A little crazy
> You're looking at your life'
> Like some book you would read on the train'
> To pass the time away

Was the experience of looking at his own life like a text part of what alienated Dan? Was it making reality into a text? Was the writing too personal? I cannot know for certain what produced Dan's anger, but what I know is that it is complicated by Dan's class background. Was this anger in part because he had to consider his class background? Does it mean that the assignment was effective for Dan or not? Maybe the assignment did work for him — maybe good teaching is painful, and maybe the results are not always immediate.

In spite of some of the successes of Dan's paper, one of the problems with many of the papers was that students felt that they could only "relate" to characters whose stories and positions were roughly similar to their own. Women wrote about female characters and experience, white women wrote about white women, and black women wrote about black women and white women. The tendency was to write about the text that was closest to one's own version of experience. For a certain portion of the class, "relating" to a text meant looking for an experience that matches yours, that "relates" to your own. But despite these goals, what happened in part was a reduction of experience, an essentializing event that did not complicate experience. Or was it? Could the essentializing experience be a necessary first step that leads to greater levels of analysis?

The greatest anger that I experienced in learning to write happened while working on a short story called "Learning." It was an attempt to bring to life the story of working-class, boring, monotonous work and to write down some of the conversations that I had when I worked alongside people who were not upwardly mobile, who were chained, at fourteen or sixteen or eighteen, to a life of poverty or subsistence or, if they were able and capable, a career in the military. These were people whom I would never know again — whether I knew that or not. The story was fragmented by having lots of voices — some sad, some comic — and by the lack of plot or unity, and I was very happy with it. The narrator's voice was not consistent, but I did not think it should be. In "Deciding to Live," Dorothy Allison writes about what it means to escape, the survivor's feelings of guilt, of being undeserving; for me, writing that story was like a prayer, a way to silence the guilt I felt about switching classes and leaving people whom I loved, whom I love, behind.[14] I left that class with a sense of purpose and the knowledge that my "working-class" and feminist subjectivities were valued.

Then I entered a fiction-writing course taught by a fairly well-known woman writer. She wanted a writing sample. I handed in what I thought was a completed story, "Learning," with the intention of moving on to different projects. Instead I received the story back with comments asking me to revise the story in a more traditional shape, with fewer characters and a more unified narrative voice. When I tried to speak with the professor to convey my distress — the story from my perspective was done; I did not want to revise it anymore — she insisted that a writer must persevere, work through blocks, and revise. From her perspective, she was teaching me how important it is to struggle with one's creative work; I had no objection to working hard, but I did have serious problems with her comments, which I thought flattened the multiplicity of voices and the sense of the working-class people that I wanted to convey. I spent a semester avoiding conferences with her and revising "Learning" half-heartedly, in an attempt to appease her so she would let me move on to something else.

In the revisions, the narrative voice began to resemble the more typical, self-reflexive voice from middle-class fiction. I was being constructed like one of the students that Linda Brodkey describes in " 'The Literacy Letters' "; both Joan and I lost "the opportunity to question the extent to which class figures in any individual's rendering of a unified self."[15] The story became less a story about the shared experiences of menial and degrading work, and more a story about one person's escape from poverty. The narrator began describing herself as separate from the people she worked with, knowing the language of the "working class" but being clearly separate from (and clearly above and distant from) those constructs. In the revision of "Learning," the narrator appropriates the thoughts of one of the other characters to describe herself as "one of those stuck up bitches, one of those girls who thought that they were better than everyone else because they were going to college. One of those girls who didn't get trashed in the middle of a field and sleep with . . . [the boys] on a Saturday night." What changed was what Zandy calls the "sensibility of community," which she defines as "more than just being connected to a community—however immediate or distant—we are also in conversation with that community."[16] It was what working-class woman writer Valerie Miner describes: "In contrast to more voguish literary obsessions with isolated relationships, working-class novels rarely situate characters alone. More likely, characters are portrayed in the workplace, in union meetings, in neighborhoods."[17] That "sensibility of community" was lost between the drafts, but something else was lost, too, the "voice" that bridged the gap and the loss between education and the people I come from, the voice that had language and words for crossing class lines. I felt tremendous anger about what was lost through that teacher, anger that felt similar to Dan's anger toward me, Dan's rage at being forced to write about what he was not ready to write about.

Elizabeth Ellsworth suggests that "because all voices within the classroom are not and cannot carry equal legitimacy, safety and power in dialogue at this historical moment, there are times when the inequalities must be named and addressed by constructing alternative ground rules for communication."[18] Alternative strategies for communication like "diverse discourse" broaden students' notions of "appropriate" or "academic" forms of discourse, and these writings can assist in the process of changing what are defined as acceptable kinds of writing in the academy. Since in the academy we learn to "think, write, and talk in a manner that shifts attention away from personal experience," the return to and theorization of the personal through stories and narratives can be an important way for people from traditionally underrepresented groups to maintain connections with the places they come from.[19] These strategies may be useful for working-class students because they allow students—if they decide to do so—to write in their "home" language. They may write versions of their experiences in classrooms, and those experiences can be a less alienating way to learn, a way to bridge the gaps between home culture and school culture.

As conscious as I try to be about what I'm doing in the classroom, I'm sure there are ways that my experiences of learning to write and my experiences with students like Dan have changed the way I teach, have pushed me in new directions. I keep returning, then, to Brodkey's conclusion of " 'The Literacy Letters' " and wondering if teaching "diverse discourse" and "stories" is a kind of "resistance . . . a practice in cooperative articulation on the part of students and teachers who actively seek to construct and understand the differences as well as similarities between their respective subject positions" and a way to incorporate social class into one's pedagogy.[20] I want to talk about—and do talk about—social class in the classroom, so I teach Dorothy Allison and bell hooks and essays like "To Have and Have Not: Notes on the Progress of the American Class War."[21] But often this is not enough; often one needs new strategies to address issues like social class in the classroom.

This is what I would do differently now, to try to get at more layers of subjectivities, to try not to teach "reductively," and to more actively engage students in issues of social class. I would work from a model that Madeleine R. Grumet uses in her educational research, from her essay "The Politics of Personal Knowledge." She writes about the gradual acceptance of narrative, of the personal, in educational research and criticism, but for her the crucial element of the work is that it does not privilege one story but works with many stories. She writes, "Most important . . . is the relation of multiplicity to interpretations. When there is one story, it becomes the story, my story, and when it is delivered to another, it arrives gift wrapped in transference."[22] Multiple stories, having both the students and me relate multiple kinds of experiences in relationship to the stories we are reading—and having multiple interpretations of those stories—might act against a totalizing narrative or "regime of truth," successfully complicating our notions of experience and our ways of "relating" to texts and to each other. Having students tell and write different kinds of personal narratives so that there are multiple ways of reading those texts, of problematizing "experience," would prevent a reduction of experience to "the experience" and would give students like Dan the opportunity to think about social class, race, and gender without having to focus exclusively on one aspect of his identity. If there are places for multiple stories, there will be more space to question the different ways we tell stories to different audiences, different ways of remembering that "reality is not a text."

I tried this strategy recently in an upper-level writing course. The assignment came from Gregory Jay's "Taking Multiculturalism Personally: Ethnos and Ethos in the Classroom." I asked students to write a "cultural identity" essay instead of standard, nonfiction autobiographical essay. A cultural identity essay, as Jay assigns it, asks students to consider their inscription in culture and to negotiate between the social and the individual or personal. This assignment was designed to complicate the telling of an individual story so that the story cannot be essentialized, reified, or stand for an individualistic, humanistic subject. Instead, it encouraged students to move "beyond identity politics" and to consider how the various groups that they belong to (class, race, gender, religion, sexual preference, and so forth) affect their identity.[23] It was an attempt to make whiteness, as well as social class, visible constructs. Certain students (white, straight, middle-class, often male) had to consider, for the first time, what groups they belonged to and why they had never before thought of themselves as belonging to any group. They often wrote about why they had no cultural identity at all, or questioned the necessity of defining oneself according to a group, or criticized the assignment as divisive.[24]

In beginning this assignment, I had students write three in-class narratives in response to three prompts: Have you ever had an experience of being "othered"? Have you ever acted in a way that "others" someone else? Describe a time when you participated in an event that made you feel proud of a group that you belong to. I did not read the writings unless I was asked to. Students used these narratives as points of entry into the cultural-identity essay. These strategies made it more possible for students to see that identity is complex, multiple, and dependent on language. It also made it possible for students to see links between different kinds of events and to decide which events would be important in cultural identity. In other words, no one event necessarily had to appear in the cultural identity piece, and in fact, none of the three events was required to appear. When I teach diverse discourse again in a literature class, I will use this same strategy of multiple stories to complicate students' ideas about identity and to allow students greater freedom in selecting the event they share with the class. I hope these strategies offer ways of "creating conversations" and inventing new ways of talking to one another, ways that bridge the categories that so often divide us.

BORDER CROSSINGS:

WORKING-CLASS ENCOUNTERS
IN HIGHER EDUCATION

RICHARD A. GREENWALD AND
ELIZABETH A. GRANT

NAMING THE PROBLEM

As working-class academics, we play a critical role in the halls of higher education. We freely cross between two seemingly opposite, perhaps opposed, worlds: the "educated" world of middle-class academic life, and the "real" world of our working-class background. Functioning within these two spheres is at times confusing and conflicting. Imagine the challenge that surviving in the academic world poses for our working-class students!

Author and socialist art critic John Berger comments on the challenge of this "alien" psychology in his acclaimed novel, *A Painter of Our Time*. The protagonist, a working-class artist, achieves well-deserved praise and acclaim from the intelligentsia in London for his paintings. In spite of it, and in spite of the fact that in his heart he knows the acclaim is justified, he cannot walk in their world feeling worthy: he feels they are of a higher class than he, and he is unable to shake off the leg-irons of his Polish factory-working background. In like manner, the contributors to *Strangers in Paradise* tell of feeling both blessed and cursed by this duality. Feeling elation for having "made it" but, at the same time, despair for not truly "fitting in."[1]

As working-class academics, we, too, exist between the borders of both worlds, feeling fully at home in neither. However, we can learn to serve as a bridge between the two for ourselves, our families, and our colleagues, but especially for our students. As the feminist movement has taught us, *the personal is the political;* therefore, the problems that we, as working-class academics, have faced and continue to face have political impact in our classrooms. Perhaps because we are afraid of talking about our "alien" status, or because there is no forum for such discussion, we let it persist. Because of our silence we are unwitting coconspirators in the classism of higher education, perpetuating the "alien" status for our working-class students.

Nevertheless, generations of working-class students have successfully entered the halls of the academy, have managed to meet and overcome the overt challenges of higher education, have graduated, and have joined the professional ranks of white-collar workers. Yet, in their overt success, they have not conquered the more internal and formidable challenge of establishing a solid feeling of self-worth. Like the painter in Berger's novel, and like James, the third-year student in *The Hidden Injuries of Class,* working-class college students and graduates are caught between two worlds. They function well enough in the outer, professional world but suffer to some degree in their inner, personal worlds.

What can we, as working-class academics, do — not only to ease the transition for our students, but also to help transform academic institutions so that they reflect awareness of the challenges higher education poses for working-class students? Let us begin to explore answers to this question by acknowledging some working-class commonalities:

Many working-class people are socially conditioned to react to authority. This reaction, on the surface, often appears as respect. What stops it short of respect is the deep skepticism about the justice of authority.

Some working people harbor cynicism toward social institutions, for those institutions do things to, rather than for, them; there is "disrespect" for work that does not produce concrete material results (such as a motor or a cake), hence scorn for intellectual activities.[2]

Many working-class people believe that middle- and upper-class people are no better than they are but have the freedom to pretend to be better because they have money: the real "bottom line" is that even the queen of England has to go to the bathroom. There is also skepticism about the worth of other working-class people who are different.

For many there is a faith that personal connections, moral or immoral, are valid means to an end. The belief that the end is more important than the means is common, and anyone who does not acknowledge this is considered to be full of bullshit.

This essay will seek to explore the discourse surrounding the commonalities between working-class academics and working-class students on a playing field that neither created but both help to shape. By initiating this long-overdue discourse among our colleagues and within our classrooms about class in the academy, we can facilitate new ways to move the academy to become more accessible to working-class students. We further believe with bell hooks that "the classroom remains the most radical space of possibility in the academy."[3] In addition, this essay seeks to affirm and act upon the wisdom of the late Paulo Freire, who asserted simply that education is always political. By rejecting with Freire "The Banking Concept of Education," which is so ubiquitous in Western culture and which insists that our students come to us as empty vessels ready to be filled with our wisdom, we recognize the educational situation as a partnership and understand our own roles as facilitating ones.[4] We must learn to learn from our students, as well as to teach them. But most of all, we must learn who we are and why that matters.

DO WE REALLY BELONG?

Greenwald recalls one student telling him: "I don't belong here." One day early in the fall semester of 1995, a struggling first-year student walked into my office and uttered those words. My reaction was to instantly visualize my grade book and frantically try to put a name, grade, and face together. But the student had not come to talk about her grade in American history. Her statement was aimed at college itself. When I realized that, I froze.

This is a telling simile for the confrontation that takes place when a working-class person enters the classically staid and orderly, conceptually neat, and entirely artificial world of academia. As the student sat down and began to talk, I flashed back to a similar scene at a not-too-dissimilar college a few years before. But in the flashback, I was the student. This was the first time I realized just how similar my students are to me. Somehow I had thought that I was the only one who had had those nagging doubts about whether I truly belonged at college.

Working-class students recognize early on how socially unprepared they are for college. But it is only if they go on and enter the world as middle-class professionals that they realize, as we have, how unprepared college is for them.

Grant reflects: As an undergraduate at a state college in the Snow Belt, I was a "townie," and this was never a positive experience. Not only were I and other townies excluded from on-campus events and "the dorm experience," but campus policies and professorial attitudes revealed extreme ignorance of and insensitivity to working-class life realities.

I lived at home two miles from campus. There was no bus system, and having a car was financially out of the question, so walking was the only way to get to classes.[5] Schedules were simply assigned to first-year students, and my first fall semester I had six eight-o'clock classes and a two-mile walk to get to them. Oswego is well-known for its winters: heavy snows from November through March with snowless "breaks" of frigid temperatures.

Strict campus policy was that female students had to wear dresses or skirts. Pants or slacks were not allowed to be worn on campus when classes were in session. I walked two miles to campus six days a week, wearing stockings held up by a garter belt, under knee-length skirts. I never had a new pair of boots, but wore boots donated to the family by an aunt who lived in North Bergen, New Jersey. Sometimes they fit. Sometimes they kept my feet warm.

I recall one Friday morning in early December 1965 when I arrived at my "Intermediate French 1" class, where I always sat in the first row. My feet were so cold, I could not feel them. The boots were wet and tight. I had to take them off and did. The professor, who had no tolerance for people "without class," ordered me to put the boots back on, to get out of the room, and not to return until I could behave like a "civilized" person. Humiliated, I did as he ordered.

Greenwald recalls a conversation with Bill, one of his advisees, thirty-two years after Grant's humiliation: This student, a rural working-class farm boy, rose before sunrise every morning to gather the eggs, to put out feed for the sheep, and to clean out the stalls — to shovel shit. He then drove fifteen miles to campus. Time was a luxury.

In my office one day, Bill recounted his own experience involving footwear and professorial ignorance; it had occurred that morning. In the past, Bill had arrived to his eight-o'clock classes just in the nick of time. To avoid being late on that particular Friday morning, he hadn't stopped to change his boots. When he rushed into the lecture hall, the professor paused to note his smelly presence by holding his fingers to his nose and grimacing — much to the delight of the rest of the class, who broke out in raucous laughter. Bill slunk into his seat red-faced. Unlike Grant, who had felt humiliated, Bill's gender conditioning prompted an immediate angry reaction. Knowing that he could not beat up his professor and remain in college, he waited till the end of class and immediately rushed into my office to vent.

Both of these episodes, separated by thirty-two years, demonstrate lack of compassion for and ignorance of the material realities of working-class students. A professor might know enough not to "poke fun" at the urban poor, but too often the rural poor are handy targets. Academics might acknowledge class as a category of analysis, but too few recognize it as a human reality. As working-class scholars, we need to force our colleagues to see and to understand the entire student/person — not just a disconnected head. Today's colleges are as unprepared for working-class students as they were just after World War II when the GI Bill flooded the universities with a new student demographic. The institutions seemed to see working-class students as only a temporary population.

The generation of GIs who went to college were special. They had survived two of the most trying crises of our century; therefore they were deserving of a break to achieve the American Dream. The college boom of the 1950s transformed higher education forever. More students meant more money. Once colleges started down that road, they were reluctant to return to more austere times. Most did not rethink their missions, much less their pedagogies, in relation to their rapidly changing student body. By 1960 many universities followed the model of the "multiversity," as laid out by University of California president Clark Kerr: students were the raw materials; colleges, the factories; and the faculty, the managers. Graduates were simply cranked out.

And they continue to be cranked out because the institutions in which we toil are trapped in a model that simply no longer works. In addition, the nature of "work" itself has changed, requiring different skills and a "new worker" to carry them out. Kerr's philosophy functions to promote a "corporate" citizenry rather than a thinking, informed citizenry. One of the reasons for this is the absence of any serious discussion of class within the academy.

RECOGNIZING CLASS: THE NEED FOR COLLECTIVE AUTOBIOGRAPHIES

We teach American literature and American history, respectively, at a small residential college of agriculture and technology in rural central New York that is part of the sixty-four-campus State University of New York. More than half the student body have incomes at or below federal and state poverty levels. Fifty-one percent are first-generation college students. About 45 percent of that group come from urban areas and another 45 percent from rural areas. The overwhelming majority of our students are working-class.

What does this mean when they arrive on campus and in our classrooms? What are their expectations? What are ours? Most likely, the students' only college experience before the start of their first semester consists of a visit to the campus in the spring and orientation in the fall — if they are lucky. They arrive bewildered and somewhat frightened. The urban students are frightened because our rural environment is alien to them, and the rural students are frightened of these strangely behaving city people who probably all carry knives and who will try to get them to smoke crack.[6] What complicates the situation is the unfathomable administrative "must dos": must have this person sign this and that person sign that, then take the blue page to this office and the pink one to that, and don't try going to class without the gold sheet, and if another student disses you, well punch 'em (for males), or shout loudly (for females), or go back to the farm and tell your father that all his warnings about college are true.

Working-class students see themselves as completely alone. One way to break the cycle of alienation and isolation is for working-class academics like us to de-cloak. If our students knew that "people just like them" exist in places like this, we could better serve as role models and mentors for them. We need to incite a dialogue with students. One way of doing this is through collective autobiography. We need to incorporate our students' stories into the college, affirming the lives of working-class students and making them part of the college experience. This process has already started for working-class academics. And though that is necessary, it is only the first step. We need to empower our students to become part of the classroom. Their individual histories need to be incorporated into the larger oral tradition of the classroom. It is when we integrate our stories with those of our students that we can come to some understanding of the process of higher education. Our experiences with students illustrate this.

Like many working-class students, we attended the local campuses of public universities, the only available option. Both were near our homes. It was a "natural" assumption that if you graduated from the kinds of high schools that we did, that's where you would go. In Greenwald's case, those who could afford to attended the private Catholic Saint John's University. Those who could not went to the local branch of the City University of New York, Queen's College. In Grant's case, those who could afford to likewise went to a private university, Syracuse University, and those that could not went to the State University of New York College at Oswego.

The only advice Greenwald's father gave him was to go into accounting, because "they make good money." Good money was anything that was not blue-collar like him. Greenwald recalls: My father worked as a splicer for the local telephone company. My parents had struggled hard to put me into private Catholic schools because they were seen as one notch above the public schools. That led me to believe that I was "middle-class."

My skills were not good, as is true of many working-class urban students. I spent hours writing papers on subjects that engaged me, only to be told my writing "sucked." Michael Wreszin, professor of history at Queens College, wrote on one of my papers, "Richard, one would think that English wasn't your primary language." He then walked me back to his office to offer me a dog-eared copy of Strunk and White's *Elements of Style*.

A few other understanding instructors also went the extra distance. They became mentors. They were usually politically committed to public education for the working class; some were socialists like Michael Harrington — then teaching at Queens. Those teachers put in extra time and convinced me that not only was I smart enough, but I had something to say — a mind-set my parents had not conveyed to me.

Grant's experiences were both similar and different. Besides the urban-rural distinction, her skills were superior. She had been a good student throughout high school and had served as editor of the high school newspaper; the required freshman composition course had been waived when she started college. She recalls: My father, like Greenwald's, acknowledged none of my college efforts. He made no comment when I received my B.A. in 1969. When I moved to Idaho and earned my M.A. in 1973, I may as well have been in a hospital for the criminally insane. In 1983, when I began doctoral work, all he understood was that somehow I was still alive and managing to pay the bills. Unlike Greenwald's father, who on the other hand constantly wondered why his son would go into a profession which paid so little for so much effort, my father wondered why I had not taken his advice: "Become an airline stewardess and marry a rich man, Ann." Then when I got too old to do that: "Get a job for the state, bend over to pick up a pencil, claim your back is injured, and get on disability for life." In his working-class worldview, I was an embarrassing failure: a well-educated daughter who paid my own bills.

Greenwald reflects on the similarities: my father continually suggested that I take every civil service exam offered by the city, so I sat through sanitation exams, answered police questions — questions and a life direction that did not fit what I wanted to do at all. Our students convey a similar tension between the expectations of their parents and their own — even if their own are not yet clear. They talk about how hard it is to "go back home." In today's economy, working-class parents and guardians recognize the importance of college — even if they do not quite understand it. And although college is encouraged, the world of college is not. This means that working-class students lack basic knowledge of curriculum and career choices. Many of us wind up in majors the same way we wound up in a particular college — by chance. That is no way to run a rational higher education system. As working-class academics we need to be more in touch with our students. We also need to advise the whole student. This means knowing them as people. How many of us are deeply involved in helping students enter the workforce? How many of us work on students' interview skills and help them prepare résumés?

Greenwald recalls: I wound up a history major simply because the faculty in the history department at Queens College recognized me as a human being and engaged my mind in ways that were unknown to me. Grant experienced the same thing with the English department at the State University of New York,

Oswego: These were some of the most caring, intellectual, and passionate people I had yet encountered. These caring teachers convinced us that we could become one of them. Once we were in graduate school, they continued to help us with letters of reference and occasional editorial comments on papers or creative projects, but mostly with the reaffirmation that we were worthy. We need to continue that tradition and enlarge it.

Graduate school was a strange experience for Greenwald: I was one of only a handful of working-class students in my program. Everyone appeared to be more confident and better prepared than I was. I continued to live in the outer boroughs. My class standing translated into a feeling of intellectual inferiority. I remember distinctly one night after a seminar in modern European working-class history that a group of grad students went out for dinner and drinks. I remember thinking, as I eyed the unfamiliar menu, that if I ate dinner, I would be broke for the rest of the week. But I also knew that I had to be there to be a graduate student. This was true, I learned afterward, for every student in that group. But we never talked about it. As I went through the program, there emerged a group of working-class students, who tended to be somewhat older, students who had started in the program before I entered. Those students, with real life experiences, provided a sense of community and reality that I needed.

Greenwald has begun to learn how to build community with his working-class students: One of my students, Carlos, recently expressed his alienation this way: "This place is so unforgiving." What he meant was merely that colleges do not forgive those who do not learn the rules or, moreover, those who have not learned them before their arrival to campus. As a first-semester student, Carlos's class schedule included a nine-to-noon chemistry lab on Fridays. At home Carlos had had high school classes that also began at nine, but aware of the "bullshit" of homeroom and the slow pace of his first class, Carlos often strolled in after ten. Yet he still passed the class. This habit did not wash well with his chemistry professor, who expected students to be in the lab and commencing to work promptly at nine. The professor mentioned to Carlos a few times that he needed to arrive at nine, but Carlos didn't take the comments seriously. He was shocked and outraged at the end of the semester to learn that he had received an F. No one had taught Carlos, or thousands like him across the country, what the expectations of college really are. These rules are understood well by middle-class students, but in communities where life exchanges function by different guidelines, working-class students may have to be taught the new rules. And who better to teach them than working-class academics?

The stereotypical professor is still white, male, middle-aged, and a person who believes that being a "professor" means that one professes; the result is lecture-based classes where students are filled up with the teacher's wisdom and experience the subject material only from his point of view. Periodically, the students "vomit" back, in exams and in papers, exactly what they learned. They are not open to new experiences and new students.

Such professors look at students as truly empty vessels (as Freire teaches us). It is sad that so little progress has been made by now, so many years after these discussions started. Maybe we could point to great changes in elite private colleges or large state university centers, but at many smaller state colleges and especially at community colleges, innovative pedagogy is the exception. Class discussions are not usually considered innovative pedagogy, but discussion can provide a forum for collective autobiographies in our classrooms. Besides class discussions, other kinds of classroom methodologies can facilitate the creation of academic communities. We need to do this for working-class students.

In her classes, Grant uses integrative strategies that invite students to take responsibility for their learning and which involve them in the class's academic decision making: For example, in my "American Literature II" class, in lieu of a final exam, the students and I discussed a full class enactment that might pull together the thematic threads they had been examining all semester. After careful discussions, they settled on a mock trial: The People vs. Ezra Pound and T. S. Eliot. These two modern poets were charged with (1) disorderly conduct (i.e., nontraditional poetics and confusing themes), (2) promoting immorality, and (3) fostering irreligious attitudes. The topics are not important here; the process is everything. The class divided itself into three factions, the prosecution, the defense, and the jury, judge, and bailiff. (Our American literature textbook served as the Bible.)

The preparation for the trial took two one-hour-and-fifteen-minute class periods, and the trial itself took a class period and a half. Students on the two teams prepared by immersing themselves in the work of the author they would portray when they were called to the stand, and the jury prepared by testing each author against each charge. The student body of the class was overwhelmingly working-class, and the students' participation in this enactment challenged them to engage the material in ways they had not been asked to do before. By turning the classroom dynamics around, I was able to turn students on to poetry.

For example, Nina Lopez, the daughter of a sanitation worker and a waitress in Yonkers, New York, "played" Upton Sinclair for the prosecution and presented a valid argument that helped to indict Ezra Pound and T. S. Eliot, who were found guilty by a unanimous jury decision. Nina commented after the class that she knew she would always remember not only the work of Upton Sinclair, but all the authors we examined (and cross-examined), and more importantly, she understood their literary efforts in an American context, which now seemed accessible to her. It is clear to me that Nina would not have felt this way if I had approached this subject in the traditional manner.

I was taking a chance by stepping away from the lectern to empower my students to participate actively in the goals of the class. Students who expected to sit passively and take notes (or fall asleep) in this American literature class are often uneasy when asked to play a role in the course. Greenwald's students experience a similar uneasiness in his "American History II" class: In my American history from 1865 course, I use primary source material (in addition to traditional texts). In the fall 1996 semester I assigned a paper and class discussion on the decision to drop the atomic bomb in 1945. After reading secondary sources, providing profiles of the players involved and other background information, I assigned a series of primary documents — most of them recently declassified. The students were to play the role of presidential advisors, writing a "position paper" to the president based on the evidence on hand.

To make this more interesting and realistic, I did not give all the students the same documents. At first the students complained about the workload. But after a few days, they got into it. During one class, after a student had presented her paper to the class, another student presented hers. The second student, using much different evidence, came to a different conclusion. After about forty minutes of discussion, another student, Ben, asked me why I had given only part of the evidence to some students. This led to a discussion on how historians work and what is "enough" evidence. I could have lectured about this or assigned readings. But by taking the risks, they experienced history rather than simply reading it.

What these experiences teach us is that we need to be flexible and creative, but most of all we need to trust our students. When they arrive in our classrooms, they are already thinking human beings with many life experiences. Those experiences have a place in the classroom and, if drawn out with mentoring care, can enrich the academic experience for both them and us.

Academic involvement in classrooms in these ways is vital for working-class students because it gives them a place in the academy. In addition, they are able to participate in meaningful activities that offer them concrete outcomes. Furthermore, their stories, although shared and added to in small pieces in enactments and class projects like the two described above, find a home in our classrooms, hence assuring the students a place at the table. For ourselves, the working-class teachers, collective autobiography breaks down the walls of alienation and self-doubt and is the first step toward building true communities within higher education. We can develop a fuller discourse on American culture.

WHAT IS TO BE DONE?

As academics, we pretend that we have enormous freedoms and choices. We delude ourselves that we choose the type of colleges we teach at; we choose our disciplines and how we approach them; we choose academic research projects; we choose the courses we teach; we choose text materials; we choose how we present a course; we choose how we evaluate students; and we choose to advocate or not to advocate on students' behalf. The reality is that we do not really have that much control of events outside the classroom. Therefore, to be true to ourselves and to be good mentors and educators, we need to be activists on campus to gain some of this control. As advocates, we need to be hyper-vigilant of our students' needs and our students' legitimacy. This might involve the following kinds of considerations:

the cost of books and tuition, including "hidden" fees; scheduling of classes

flexibility in testing situations; accessibility of campus facilities (e.g., bookstore and library hours)

availability of faculty for advising

faculty involvement in extracurricular activities

knowing who our students are and being sensitive to their realities

approaching each learning situation as a new experience with new strategies

inviting students to participate in academic discussions and decisions

holding formal and informal discussions with faculty, staff, and administrators about working-class student needs and realities

In conclusion, most centrally, we need to think about how colleges function in the economies of our nation. How do colleges treat those who work for them? How can we bring students to the recognition that collective identity can be empowering? Taking considerations like these seriously means becoming activists as well as intellectuals.

REVERSALS OF FORTUNE:

DOWNWARD MOBILITY AND THE WRITING OF NONTRADITIONAL STUDENTS

ANNE ARONSON

Nontraditional students of all ages entering college in the late 1990s often have uneven if not volatile socioeconomic histories. For older students, it is often a change in career or income — almost always for the worse — that provokes the return to college. Some, particularly women, seek out higher education as the result of divorce, an event that usually causes a sharp drop in income. Others return to college because of layoffs or because a disability has made it impossible for them to continue at a job. Others are simply stagnating in their jobs; a bachelor's degree might lead to a promotion, their only hope for maintaining their standard of living. Although we typically think of younger students as having quite different work and family histories from older students, in fact nontraditional younger students have much in common with returning adults.[1] These are the students who work one or more jobs, commute to college from rented housing, have very young children, or carry some other responsibility that is the hallmark of adulthood. Like their older counterparts, their socioeconomic status is subject to the volatility of the job market, personal health, and family circumstances. Some of these younger students may also experience significant changes in class status because of the effects of the economy on their parents. Still others may feel the downward pull of entering a job market that holds only dim prospects for a prosperous future. For these students, whether young or old, upward mobility — the promise that all Americans can move up the socioeconomic ladder if they work hard enough — is not a reality. Instead, they and their parents have worked hard at one, two, or three jobs; have watched their work weeks lengthen; and have still not seen a change in income that would significantly alter their life circumstances. For many of them, downward mobility is more a reality than upward mobility is.

This essay examines how students' experiences of downward mobility affect their sense of self and their ideas about class inequality, success, and work. The students featured here attend the urban state university in the Midwest where I teach; this institution serves almost exclusively nontraditional students, most of whom have one or more jobs. Although the university has historically served older students (over the age of thirty), in the last two or three years the student population has included more nontraditional students in their twenties.

The socioeconomic paths of the students examined in this study are reflective of national and international trends. Students entering or reentering college in the mid-'90s are strongly influenced by the enormous economic changes of the '80s and early '90s. Both students who have themselves been displaced because of economic changes and those whose parents have been displaced have felt the consequences of massive corporate merging, restructuring and downsizing, the relocation of manufacturing to cheaper labor markets, the shift from higher-paying industrial to lower-paying service jobs, and the declining influence of labor unions. The statistics are impressive. For example, in an annual survey by the American Management Association, of the 1,441 large and mid-sized firms responding, 49 percent indicated that they eliminated jobs between June 1995 and June 1996. Although job loss among these companies was slower in the mid-'90s than it was in the early '90s, nearly one-third said they had a smaller workforce in 1996 than they did in 1990.[2] Downsizing has been accompanied by a sharp increase in the number of part-time jobs. Part-time work, which offers lower pay, fewer benefits, less security, and less chance for promotion than full-time work, increased 70 percent between 1974 and 1994, while the total workforce increased by only 42 percent.[3]

Another issue is the dramatic change in the economy between the post–World War II years and the years following 1973, the year of the oil cartel. Wages climbed sharply and consistently in the twenty-seven years immediately following World War II, but they stagnated between 1973 and the early '90s. Even as the economy grows in the late '90s, productivity, which is closely tied to income growth, is far below where it was in the '50s and '60s.[4] In other words, the parents and grandparents of today's students experienced a kind of prosperity in the postwar years that our students will probably never even approximate. As anthropologist Katherine Newman puts it, "On virtually all counts it was better to have reached adulthood by the early 1950s than at almost anytime afterwards."[5] In *Declining Fortunes,* Newman chronicles the economic "fall" of the baby boom generation. She uses the pseudonymous community of "Pleasanton" as the lens through which she captures the anger, frustration, and disappointment the baby boom generation experiences when they compare themselves economically with their parents. The example of one of her subjects, Mary Flory, is revealing. Flory's father was an unskilled worker who was nonetheless able to buy a home in the new suburb of Pleasanton in the 1950s. Because of increasing real estate values and declining earning power, Flory and her professional husband are now unable to buy a home in the same community. Flory says, "My father was an elevator operator all his life. My husband is a teacher. I would have thought right away of course we could afford to live in Pleasanton. We have better jobs. But we couldn't. There is no way we could live there. I really couldn't believe that I couldn't live in the town that I grew up in."[6] Flory is confused by the fact that her working-class parents were able to acquire more than the middle-class family she is now a part of. Like Newman, Jean Bethke Elshtain sees experiences like Flory's as emblematic in an economy that dislocates, downsizes, and generally diminishes workers. She says of her grandparents and other generations of immigrants, "They dreamt about . . . improving their lives and the lives of their children . . . of passing something on to their grandchildren. No more. Now you're a sucker if you believe these things, or so those calling the economic shots are, in effect, telling people, and showing them in the crassest of ways. What is rewarded now is maximum flexibility, which means, in practice, no particular commitment to a job, a skill or a place."[7]

One outcome of class mobility — whether upward or downward — is a sense of conflicting class identities. In moving from the middle class to the working class or vice versa, one may end up feeling that one belongs to two socioeconomic classes. Patricia Hill Collins calls the experience of simultaneously occupying two different locations on a spectrum of power the experience of the "outsider within."[8] As a middle-class professor on the one hand and a black woman on the other, she is both inside and outside the academic circle of power. Collins's analysis is confirmed by a sizable body of literature on the psychological consequences of upward mobility. Richard Hoggart's *The Uses of Literacy,* Richard Sennett and Jonathan Cobb's *The Hidden Injuries of Class,* and Richard Rodriguez's *Hunger of Memory,* among other works, examine how the upwardly mobile individual experiences dual and conflicting allegiances, a feeling of betrayal of the working-class family, a sense of being an impostor when assuming a middle-class identity, and a sometimes powerful insight resulting from the dual perspectives.[9] These experiences are captured most recently in *This Fine Place So Far from Home,* a collection of essays written by academics from the working class. In the section "Border States," writer after writer articulates the pleasures and perils of "outsider within" status. Nancy LaPaglia, for example, captures a sense of being trapped: "When I think of the impact of this background on my life and work, I picture someone with one foot in the working class and one foot on a ladder going up, unwilling to commit to a single, more stable stance. To do so would mean betrayal and treachery in some nebulous way."[10] Dwight Lang sees his dual class identity as a source of insight: "My self-image is, in part, that of a traveler. I have left one social structure and am now making my way within another. . . . I am a link in social time and space. I am both insider and outsider in my new and old worlds. . . . Having traveled across class lines, I am conscious of the realities and meanings of social class in America, perhaps more than others who remain in their class of origins."[11]

Although these accounts question and critique the process of upward mobility, they also assert that upward mobility is alive and well in America; in other words, these narratives of movement from the working class to the professional middle class cannot help but contribute to the perpetuation of the myth that smarts and hard work will lift a person up the ladder of success. It may not be surprising that accounts of the dual identities resulting from *downward* mobility are harder to find. The experience of the fall from the middle class is part of our literary heritage (Theodore Dreiser, William Dean Howells, Arthur Miller), but personal essays and sociological studies of downward mobility are less common as reading material in composition classes. Yet, for many of our students who have experienced job loss, disability, divorce, and other catalysts to declining fortunes, narratives of downward mobility may be far more relevant to their lives than the poignant success stories of intellectuals like Mike Rose and Richard Rodriguez.

To learn more about the class histories of students at the university where I work, I collected essays on socioeconomic class from students in an intermediate composition course taught by another instructor. This section of "Intermediate Writing" had as its theme social class.[12] The textbooks included *Created Equal: Reading and Writing about Class in America* and *Rivethead: Tales from the Assembly Line,* a book about working-class experience in Flint, Michigan.[13] Students wrote four essays during the quarter: an essay in which they developed their own hierarchy of class, an essay analyzing how class had affected their personal histories, an essay comparing several articles on the "power elite" in America, and an essay involving research on a topic related to class. My study focuses on the first two essays because they are the most explicit on the topic of class identity.

In addition to collecting essays composed by students in the course, I asked the students to complete questionnaires on their class histories and aspirations (see Appendix). One of the questions asks students to identify the socioeconomic class they consider themselves currently a part of. A follow-up question asks, "Do you think you've ever been a part of another socioeconomic class (e.g., when you were growing up, five years ago, etc.)?" Most of the students indicated that their class status had changed at some point in their lives. A few students indicated that their class status had improved. Denise, for example, grew up in a home that she considered "lower-middle class" because her mother was a struggling single parent. Denise is currently a human resources assistant, and she aspires to be a human resources manager. She now considers herself a member of the "non-struggling middle class." In a couple of cases, students had traveled widely up and down the socioeconomic ladder. Paula, for example, a fifty-year-old woman, described how she grew up in a "lower bracket" (her father was an unskilled laborer and her mother did domestic work) but married a professional athlete, greatly increasing her class status. She was divorced from him after twenty-five years, however, and now says her income "dictates that I am in the lower class."

Another group of students indicated that they were in a lower social class than they had been in previously. One student, for example, says she is currently in the "low class" but that she used to be in the middle class before her father lost his job seventeen years ago. These students tended to be cautious in asserting that their class status would improve in the future. When the survey asked students if they thought they would be in a different class in the future, one student responded, "I hope to be able to at least maintain middle class status." Another said, "I don't know. I hope so." There is a tentativeness in these responses that suggests students are less than confident about their prospects for riding the American trajectory toward success. Though a college education is usually regarded as a class booster, these students did not seem entirely certain that college would bring them the success to which they aspired.

In order to find out more about this last group of students — those I identified as downwardly mobile — I chose to look in depth at the essays and surveys of three students. Each of the three had experienced a change in socioeconomic status — in one case because of a parent's job loss, in another because of the decision not to complete college, and in the third because of the generational "declining fortune" featured in Newman's book. My reading of the essays and surveys suggests that the topic of class was an extremely challenging one for the students. They had difficulty developing and expressing coherent beliefs about what class in America is and how it affects their lives. This incoherence may be more than just a consequence of a struggle with new material and language practices. In their study of adult basic writers, Coles and Wall examine how student writing is fraught with conflicts, particularly about the ideologically charged issues of "work" and "success." They explain that these tangles may indeed be ideological in nature: "Features of a student's text that we might customarily treat as misreading or rhetorical incoherence may originate as much in ideological conflicts the writer is experiencing as in unfamiliarity with academic reading and writing."[14] Following Coles and Wall's cue, when I read the work of the students in "Intermediate Writing," I paid particular attention to places in the essays where the logic sagged or the ideas conflicted and where students attempted to avoid or resolve an apparent incoherency. I found that the most significant conflict in the students' essays was between a recognition of class inequality on the one hand and a belief in upward mobility and equal access to the American Dream on the other hand.

PATRICK

Patrick is twenty-eight years old, white, and single. He works as an administrative aide for a large school district in the metropolitan area. Although he identifies his current status as "lower middle" class, he considers that he grew up in a middle-class environment. His father is a pastor and his mother a homemaker; both of his parents have bachelor's degrees. He says of his class identity, "It is when I think of my education level that I consider myself lower middle." Patrick did not complete college, although many of his good friends did earn bachelor's and master's degrees.

In his writing, Patrick vacillates between a keen understanding of class difference and inequality and an apparent desire to repress that understanding. In his first essay he attempts to define class in two different ways: in terms of "character" and in terms of money. Overflowing with questions that never get answered, his essay is noncommittal at best. At one point he asks, "Is it beneficial to society as a whole for people to judge other people they do not know based on their own experiences, prejudices, and media exposure? These are difficult questions that do not have simple solutions. Is class something we should try to ignore? Is ignoring class distinctions as harmful to our society as overemphasizing them? If we ignore the problems of economic struggle and social situations in which the lower classes find themselves, are we better off?" His first question begins to discuss classism. No sooner has he opened up the possibility of discussing class prejudice, however, than he dismisses it as a "difficult" question and goes on to interrogate the value of "ignoring" class altogether. It's unclear from his questions whether Patrick wishes to ignore class or not, but he certainly entertains the possibility that being oblivious to class might be a good thing. In this first essay, Patrick appears to hide from issues of inequality and prejudice with respect to class by asking a series of questions that go unanswered.

His next essay — a personal narrative about class — delves much more deeply into the issues he touches upon in the first essay. In the opening section, he discusses his experience of participating in a "Big Buddies" program, which provides mentoring for children living in poverty. That experience has allowed Patrick to "empathize" with people in poverty. Though his language is at times patronizing and vague ("The experience has formed many of my thoughts on the class issue that so many of us struggle with"), he goes much further in acknowledging class inequality in this paper than in the first one: "When poverty is witnessed face-to-face, it has an effect that does not vanish by turning the page of the newspaper."

The heart of the essay, however, begins when he describes a second significant experience with class. Patrick says that some of his high school friends are making quite a bit more money than he is. One in particular — Chris — his best friend in high school — is a stockbroker who "married into a wealthy family." In recent years, Chris has requested Patrick's help in installing a dock for Chris's in-laws, a task that requires "a certain degree of muscle power." Here is Patrick's account of this yearly event:

> Each time I have been out to their house to help, they say they will invite me for a day on the water with them. When I lived in Boston I learned to sail and being a veteran of the Coast Guard, consider myself competent on a boat. Well, I have never been sailing with them and each autumn, when the weather starts turning sour for sailing, Chris asks for my assistance in removing the dock and boat lifts. I am not bitter. I think it is an interesting situation. Are our schedules to busy to figure out an agreeable date to sail? It is hard to say because I have never received a call from them or initiated a call about going sailing. Is it a class issue? Am I good enough to assist in the dirty work but not good enough to enjoy a day on the water with them? Is this a case of intentional class segregation or simply a lack of consideration? I think it is the latter. The question I ask myself is this: Do I exhibit the same type of behavior towards members of an income level below mine?

Patrick once again uses questions to explore a difficult topic. The issue he takes up this time is whether he has been used by Chris's family for the "dirty work" of installing a dock because of his lower class status. In his references to muscle power and dirty work, Patrick invokes a stereotype of the working-class male.

Although Patrick goes much further in this essay than in the first one toward asserting class inequity, it is interesting how careful he is to back away from any strong statement about the subject. Again he asks the trenchant question, "Am I good enough to assist in the dirty work but not good enough to enjoy a day on the water with them?" at the same time that he insists that he is "not bitter." He asks a crucial question when he puts the problem in terms either of class segregation or of lack of consideration: is Chris's behavior part of a widespread, institutionalized outcome of class stratification, or is it the result of one person's insensitivity? Obviously Patrick believes that the problem *might* be about classism, not personality, but he backs off this insight when he says, "I think it's the latter." And although Patrick appears to have a strong sense that the incident is about exploitation of the working class, he codes his exploration once again in questions, thereby dodging commitment to any viewpoint.

As Patrick's story of Chris and the boat dock illustrates, one of the consequences of downward mobility (or any class mobility, for that matter) is that one loses connections to people from one's past. The guy you cruised with in high school now asks you to fix his car, or vice versa. That is, of course, an exaggeration of Patrick's situation. In fact, Patrick has a good office job, what he describes as "a relatively well-paying, challenging job for a non–college graduate." But Patrick would probably be sipping drinks with Chris and his family if he had completed college and become a manager rather than an aide. Patrick's essay reflects at once a recognition of this inequity (and of his own role as a potential exploiter of those less privileged than he is) and a desire to look the other way, to label the whole thing as no more than an "interesting situation." His inclination to repress or deny the pain of class conflict is common in a nation captivated by the belief that upward mobility is available to all. The experience of downward mobility may be too bitter a pill for the American worker to swallow; perhaps it is better not to answer the hardest questions.

LISA

Lisa is twenty-three years old, white, single, and a registered nurse. She is seeking a bachelor of science degree in nursing and expects to stay in the nursing profession in the future. Her parents had very little postsecondary education: her father had one year of technical school and her mother about the same of nursing school before they "dropped out." Currently her father is a captain in the fire department and her mother is a medical transcriptionist. In her autobiographical essay, Lisa expresses her belief that her parents' hard work lifted them from the working class to the middle class: "As time passed and as a result of hard work, my father was promoted and both parents received yearly raises. As I approached high school, my parents were considered middle class. With hard work and time, they were able to upgrade their class status." Lisa points to the fact that her parents could help finance her college education and that they have a cabin in Northern Minnesota as evidence of their middle-class status. Lisa's view of class is firmly tied to income and property; although she alludes to the importance of education in determining class, she believes that her parents' increased financial resources led them to be "considered" middle class.

Lisa, however, is not sure that she is as firmly ensconced in the middle class now as she once was. She says, "As I am making the transition from my parents' life to my own life, I found that class issues arise. It is very hard to be living in the environment your parents have worked years for and thrown into a lower class status because you are just starting out in your career." Lisa identifies the generational downward mobility that is the focus of Newman's *Declining Fortune*.[15] She is not yet demoralized by the generation gap, however, because she sees herself as starting out in her career. She attributes the class difference between her parents and herself to how little time she has spent in the workforce, rather than to the generational disparity of fortunes. Yet, at the end of the paper, she concludes, "The class your parents are in may or may not determine the class you find yourself in." Lisa may not be confident that she will equal or exceed the success of her parents, even though she already has more education than they. When asked how she sees herself in the future, she says, "I think, or hope to be, a part of the same [middle] class." Despite Lisa's belief in the work ethic, upward mobility, and the reality of the American Dream, there are moments in her prose when she indicates some doubt about the dominant class ideology.

Like Patrick, Lisa recognizes class difference and inequality. She is much more explicit in discussing the unequal distribution of goods and opportunity, however. In her first essay she likens the American class system to the hierarchy of health professionals in a hospital. The four tiers differ according to type of work, amount of education, and degree of responsibility. On the one hand, Lisa seems sensitive to some of the hardship and even injustice that characterizes this system. She says of the nursing assistants that they "are found to be working many double shifts and overtime just to make it financially." On the other hand, Lisa seems to want to palliate the struggles of this group. In describing the working class a few sentences later, she says: "Although these people are very important to society, they are not as financially rewarded. . . . The working class consists of underpaid individuals who often do not get a lot of job satisfaction but, hopefully, have a good homelife to fall back on." It might be difficult to have a good home life, of course, when one is underpaid and working double shifts and overtime. Like Patrick, Lisa seems both to engage with class difference and to avoid it.

This conflict in beliefs about class appears in other parts of Lisa's essays. When defining the class system, for example, Lisa notes that although Licensed Practical Nurses (LPNs) have very similar qualifications to RNs, they do not have the same responsibilities or salaries:

These nurses, or LPNs, do much of the same work as the RNs, or Registered Nurses, but they lack the decision making authority and the additional education. Their education consists of an 18-month training program. As a result, they are lower on the pay scale than the RNs. Where much of the tasks are the same between the two nurses, many LPNs lack the power to make decisions in relation to their patients. . . .

The RNs make up middle class individuals. These people have as little as two years of education. Although this is not much more than the LPNs education, RNs do earn the higher salary. The basic difference between the two is the level of responsibility. The Registered Nurses come into the job having a lot of responsibility regardless of their experience. . . . Although RNs and LPNs have much of the same tasks, RNs have more leadership responsibility which places them in a higher class.

Lisa suggests that the two classes of nurses — RNs and LPNs — are quite similar in education and in the tasks they are assigned. The main difference is that the RN is given more responsibility (although it's not clear *why* they receive this additional decision-making power, since their backgrounds, according to Lisa, are quite similar to those of the LPNs). Later in the essay, Lisa indicates that she does not approve of lower classes who express "hostility and condemnation" toward upper classes: "For example, I have heard many LPNs comment on the unfairness of the RN's higher salary. There is often bitterness toward job status among the LPNs toward the RNs. Even though the job tasks may be similar, many LPNs do not realize the responsibility and stress level the RNs have to encounter. As a result, there is often an underlying resentment towards those of a higher class." Again, Lisa's position appears to be incoherent. On the one hand, she seems to emphasize the similarities between LPNs and RNs. On the other hand, she condemns LPNs for being angry about the higher salaries and greater prestige of the RNs. On the one hand she seems to recognize a potential injustice in the system, and on the other hand, she seems to condemn anyone who might be bitter about this injustice.

There is a pattern in Lisa's essays, then, of at once acknowledging and re-pressing the pain of class difference. In her second essay she begins by describing how her cousin, an engineer, was able to afford special medical attention for her newborn baby. She compares the affluence of her cousin to the poverty of another parent she met at the hospital, a man whose baby died because he could not afford prenatal care. She uses this example to make a point: "Class differences do exist. The more money and education one has, the more oppor-tunities are available to that person." The contrast of the two parents power-fully instantiates her point about the inequities of class. Once again, however, Lisa seems to back away from her insights about class difference. By the end of the essay, Lisa asserts that success is not tied to money. She gives the example of the Alberts, a couple profiled in an interview piece in *Created Equal*. The Alberts are a poor rural couple who became rich when oil was discovered on their property. Despite their newfound wealth, the Alberts maintained a life-style identical to the one they had had for over fifty years. Lisa says of this couple: "They never attended college, they did not speak with the correct grammar, and they did not exploit their wealth. . . . Throughout the essay, Harold and Louise Albert were depicted as being truly happy with their lives. It did not matter to them if they had one dollar or a million dollars." Lisa greatly admires this couple, holding them up as an example of how money and happiness are truly separate phenomena. What happens, however, if we put the pre-oil Alberts into the scenario that opened Lisa's essay? What if Mr. Albert is the one who cannot pay for prenatal care for his infant? Who cannot communicate effectively with the doctor, because of his backwoods dialect and his lack of education? Would the Alberts be happy then? The Alberts provide a sentimental wash that blurs the astute class analysis with which Lisa begins her essay.

There may be many reasons for Lisa's and Patrick's unwillingness to sustain an analysis of class inequality. Certainly it is much more comfortable to think about the Alberts shunning all materialism than it is to think about babies dying because their parents do not have health coverage. I would like to hypothesize that one reason for the simultaneous recognition and avoidance of class inequality in the work of these two students is the particular circumstances of downward mobility. I believe that downward mobility provides those experiencing it with an acute understanding of class inequality. For many who are born in the working class and who stay there, there may be only a general awareness of middle-class privilege. Those who travel from a higher to a lower class, however, have the benefit — and the bitterness — that comes with a view of two worlds. Why, then, would they be so interested in avoiding or repressing this anger? Perhaps Patrick and Lisa discover that a belief in class inequality is not compatible with a belief in equal opportunity for all. They can either choose to let go of the myth of upward mobility, or they can downplay their bitterness about class inequality. They choose to hang onto the myth. For Lisa, the image of the Alberts allows her to accept the possibility that though she may not live as well as her parents, she may still be happy.

CHARLIE

Charlie is a white, twenty-three-year-old housepainter. His mother, who started but did not complete college, stayed at home while he was growing up. His father, who has a bachelor's degree, has been in sales, real estate, and customer service. He describes his upbringing as "dead solid middle class — house in the suburbs, one parent working, never in need of anything, but never having too much." Charlie's story has a number of economic ups and downs. Although he grew up in the middle class, he became a roofer briefly after he graduated from high school. He then entered a local private college to study music. When his father lost his job at a large company, Charlie's family could no longer afford the private college. He left college, returned to working blue-collar jobs, and recently entered the university, where he plans to become a writing major.

Charlie's first paper has some similarities to Patrick's and Lisa's essays in that he introduces the problem of class difference but never really commits to exploring it. The paper begins with an astute observation about the socially constructed nature of class: "We make class distinctions based upon what we value. If society values wealth and ownership, then the amount of money you make and the number of possessions you own will determine how society rates and perceives you." He also acknowledges the divisive nature of class. But as the paper progresses, the writing seems to get away from Charlie. He starts to pile up metaphors for class difference, but the metaphors do not develop his ideas further. He concludes, "Class is like a human price tag; it measures how much you are worth to society. Class is like having a membership to an exclusive club; it gives you a sense of identity and belonging. Class can also be a curse or a blessing. It can open or it can close doors of opportunity; it can give you a sense of pride or it may humble you, depending on where you place in the pecking order. Class is what distinguishes between who is master and who is slave." In contrast to Patrick and Lisa, Charlie does not appear to be outwardly ambivalent about class inequality. But his analysis stagnates, and he seems more interested in producing metaphors than in looking deeply at what class inequality really means.

Charlie's next paper, "No Guarantees," is much more assertive in its analysis of class. In it he examines his own uneven class history, beginning with his confusion about what to do after high school. His first impulse when he graduated was to go out west — "That was what the American Dream meant: happiness and freedom and adventure." He rejected this plan as too risky, however, and ended up taking a job as a roofer. Soon after, he found out that he would be going to college. "The guys on the crew often criticized me for wanting to go to school. . . . I had plans in the works, and they had nothing to do with tar." Charlie's brief experience among the working class leaves a mark on him. When he gets to college, he feels out of place: "Every time someone passed me I caught the unfamiliar smell of fresh laundry." This discomfort turns into a startling insight about the nature of privilege when, one day while walking to class, he looks up and notices several roofers working on a campus building:

An odd sense of exhilaration filled me as I thought: roofers! I remember having to restrain myself from rolling up my sleeves and joining them. I wanted to grab somebody and tell them what those guys up there were doing and how hard they worked. I stood frozen for a long time, watching the men at work. None of my fellow [students] seemed to notice what was going on up there. Didn't they care that these people were responsible for keeping the rain off our heads while we sat at our desks discussing life's Big Question?

It was at this moment when I first began to realize the meaning of privilege. Here I was holding a load of books while kids my own age were busy doing shit work in order to make a living. I couldn't help but think that if our circumstances had been different, I could be up there working and one of them might be carrying a stack of books looking up at me.

Instead of backing off from this insight into the nature of class and privilege, Charlie's paper enters further into it. Shortly after the roof incident, Charlie's father lost his sales job at a large company and was unable to find another job; Charlie was forced to leave the private college.[16] This reversal of fortune brought Charlie more disillusionment. His father, it turns out, was a strong believer in upward mobility. He had taught his son that "as long as I worked hard, it didn't matter who I was or where I came from—a person could do anything or be anybody." This is precisely the message Lisa learned from her parents. Unlike Lisa, however, Charlie enters fully into the bitterness and anger that is a natural outcome of downward mobility: "To put it straight and simple, there are no guarantees. A boy might dream of one day becoming a doctor and may end up cutting cow's throats in a stockyard. . . . Why is this? It is because the American Dream is not for everybody. There is not enough 'success' to go around. . . . If you are lucky enough to have the winds of fortune give shape to your sails then you probably have a bright future ahead of you. If not, then the American Dream can become the American Nightmare." Charlie's disillusionment takes on a grim, even violent form in this conclusion to his essay. The image of the boy who grows up to cut cows' throats is particularly disturbing; its specificity is in striking contrast to the vague images of his first paper. In abandoning the belief that individual hard work will bring one success, Charlie swings to another extreme—a belief that, ultimately, only luck determines one's socioeconomic fate.

Charlie's response to downward mobility, then, differs considerably from that of Patrick and Lisa. Whereas Patrick's and Lisa's texts are characterized by incoherence and even contradiction when they address class differences and inequality, Charlie's second paper confronts the contradictions in the myth of upward mobility and presents a coherent class analysis. The differences in their analyses have a great deal to do with the differences in how they see themselves with respect to the rest of society. Patrick and Lisa seek to belong to the mainstream, to have the lifestyle that places them firmly in the middle class. When Patrick, for example, addresses his future class affiliation in the survey, he says that he wants to maintain middle-class status but would "prefer to have a larger income. Possibly through marriage, I hope to achieve a higher level of socioeconomic class and also through job promotion or getting a higher paying job after graduating." Charlie, on the other hand, says, "I see myself maintaining some distance between myself and the rat race." Charlie does not seem to want to engage in the same quest for middle-class security as the other two students. As an aspiring writer, he may be someone who prefers marginal status because it allows him the perspective to see from many angles. Patrick and Lisa simply do not seek this position.

CONCLUSION

In analyzing the writing of Patrick, Lisa, and Charlie, I have been examining how the experience of downward mobility influences beliefs about class. In particular, I have looked at how these students try to reconcile the fact of class inequality with the dominant American belief that the ladder to success is available to anyone willing to put in the time and effort to climb it. My analysis suggests that these students are deeply challenged by the task of looking at class in their own lives and in the larger society. Their uneven class histories create conflicting feelings about class; their experience of downward mobility gives them insight into the injustices of the system, but they are still strongly tied to the belief that upward, not downward, mobility is the norm. Although Patrick and Lisa simultaneously express their bitterness and dodge the implications of that bitterness, Charlie confronts his own anger head on. I do not mean to suggest that Charlie is on a higher moral plane than the other two students, that he is the "good" student who successfully attains critical consciousness while the others wallow in a kind of false consciousness. The violence and despair at the end of Charlie's essay are not necessarily a better place to be than the ambivalence of the other two writers. Rather, my point is that class is a deeply challenging subject for students and that the ideological tensions generated by their class histories will influence the writing they produce. In particular, apparent problems with logic and coherence in student writing about class may have as much to do with ideological tension as they do with poor writing skills.

Many of us who devote our lives to education believe that the work we do will contribute to the upward mobility of our students. Every term I find myself telling students that expanding the scope of how they use language will open doors for them both intellectually and professionally. Perhaps in claiming that writing has something to do with success, I am touting just another version of the myth that hard work will lead to economic and social opportunity. Lynn Bloom says this is what American education has been about, "not putting the 'finishing' veneer on an elite class, but enabling the transformation and mobility of lives across boundaries, from the margins to the mainstreams of success and assimilation on middle-class terms."[17] The fact is that a college education is no longer a ticket to the "mainstreams of success." A student graduating from college now may know a great deal more about Immanuel Kant than her working-class parents know, but she may not be able to surpass her parents' earning power. Even if today's students do achieve middle-class success, divorce, job loss, disability, legal entanglements, or the illness of a parent may, in an instant, cause a reversal of fortune. Shirley Brice Heath captures the deep sense of insecurity among younger students: "Though they often cannot talk in terms of 21st-century capitalism, they see that in their late 20s and 30s, they are highly likely to face joblessness, despair, and family problems, even if they should be able to gain college educations."[18] These grim images call into question a traditional goal of American higher education — to assist students in achieving economic success.

How, then, do we teach in a climate where downward mobility or, at best, economic stagnation is the norm for many of our students, even with the benefits of a college education? I would like to make two suggestions for directions that literacy and communication curricula might take, given this climate. First, literacy education should respond to the needs of students who will likely face economic changes if not economic hardship during or after their years in college. These changes, as I have noted above, can involve divorce, disability, unemployment, care of an aging parent, and many other scenarios that require people to interact with a wide range of bureaucratic systems, all of which use language that confounds even sophisticated readers and writers. Students need to understand how this language creates and recreates an unjust class system, but they also need to learn how to read, decode, process, and respond effectively to the language of the law and of other bureaucracies, so that they can best manage life crises that force them to interact with these institutions. Such a curriculum would supplement the usual texts studied in composition classes — literature, essays, and artifacts of popular culture — with an array of bureaucratic texts, including, for example, applications for unemployment compensation, hospital consent forms, and community planning documents. In such a course students might discuss how these documents construct the subjectivity of the reader, how linguistic and rhetorical forms are used to create and perpetuate class differences, and how specific reading and response strategies might help students "speak" this discourse, rather than being "spoken by" it.[19] Students could also learn to rewrite this material in such a way that readers were empowered rather than diminished by the texts. Although a curriculum of this kind cannot prevent students from experiencing downward mobility, it can help them understand and manage economic hardship if and when it enters their lives.

Second, as is obvious from this study, I believe that writing and other communication courses should fearlessly tackle the subject of class. The readings and discussion should examine not only the familiar trajectory of upward mobility, but also the often hidden experiences of downward mobility and class stagnation. As the student essays in "Intermediate Writing" suggest, the subject of class may provoke anything from an anxious avoidance of the topic to conflict and ambivalence or gloom and despair. All the students in the course I studied, however, moved forward in their understanding of how class shaped social institutions; all of them learned the value of interrogating (if not entirely displacing) beliefs about success, hard work, and mobility. Perhaps this act of questioning sacred beliefs about class will help students as they confront more of the socioeconomic disappointments of adult life. We may not be able to educate students so that they will be in positions of security regardless of disruptive life events, but we can do what James Berlin proposes: "Education exists to provide intelligent, articulate, and responsible citizens who understand their obligation and their right to insist that economic, social, and political power be exerted in the best interests of the community as a whole."[20] Through such an education, we can perhaps prevent or at least mitigate the dashed hopes and damaged lives that accompany reversals of fortune.

APPENDIX

Questionnaire for Intermediate Writing Class

Thank you very much for filling out this questionnaire. It is designed to get some basic background information about our students. If I use any information from your questionnaire, I will not use your name.

1. When did each of your parents or guardians leave school (e.g., when they finished high school, after 8th grade, after a year of college, after receiving a master's degree, etc.)?

2. What jobs did (do) your parents or guardians have? You may include working inside the home as a job, if you wish.

3. What are the last two or three jobs that you've had (including the job(s) you have now)? You may include working inside the home as a job, if you wish.

4. What jobs might you like to have in the future?

5. I understand that you've been studying socioeconomic class this quarter. What class do you currently think of yourself as a part of?

6. Why do you think you're a part of this socioeconomic class?

7. Do you think you've ever been a part of another socioeconomic class (e.g., when you were growing up, five years ago, etc.)? Explain.

8. How do you see yourself in the future? Do you think you'll be a part of a class other than the one you're a part of now? If so, how do you think your life will be different?

9. Do you have any other comments related to these questions?

THE (DIS)LOCATION OF CULTURE:

ON THE WAY TO LITERACY

JOANNA BROOKS WITH FERN CAYETANO

For working-class college students, literature means work. Paper writing is a demanding, time-intensive process; poems require multiple readings; novels swallow hours already designated for part- or full-time jobs and family responsibilities. And everyone knows that English will not get you a job. Long before students make it to a general education literature class, economics has taught them their first literary critical lesson: since time is money, there is no time to collect books during one's four-year transit through college. Tools, maybe, but not books.

This practical view may seem to signify a "lack of interest" in or a "lack of appreciation" for literature. Read as a class issue, this "lack" joins a long list of reasons — no financial support, no leisure time, no word processor of one's own — that working-class people supposedly do not "do" literature. Teachers feel that they are working against mounting odds. Teaching literature assumes a redemptive urgency, a proselytizing drive reminiscent of the colonial "civilizing missions" that founded our discipline.[1] And thus, even class-conscious pedagogies can unwittingly confirm a reactionary "deficit model" of literary education.

As a step toward a more progressive way of "doing" literature, we might — like our students — take a few lessons from economics. Economic restructuring has brought fundamental changes to the way universities operate, from the part-timing of faculties to the commuterization of student bodies. Literature departments sense crisis as the field fractures into ever finer specializations, as content-heavy literature courses struggle to keep up with process-driven writing programs.[2] The way we understand class is changing too — it is no longer a stable identity but a "modality," a way of getting around. In short, teachers of literature are facing what working-class folks — from Dust Bowl Okies to Mexican *maquiladoras* — have known all along: that change is the only constant thing, that disruption and displacement are the most familiar landmarks.

Children of refugees may have little sense of a "home" literary culture; some can speak their parents' language but not write it; some cannot spell their grandparents' names. Migrant workers have no space in the truck for books — for tools, maybe, but not for books. Culture is not something one acquires or collects; it survives the trip and the translations. How will this translate into literary pedagogy? This paper will suggest that teachers of English can better serve working-class students by restructuring the study of literature in terms of literacy: decoding texts by identifying their conventions and contexts, reading "style" critically, and recognizing cultural boundaries.

POINTS OF DEPARTURE

Thinkers from many disciplines have recognized the profound cultural effects of economic restructuring. Sociologist Manuel Castells claims that the remapping of economies along ever more diffuse and transnational information networks will put "place-based" labor — that is, people tied to local sites of production such as factories or farms — in a vulnerable position.[3] Working people can gain leverage where local and global cultures intersect, Castells claims, by learning to navigate parallel social and cultural exchanges. This can mean recognizing subcultures, establishing "communication codes" with other subcultures, and building new local alliances among displaced groups; this can also mean learning to close-read the signs of political and economic change. In Castells's "informational city," economic and political practice are closely linked with symbolic practice.

The kind of symbolic practice that happens where the local meets the global — syncretic, multilingual, double-coded — is as old as the trade routes. And yet only recently has literary theory developed the vocabulary to appreciate it.[4] Literature's claims to essential or national significance have kept scholars and teachers busy defending the storehouse of "meaning" and depositing "meaning" in their students;[5] the claim that there are other texts, other meanings "out there" — as advanced during disputes over the diversification of the American literary canon — has been seen as a fundamental challenge to literature itself. But the restructuring we are talking about is not about the canon; it is about how and where meaning is made. It is about pulling up stakes from the fundamental assumptions of literary study and making ourselves feel at home in the work of translation and exchange.

Fundamental assumptions of ontology and epistemology have already undergone substantial change. The migrant or nomadic postcolonial subject has tracked her way across the pages of poststructuralist theory, breaking up old philosophical camps and calling for new, more ethical modes of thinking. Iain Chambers summarizes the effects of this movement:

> a movement in which neither the points of departure nor those of arrival are immutable or certain. It calls for a dwelling in language, in histories, in identities that are constantly subject to mutation. . . . in breaking into my own body of speech, opening up the gaps and listening to the silences in my own inheritance, I perhaps learn to tread lightly along the limits of where I am speaking from. I begin to comprehend that where there are limits there also exist other voices, bodies, worlds, on the other side, beyond my particular boundaries.[6]

Chambers's comments demonstrate his awareness of the critical and interpretive symbolic work that happens "on the way" to meaning — working across "gaps," working with fractured and sometimes silenced "inheritances," working at "limits," and working among "histories." This is how meaning is made where little is familiar except movement and change.

Pedagogical theory has kept up with the changes. Displacement, migrancy, and economic restructuring, after all, affect not only the status of knowledge but also the way it is produced. Claiming solidarity with working-class people, educators doing "critical pedagogy" have sought to effect a redistribution of these means of production. They point out the relationship between knowledge and experience, advocate a dialectical model of student-teacher interaction, and emphasize language — story-telling, dialogue, writing — as the place where it all comes together, the (possibly revolutionary) place where students make meaning. Peter McLaren and Tomasz da Silva write: "Stories help us to remember and also to forget. They help shape our social reality as much by what they exclude as what they include. Narratives provide the discursive vehicles for transforming the burden of knowing into the revolutionary act of telling."[7] Students who can tell their own stories about how truth is made can negotiate (and renegotiate) their own relationships to a rapidly changing world. In this process, textual and even literary skills are critical.

Accordingly, critical pedagogues call for a renewed conceptualization of and emphasis on literacy — a literacy, in the tradition of Paulo Freire, firmly situated within a wider commitment to social change. Henry Giroux explains, "In the United States, the language of literacy is almost exclusively linked to popular forms of liberal and right wing discourse that reduce it to either a functional perspective tied to narrowly conceived economic interests or to an ideology designed to initiate the poor, the underprivileged, and minorities into the logic of a unitary, dominant cultural tradition."[8] This functionalism, Giroux rightly observes, represents the interests of those who would perpetuate through "jobs training" the stratified status quo economy. A more transformative, critical literacy reads not only the words *interests, jobs,* and *economy,* but the networks of power that give them meaning; it reads the artwork on the cover of the textbook and its price tag; it reads the way the words are taught, the silences that punctuate class time, the way students pause, the way the teacher responds; it reads the color of the teacher's face, the color of the students' faces, and the color of the faces of those who clean the classrooms at night; and negotiating and translating among all these, it makes meaning. Also legible to critical literacy are the limits, gaps, and barriers that determine its own enterprise. Giroux's critical definition of illiteracy — "forms of political and ideological ignorance that function as a refusal to know the limits and political consequences of one's view of the world" — makes it clear that pedagogies must know their own limits.[9] Teachers, too, need to read their students, to recognize the networks of power operative within their classrooms, to sense which lesson plans work and which lesson plans do not, and to watch for the subtle signs that indicate that meaning-making is under way.

Reading signs, recognizing the migratory, locally negotiated nature of meaning, translating among discourses, and constructing new codes — the concepts and keywords that emerge from this review of recent theory seem familiarly literary. And yet, most literature classes do not work this way. Teachers teach books; students are expected to translate their ideas into literary jargon; historical consciousness is more about the archives than it is about where in space and time the classroom is located. The status of literary knowledge remains static; books are sold back at the end of the term. What use are they anyway? We're all just trying to get through.

A transformative literary pedagogy is a self-conscious literary pedagogy, one that asks itself the unsettling economic questions — "What is this for?" "Where are we going?" "How are we getting there?" — that economic restructuring, displacement, and forced migrancy have taught working-class people to ask. A transformative literary pedagogy recognizes that students do not come out of nowhere; before they take our "Introduction to Literature" classes as college freshmen, they may already be master practitioners of the symbolic — expert translators, trained to read the charged boundaries of race, class, and gender and to discriminate among subcultures, critically attuned to the fluid codes of hip-hop. Transformative literary pedagogy works through dialogue, translation, and code-switching, negotiating the production of meaning and not "meaning" itself. It reminds itself that meaning is being produced, in each classroom, in each session, by teachers and students who — either acknowledging or denying each other's presence — form a reading community. It claims, against widespread academic Darwinism, that community-building, not book-collecting, is literature's best use. It values methods over topics, critical tools over texts, literacy over literature.

WHERE WE'RE COMING FROM

The pedagogy we are working out knows theory, but it does not come from theory. A conversation with my grandmother started me thinking about literature and migrancy. One day, after reviewing my own bookshelves, she asked, "What do you do with all these? Can't you sell them back when you're done?"

It was a good question; we talked about books, family reading habits, houses where she had lived. Her grandparents, Mormon pioneers, had pulled hand-carts across the plains; her own family followed the sugar beet harvests between northern Utah, Idaho, and South Dakota; during the Depression, her brothers set out for WPA jobs in Nevada or joined the navy, while she and her mother came to Los Angeles looking for work. Most of my family came to Los Angeles about then — my father's people followed heavy construction jobs here from the WPA Boulder Dam project, from the Arizona cotton fields before, and from Oklahoma sharecropping before that. Books, had they been a part of family life, would scarcely have survived the trips. In the mid-1960s, my parents were the first of their families to go to college; they took degrees — teaching and engineering — from Brigham Young University that suited their own hard-driving, practical instincts. They now read church publications and manuals; a large set of National Geographic picture books fill out the family room shelves. And although they are nothing but supportive, my study of literature remains an utter mystery to them. I attribute it to a childhood immersed in Scripture; the first books I bought for myself were discarded textbooks, which I read over and over and over again.

My literary and pedagogical instincts have been sharpened and better defined through interaction with the students I teach at the University of California, Los Angeles. It was in conversation with a student, Fern Cayetano, who now joins me in the writing of this essay, that more connections between migrancy, literacy, and translation became clear.

I was sitting in office hours one day when a classmate of mine was having difficulty with poetry. He also believed it was beyond him and completely unrelated to his life. I tried to get him to see that he had the interpretation skills necessary to understand, using graffiti as my example. What is graffiti? Who is it for? What is literature? Who is it for? Depending on who you ask, you'll get mixed responses. People from outside the community look down on graffiti as useless scribblings or destruction of property. People from within the community will be quick to tell you that it is very significant. Being able to interpret it comes from being able to understand its codes and context. If you can read the codes of graffiti, then you can read literature. Both graffiti and literature get a bum rap; and yet both are used to conjure up a sense of pride in who we are and what we represent — literature in one world, graffiti in the hip-hop world.

My grandparents immigrated from Belize, looking for work. My own parents work for the military, and our family has moved around quite a bit. In teaching us to read, my dad was not into names and the fifty classics; he just wanted us to be able to understand what we were reading and the world around us. Before I began school, my father would pull out a newspaper and have me pick out the letters I had learned. As the letters became words, my excitement and love of reading grew. We were not allowed to take trips to the grocery store without a book in hand! Through my conversations with my parents and immersion in my stories of choice, I learned about people and how they relate. I learned how to understand and appreciate the lives of others, even if they did not directly involve me.

This kind of literacy is essential at UCLA, which, with its sister institution at Berkeley, ranks as the most ethnically diverse research university in the nation. Because UCLA is a public institution, its combination of relative affordability and prestige makes it especially attractive to students from middle- and working-class backgrounds. Many are the first from their families to go to college; many are commuter students with strong home ties; most feel a tremendous amount of pressure to succeed, pressure that sometimes has more to do with survival than with pride. These are they who Richard Hoggart, in his classic book on working-class literacy, called "the anxious and uprooted."[10]

Rather than promising these students an escape from anti-immigrant sentiments and class distinctions, university life often brings these issues to the foreground. Politicians play out the state's diffuse and difficult socioeconomic anxieties through very public, dramatic episodes in the University of California system — including the 1995 abolition of affirmative action practices and the system's protracted labor dispute with its own academic student employees. In addition to the usual campus political tensions — the exposure of racist and sexist fraternity songbooks, the struggle to establish and maintain ethnic studies programs — UCLA students face challenges unique to California's emergent immigrant communities. Southeast Asian groups, for example, lobby for support for students recovering from war trauma; student coalitions struggle to adequately serve and respect differences among highly differentiated constituencies — Salvadoreans as well as Chicanos, recent Chinese immigrants as well as Filipinos. At UCLA working-class stories, migrant histories, are told in dozens of languages.

BAGGAGE

What we bring to the literature classroom — be it baggage or equipment — depends on where we have been. This baggage becomes palpable in the moments of silence that punctuate class time, moments that panic many progressive teachers of English who idealize the loud, eager literary discussions one sees in movies. We would like to claim, to the contrary, that silence marks the places where students are making meaning — articulating their loaded relationship to their course of study and their educational environment.

Teachers should be willing to identify, accept, and honor student silences. Never should the goal be to draw a response — feeling pressure, some student will eventually respond, and usually in ways that confirm rather than transform classroom economics. Rather, teachers can make silences productive by paying sympathetic, critical attention to them and by encouraging their students to do likewise. It's a literary practice, really — noting pauses in poems, reading what characters don't say. It's good pedagogy too, pedagogy that, as Bonnie Smith suggests, "opens the possibility for drawing competing meanings and competing discourses out of social relations."[11] When talk breaks off in English class, it means paying attention to the context of literary study, not necessarily to the text at hand.

Some working-class students may explain their silence by claiming not to care about the subject: "I'm a business major"; "I'm a science major"; "this poetry stuff seems kind of pointless." What seems like apathy may really be careful calculation. *Just mass memorize for four or five years; you'll get your degree, pass go and collect $200. It costs a lot of money to go to school to get this "wonderful" knowledge; a common argument for taking kids out of school is "books don't feed you." Poor people don't want to admit they don't know something; the elite have no problem letting it be known who's running things; and everyone knows the middle class is trying to get there. Look at the grading system and the vicious competition it creates. It discourages communication and interaction; it cuts down on all the questions. We become academic enemies and slaves to our stereotypes. We play it safe and assimilate or "pass" in academic society.*

Driven by necessity to make learning an efficient enterprise, one that promises a material reward — a better job, a better standard of living — many working-class students place a premium on this kind of academic "passing." *We would rather know Shakespeare and Longfellow because that will make us seem like our boss and we'll get the promotion.* Some balk at literary methods that romanticize the sublime pleasures or supposedly deconstructive virtues of cultivated confusion. After all, when displacement and disruption characterize "real life," finite and stable disciplines seem very attractive — numbers do not lie. These are not attitudes to be "corrected" in the name of better English. Peter McLaren reminds us, "Ideology needs to be understood as lived experience constructed as common sense, and hegemony as the process whereby students not only unwittingly consent to domination but sometimes find pleasurable the form and content through which such domination is manifested."[12] By stepping back and speaking to the expressed apathies, acknowledging and engaging them, teachers can create an environment where dialogue replaces domination.

Connections between subjects always make things easier. When I was battling with Marianne Moore's poetry one quarter, there was a line that jumped out at me: "When they become so derivative as to become unintelligible, the same thing may be said for all of us, that we do not admire what we do not understand." The derivative — there it was, in the middle of a poem, the same derivatives that I battled with in calculus. I could translate math, my major, into English, my former nemesis, and enhance my understanding of both. People always say they hate math because they don't understand it, and I've always felt the same way about poetry. Poetry and math related? Something outside math could definitely be manipulated to the point where I can't tell where it came from. It is an experience I know all too well. In literature, it is important to find the familiar and make a bridge, through instruction and dialogue with the students, to the unfamiliar.

Many students' silences represent anxieties accumulated from or resistance developed in response to previous negative experiences. Students coming out of California public high schools, where English class sizes regularly run into the forties and overworked teachers develop pedagogies driven by the need for efficiency, bring crippling assumptions to their college English classes. Poems, in their experience, have one mysterious "deeper meaning," available only to the teacher. *I always thought all of the English teachers in the world had the right answer handbook. I thought I would never be able to understand it and it wasn't meant for me. The books they chose — all European-American authors — seemed to confirm my instincts.* Essays have one acceptable five-paragraph form; overgeneralization and sweeping summation are always preferable to multivalency and discussion. Bilingual and dialect English speakers carry huge burdens — especially in a state where anti-immigrant and racist sentiments color public debate over English as a Second Language (ESL) and Ebonics instruction.

Many teachers choose to ignore these conditions, naturalizing them to categories of race or class, believing that such issues are best handled in private "remediation." However, when the majority of the students in my classroom are coming from homes where English is not the only or even the primary language, these anxieties constitute an almost tidal undercurrent to every class discussion and every writing assignment. If this is the way meaning is produced, if this is the nature of literacy in California public schools, my public university classroom needs to acknowledge and address that. Of course, the system is set up to privatize the guilt on these issues — every student thinks he or she is the only one with such worries; the way things work needs no justification.

It is up to the teacher to identify that dominant pedagogy as a pedagogy, as one way of doing things. I often remind my students that our classroom is not a bank, a jail, a taxicab, or a convenience store; there is no plexiglass divider between me and them; I can see their faces, their discomfort. Faced with anxious student silence, I realize it is up to me to cross over to their side of the classroom. I do this by indirectly narrating their fears and anxieties about the task at hand. I might say to the class, "You're thinking, 'I have to have one right answer, the one in the secret teacher's manual,'" or "Are we allowed to be confused in here? You're thinking, 'Confusion is bad and I'll never get an A if I admit being confused.'" Students often laugh, recognizing these thoughts as their own; seeing other students around them laughing as well helps folks realize that they are not alone. "A+ for honesty" and "confusion is good" become class refrains. Early in the quarter, I speak directly to ESL fears, saying, "You are welcome here. And if I were reading literature in Cambodian, I'd be asking for your help." To refuse to identify and speak to these issues, especially when they affect so many of our working-class students, is to comply with a politics that silences immigrant voices.

Formal discussions of race, class, or gender may send many students into silence. At a place like UCLA, this silence has its practical purposes; no one believes that even a well-meaning class meeting will "solve" anything; these issues are too real, too present, and too costly to be just "academic." Students who want to play it safe may offer a Rodney King-esque plea: "Can't we all just get along?" Truth is, no — the classroom is not always a safe place to speak. Elizabeth Ellsworth, writing about teaching during a campuswide racism controversy, explains: "What they/we say, to whom, in what context, depending on the energy they/we have for the struggle on a particular day, is the result of conscious and unconscious assessments of the power relations and safety of the situation."[13] Ellsworth reminds us that, critical pedagogy's optimistic moments and brave commitments notwithstanding, not all talk is done in the spirit of sharing.

When Proposition 209 — the antiaffirmative action ballot initiative — came up for discussion during an education class of mine, everyone turned around to look at me. I wanted to say, "Why are you making me the anti-209 representa-

tive? I'm sure there are some black people voting for it too." It's just a self-preservation thing — you don't want people to base their image of you on one comment, in a discussion you'd never be having with them outside of class. And what if the teacher disagrees? There's a big fear of being wrong, or of the teacher being indifferent. It all comes from who believes who belongs; poor people aren't used to being heard.

And I am not sure college teachers are used to dishing out the kind of positive follow-up that frames cohesive, productive class discussions. Many take a laissez-faire approach, thinking that it is okay for a comment to just hang there, waiting for response from other students. That can be crushing for students not used to being heard, replicating more familiar and more threatening types of silence. English teachers who recognize the limits of their project understand that a tearful confession is not necessarily a sign that the class is "getting real." Expected moments of revelation often replicate the overexposure working-class people endure on *Ricki Lake* and *COPS*. If we want to encourage students to represent themselves, to be skilled practitioners of the symbolic, we must leave it to them to determine what their experiences will mean and to whom.

WAY STATIONS: METHODS AND MEANS

In order to move toward a participatory, process-conscious literary pedagogy, we need to reexamine our existing concepts of literary analysis. Well-entrenched in our discipline is the idea that a "deeper meaning" lies in literature awaiting skilled excavation; this assumption confirms the authority of teachers as archaeologists, anthropologists, and/or ethnologists and forecloses student-generated avenues of approach and investigation. It perpetuates the sense that meaning is already made, not in the making; it subjects students to a textuality that is "found," not participatory.

Students come to the classroom with analysis and interpretation skills, but many teachers ignore those skills. Many students never realize what they can accomplish once the bridge is built. We have to include students in the discussion by making them comfortable. They have to see that they already have the skills necessary to "decode" literature; they just have to learn about the context and keywords of the literary community. If we could get students to appreciate literature not just as a set of names but as a way of viewing and understanding the world, I think they would be more interested.

In order to open up the work of analysis, I have structured my classes around keywords. My method is something like a cross between Paulo Freire's literacy program — "Culture Circles," which decode and recode lists of "generative words" — and Raymond Williams's emphasis on invested etymology, the historicization of text and the textualization of history.[14] I choose words that dwell somewhere between culture and method, words that call attention to the constructed nature of the "literary" — *writing, author, story, persona, romance* (in terms of the novel), *performance;* if words or phrases emerge during class discussion, I incorporate them into the next quarter's syllabus.

Making my methods as explicit as possible, I tell my students that analysis means taking these keywords apart and putting them back together on their own terms. In taking apart, I emphasize contextualization and close reading. In putting concepts back together, I encourage students to work, literally, from their own intellectual genealogies, to put their family history side-by-side with received etymology. What does "literature" mean to their parents and grand-parents? How are "stories" told in their family — who is "authorized" to talk and what is not open to interpretation? Bringing family history into analysis puts history next to history, toward a negotiation of migrant "histories." It exposes the particular genealogical development of seemingly absolute literary standards, and it brings the study of literature, quite literally, home. It calls attention to the many parallel histories existing in our classroom — some of which dominant literary discourse deems "illegitimate" — and presents the pos-sibility that, through discussion, common concepts can be negotiated.

Because literary conventions are freighted with ideology, genres can also be opened to critical redefinition. For example, conventional plot assumes the radical individualism of the heroic protagonist and a Horatio Alger ideal of progress and class mobility in its linear development. Conventional pedagogy is embedded in the structure of plot, too — the idea that one reads straight through a novel to find a meaning at the end mirrors the idea that one goes through school to get educated. Such notions fail when tried out on books like William Faulkner's *As I Lay Dying,* Louise Erdrich's *Bingo Palace,* and Gloria Naylor's *Bailey's Cafe,* all of which combine unconventional structure with working-class stories. Of course, students worried about "getting through" are not always eager to "get lost" in unconventional fiction. Framing the discus-sions can prevent frustration — I use television plots (the conventional *A-Team* versus the soap opera *Melrose Place*) as points of reference. Sometimes I ask the class's permission to "get lost," assuring them that they will not be expected to come up with "an answer" independently, that such stories are meant to be read and understood in community.

The conventions of poetry also bring out issues of community and transla-tion. I choose to teach texts whose formal qualities negotiate between "high" literary and peculiarly cultural sensibilities, between global and local — Lang-ston Hughes, Americo Paredes, Lorna Dee Cervantes, for example. Reading for meter, line-break, and metaphor, usually a dreaded exercise, turns into an adventure in decoding. How did these authors use poetic techniques to repre-sent experiences that the established literary audience would not otherwise see or hear — police brutality or lynching, displacement, racism? How does poetry, using "denotation" and "connotation," work "between worlds?"

I encourage students to take these questions on together, to form groups focusing on one author. Those who identify with an individual author's "local" culture feel a sense of ownership and learn how experience can be encoded and represented; everyone is required to do historical research, to understand what socioeconomic conditions shaped the way the author represented himself or herself. The presentations they produce together bear the fruits of intercultural collaboration: one group used the music of Nina Simone to demonstrate the loaded significance of Langston Hughes's jazz rhythms; another group performed a traditional *corrido* to explain the tension between oral tradition and print culture in Americo Paredes. One of the best presentations led into a discussion of how to deal with the Spanish portions of Lorna Dee Cervantes' bilingual verse. Comfortable in class discussion, students were able to acknowledge some frustration and to come to the realization that not all discourses are meant to be available to all readers. The realization that cultural boundaries have their own significance and deserve respect is a transformative realization in this city of transplants.

The study of drama can expose how literature itself establishes cultural boundaries — through ritualizing the social order and/or allowing marginalized communities to stage otherwise unavailable freedoms and justice. Correspondingly, keywords for this unit have included *performativity, staging,* and *community.* In plays like Ntozake Shange's *for colored girls,* Anna Deavere Smith's *Twilight Los Angeles,* and Eric Bogosian's *Suburbia,* we examine how groups determine themselves through dramatic means like costume, speech, and movement. Students from immigrant families often latch onto the idea of "performed" communities and "staged" identities; many choose, for their final paper, to write a play (with summary analysis) about their own "home" communities.

The results have been remarkable: one woman, combining Shange's and Smith's methods, interviewed twenty UCLA students about black/white interracial dating and crafted her play from their responses; one woman staged the issue of pan-Asian ethnic solidarity as a dialogue between a Korean woman and a Chinese man at a college dance, with the dance's quasi-omniscient Filipino deejay intoning subtle narrative editorial over their flirtations; another student dramatized the three faces of Mexican American identity — the *Mexicano,* the Chicano, and the *gabacho,* using puppets to stage the *gabacho*'s attempts to "pass" during a fraternity margarita-fest at a mainstream Mexican restaurant. In writing these plays, working-class students can transgress the border between those who write literature and those who study it, in turn challenging the class distinction between workers and aesthetes.

HORIZONS: YOU CAN'T GO HOME AGAIN

JEFF: Go home. Stop drinking. Go home and sleep it off.

TIM: Sleep what off? What should I sleep off, Jeff? My life? I should go home and go to sleep and when I wake up, what will I be? A pilot? A Super Bowl quarterback? Maybe a rock star? I don't think so.

JEFF: Just go home.

TIM: This is my home.[15]

This exchange, from Eric Bogosian's play *Suburbia,* occurs in the parking lot of a convenience store. Throughout the play, loitering local dropouts argue with the store's Pakistani-immigrant proprietor and with each other about who belongs "there" — at the store, in the social crowd, in America. All of the characters seem to feel displaced — the Pakistani immigrant claims a literal displacement; the kid discharged from the army, the recovering alcoholic, and the kid who takes a class at the community college and works at the cardboard box factory try to articulate their sense of virtual homelessness.

Who says what "home" means? Who belongs? Who owns the enterprise? Economic restructuring and its accompanying migrations can leave English departments similarly uprooted — not always sure how to negotiate between the discipline's need for cohesiveness and the needs of our students. Working between these worlds may mean reconceptualizing literature in terms of the cultural work it does and teaching in terms of literacy. For teachers, this might feel like voluntary displacement — it is a risky pedagogy, which rests less on its own conclusions and more on students' willingness to make class work. But we all know you can't take your bookshelf to class with you; diplomas stay on the office wall.

More portable and useful are the subtler lessons of our literary training — the ability to decode, translate, and negotiate, to deconstruct concepts and to reconstruct history. To teach like this is to reinstate the imaginary in our profession, as a tool and not just an object of study. It is to imagine common grounds on the horizon of literary study, a classroom where privilege does not necessarily signify power. It is to cultivate a literary method, a literacy, that welcomes working-class students to join the journey.

BETWEEN DIRTY DISHES AND POLISHED DISCOURSE:
HOW WORKING-CLASS MOMS CONSTRUCT STUDENT IDENTITIES

EILEEN FERRETTI

Can you imagine being in college for eight years before you get to take fresh-man composition? Some might ask, "Is it worth the wait?" Well, the para-professional women I teach at Kingsborough Community College, City University of New York, have little choice but to wait. When I came to Kingsborough in 1992, I was astounded to learn that my students, adult women paraprofes-sionals in the New York City public schools, had been in college as long as I had — the only difference being that my eight years earned me a B.A. and an M.A. in English, while their eight years were spent in piecemeal vocational courses qualifying them for Board of Education pay raises. These adult women initially come to college to obtain "Board Certification" in their job title, which requires them to have a high school diploma plus six college credits in educa-tion within two years as a condition of continued employment. Most remain in college beyond six credits to accumulate electives in education and related fields, for which they receive regular salary increments. After their long-term odyssey with career-based classes, some of the paras finally enter the liberal arts track of the college and become my students in first-year composition or basic writing. Although these liberal arts paras represent the academic "survivors" in a group where most don't get that far, they are not on a fast track to aca-demic learning, and their delayed entry into liberal arts education presents a range of conflicts for women already encumbered by full-time jobs and family responsibilities.

Not only do their jobs and their families interfere with their academic lives, but also my critical pedagogy (drawn from the work of Paulo Freire and Ira Shor) looks to them like a writing class from Mars — basically a Star Trek departure from the fill-in-the-blank education they received.[1] As Carlene, an African American mother of two who was a student in one of my basic writing courses, said, "In this class, you can't check your answers. No one seems to have the right answers, the same answers, or even the same questions." Carlene's need for definitive answers conflicted with my pedagogy of questions, but this did not surprise me because the paras' sturdy desire for *the facts* had been permanently stamped in my memory on my first teaching day at Kingsborough. I had barely uttered my name before a designated para spokeswoman announced that the women in the room already knew all about me — where I lived, where I attended school, where I had previously taught. Even my date of birth was announced to the class by a second para who had a snooping friend in personnel. As soon as my life facts were disclosed, a third para said, "As you can see, we know all about you. So, hand out the syllabus and let's go home." The students I had hoped to empower with a critical pedagogy were already walking all over me and were eager to walk out the door. It is fair to say they had done their homework on the facts of my life and were ready to give me, the teacher, a lesson on the facts of para life. What I eventually discovered, though, is that after several years of *slightly* higher education, the paras find themselves still at the starting gate (that is, in entry-level college composition). In addition, their pay raises abruptly terminate after they complete sixty elective credits;[2] so the paras are left sliding sideways through college and downhill through their paychecks. Thus, I sensed that without regular pay raises as an incentive, the paras might gain access to a new relationship to higher education, repositioning themselves from workers who attend classes for pay raises and narrow technical knowledge to student intellectuals who aspire to a liberal arts degree. But how do adult working women adjust to high expectations and liberal arts after a lifetime of low aspirations in service to other people's needs?

These multiple conflicts and dilemmas have become the thematic center of my composition classes.[3] My critical teaching invites the paras to compose literacy narratives in which they reflect on their own academic development. The literacy narrative genre now emergent in the field of composition and rhetoric offers accounts of assimilation into academic culture from the perspective of working-class academics. These impressive stories, typically focused on the dissonance between the writers' home and school cultures, have been used effectively by Linda Brodkey, Lorene Cary, Keith Gilyard, Mike Rose, Victor Villanueva, and others to illuminate the unique cultural conflicts of upwardly mobile working-class students.[4] The published literacy narratives of these "Scholarship Boys and Girls" show that coming to college young and unmarried enabled them to use higher education for a faster climb out of their working-class roots than is available to or possible for older adults like the paras, whose multiple roles include family responsibilities that keep them rooted in their home culture despite their long-term exposure to campus life.[5] In this way, "class" is gendered as well as age-related in its impact on the upward mobility of these working-class students.

The "para literacy narratives" I will discuss in this essay are classroom journals written in two forms: autobiographical accounts of conflict caused by the paras' multiple roles in the home, the school workplace, and the college campus and their written reflections on readings about gender issues, class conflicts, and/or race relations. The journals vary in length from a few paragraphs to a few pages and comprised approximately one-third of the students' writing in this course. As Joseph Harris points out, "Our goals as teachers should be to offer [students] the chance to reflect critically on those discourses — of home, school, work, and media, and the like — to which they already belong"[6] Constructed in their own idioms and situated in themes, knowledges, cultures, and conditions of para life, the narratives represent a group experience with higher education significantly different from that of working-class academics, because of the paras' age and gender roles. In highlighting their texts in this essay, my goal is twofold: first, to raise the profile of some average adult working students whose progress from domestic life and school employment to higher education has not been triumphant (or documented) like the stories of "Scholarship Boys and Girls," and second, to offer a consideration of critical pedagogy as a means to help these adult working women explore their cultural conflicts, question their subordinate social construction, and transform their marginal encounters with campus life.

To begin, I should say that my life story is close to theirs. As a working-class mom who came to college after spending eight years as a lunch mother in the elementary school my children attended, I looked forward to teaching in the para program. Given the common conditions of our domestic experience, our shared histories as subordinate workers in a school setting, and our mutual decision to return to school as adults, I hoped that my writing class would offer the paras a chance to critically reflect on their home, work, and school experiences so as to help them mediate between the limited vocational curriculum of their past and the liberal arts classes ahead. Since the goals of my pedagogy for the paras center on a critical inquiry into *their* lives, issues, and concerns, I had carefully planned a course that would use autobiographical narratives to initiate the writing process.

I soon discovered, however, that no amount of planning could have prepared me for my initial encounter with these women. Assertive despite their subordination, these long-term veterans of the community college system were completely at ease with their surroundings, even if I was not. Standing alone in front of them on that September day, I was in awe of their *presence* in the classroom and intimidated by their collective upset of my agenda for the first day of class. Intuitively, I turned to the blackboard, transcribed the list of *facts* the first speaker had offered about me, and composed a short narrative about myself beside it. I do not recall exactly what I wrote, but my story contained the statement, "Eight years ago I was a lunch mother at my children's school." This new fact got immediate attention and generated a barrage of questions that I refused to answer until each student had compiled a similar list about herself with an accompanying autobiographical narrative.

As the women read their lists, I made a composite sketch of the thirty students, twenty-six of whom were paras, the remaining four being students in the school secretary program. The women ranged in age from twenty-eight to sixty-four, all had at least one child, and nineteen were married. Of the eleven nonmarried women, six were single mothers and five were divorced parents. Fifteen identified themselves as white. Of those, approximately half said they were ethnically mixed (the most common being Italian/Irish and Italian/Jewish). Of the remaining fifteen, six identified themselves as Hispanic, three said they were African American, two claimed Asian origin, and four said they were first-generation immigrants — one from Haiti, one from Guyana, and two from Russia.[7]

As their narratives unfolded, I noticed that the women's multiple roles merged in their texts. Angelica, a forty-two-year-old Hispanic mother of four, captured the collective attitude quite succinctly when she wrote, "I became a para to supplement my family's income, and I came to college to supplement my para paycheck."[8] Angelica's comment highlights how the paras' work/study experience encourages them to accept a preordained hierarchy among their multiple roles, one that subordinates education to finances, limiting their capacity to reflect on the challenges and rewards that college attendance can present to adult working women. Although the paras' early autobiographical narratives clearly illustrated this subordination of their student identities to the demands of their domestic and working lives, their verbal comments suggested that many were beginning to embrace a "now or never" philosophy about the prospects of earning a college degree. They also used their narratives to explore the connections between college attendance and the conditions of everyday life. In this way, the paras' autobiographical accounts served to recast their multiple roles in ways that challenged their previous assumptions. For example, Cassandra, a thirty-one-year-old African American mother of six, wrote, "I've reached the point of 'no return' in my desire to become educated; my daughters watch me struggle, and they see a role model for reaching higher than cleaning other people's houses. For my sons, though, it's not so easy. . . . I hope that they will eventually see [in education], an alternative to the gang-violence in the streets."

Cassandra's narrative introduced a Freirean "generative theme" for the group — fear of "external threats" emanating from outside the home.[9] As her narratives centered more closely on the dangerous streets near her public housing project, many other women cited "fear of violence" both outside the home and within it as an impediment to their college attendance.[10] Leaving children at home alone after school was a major stress factor reported by most single mothers; frequent, sometimes violent confrontations with spouses over college attendance was mentioned by others. My critical pedagogy curriculum took up this generative theme to provoke deeper inquiry into their domestic conditions and their neighborhoods. Critical discussion of these narratives shed light on the possible connections between going to college while raising a family and the larger social issues of domestic violence, teenage gangs, inadequate child care, and dangerous streets. For example, some paras asked, "Does a mother's decision to attend college cause or contribute to these family and community problems, or does exposure to higher education just make the threats posed by violent and unsafe conditions more visible?" A number of follow-up narratives focused on the positive aspects of working and going to college despite domestic and neighborhood obstacles. In fact, some women said they felt "more prepared" to face the challenges presented by their gendered/classed position in the university because they had already successfully mediated between domestic duties and paid employment.[11] As Svetlana, a forty-eight-year-old Russian immigrant and mother of two, explained, "Coming to college at forty added one more fly to the ointment that is my life, but it was a small one — more like an annoying little gnat as opposed to the gigantic horse fly I took on when I left my drug addicted husband and returned to work. As I see it, my life experience (working full-time while raising my two boys in a poverty neighborhood) prepared me for anything." Although this comment was intended to project self-confidence and optimism, it also revealed the marginal status Svetlana assigns to her student identity. However, through acknowledging and questioning the words they used to describe and compare their roles, the women began to interpret them from multiple perspectives, calling attention to both existing and alternative relationships among them. As Mary Soliday suggests, "When they are able to evaluate their experiences from an interpretive perspective, students achieve narrative agency by discovering that their experience is, in fact, interpretable."[12]

Although the narratives on family life explored a variety of obstacles and incentives to academic success, the paras' descriptions of student life made it clear that my high expectations for reflection and textual literacy had placed college in direct conflict with their primary roles as wives and mothers. As Janice, a thirty-six-year-old mother of three, wrote, "The worst aspect of this course is the endless stream of drafts and revisions. I'm used to a mid-term and a final exam. I study for a week, I take the test, and that's that. Now, I'm writing and revising every single weekend. My family is fed up with me and I can't even justify all this extra school work because I'm not getting a pay raise for being here. . . . When my husband used to complain about school, it felt good to shove my 'higher' paycheck in his face every now and then. But now, I don't want school to cause any further conflict, so I just try to write before class or when no one is home." The last line of this journal provoked an immediate response from the other paras, who asked in unison, "When *is* no one home?" During our discussion of this narrative, I asked Janice what she resented most about her situation, revising her drafts, not getting a raise for being in the writing class, or living in a domestic setting that allowed her so little time for schoolwork. She backed away from the complexity of this question, saying that she had "gone off the topic" by emphasizing her financial and family conflicts in a journal on "student life." I replied that financial and family conflicts impact a student's college experience and are appropriate in a narrative on student life.

I also noted, though, that perhaps the connections among her multiple roles needed to be revised along with revising her papers, referring to the idea that critical reflection revises perception, not just writing. Consequently, I said in class that the study strategies and pay incentives of the past no longer applied to her situation and that more appropriate strategies and incentives needed to be created. This comment was met with a great deal of collective skepticism by the paras, who resented my advice to revise their priorities. They ignored my challenge in their follow-up journals, responding instead to what they perceived as Janice's need for more effective study strategies. For example, Stephanie, a thirty-eight-year-old Italian-American mother of four, offered a personal solution to the conflict between domestic duties and study time: she taped index cards to the splashboard above the kitchen sink; that reminded me of the way Celie in *The Color Purple* learned to read by pasting words on the kitchen walls.[13] Stephanie wrote, "Last night I studied Erik Erikson's stages of psychosocial development while washing the dirty pots and pans. Eventually, I moved on to the clean pots and pans that I keep under the sink because I wasn't quite finished memorizing. The noise of the water running into the sink drowned out the sound of the portable T.V. on the counter next to the stove that my husband was watching and the noise of my kids fighting over the last piece of cake at the kitchen table." This journal generated some lively response from other paras who shared original and hilarious techniques on where and how moms could study, drowning out family life with transistor radios and ear plugs, using audio cassettes in the car while commuting, and taping oaktag paper inside the bathroom door (if only the paper were water proof!). But the tone of the conversation grew more serious when other women pointed out that these suggestions failed to solve the problem for the composition class, where and how moms could find the peace and quiet they needed at home to accomplish the kinds of reading, writing, and reflecting that the composition class demanded—activities that placed the process of education in direct conflict with their domestic roles.

The lack of quiet and privacy in the working-class household is also mentioned in published literacy narratives. Linda Brodkey reports that she learned how to read "in the social space of the kitchen." Richard Rodriguez, armed with a flashlight, secreted himself "in a closet . . . or under a bed with a book."[14] But, unlike Brodkey and Rodriguez, who had to create space for themselves amid the cramped quarters and chaos of the working-class household as children (but moved on to the more private spaces of the university dormitories and libraries as college students), these adult paras in college come home to a domestic setting that permits no rendezvous with books for them—not in the kitchen, or in the closets, or under the beds. Can you imagine mom hiding under the bed with a book and a flashlight? I confessed to the paras, though, that when I was in college I had done my reading with a flashlight, not under the bed, but in bed (under the covers). They said that there were more interesting things to do under the covers and implied that my marriage must be pretty boring if I took my schoolbooks to bed. I assured them that my marriage wasn't boring and reported that the flashlight strategy had worked quite well, indeed, eventually prompting my husband to furnish a well-lighted and spacious office for me to do my schoolwork (if for no better reason than to get my schoolbooks out of our bed).

Overall, the recurrent conflicts emerging in the paras' narratives on home, work, and student life became material I wanted to pose as problems for changing their aspirations, intellectual habits, and literacy style. For most of them, college attendance had become routine, filling a small slot in their daily schedules, much like doing the laundry or going grocery shopping. The courses were complementary to each other and the work load predictable; student life was therefore manageable. By contrast, my critical writing class suddenly presented their everyday life as a problem for successive levels of reflective inquiry. It is not easy to grow into the uncertainty of skepticism and the habit of inquiry from several different perspectives. Because they are used to the old "banking" routines of education, which ask them to memorize and return facts, not to think critically about issues, my invitation to reflect on their themes is resisted because it asks something more of them, something new, something threatening.[15]

Critical pedagogy directly confronts student resistance to complexity and inquiry. I hope to foster the type of critical literacy Mike Rose describes as "an ability to frame an argument, take someone else's argument apart, systematically inspect a document, an issue, or an event, apply a theory to disparate phenomenon, and so on."[16] To do this, I involve the paras in all aspects of the learning process, including the design of the syllabus. Collectively, they decide what we read and when we move from one text to another. The criteria for these decisions are the students' perceptions of what the class is actually talking and writing about at any given time. I do this negotiating because it involves the students in a decision-making process; no longer merely spectators or subordinates, they are invited to become participants in an educational setting. As Ira Shor points out, "Education for empowerment is not something done by teachers to students for their own good, but something students codevelop for themselves, led by a critical and democratic teacher."[17]

But no matter how I negotiate with the paras, we invariably reach a moment when the conflict between their working-class culture and the world of college erupts (usually in the midst of a philosophical debate among themselves). When we do not reach consensus on an issue reasonably soon, one of them will inevitably voice her frustration with the whole process of negotiation and discussion in the composition class. As Monique, a forty-two-year-old Haitian mother of five, put it, "Who cares? None of this is relevant to my life, anyway. I don't need all of this philosophical debate to teach second grade. They don't pay school teachers to voice their opinions about this and that — they pay them to apply a particular set of methods laid out by the Board of Ed. . . . That's what I came to college to learn, that's what I want from this class, a method for writing my term papers." This resistance to complex, critical thought has been discussed by Rose Zimbardo, formerly of City College of New York's Center for Worker Education, who notes that her students have "suffered at the hands of the educational establishment and if they believe they have little or nothing to offer, it is because they have been taught to believe so." The paras' narratives on work and student life support Zimbardo's findings.[18] For example, although they claim that the fear of losing touch with the familiar rhythm of their vocational classes causes their resistance to academic work, turning them from "aspiring teachers" into "career paras," they typically view this fear as a self-imposed limitation, not as the result of social, economic, and cultural forces that limit their intellectual and professional development. It is only through discussion and analysis of their narrative stories that they begin to question the relationship between their domestic and work experiences and their academic progress.

Whereas their self-generated narratives provide a space for the paras to reflect critically on the conflicts among their multiple roles, their narrative reflections on readings about gender issues, class conflicts, and/or race relations encourage them to develop individual perspectives and to express opinions on a wide range of social issues. Because the paras have been working at similar job sites and taking college classes together for a number of years, they assume an intimate knowledge of each other based on their common experiences on the job and the college campus (where antidialogic teacher talk and one-way banking classes have silenced their exploration of their own voices and diversity). By contrast, their narrative responses invite philosophical debate about readings, debate that inevitably leads to some disagreements. In this way critical inquiry brings out the diversity in this seemingly tight-knit group. For example, in response to Judy Syfers's "I Want a Wife," women of color, almost without exception, attacked Syfers's elitist stereotype of the family as a unit with a gainfully employed male at its center who could afford to keep his wife at home to wait on him and dote on his children.[19] Some of these women wrote narratives in which they imaginatively changed places with Syfers and concluded that they preferred affluent homemaking to the low-pay, low-status jobs they must take. This response shocked the younger (under forty) white paras who agreed with Syfers, many insisting that they would be in graduate school by now if only they had a wife to take care of their domestic needs. However, the responses of Carol and Margaret, both white women over fifty, engendered the most controversy because they contended that Syfers's essay reduced the most significant identity of women in the family to a composite sketch of its "working parts." They argued, as well, that being a wife and mother was not a "role" in the same way as being a para or a student. Carol explained her position as follows: "I used to be a hairdresser, now I am a para, someday I hope to be a teacher. I'm a student today, but I won't always be in school. These aspects of my life I consider roles because they are temporary. On the other hand, being a mother is a permanent identity, not just a role. . . . When I became a mother, I made an irrevocable decision . . . no matter where I go or what other roles I play, I'll always be 'mom.' " Carol's response to her multiple roles confirmed her resistance to intellectual life, revealing a mythology of "self-sacrifice" via her motherhood identity. Many paras challenged Carol's distinction between a role and an identity on the basis that although her job title had changed over time and might change in the future, her role as a worker was not temporary, but every bit as permanent as the role of mother. At this point I asked the class why all of the narratives had taken Syfers's satirical description of women's roles in the family for granted? Why did no one challenge the notion that the tedious chores of domestic life should be relegated to women exclusively? Some paras argued that Syfers's essay defined the family as they know it, with one exception: women can no longer afford to stay home with children because they must take care of the family and earn a salary to help pay the bills, as well. Others challenged *me* for suggesting that they revise their domestic roles just as I insist that they revise their papers. "Can a family be revised like a college paper?" they asked. I said, "No, family life is old, complex, and conflicted in ways that a college paper is not." Conscious of my own struggle to balance my needs as a student and aspiring professional with the realities of family and working-class life, I cannot tell my students that their role conflicts will be resolved easily or soon.

Nonetheless, my critical pedagogy does not stop where my students' questions begin but employs a "problem-posing" approach, which was useful in helping the paras interpret "revision" from multiple perspectives. I asked the class to come up with a collective definition of the term *revision* as it is understood in the writing class. After some debate, they agreed that revision changes the organization of a paper, develops its ideas, and corrects surface features of writing. From this definition, the class drew some parallels for Carol's role as a mother. Posing some common problems mothers encounter in raising children (the "terrible twos," sibling rivalry, teenage autonomy, and so forth), the class eventually concluded that Carol's mothering role had been reorganizing, developing, and correcting itself for decades in order to accommodate the changing needs of her children. Although most were eager to point out that the process of "revision" is much slower and infinitely more complex in families, some also noted that revision of our mothering roles is inevitable; the real issue is whether we actively participate in the process or resist it until our children make the changes for us.

Despite these moments of collective insight, however, multiple conflicts continued to emerge in the women's responses to gender issues. Because the paras are working-class women whose folkways consider a college education unnecessary (or even impossible), they typically harbor some resentment toward highly educated professional women, and they cringe at the word *feminism.* Although most of them came of age during the recent women's movement, they did not have access to the wider educational and professional options that their middle-class counterparts fought for. In fact, while the middle-class baby boomers were marching on the college campuses, the working-class paras were pushing baby carriages, just as their mothers had done a generation before them. But, unlike their mothers, they were told (by social, cultural, and economic forces) that the roles of wife and mother were no longer enough; more was expected of them — a job outside the home, an economic role in the family. Because they live in a culture still dominated by patriarchy, though, their ideas about women's roles in society conflict with those shared by most academic women. They see their positions in low-paying, low-status jobs not as a function of gender oppression but primarily as a result of economic conditions that have negatively impacted the working-class. Their worker husbands, no longer earning enough to support the family, have sent them out to work or have left them (turning them into single mothers). As bell hooks explains, "Women in lower class and poor groups, particularly those who are non-white, would not have defined women's liberation as women gaining social equality with men since they are continually reminded in their everyday lives that all women do not share a common social status . . . and that many men in their social groups are exploited and oppressed."[20] Although the paras' everyday lives reflect the circumstances hooks points out, most of them are unfamiliar with women writers (such as hooks) who address issues of race, class, and ethnicity. Therefore, their initial responses to these texts often stress differences, not common conditions. For example, Monica, a forty-nine-year-old African American mother of two and grandmother of six, suggested that we read something by Audre Lorde after she saw a documentary about her on public television. In response I chose "Age, Race, Class, and Sex: Women Redefining Difference." In the opening lines of this essay, Lorde defines herself as "a forty-nine year old Black lesbian feminist socialist mother of two and a member of an interracial couple." All of the paras responded negatively to Lorde's self-definition, and black women, in particular, were repelled by her lesbian/interracial identities. In addition, when many of the women saw the word "socialist," they envisioned a potentially deviant combination of two politically active lesbians raising children and immediately declared Lorde a "radical" and a "subversive." Lorde offers this brief self-description (with all the wrong labels attached to it) in order to critically analyze what she calls "the systematized opposition of Black and Third World people, working-class people, older people, and women."[21] But the paras' response narratives acknowledged no common ground with Lorde on issues of race, class, age, or gender, and women of color said that they were both annoyed and offended by this reading selection, which they described in their narratives as "degrading to black women."

Because I was surprised by their negative reaction, I can say that these women were educating me, the teacher, about how they see the world, but I was not yet willing to give up. I decided to move deeper into the issues presented in the text. After much discussion of lesbianism and social activism, the class agreed to compose self-definitions and compare them to the "mythical norm" that Lorde identifies with "the trappings of social power: white, thin, male, young, heterosexual, Christian, and financially secure."[22] Gloria, a thirty-eight-year-old African American mother of five, summarized the consensus of the class most succinctly when she wrote, "I'm not white, thin, male, young, Christian, or financially secure, but I am heterosexual. . . . I still believe that being a lesbian is a sin against God and I wonder how those children with two mommies and no daddy will ever grow up normal. However, at first, all I saw in Lorde's identity was the label 'lesbian' . . . that separates us. . . . But in all the other categories she mentions, I, too, am an 'outsider,' and I share her position as a member of the powerless groups."

Some of the readings suggested by the paras themselves raised the profile of working-class life, particularly those aspects that represent the diversity of the female experience in the workplace. Before they came to my writing class, most of the paras were unaware that women without formal education wrote published accounts of working conditions in a variety of job settings and historical eras. For instance, a few had heard stories of the famous 1911 "Triangle Fire" in New York's garment center, through the oral histories of their grandmothers and great-aunts who had worked there, but they had never read accounts of the tragedy by survivors or witnesses until they saw an exhibit on campus during Women's History Month in 1991, commemorating the eightieth anniversary of the event. Some suggested that the class use material from the exhibit as a focus for reflective essays. Once we began to examine firsthand accounts of the fire, many of the paras' narratives on "work" centered on their previous employment in filthy and unsafe factories. Diane, a thirty-four-year-old mother of three, wrote a narrative in which she described her former work setting in a factory and summarized a common para experience — the joy of finding "work" in the field of education:

> Being hired by the Board of Education was the best thing that ever happened to me. Even though many other paras complain about the conditions on this job, I know that I have it good, now. From the age of sixteen, I worked sixty hours per week as a seamstress in a sweat-shop on the lower east side where there was no fresh air (mostly because of the cigar smoking boss who shut all the windows and fans whenever the line got held up and production slowed down). He screamed and cursed at the women workers and he wasn't above taking sexual advantage of the younger girls who had no green cards. Being a para is being in paradise compared to this occupation, and I can't believe that I'm working with children, now, and going to college.

Diane's narrative (and others like it) made me aware of the vast distance some of these women had already traveled to reach the point at which my education began (freshman writing) and made me conscious of how much I had taken for granted in my own life. Although some of the women were housewives (like me) before coming to college, others had a long, painful history as marginal workers in a variety of settings, including the needle trades. Our discussion of these personal accounts sparked vivid written reflections on the conditions of factory life (rats and mice in the lockers, cockroaches running through the sewing machines, verbal and physical assaults by male supervisors, mandatory overtime, unexpected layoffs, and so forth). From this perspective, the stresses and conflicts of para life seemed much less onerous because cleaner working conditions and the opportunity to go to college represented a giant step up for these women. I was moved by these narratives and gained much needed insight into the diversity of female working-class experience.

Then the class moved on to "The Fire Poems," and a few pieces of writing that had been tucked away by a previous generation found their way into the writing class.[23] Rebecca, a fifty-two-year-old mother of three whose family had escaped the pogroms of Russia at the turn of the century, offered a glimpse of her grandmother's scrapbook. It was filled with pictures, newspaper clippings, and handwritten vignettes jotted down by a number of women who wanted to record memories of friends who were victims of the terrible fire. Rebecca told the class, "My grandmother worked in a factory across the street from Triangle. She wrote a few lines in her scrap-book about women she knew (who died there). But, it was only something she wanted to do for herself (to remember them). Later, other women she worked with wrote remembrances in it as well. She never wanted to part with this book or to make it public because it records a very personal memory."

This comment illustrates the borders that many working-class women maintain between public and private discourse. These public/private conflicts also emerge in published accounts by working-class writers. For example, in "The Mighty Wedge of Class," a moving essay on the dissonance between "middle-class packaging" and "working-class core," J. Todd Erkel, discusses his mother's discomfort with his willingness to expose (in his professional essays) personal details of his life "where anyone might read them."[24] In a subsequent narrative, Rebecca wrote about a similar conflict: she had a sense that she was betraying her (now deceased) grandmother by showing this scrapbook to "strangers," while at the same time she felt compelled to do so by her desire to share something that had "historical and social relevance in a college course." David Bleich has pointed to the potential benefits of such public recollections: "If one task of the literacy classroom is to try to reconstruct [our] history then many hours can be spent thinking and asking friends and family about what one only partially remembers, and a surprising number of salient events of the past can be assembled. While it is never clear how 'accurate' our memories are, the fact of having remembered something important always facilitates new reflection and analysis."[25]

Collectively, the paras' narrative reflections on readings also revealed their need to separate "objective" opinions on social issues from the conditions of everyday life. To this end they employed a number of rhetorical strategies to distance their critical commentary on readings from their own lived experience. A clear example of this tendency appeared in their responses to Adrienne Rich's "Taking Women Students Seriously." Although no one disagreed (in principle) with Rich's arguments on the influence of gender stereotypes on educational opportunities for women, most exempted themselves from the group of women to whom she refers. Janice, whose autobiographical narrative focused on the conflicts between her domestic responsibilities and schoolwork, summed up the thoughts of many: "I absolutely agree with Rich . . . women have a right to develop their intellectual potentials. However, the author points out that her successful female teachers were single, by choice. . . . Women who choose to marry and have children no longer have a right to be autonomous individuals . . . they belong to a family." The problem with this position is that men are exempted from the restrictions of family life.

Only two narrative responses directly addressed Rich's claims about the special restrictions on women in families, in a society that insists that "doing the dishes" is more important for women than "studying."[26] These two responses did, in fact, refer to Stephanie's journal entry on the connection between dishwashing and studying, recalling that Stephanie's husband was watching television while she washed dirty pots and pans. They pointed out how her story supported the patriarchal assumption that all family chores like doing the dishes are "women's work." However, they did not address the role conflict between household chores and academic work also encoded in this domestic scene. A third response offered by Karen, a twenty-eight-year-old mother of two and the youngest para in the class, took a novel approach to Rich's text by depicting her own chronological history with dishwashing:

> When I was very young, I loved to wash the dishes. Mom would stand me on the stepladder and I would spray the rinse water; the reward was getting wet. In elementary school, I washed the nuns' dishes after lunch; the reward was getting out of math class. In high school, I washed dishes after card parties, PTA meetings, and school dances; the reward was "school service credits." By the time I got married, I realized the only reward for doing dishes is more dirty dishes. . . . It's not that doing the dishes is a big deal, but Rich made me think about the alternative "rewards" I didn't get, like playing outdoors with my brothers after dinner, like learning math, like getting "school service credits" for more important activities like community service. . . . Because I was brought up to value doing the dishes, I missed out on more interesting options.

Karen's story of her gendered/classed connection to dishwashing prompted a class discussion of the role that dirty dishes (and other domestic duties) played in their lives from childhood to adolescence to adulthood. Most reported that they had assumed they would get married, have children, wash dishes, and perform other household chores. Many recalled being taught by their mothers how to play their future domestic roles beginning in early childhood (because this kind of knowledge was expected of them). But none of us in the room, including myself, assumed we would go to college, nor did anyone else expect us to (or prepare us to acquire this other kind of knowledge). Thus, our student identities were never rehearsed or even imagined until we inhabited them as adult women with a whole set of previous role commitments competing for our time and attention.

This discussion of our access to gendered knowledge opened a dialogue on how gender expectations in working-class culture shape attitudes toward family, work, and student life. At the same time the class uncovered a number of distinctions among learning environments — various settings where different kinds of knowledge are available to women. Most claimed that formal schooling was the least effective model for learning in their lives, and many reported gaining the academic or professional skills needed to pass school exams or to advance themselves in the workplace from teachers or friends *off campus.*[27] Nevertheless, the need for formal credentials designates the college campus as the official setting where "knowledge" must be acquired and certified (if a person wants to advance financially and professionally).

The dissonance between home and school cultures was articulated by most of the women through comparisons of "learning from experience" versus "learning from books." Julie, sixty-four and the oldest para in the class, after ten years in college had accumulated only twenty-six credits, four less than she needed for her next pay raise. She explained her dilemma with the structure of higher education in a narrative entitled "Actions Speak Louder than Words":

I've been working for almost fifty years, twelve of those years I have spent as a paraprofessional. In all of my other work settings, the supermarket, the drug store, the office supply outlet, and the day-care center, I learned by experience and I was judged and rewarded financially by the quality of my work. As a para, I had to get my GED (which took me two years) and take college classes just to keep a job I already knew how to do. I love working with the children in Special Ed . . . and I'm very good with them. . . . But, on the college campus, I can't find the right words to fill in the god damn blankety blanks on tests. On my final exam in Special Ed. last semester, I couldn't fill in the different categories of special ed. students because I forgot the designations. So, on the back of the sheet, I described a number of children I work with who fit those categories. The professor would not accept my answers — and I failed the course. I don't need these credits to keep my job, but it seems to me that after twenty-five years of working with children (thirteen in day care, and twelve in the school system), I deserve to be judged and rewarded on whether or not I know the needs of the children I work with, not whether or not I can fill in the blankety-blanks on a college test.

Julie took composition (despite the disapproval of her academic advisor) because she wanted to take a course that involved "explaining in her own words."
She was still clearly struggling with surface errors and organization, but she
thought her ability to develop ideas and use rich details more than compen-
sated for these problems, and I agreed. Yet she remained at the low end of the
para pay scale because she could not connect official categories used to name
children's disabilities with her concrete experiences with these same children.
Due to her older age and few educational opportunities, Julie represents a
special circumstance (most younger paras adjust to the use of technical jargon
in their field and move along in the vocational courses). However, like Julie,
many paras experience test anxiety and perform poorly on standardized exams
because academic culture values ways of knowing and forms of expression that
these adult working-class women have been prevented from developing.[28]

Although the paras' experiences are tied to a specific situation, their narratives reflect tensions that affect a number of nontraditional working-class
women students. Juggling full-time jobs and family responsibilities, adult
working women students lead lives of frantic commuting from home to work,
to school, and back home again. In this stressful daily routine, campus life is
sandwiched between an eight-hour work day and a return to domestic and
child care duties. The ways of learning and knowing they bring to class are
different from those of other working-class students — more rooted in the interpersonal relationships and caretaking activities they participate in at home and
limited by the subordinate roles they play in the workplace. Thus, the critical
pedagogy I offer the paras begins with their own written accounts of their
families and working lives, the settings where their most frequent encounters
with language and learning take place. The production of literacy narratives
about their multiple roles inscribes their life experiences as wives, mothers, and
working women. At the same time, interpretation and comparison of their
narratives provide critical insights about their gendered/classed position and
its relation to issues of culture and social class. As a working-class wife, mother,
student, teacher, and writer, I do not believe that the construction of a student
identity with its attendant knowledge and experiences necessitates the erasure
of other existing identities. Therefore, my goal is to open a forum for my adult
women students to express their cultural conflicts with academic life, to examine the connections and conflicts among their multiple roles, and to analyze
how their women's experiences relate to academic knowledge, career goals,
and the larger issues in society. Maybe no one else honors them for washing
dishes, but I do, and I also honor their struggle for "a voice of their own" in
higher learning.

THE SHAPE OF THE FORM:

WORKING-CLASS STUDENTS AND THE ACADEMIC ESSAY

LINDA ADLER-KASSNER

At the beginning of the term, I ask students in my basic writing classes to write about their previous experiences with writing and reading. Did they like to read? To write? What was the last thing they read or wrote? I stress that students shouldn't worry about spelling, punctuation, or grammar; that they should work instead on developing the content of their response. By way of introduction to the students whose writing will illustrate some of the points raised later in this essay, here are excerpts from two of their essays:[1]

> Starting on an empty page, a white leaflet of nothingness, seems to be a little difficult for me, only because I find myself reflecting too much on the issue at hand, and even sometimes not sure of my opinions. . . . Expressing my opinions in a perfectly harmonious fashion while using others perception and continually developing a personal touch, has proven to be an artistic way of simplifying ideas and proposes questionable thinking.
>
> —Ned

> Well the last thing I read was my first chapter of math. The last thing I have wrote was a letter to my Grandmother in Florida. . . . I don't know what type of writing I like best because I don't know. I write when I have to. It's not like I write just for the fun of it. I just sometimes have a hard time trying to write

about things I don't like. I like writing papers about things I like, whatever it may be. I really don't read books unless I'm reading for class other than that I don't read books too much.

—Frank

Little exposure to or experience with writing was the rule for these basic writers, both from working-class backgrounds. But note that I'm not referring to them (at least, not yet) as working-class students, because I am not comfortable saying that all working-class students are basic writers, and I know that not all basic writers come from working-class backgrounds. Nevertheless, it is safe to say that working-class students like the ones discussed in this essay, who were enrolled in a basic writing course, traditionally come out of schools where they get very little experience with composition, and this inexperience leads them to struggle with academic writing. Mina Shaughnessy's pioneering work on basic writers, *Errors and Expectations,* was among the first to point out what now seems commonplace, that "the single most important fact about B[asic] W[riting] students is that, although they have been talking every day for a good many years, they have been writing infrequently, and then only in such artificial and strained situations that the communicative purpose of writing has rarely if ever seemed real."[2] Other researchers like Sondra Perl, Mike Rose, and David Bartholomae and Anthony Petrosky, have built on the foundation laid by Shaughnessy, studying the composing processes of inexperienced writers to examine the ways in which this inexperience leads them to processes different from what we might expect.[3]

The argument advanced by these basic writing researchers that some of these students' issues with academic writing come from their inexperience with the genre has been an important one for compositionists because it has helped us look closely at the relationship between basic writers' prior experiences and their performance in our classes. But I'd argue that issues connected with these students' success or failure with academic writing go beyond lack of exposure to the acts of reading and writing. They extend to a disjuncture between students' own values, reflected in their literacies, and the values and literacy reflected in the shape of the essay itself, as a genre. If we are to successfully help students from working-class and other nontraditional backgrounds whose values and literacies differ from those reflected and refracted in the essay, it's important to take a step back and examine the essay in order to pinpoint some of these differences and discuss their implications for the teaching of essays in any course, not just composition.[4] This essay is a step in that direction. First, it contextualizes the contemporary expository essay in the culture from which it emerged, looking at the relationship between that culture and the form of the essay itself. Next, it looks at writing by working-class students to examine potential issues that might arise between such students and the essay. Finally, it suggests some possible solutions for bridging the gap between student and academic literacies.

COMPOSITION AS COMMUNICATION

First, an assertion: The essay is a form of communication in the same way that newspapers, television shows, or movies are forms of communication. People participate in these forms (they read the paper, listen to certain kinds of music, watch certain television shows) because they find that these media confirm the ways that they see the world and reaffirm that what they perceive as reality is, indeed, real. And they're not alone — they belong to a community, not of people in the same geographical area, but of people who also find their values confirmed in those media.

As a form of communication like these other media, the essay also mediates the existence of a distinct community of people who interpret communication in similar ways. Here, as above, I define *community* as a group sharing a common interpretation of mass-communicated symbols, in this case the essay itself, and the words that comprise it. While two people in the academic community may not interpret an idea in the same way — for example, I may believe that John Dewey meant one thing when he wrote about the purpose of education and you may believe he meant another — this disagreement is carried out in a broader context of understanding that we both share.[5] This is the sort of "cultural literacy" of academe, a common understanding underscoring our differing interpretations that ensures we're basically in the same ballpark. Although we may be on different teams, sharing this ballpark means that we use language and form to express our allegiances in ways that we (and our millions of teammates) see as "correct" within the context of the academy.

The question is, What are the values shaping the walls of the ballpark, the ones that we unwittingly participate in when we participate in academic writing? Lynn Z. Bloom argues that this "correctness" reflects middle-class values; that, in fact, academic writing (and first-year composition especially) is a "middle-class enterprise." It is

> taught by middle-class teachers in middle-class institutions to students who are middle class either in actuality or in aspiration — economic if not cultural. Indeed, one of the major though not necessarily acknowledged reasons that freshman composition is in many schools the only subject required of all students is that it promulgates the middle-class values that are thought to be essen-

tial to the proper functioning of students in the academy. When students learn to write, or are reminded once again of how to write . . . they also absorb a vast subtext of related folkways, the whys and hows of good citizenship in their college world, and by extrapolation, in the workaday world for which their educations are designed to prepare them.[6]

The recent debate over the Oakland, California, school district's decision to designate Ebonics as a separate and distinct language is an excellent example of Bloom's claim: those who objected most stridently to the policy to designate separate classes for speakers of this dialect did so because they believed that allowing Black English Vernacular in the classroom would somehow interfere with students' abilities to master Standard English and therefore prevent them from functioning as fully vested citizens in a culture based around middle-class values and norms. For example, Syl Jones, an African American commentator for the *Minneapolis Star-Tribune,* wrote that "the failure of many black students to connect with the outside world, particularly the business world, is directly connected to language choices. Those who do not learn standard English may remain isolated economically and, as a result, mired in poverty. Therefore, the goal must be to teach standard English by any means necessary, to borrow from Malcolm X, so that our children prosper."[7] Clearly, Jones and others like him see a strong connection between language, as a form of communication, and culture. They view participation in Standard English as a key to entrance into middle-class culture and its concomitant benefits — economic security, some element of social stability, access to opportunity. While academic writing doesn't enter into Jones's argument directly, many have made the same argument with regard to this medium as well — students need to master it to do well in school, and that success is one step toward economic success. Because composition is the site charged with teaching students this language, composition classes are by default where struggles over the relationship between students' languages and cultures and academic language and culture are played out. As a result, composition often becomes both a dumping ground for the problems of the academy and a fertile site for investigating the tension between academic and student literacies.

But in our haste to examine the (mis)connections between student and academic language in the present, we sometimes forget two crucial points. First, it is not only the language, but also the form of the essay that reflects and refracts the culture in which the essay exists. Second, the essay, like all other forms of communication, has a "significant past" in which it is deeply rooted and which continues to affect its present. Therefore, it's relevant first to examine this past, looking particularly at the historical relationship between form and the contemporary expository essay as it emerged during the early twentieth century.

THE SHAPE OF THE FORM:
THE EVOLUTION OF THE CONTEMPORARY EXPOSITORY ESSAY

The contemporary academic essay is something most readers of this essay know well. It begins with a thesis that introduces and summarizes the writer's argument, moves on to evidence supporting the thesis, and ends with a conclusion that might summarize the essay, demonstrate the relevance of the paper, or suggest avenues for additional investigation. The writer is expected to draw the reader through the argument, demonstrating how the evidence in the essay is related to the thesis.[8] For those of us immersed in this kind of academic writing — because we write it ourselves, grade stacks of it on a regular basis, or read it in academic texts — it is familiar territory. As successful survivors of multiple components of the educational system (elementary school, high school, college, graduate school), it feels fairly natural because we've done it for so long and because, for many of us, the essay reflects the values that we've (willingly or unwittingly) adopted in our own lives.

Too often, however, we forget that the values reflected in that form don't represent everyone's culture. The essay, like all forms of rhetoric, has its origins in the work of classical rhetoricians. But, as Jasper Neel writes, those ancient scholars really aren't who most us think about when we think about composition. They "remain . . . shadowy, subliminal presences. They 'exist' merely as unknown influences whose ideas appear . . . from the dimmest recesses of our discipline's history."[9] Although Neel insists that compositionists should understand the logic of the ancient rhetoricians, I find it far more significant to look to our more immediate ancestors, those compositionists working during the period around the turn of the century known as the Progressive Era. In their belief that the strict lessons of their predecessors were not the most effective way for students to learn how to write, progressive compositionists instituted a new way of thinking about writing that has shaped our work into the present.[10]

The most prominent of these pedagogical trailblazers was Fred Newton Scott, creator and chair of the Department of Rhetoric at the University of Michigan and an outspoken critic of nineteenth-century pedagogy, which he believed stifled student creativity. Rather than write about subjects remote from their experiences, Scott argued, students should write about things that were familiar to them. In this way students' natural tendencies toward self-expression would find outlets in the classroom. Scott's intellectual descendant, biographer and compositionist Donald Stewart, wrote that Scott believed "students are never deficient in the impulse to express themselves . . . or in the desire to communicate what they have to say to someone else."[11]

But the rationale for wanting students to feel that their essays represented something of themselves went beyond a desire to have students enjoy their composition experiences. In fact, it is possible to outline a trajectory in progressive composition scholarship from ownership of content, to mastery of form, to participation in Progressive Era culture.[12] Scott, for example, insisted that "every pupil uses his own language, every pupil is witness to the power of his own words upon his fellow-pupils. To reveal to him the effectiveness of the tools which he already knows how to use and to show him how to sharpen them and use them more effectively, is the language teacher's first task. . . . What more is there to do than to go straight on in the same direction cultivating more power and realization of power as long as education lasts?"[13] But as students wrote about subjects familiar to them, they were also expected to become more proficient academic writers. With their mastery of the academic essay, Scott insisted, also came "the obligation to use this great instrument for the training and instruction of the souls of the citizens."[14] Composition, he wrote, would become a place for "growth in power to do the world's work."[15]

Clearly, Scott believed composition vital for the perpetuation of a specific vision of the American experience. But that vision was linked to Scott's own position as a Progressive reformer, one who believed that the nation was progressing toward the achievement of some kind of virtuous democracy. And although Progressives believed that achievement of this goal was in some ways America's destiny, they were simultaneously concerned that the nation could veer from the course leading toward it. Thus, they believed that for the nation to achieve this goal, it was vitally important that all Americans embrace a common ideology. Broadly summarized, the most prominent characteristic of that ideology was commitment to a set of political and civil ideals stemming from the legacy of republicanism: commitment to the public good and the health of the nation; a belief in liberty so that all could be free to participate in public affairs; and the creation of community, so that all would share an equal existence among others who shared and participated in the same commitments. Despite the dominance of Progressive ideology, however, another characteristic of Progressivism was the belief that the virtuous democracy was always a step too far away. Thus Progressives believed it was vitally important to bring others into the Progressive fold.[16] Therefore, when Scott linked ownership of content to mastery of form to participation in the culture, it was Progressive culture that students would participate in. Yet, Progressive Era culture was nothing if not middle-class — as countless historians of the period have argued, the contemporary middle class is firmly rooted in the fin de siecle period.[17]

The trajectory from ownership of content to mastery of form to participation in values essentially endures, in different shapes and forms, throughout much of this century's composition scholarship. Much of it revolves around the vital importance of having students write about what they know in order to more easily master the form of the academic essay. Even in paradigms like expressivism, where good form was seen as less important than helping students work toward self-knowledge and self-understanding through writing, the idea that producing "good" writing will move the nation closer to the achievement of a laudable goal always hangs in the background.[18] As expressivist Stewart put it, the development of an honest, ethical culture was predicated on students' developing self-knowledge and self-understanding. For instance, Stewart argued that "rhetoric should persuade men to desire the good. To do that, the words of the persuader must be true in the broadest and intensest meaning of that word. . . . The user of words must believe that they are true, that they describe things as they are, within the limits of his capability to perceive them." Quoting psychologist Robert Zoellner, Stewart argued that the student must use "words for me" instead of "words for teacher" by using "*his* words to describe *his* experience."[19] But it's important to remember that neither words nor experiences are value-free. Throughout the twentieth century, writing about the *right* experiences in the *right* ways to prove their authenticity also meant that the student had to participate in the (middle-class) culture's definition of "authentic truth."

CITIZENRY AND COMPOSITION TODAY

The legacy left by progressive compositionists to contemporary teachers is complicated. On the one hand, they moved composition away from a model that asked students to work with texts completely unrelated to their daily experiences; one can only imagine that the themes based on those experiences were painful to write and read. On the other, the ideological baggage associated with composition remains as heavy today as it was in the Progressive Era. Since the progenitors of the composition program at Harvard University insisted that freshmen whose writing was not up to snuff take a course called English A, composition has been charged with preparing students to write for the academy. But the argument here is that composition, like any other form of communication, is intricately bound up with the academic culture; therefore, we have also taken on the responsibility of helping to prepare students to enter the (middle-class) culture of the academy in all of its complexities.

Here, then, is one of the fundamental dilemmas facing not only composition instructors, but also those in many other disciplines. In addition to teaching students the "content" of our courses, we are charged with helping them become good academic citizens, and part of the qualifications for that citizenship is reflected in their use of "proper" academic writing. Yet, because this form reflects the middle-class values of the Progressive/pragmatic culture from which it developed, many of our working-class students might not find it a comfortable mode of expression, because their values are different from the ones reflected in it. We know that in preparing students, we ask them to work with academic language and form that may be alien to them. Composition instructors are caught in a trap: whether we agree with it or not — and most of the compositionists whom I know wrestle with this dilemma on a daily basis — our survival is in part contingent on our success in this preparation. Too often, we hear colleagues teaching "content courses" insist that the responsibility for teaching students to write for the academy lies with compositionists; too often, those complaints trickle up to administrators, who question whether composition programs are successful if students don't meet the expectations of instructors throughout their college careers based on one or two terms in our classrooms. Thus, although the current paradigm of composition instruction may not serve all of our students as effectively as we might wish, the cycle continues — our survival is contingent on perpetuating this discourse to some degree, and so on.

In my own classes this dilemma is something I think about every day. In one of my courses, it's also the subject we study for the term. Looking at examples of writing from this course by the students whose excerpts opened this essay, it's possible to see how the disjuncture between students' values and the values implicit in the essay can pose a difficulty for some in the composition classroom.

The theme of the course, broadly speaking, is language and education. The writing in the course builds on the reading and reflects ideas that I share with progressive compositionists, such as Scott: it's easier and more meaningful for students to write when they write about something that they know. It's also easier for students to begin mastering the skills associated with academic writing (like the thesis-evidence-conclusion form of the essay, integrating quotations from other sources) in a context of some familiarity. Therefore, the reading and writing here simultaneously introduce new ideas to students and ask them to build connections between what they know and what we are studying. We begin the quarter by reading Keith Gilyard's *Voices of the Self,* which alternates between a narrative of the author's experiences as an African American student in predominantly New York public schools during the 1950s and 1960s and an analysis of the sociolinguistic and cultural contexts in which those experiences took place. Halfway through the term, the course focus shifts as we begin looking at the relationship between another kind of language, graffiti, and its reception in the broader culture. After a "taste of the library" paper that is related to the subjects of study in the course, we end the quarter by working with the "Students' Right to Their Own Language" resolution, a statement approved by the Conference on College Composition and Communication in 1974 "affirm[ing] the students' right to their own patterns and varieties of language" — the dialects of their nurture or whatever dialects in which they find their own identity and style."[20] For each formal essay assigned in this course, students write two shorter, informal ones in about an hour of class time. As in the assignment described at the beginning of this essay, I encourage students to focus on content and not worry about form. The differences between these assignments speak volumes about the difficulties that these working-class students have with the essay.

WORKING-CLASS STUDENTS AND THE ACADEMIC ESSAY

David Bartholomae has argued that students' success with academic writing depends, in part, on their abilities to strike a balance between their own modes of expression and the discourses they're expected to produce. According to Bartholomae:

> The student has to appropriate (or be appropriated by) a specialized discourse, and he has to do this as though he were easily and comfortably one with his audience . . . ; has to invent the university by assembling and mimicking its language while finding some compromise between idiosyncrasy, a personal history, on the one hand, and the requirements of convention, the history of a discipline, on the other. He must learn to speak our language. Or he must dare to speak it or to carry off the bluff, since speaking and writing will most certainly be required long before the skill is "learned." And this, understandably, causes problems.[21]

For working-class students, this issue is especially pronounced. As the excerpts below demonstrate, these students are aware — consciously or unconsciously, although I suspect the former — that their expression does not look like academic expression. They try to compensate for what they see as the difference with the language they use in their essays. But these excerpts also show that as much difficulty as these students have with language, they also have problems with the form of the essay, about which they are less conscious.

This is evident, for example, in the differences between students' short, in-class essays that focus only on content and formal essays (the more "traditional" essay). But as much as these papers illustrate the differences between these literacies, they also illustrate the steps that students took in the course toward finding some compromise position that worked for them. For example, here is an excerpt from one of Ned's short essays, written as one of the steps toward a formal paper in which he was analyzing why Keith Gilyard split himself into two "selves" when he entered elementary school and reflecting on similar experiences he'd had or witnessed.[22]

Much like Keith, I had two different "halves." But unlike Keith I was this way because I was ashamed of who I was and where I came from. . . .

* * *

. . . [T]hroughout [my childhood] we were moving from town to town, suburb to suburb. Nothing was consistent in my life I was continually having to regain my stature as a student. I noted that as I got older things were changing. I was beginning to lie more and more about who I was. . . .

After several moves I started to notice . . . that things are not going to change as far as the moving around. So I began to tell wild stories about who I was. My friends were, alot of the times, under the impression that I was from "France." . . . My class mates were always impressed with me, and so were my teachers. I think what helped me as well, with the impression that I was trying to portray was that my transcripts were always getting lost. My mom couldn't keep track of the records so alot of times the teachers had no files on me so I was free to do whatever I wanted so long as no one was harmed. . . .

* * *

I was born in St. Paul, Minnesota. We first lived in a project kind of housing. There was no way I was going to let on that that was where I lived so when my "friends" asked me, I would tell them that we lived in a nice house.

This excerpt demonstrates Ned's acumen with the application of theory (from *Voices of the Self*) to his own experience. He's not describing the invention of his "French" origins as aberrant behavior, but as an act of "switching" that he performed to ensure his survival in school. This is an important part of mastering academic reading — it shows that he not only understands the concepts in the text but is applying them to his own experiences and thus gaining new insight on them. Furthermore, he is able to write these experiences in language that is easy to read and understand and communicates the complexity of his experience.

When Ned moves from this short essay about his own experiences to the part of the formal essay that focuses on analysis of Gilyard's experiences, it's clear that the same quality of analysis is present. But because the writing in the essay changes, it's more difficult for the reader to fully understand that analysis. Here's an excerpt from that piece:

Keith Gilyard in "Voices of the Self" provides several examples of separating his cultural life from his school life. The first time that the separation of the self was evident was when Keith was brought to a classroom predominantly consisting of white children by the principle of the school. . . . Keith in preservation of his identity uses Raymond as a scholastic tool. Raymond suddenly became Keith's school identity, a role that Keith is going to play until he can get to know his classmates. Which was the first step of Keith's survival plan and a separation of self.

Later as school progresses Raymond begins to develop socially. He began to pry into other students lives, made friends and dominated the playground, and was the class clown. His only down fall was the dotting of his i's.

* * *

"Keith was developing as well" p 51. Keith met a boy by the name of Lonnie. Lonnie was throwing pebbles at a house when the two intercepted. . . . Their first interaction seemed threatening and up frontal, which prompted Raymond's change of identity to Keith, which is the name that Keith goes by when he is around other black people p 52. Both of them were trying to gain ground on each other but because Keith "made up" stories of him getting stabbed and being involved in harlem gangs helped him to gain respect from Lonnie. Lonnie was impressed by Keith. Keith expresses that although his friends are violent he preferred to "spar with words" p 53. Which helped him from brawling with the more aggressive kids p 53.

In the excerpt from the formal essay, Ned's struggles with the essay are clearer. For example, there are interesting syntactical turns here that occur when he uses language that he thinks "sounds" more academic than the language he uses in the earlier excerpt: "Keith in preservation of his identity uses Raymond as a scholastic tool"; "Keith met a boy by the name of Lonnie. Lonnie was throwing pebbles at a house when the two intercepted. . . . Their first interaction seemed threatening and up frontal, which prompted Raymond's change of identity to Keith."

But in addition to using a different kind of language than he did in the short essay, Ned is struggling with the form of the essay itself. The first paragraph of the excerpt is strong and establishes a good thesis for the remainder of the paper. But the next two paragraphs, reprinted here as they appeared in the essay, are missing some of the crucial formal components that readers expect of an essay.[23] The second paragraph begins without the kind of leading topic sentence that helps the reader follow Ned's analysis of the situation: why this piece of evidence, about Raymond's social development and his interaction with friends in the classroom and on the playground, supports his argument that Keith split himself into two selves as a "scholastic tool." The third paragraph begins with a quote from the book, but there's no explanation regarding the relationship of the quote to the thesis that Ned established at the beginning of the paper regarding Keith's split into two selves. What Ned is doing here is giving the reader the skeleton of an essay, the evidence that he's found that supports his thesis. But the form in which he's presenting this content is askew — it's missing the signposts that readers of academic essays come to expect.

This absence is pronounced in other essays by other working-class students, as well. In Frank's first short essay of the quarter (which appears at the beginning of this piece), he allowed that he had little experience reading or writing in an academic context. Yet, although that first essay is about the fact that he doesn't like to write or read, it's a fairly fluid piece of writing — sentences are complete, ideas in the selection are connected to one another, it carries the reader through the piece of writing with a clear idea of the relationship between the assigned question and the resulting essay. In a more formal piece of academic writing, Frank's analysis of the issues involved with the question he created for himself (What are graffiti artists trying to teach people through their language?) is excellent. As in Ned's essay, it's clear that he's making connections across a number of contexts, reading the texts through his own experiences, and reading those experiences through the text. But in the essay, the language and form required seem to interfere with the expression of these ideas:

> What is graffiti artist trying to teach people through their language?
> Graffiti artist are trying to bring their language to a main stream. Taggers (graffiti artist) are trying to reach out to their community and with their environment. One tagger had several words about the urge of tagging.

> > On a [gray]-skied Wednesday afternoon within the confines of my first floor lab, I recline my had on a soft blue cushion, relaxing, pondering life's poisons over a glass of mango snapple. An excessive dose of underground hip hop seeps thickly out of my make shift boom box. As the beat hits the audio canals and liquid trickles slowly down my esophagus, I allow my eyes to wander over two hundred cans of Krylon, American Accent, Plasticote, and the old time favorite, Rustoleum. (33) *As the sun sets, we rise*

> That is artist pleasure about the whole thought of performing graffiti. Taggers would love to have the chances to have abundant of cans and nozzles, to perform their great art. One of their first love of many artist is their names, lots of artist start out just writing names in bold form.
> Taggers plan weeks in advance to tagg a spot. Typically like cases frequently in New York Taggers plan to hit a Whole train which is ten cars deep. When taggers are trying to tag a whole train, they usually are trying to make a

statement. Many taggers get respect when they can tag a whole train. Once a tagger tag a train they know if they want people to keep seen their work they . . . have to keep tagging.

* * *

Chris a tagger said "When I first became Christian I realized on my own that I would have to stop tagging because it defaced other people's property." (30) *Internet.* Chris who was going through some changes at the time of his initial tagging. . . . Chris after stopping his work of art, he wanted a place where he could display his work. Jude a mentor to Chris . . . finds Chris and other artists a alleyway where drug dealers and prostitution use to go on. Jude told the artist that they can paint a mural in the alley but she would have to see the mural on paper first. Chris and friends went on to paint the mural after Jude approved the draft. After Chris finished the mural he went on to add "It made me feel important to have my name on walls. It was my escape." He goes on to say "the fear and risk of tagging numbed the pain of loneliness." Chris also loved the fact that all the neighborhood taggers knew who he was. Chris like so many other tagger uses graffiti for a outlet out, another form of communication so to *draw.* Chris was trying to let people know that he was going through some problems with his graffiti. Rather than fighting with people, he chooses to tag buildings, trucks, and many other objects, Chris takes pride in his tagging, it's a piece of art. Using graffiti to express his feeling was hard but, by expressing his selves he was able to maintain. Graffiti is a expression that everybody doesn't understand. Taggers don't want to be called vandal but artist.

* * *

In my conclusion I feel I have shown you many reasons why taggers tag building. I also have gave many reasons why taggers tag. After understanding why taggers tag I had a better understanding of what goes through a taggers mind. I've also shown many causes of different tagger and different experience. In my final statement I feel that all *art* should be accepted as *art.*

As a reader, I can almost feel Frank wrestling with the form of the academic essay in this excerpt. He begins with the question he's answering, which he's using as part of the thesis for the paper: "What [are] graffiti artist[s] trying to teach people through their language?" He then moves to an answer, an additional part of that thesis: Graffiti artists are trying to bring their language into the mainstream. They're "trying to reach out to their community and with their environment." In the next sentence, Frank sets up and contextualizes the quote that follows it, about the "urge of tagging," which certainly fits the form of the standard academic essay. But in doing so, he fails to make clear the relationship between the quote, which seems itself to contextualize the tagger's culture and mind-set, and his thesis, about what graffiti artists are trying to teach through their language.

After this opening paragraph, Frank shifts the paper away from analyzing what graffiti writers are trying to teach and begins a section about the act of tagging, one kind of graffiti writing. Although the first paragraph of the paper was analysis (which the assignment called for), this one is a narrative about what's involved in tagging a train. Although a relationship certainly exists between these two pieces of information, Frank doesn't make clear what that relationship is — as in the previous example, the kind of signposts (like topic sentences and even indentation) that the reader expects to guide her through the essay are missing here. However, embedded in the narrative are statements about what graffiti artists are trying to teach through their language: for example, they're "going against the norm and trying to relate to other artist[s]." In the third paragraph Frank focuses on a specific tagger, Chris, and uses him as a case study around which to focus this section of the paper. In this paragraph are statements linking the example to his thesis: taggers are asserting their own presence (Frank writes that Chris says "It made me feel important to have my name on walls. It was my escape.") and they're "trying to let people know that [they] are going through some problems with [their] graffiti."

Throughout this section of the paper it becomes obvious that although Frank has a clear sense of the relationship between each piece of evidence in the paper and the thesis he outlined at its onset, the essay is missing structural components that help the reader make the same kinds of connections. This becomes even more clear with the paper's conclusion, where Frank wraps up everything he's tried to show in the paper in a concise and clear statement. There *is* a structure here; it's just not the one that we expect to read in the standard academic essay. Instead, it's a step toward a hybrid text. In some ways this essay reflects a form more familiar to Frank: he's not accustomed to having to make his argument this clear, or connect all of his ideas explicitly, or pull the reader through that argument using certain (idiosyncratic) formal conventions in the way that the essay requires him to. In other ways, though, it's clear that he's working toward inserting his ideas into the form of the conventional academic essay; it's just that he hasn't completely succeeded yet.

Excerpts from Ned's and Frank's papers demonstrate common points of difficulty that working-class students seem to have with academic writing. The model we expect in the essay — thesis, evidence, conclusion, with topic sentences and other points of reference that help the reader follow the writer's argument — seem less accessible to these students than they do to others who might have more academic experience with writing and reading. But by examining examples like these side-by-side with the historical context in which ideas about what an essay should look like evolved, it becomes clear that some of the reasons for this inaccessibility go beyond lack of experience with academic writing, perhaps to differences in ideologies and values reflected in the forms of expression most commonly used by students. As the excerpts from early-twentieth-century compositionists demonstrate, mastery of the essay's form has long been integrally linked to assimilation of cultural values that they consider to be reflected in and perpetuated by the form of the essay. If students come to that form with different values, it might seem far less "natural" to them than it is to students who already participate in those values.

BRIDGING THE GAP

When I started teaching composition, I would suggest that authors of papers like these sit down with me so that I could help them find ways to transform what they had into something that conformed to the formal conventions of academic writing. Working through the essay one piece at a time, I'd begin by talking with students about what an essay (or paragraph) should look like. When I finished my short explanation, I'd ask, "See what I mean?" Most students would nod and say yes, and we'd move on to the next chunk of the paper. But after loads of teaching and grading and extensive research into the roots of conventions of different disciplines, including composition, I've learned that "seeing what I meant" sometimes involved asking students to conform to a whole set of unspoken values that are part of the ideology reflected in the form of the essay. Now, I do things differently. I still sit down with students who write papers like the ones above and work through them piece by piece. But I'm explicit about what might seem to them the illogic of the essay, and I talk with them about how they might use what they have within the formal confines of what they need to produce in the class.

But these conversations are really only a small part of bridging the gap between student and academic literacies — which, after all, is the problem underscoring the differences between the ways that students express themselves and the (il)logic of the academic essay. There are other solutions that make this gap more manageable and that bear investigation as well. To conclude this essay, I'll discuss some of those solutions, each of which builds on the idea that though the essay reflects middle-class culture, we should remember and take advantage of the fact that it can also refract it, thereby allowing students spaces to create a hybrid within the form.

Solution One: Change the Way We Think about Academic Writing

I regularly receive readers and books on rhetoric that focus on the teaching of academic writing. They vary wildly in quality — the very best are very good, indeed. The editors have considered their audiences of students and, certainly, instructors carefully; they reflect broad consideration for what "students' cultures" are and try to represent them in the reading and writing assignments in the books. They provide stimulating, challenging readings for students to use as a basis for investigation of a variety of topics and ask good questions to push students to broaden their consideration of these topics. They help students "write to learn," asking them to interrogate their own experiences as they analyze the experiences of others whose work appears in the collection.

But not all of these readers demonstrate this attention to student culture and the nature of writing. Others present academic writing as a formula to be mastered and provide content that can (and presumably should) be "inserted" into this form. One of the chief differences between these readers, too, is the way they conceptualize writing. In the good readers, writing is seen as a vehicle for learning and a tool for communicating. In the less stimulating ones, writing is seen as little more than a form, and the primary purpose of composition classes appears to be to demonstrate competency with this form to a reader who has not only expertise in it, but also mastery of the knowledge being communicated.

If we are to help students from backgrounds whose values are different from those reflected in the academic essay — students from working-class backgrounds, as well as others — we need to move away from framing the essay as a vehicle through which mastery of knowledge is proven. Instead, we need to think of the essay as a form of communication, a medium that guides a reader who might not know about this particular subject or aspect of the reading, but who *does* participate in the academic community through a writer's consideration of a question, understanding of a subject, investigation of connections between different worlds or ideas. This means assigning questions that really have the widest possible range of answers. Those who assigned the questions may have our own ideas about how to answer them, but our answers are not necessarily "right," because they're based on our interpretation and understanding of the texts we are studying, and those are shaped by *our* experiences. Students, whose experiences likely differ from our own, may come up with different answers from the ones we have because they interpret the material we read together differently than we do. For me, these questions frequently include a lot of "whys": what is the purpose of education and why is it that; why did Gilyard split himself into two selves; why do people use different forms of language in different situations; why should students have a right to their own language in the classroom, or why should they not?

This approach has several benefits for students who struggle with academic literacy. One of the most important ones is that composition classes become less about helping students "match" an instructor's idea of what an essay should be — how it should look and sound, exactly what evidence should be included in it — than they are about using evidence from texts and experience to investigate topics mutually relevant for students and instructor alike. The essay becomes the vehicle through which students' understanding of a question or a topic is communicated, and questions about the form of the essay become honest ones — if the reader really can't understand the connection between different ideas (or even if that connection is explicit), it's no longer a sort of well-meaning fallacy when we write, "It's hard for me to see the connections between these two ideas. Can you help me here?" or "I think I see what you mean here, but can you help me better understand it with evidence from the readings?"

Solution Two: Design Assignments That Invite Students to Find Connections to the Material Being Studied in the Course

This solution is hardly a new one: designing curricula that encouraged students to make connections between their "real lives" and school was, after all, one of the central tenets of John Dewey's work, and it is certainly central in the work of progressive compositionists like Scott. But because composition courses are one of the sites where students learn how to "do" academic culture, sometimes it's assumed that part of that "doing" means leaving real lives behind, particularly for students whose real lives don't match academic culture particularly well. When this is the case, however, it's all the more important to help students make that connection: after all, one of the reasons that we've all made it as far in the educational system as we have is because we found some reason to care about what we are doing. Don't we owe it to our students to help them create the same kinds of connections? For example, I invite students to examine their own experiences or the experiences of those whom they know side-by-side with our investigations into text-based subjects. This doesn't mean that they need to produce personal narratives or confessional writing — in fact, it dissuades them from that kind of writing. Instead, it asks them to analyze these experiences through lenses provided by readings, or in response to those readings.

Solution Three: Allow Students to Incorporate Their Own Ideas and Language into the Academic Essay

One of the themes of Bartholomae's "Inventing the University" is that students have to find some compromise position between their own forms of expression and the discourse they're expected to use in academe. Although Bartholomae has written elsewhere about the importance of movement by both academy and student, the conception of the "compromise" in this essay seems to put the burden of the code-switch (which is really what it is) entirely on the student.[24] Why not have academic writing generally, and composition classes specifically, meet students halfway? One dilemma of compositionists, discussed earlier, is that we are charged with helping students master the language and form of the essay, but the argument here is that this language and form reflect and refract a community different from the ones our students belong to. Within the form of the essay, however, there is some room for maneuvering—it can be taught as something akin to what educational theorist Basil Bernstein has called a "consensual ritual," where the potential exists for both student and institutional cultures to be represented in the content and form of the subject being taught.[25] This idea is similar to basic writing pioneer Mina Shaughnessy's suggestion that the basic writing teacher should "remediate himself, to become a student of new disciplines and of his students themselves in order to perceive both their difficulties and their incipient excellence."[26] But it goes beyond Shaughnessy's idea in its attempt to incorporate student language and form into the classroom to work toward a kind of collaboratively constructed literacy that incorporates both academic/instructor literacy and students' literacy.

One way to create opportunities for this kind of multivocal, hybrid text is to assign different kinds of writing in the course, such as the short and formal essays described here. In short essays, for example, I encourage students to forget about making sure that their language "sounds" academic or that they have a strong thesis and topic sentences that help lead the reader through the essay. Instead, they focus on content—getting down on paper what they want to say about whatever they're writing about. Furthermore, although the excerpts from short essays here have students' own experiences as a subject, only about half of the short essays in the class focus on student narratives. The other half ask students to focus on how they will use class readings in their formal writing assignments.

Students often produce their best writing in these more comfortable, less intimidating "spaces" where they don't have to think about connecting everything together in a way that looks academic. Then we work to move this less formal writing into the formal papers. Sometimes this means taking an entire short essay and using it as the basis for the long essay. Since the content is there, we focus on shaping the structure of the essay and building in "signposts" such as theses, topic sentences, transitions, and citations that help the reader follow the writer's arguments. Other times, it means taking ideas from the short essays and expanding on them for the long essay, building in connections between them so that it is clear how they relate to the thesis (and the assigned question).

Because the writing produced in these short assignments is usually so rich, the possibilities for helping students build on it for the long essay are myriad. As the excerpt from Ned's short essay shows, students sometimes produce some very eloquent writing when they don't have to worry about how what they're writing sounds or the form it takes; as the excerpts from the long essays show, when they do worry about these matters, the results can be mixed.

Ideally, students work from the short essays to the long and produce a kind of mixed-genre essay that combines analysis of their own experiences and language and the language of the academy. One working-class student, Sarah, did this extremely well. Here are excerpts from two of her short essays, written on the same question as Ned's was, why Gilyard split himself into two "selves": Excerpt one:

> I am going to write about why I feel he split his life into two different lives. I felt he did it to fit in. pg.43: it talks about his new school and how in his class room he was the only black student other than a saundra meritt the girl with the pig-tails. he talks about how he felt trembled and fearful and wanted to grab hold or mr. prices pant legs ad if it were his moms apron. I think he thought doing so might comfort him cause when I think mothers and kids I think of security and comfort. then he wanted his sister but realized she wasn't coming for him either. then when given the question ??raymond?? or??keith?? he felt as if he (keith) were a share or a fifth wheel. (pg43) he said that they couldn't meet keith now and that he would put someone else together for them and he would be their classmate til further notice. and that was his first step in survival. so he choose raymond. I felt out of this he changed his identity so he could create a person that he felt would fit in more with the class than keith. keith to him was different or like he said a fifth wheel and being a new student and one of the only blacks in a white dominated school can be difficult. especially at a young age.

Excerpt two:

> Even though I didn't give myself a new name like keith did (to raymond) I have also had times in my life when I made up a new character that I felt would fit in better with the surrounding then myself.
>   moving: in the middle of 9 grade I moved from a jr. high [in one suburb] to a high school [in another]. jumping from the middle of my last year in jr. high right into my first year of high school was difficult for me at first (old jr high 7-9 and high school 9-12) through moving I learned that even though at first I didn't realize what I was doing, I hide my whole self from my classmates to cope with and fit into my new environment, but in the end I broke free from my bubble, let myself out and found my true friends.

In both of these excerpts, Sarah uses the space of the short essay to cram in as many ideas as she can. The language here is clearly hers — she doesn't even pay attention to punctuation, much less grammar. And here's how these parlayed into the formal essay:

Code switching in ones life sometimes has advantages as well as disadvantages. Different people code switch for many different reasons and at times they don't even know it. I felt that Gilyard separated himself into two different people to help him cope with his new and different environment in his school community by fitting in with people. I felt that him leading two different lives at times was his way of coping with the feeling of being different.

* * *

The first day that Keith Gilyard walked into his new classroom he started his first coping strategy. That's when he noticed the majority of his class were white students. Gilyard became the second black student in his class after the little girl with pigtails, Saundra Merritt, who too was staring just as hard as the white kids. He felt as if he were a fifth wheel or a spare tire to his class. He talks about the fear and trembled feelings that came over him as the principal, Mr. Price, walked him into his new classroom for the first time.

* * *

Like Gilyard there have been times in my life where my surroundings were new and I just didn't feel like I fit in. Sometimes I felt like I had to change my character in order to fit in better. But being someone else did not help me cope with my classmates. One of the biggest step that I took in my life was when we moved in the middle of ninth grade and my last year of junior high school. We moved from [one suburb to another] where I was about to start High School in the middle of my Freshman year. I was terrified because I was not even done with junior high school and now as to be in high school. Through moving I learned that even if at first I didn't notice what I was doing, I hid my real self from my classmates to cope with my new environment and fit in better.

This essay is less of a "frankenstein text" than either of the two previous formal-essay excerpts. Sarah's formal essay sounds like her, but it also sounds like an academic paper — she's worked in the content *and* the language she developed in the short essays there. This is not to imply that the writers quoted above didn't also work toward the same achievement — without seeming harsh, it needs to be said that the gap between student and academic literacies is easier for some students to bridge than for others. And from the points from which the other students' work started, the essays that they wrote represented significant steps toward creating formal academic essays.

These three solutions — changing the way we think about academic writing, designing assignments that facilitate connections between students and material, and making space for students to include their own language and ideas in the essay — involve a lot of listening in order to learn more about why students wrote things as they did and thinking about what values and ideologies are reflected in the forms they use. I think all of these can help working-class students find some way into a form that represents values different than the ones that they might embrace. But I also think that we in composition can work on pushing this discourse from within, trying to help our students into it in the best ways we know, and working with colleagues in other disciplines to expand ideas of what academic writing can be. The culture of the academy, like any other, is constantly in a slow and steady state of transformation — as the values surrounding it are transformed, the communication that reflects those values is, too. Thus, expectations for what academic writing is constantly shift and move with the transformations. The more we work with and understand working-class students, the greater the possibility that together with them, we can incorporate their positions in academic writing, as well.

WHAT KINDS OF TOOLS?
TEACHING CRITICAL ANALYSIS AND WRITING TO WORKING-CLASS STUDENTS
JOSEPH HEATHCOTT

One of the great but ambivalent accomplishments for a working-class family is to send one of its sons or daughters to college. It is a great accomplishment, because by so doing the family can imagine itself within a flow of progress, moving upward socially and economically through its offspring. The family might feel rewarded for decades of hard work and miserly savings, gratified finally to have produced an aspirant to the middle or upper class. Parents and grandparents, aunts, uncles, and cousins can bask vicariously in the legitimacy that a college degree confers on those who earn it.

It is an ambivalent accomplishment because the process of higher education acculturates these sons and daughters into new peer groups, different standards and criteria for success, alien vocabularies and views, and even new class identities. For those back home, in the old neighborhood or on the farm, college is perhaps a distant dream. They are at once proud of and envious toward their educated offspring, and they feel the gap in horizons widen as the years go by. When the prodigals return, perhaps for Spring Break, maybe for Christmas or Passover or Thanksgiving, they are changed. They have new habits. They see the world differently. But they still must relate to their families, their friends, the world from which they came.

The weight of obligations to families back home coupled with the tension and ambivalence working-class and first-generation college students experience on campus, in the classroom, and in their new living spaces puts enormous pressure on them to succeed and to excel. Yet they are cast into their new circumstances with little preparation and are expected to take to the institution as if they had been bred for college life and a professional career. This is the primary reason that so many of these students drop out after one or two semesters. They do not fit the institution, and rather than changing the institution to fit their needs, university managers and planners demand that such students either reorder their lives or drop out. Rare is the college program that asks the provocative but crucial question, How can we change the way we do things to accommodate and to meet the needs of nontraditional students? This question, however, is at the heart of a program that I worked for in the summer of 1994, called Groups.[1]

THE GROUPS PROGRAM AND THE
STUDENT ACADEMIC CENTER, INDIANA UNIVERSITY

Founded in 1969 with funding from the Department of Education and Indiana University, Groups has provided support for more than six thousand students from around the state. Its mission is to recruit students from low-income and minority backgrounds, most of whom are in the first generation of their families to attend college, and to provide them with a comprehensive and ongoing support network that includes preparatory summer course work, academic advising, tutoring, financial aid counseling, and mentoring. Students who are admitted to the Groups Program come to Indiana University in the summer before their first year for an intensive session of three courses. These courses, offered through the English department ("Composition"), the Department of Mathematics ("Pre-calculus"), and the Student Academic Center ("Critical Reading and Research"), are designed to give students a jump start in college-level work.

This is where I come in. In the summer of 1994 I worked for the Student Academic Center, under the administration of Dr. Sharon Pugh, teaching X152 Critical Reading and Research. The theme for that summer's X152 course was "Racism and Prejudice," an excellent point of departure for engaging students in issues meaningful to them. Dr. Pugh and the Student Academic Center staff chose the theme and assembled a course reader for students, though X152 teachers were not bound to cover any set amount of material. Our mission was to teach the skills of critical reading, analysis, research and writing using whatever means we thought most appropriate for our classroom. My participation in Groups, then, allowed me to pull together a number of different teaching strategies and approaches that I had used in one form or another in the past, whether teaching skills-based or content-based courses.

The broad question posed by Groups is how to change the classroom itself to fit the needs of working-class and first-generation college students. How can we recruit and retain students from low-income backgrounds, from families within which higher education is not a tradition or an expectation? Our task at the Student Academic Center was to transmit critical reading and writing skills to these students in ways that made sense to them.

I felt that if we really wanted to make sense to students, to reach them on their terms, there was no way we could divorce the course content from the actual experiences and lives of the students themselves. How would a remote and didactic approach, in which I merely instructed on the "right" way to unpack arguments and write research papers, serve the intense curiosity and intellectual needs of a group of men and women for whom college was already a tense and anxious experience? Simply imposing alien vocabularies and requirements would not only lead to dissonance and failure on the students' part, but would also reflect my own larger failure to make the course relevant — at a crucial moment in students' lives when course work had to compete with a whirlwind of emotions, challenges, and anxieties. Instead of fitting students into a curriculum, then, I was compelled to organize a curriculum around the students themselves, drawing upon their backgrounds, experiences, needs, frustrations, fears, hopes, and goals.

Thus, I had three major priorities for the summer. First, in order for learning and teaching of any value to occur, I had to build an appropriate context for learning and teaching. Second, I had to provide students with ways to bridge their backgrounds to the academic present and to their future aspirations, so that they could make sense of their place in "higher" education. This would allow them to locate appropriate and empowering interpretive frameworks so as to come into college from a position of strength, rather than bewilderment. And third, with the establishment of this sense of place and context, I wanted to teach practical tools for critical thinking and writing and equip students with solid skills for the years ahead.

My grounding assumption was that every student already possessed significant critical abilities but that they needed my support, each other's support, and the support of the Groups Program in order to translate their critical abilities into academic work. This translation process constituted the major focus of my teaching and interaction with these twenty-five amazing and brilliant individuals. I viewed our work together as no less than an empowerment project, with the students and their needs, their backgrounds, and their interests as the central focus of the course.

What Kinds of Tools?

PROVIDING THE CONTEXT FOR LEARNING

The class itself was a curious mix of people from Indiana's most marginal groups. Out of a total of twenty-five students, seven (two men and five women) were from Latino backgrounds. They were all of Mexican descent; some came from families long established in the United States, while others were first-generation Americans. Five of the Latino students were from urban backgrounds, the sons and daughters of factory workers, laborers, domestics, and truck drivers. The families of the other two were migrants, who lived in rural areas and worked as farm laborers. Fourteen of the twenty-five students were African American, only two of them men. In fact, within Groups as a whole there is a distressingly low rate of participation by African American males. This may reflect problems and biases in the recruiting methods, but more likely it testifies to the ongoing, racist criminalization of African American men, most of whom by the age of seventeen or eighteen are incarcerated or on probation, or have dropped out of high school. Finally, there were one male and three female European Americans in the class, all of them from rural poor backgrounds. This is, of course, a small number, considering the high proportion of people living below the poverty line in rural areas of Indiana — particularly in the southern part of the state. Though educational institutions have traditionally stereotyped blacks and Hispanics as poor, the fact of rural white poverty has only recently motivated special provisions within university recruitment programs. Indiana University, like most Big Ten state schools, continues to draw the overwhelming bulk of its student population from the white middle class.

The most important initial goal in X152, then, was to create an environment, a "safe place," for learning and teaching — not a light task within such a diverse and potentially conflictual group of students. I wanted students to become familiar with the idea that they could speak up on issues that moved them, throw out ideas, challenge one another, have the space to speak their minds without interruption or intimidation, and make mistakes. The difficulty one might ordinarily expect in fostering an equitable forum for women in a classroom was absent from X152, since fully three-fourths of the students were women. Several women, in fact, quickly assumed prominent leadership roles, providing much better role models for the quiet and reserved women in the class than I could ever have provided. The first week was spent in discussions and exercises designed to bring people to a point where they respected the differences among them. Even if they chose not to hang out together outside of X152, I wanted them to consider their four hours of class with me each week as a time for working together and learning from one another.

To this end we spent much of the first week familiarizing ourselves with each other's grammar, speech patterns, and pronunciations (I am, for example, the product of a southern Indiana working-class family, which comes through in my own speech). Students took turns describing their slang terms, the way they pronounced certain words, and the varieties of their grammar. We put these all on the chalkboard and then went through them in order to figure out which ones were distinctly Latino, African American, or European American and which were shared by two or all three groups. In addition, I asked the class to think of situations in which they found themselves code-switching, that is, adopting a different speech style from the one they used ordinarily with their peers. Without exception, the students could easily recall dozens of scenarios in which they moved into different styles of communication, from talking with grandparents to confronting police officers or school officials. They kept track of these slang differences and code-switching moments in journals. We discussed why some styles of speech and communication were valued over others and decided together that all of our styles were equally valid and that all enrich our culture.

Many students felt, however, that it would be valuable for them to adopt a certain style of communication — especially in their writing — that would help them in their university studies. Most expressed some anxiety about having to learn and communicate in this style. "I want to get in the habit of talking proper," one woman said, "because I know that the way people speak in college is different than I might speak normally. But it's going to be hard to break old habits." This woman articulated in crystal-clear terms the ambivalence many of the students felt about learning a new code of communication. I seized on her remarks to make what I consider to be a fundamentally important point: the idea that collegiate English is not necessarily "proper" English. If proper means appropriate, I asked, would it be appropriate to speak to your grandparents that way? Your friends on the street? The bus driver on your route? If it would not be proper in those circumstances, why should we call it proper English? This touched off a lively debate in class over what is proper and what is not in given circumstances.

For fun, and to demystify and satirize this so-called proper brand of communication, we resolved to call it "the King's English" in order to distinguish it from other varieties of English that we spoke. Though these discussions about communication took up nearly two class periods, I feel that it was well worth our time to work through "proper" and "correct" English as issues. Our conversations allowed us to critique these notions of what is "standard" and "acceptable," and to bring all of us to a view that academic writing and speaking is not necessarily superior but rather another variety of communication that we could each add to our repertoire. Just as we might code-switch to talk to different family members or to our employers, we could shift our styles to write for professors and each other. Moreover, some students argued, the academic voice need not be the only one in the classroom. It has its time and place, like other kinds of communication.

In addition to exploring various codes and styles of communication, we also spent a good deal of the first week discussing our backgrounds and our experiences. X152 provided a very special and nearly unprecedented environment for encounters, conversations, and learning. Rural whites shared their experiences and ideas with urban African Americans and Latinos, as well as Latinos from rural, migrant-worker families. For many of the students of color, it was the first time in their lives that they were confronted by the fact of white poverty in America — and not in an abstract sense, but by living, breathing people who could speak directly from their own experience. When the subject first came up, a white woman from Vigo County described to the class her own pain at having to see her parents struggle to make a living on other people's land, and at growing up on "poor relief." One Latina from East Chicago replied that "all the white people I knew were rich, like they owned our building and the stores that we shopped at. I just never thought there were poor white people." An African American woman from Indianapolis said she "knew about poor whites — we call them crackers or rednecks" but had never actually known or talked with any. "All the white kids at my school were from the suburbs, and had lots of money. All us black students came from the city, and didn't have nothin'."

At the same time, African American students could assert their own perspectives in a mixed-ethnic environment where they were, unusually, in the majority. They offered counters to the racist stereotypes that European Americans, and even Latinos, brought to the classroom. Each African American and Latino student, moreover, contributed particular stories and experiences of discrimination and racism. A Latino from East Chicago recalled his experience of dealing with his white bosses as "humiliating" and full of hurt. He powerfully described an instance in which his white coworkers and bosses ridiculed his Mexican heritage and Spanish accent, calling him "bean eater" and "wetback," deriding him for "taking an American's job" despite the fact that he was a third-generation American citizen. For many African and European Americans, this was the first forum in which they had heard such moving stories of discrimination from Latinos.

The students differed widely in their personalities, their temperaments, and their goals and interests. Some wanted to go into fields such as accounting, law, or international affairs. Others wanted to prepare themselves for careers as social workers, journalists, scientists, criminologists, even FBI agents. Several of the men and one of the women were considering ROTC as a possibility. We spent the better part of a session that first week going around the room and talking about what we wanted to do and why, what each person wanted to get out of Groups and out of college generally.

Most students were self-conscious about their presence in the Groups Program, because it can carry a stigma within the larger student population. Yet they were mindful of the reasons why programs like Groups are necessary in the first place, and when we discussed these issues, few of them failed to blame racism, government neglect, and lack of advantages in crumbling, poorly funded inner-city and rural schools. Yet they differed in their analyses and opinions of what minority groups — and ultimately each of them — should do to challenge oppression. Many felt that minority groups should concentrate on the uplift of their own people, despite the racist trends of dominant society, while a few believed further social integration was key. Some African American students believed that they should focus primarily on their own personal lives and careers, since their success would have an uplifting effect on the communities from which they came. Others, however, felt that it would take more than just individual success to improve the lot of African Americans in the United States.

European Americans, though generally acknowledging the severity of racial oppression, uniformly touted integration and "putting difference behind us" as the best ways to alleviate racial problems. Needless to say, they received a much-needed education from their fellow students on the complexities and problems with such approaches. African American and Latino students almost unanimously valued differences and pointed to the problems that arise when society ignores difference — whether in schools, workplaces, courts of law, cultural institutions, or mass media. At the same time, European American students were very effective in making cross-racial, class-based connections. "Really, all of us come from backgrounds that are discriminated against," one European American woman argued. "So when are we gonna act together on these problems instead of separately?"

These discussions continued throughout the summer, of course, given that the theme for X152 was "Racism and Prejudice." But the first week was crucial, because we did more than merely raise issues or exchange ideas. Our conversations, arguments, and deliberations cleared a space in which all of us came to feel safe, in which all of us felt we had a stake. A small amount of emotional and intellectual investment can go a long way in fostering an appropriate and powerful learning environment.

BUILDING BRIDGES BETWEEN THE PAST AND THE PRESENT

Closely related to the creation of a safe space in which to learn was the need for ways in which students could value their own backgrounds and experiences and see them as strengths rather than weaknesses in tackling the immense challenge of college. Too often, working-class and first-generation college students see or are made to see their backgrounds as liabilities, and their student status as a radical break from the past. As a first-generation college student myself, I can attest to the feelings of isolation and anomie that accompanied my own immersion into the academic world. Today, I realize that the abruptness of the transition closed me off to a full awareness of and pride in my own background that could have served me well in college. Instead, my working-class background was a stigma within the university, and I took pains to hide it as best I could. Without the comfort of a strong peer group with which to weather the transition, I felt as though I had been cast adrift with no support.

Groups, however, provides an excellent context in which students can work together to connect their past and their present and to see that they are not alone in the university. In order to build this crucial bridge, during the second week we created family genealogies. I passed out family tree charts and asked students to list their parents and grandparents, aunts and uncles, noting where they came from, their educational levels, and the things they did to earn a living. When we were done, we took turns sharing our genealogies with the rest of the class. This was voluntary, of course. I assumed from the start that family pasts might be a sensitive topic for some people and that students should not be compelled to share their charts with the class if they did not feel comfortable. Nevertheless, most students clamored to discuss their family backgrounds, and their enthusiasm was enough to put at ease and pull in some of the more reluctant students. A few of the most reticent students did not share their charts with the class, but I suspect that the exercise empowered them anyway, because they began to speak up on other topics later in the week.

Truck drivers, coal miners, farmers, laborers, laundresses, clerks, secretaries, ushers, factory workers, bartenders, carpenters, railroad workers, barge hands — these are only a few of the tremendous variety of livelihoods that students revealed from their families' pasts. Using Howard Zinn's concept of "People's History," I referred to the three or four dozen occupations I had written on the board as a vital cross-section of working people who actually built America.[2] Students took off with this idea at once, and we spent an entire class period discussing why history and society might forget or devalue the masses of people who actually labored to create the farms, railroads, highways, buildings, towns, and cities in which we live.

My basic aim was simple. I wanted to create a context in which students could recognize both intriguing differences (his grandmother was a seamstress from Northern Mexico, her father is a mechanic in Gary) and important commonalities in their pasts. In this way, students can see that they are not alone in coming from working-class backgrounds and, more importantly, can learn to take pride in the fact that their peoples' histories are important. In the context of the Groups classroom, twenty-five men and women were able to see and hear each other talk about their nonliterate grandparents, their working parents, their struggling aunts and uncles — some of whom might be in prison, a few of whom might even have died in the jungles of Viet Nam or served in the Gulf War. Without this crucial, collective context, students remain isolated and unsure about the value of their pasts. The rupture between family past and collegiate present is then so difficult, so onerous, that it often leads students to devalue their own backgrounds in order to adopt new identities. This can throw many of the students' own values and sensibilities into question, creating confusion, turmoil, and anxiety in their new surroundings. In addition, and perhaps most tragically, it can lead to a dreadful distancing from families and friends back home. As that distance increases, students lose important systems of support that might otherwise sustain them psychically and materially through college.

The Groups classroom, then, can empower students to take pride in their families, their heritage, their pasts while they work to attain new skills and ideas in college. The transition will never be seamless unless the research university becomes a working-class institution, responsive to (rather than merely sensitive to) racial and ethnic diversity — which is unlikely. But the transition can be made easier, and people's own experiences can be meaningful in the context of the classroom. Moreover, students who go through the Groups Program can, if they choose, provide each other with a support network for the next four years, with a network of people who understand the challenges of new values, new ideas, new mobilities. Even if a student opts out of such ongoing connections, she will always know that there are others going through similar changes, encountering similar discontinuities and challenges.

SHARPENING THE TOOLS OF CRITICAL THINKING
AND WRITING FOR COLLEGE

No one tool will ever fit the needs of everyone in a classroom. Yet some tools can provide nearly all students with a place to begin, a procedure by which to construct their own methods of thinking, reading, research, and writing, and to develop their own critical lenses. For all students, but especially for nontraditional and first-generation college students, it is important to introduce a variety of methods and ideas for critical thinking. If the first approach works with many but not all students, then the next exercise will capture still more, and so on.

My basic approach is to start simple and make assignments and concepts gradually more complex. In addition, I tend to deal with issues and concepts with which students will be very familiar and in which they will have a stake or interest. In this way students can practice methods of critical analysis using texts whose contents resonate with their own experiences. This enables students to focus more on developing and honing their skills, rather than overburdening them with new content. However, once students have gained and are comfortable with a variety of analytical tools, I gradually begin to introduce new and challenging content — even bizarre texts that ply the strange and unfamiliar. I feel that the introduction of unfamiliar texts and ideas into the curriculum is extremely important, because it allows students to develop their creative, interpretive abilities. In other words, we should never make the assumption, just because students are working-class or first-generation, that they cannot handle material outside of their experience. Failing to introduce them to new and challenging material does them a disservice, since this is what college is all about — for everyone.

My supervisor, Sharon Pugh, introduced me to a useful heuristic to use when teaching critical analysis. The application of this heuristic, called IPSO (Issue, Position, Support, Outcome), is an effective way for students to take apart arguments, to reduce them to their most basic elements, and to make critical judgments based on the available evidence. In Pugh's estimation, the use of simplistic pro-con arguments when teaching critical analysis fails to attune students to nuances and complexities or even multiple arguments within a single piece of writing. IPSO, however, is a tool that can be used to root out and analyze as many arguments as one can find in a text. I decided to introduce IPSO at the end of the second week of X152, but not in a way that made it seem like an alien imposition or "textbook" method. Instead, I wanted to allow the students to develop IPSO on their own while working together to analyze an argument.

To this end, I brought in a jam box and played a tune by Public Enemy (then quite popular) called "Burn, Hollywood, Burn." I asked them to listen carefully to Chuck D's lyrics — among the most profound in rap music of the 1990s — and to think about the argument he makes in the rap. The first reaction from several students came as soon as the song ended: "What does this song have to do with college learning?" This sparked a wonderful discussion among students as to what constitutes "proper" material to study. "I think the song is dope," one man argued, "but I don't believe it should be in the classroom, you know, because it is something that we listen to for our entertainment." A woman who up to that point had remained pretty silent, countered this opinion: "But Chuck D is making an argument. It's not just entertainment. There is an argument there." Others seemed to agree.

"Well, if there is an argument, what is it? What is the main issue here?" I asked. Students quickly identified racism in Hollywood movies as the issue.

Chuck D's position, they agreed, was that Hollywood representations of blacks are racist. "Does he just say this, or does he give reasons why he believes this to be the case?" I asked. Students responded by throwing out a number of lines from the rap that provide evidence: black men are shuffling clowns, contented servants, or violent criminals; black women are maids or whores; whites control the movie industry, from casting to producing and directing. This led, of course, to a barrage of further evidence from students' own memories. Though it was important to let this provocative conversation play itself out, I took care to write only evidence from Public Enemy's song on the board.

Finally, when we had exhausted the considerable amount of evidence from "Burn, Hollywood, Burn," I posed another question: "So, does Chuck D propose a solution here?" One student immediately shouted "Burn Hollywood," to the laughter of the class. To their astonishment, I wrote it on the board. "That's right," I said. "That is one possible solution he suggests. Are there others?" Another student replied, "Boycotting movies made by Hollywood," and a student sitting next to her added, "but only if they don't portray black people positively." I wrote these on the board. Finally, a student who had been mostly silent up to that point blurted: "I know! He said that black people should make their own movies, like Spike Lee!" Excellent. "Not one, but three possible courses of action," I said, adding that this was the hallmark of a well-thought-out argument.

"But I think that's terrible, that he says blacks should burn down Hollywood," a black woman protested, with nods of agreement from a few students. "That's not right. Just because you don't like the movies, doesn't mean you can burn Hollywood down." A Latino countered, arguing that "Chuck D is saying that after hundreds of years of gettin' screwed over, blacks have a right to respond that way, since it hurts them so much." A heated exchange ensued, which ended in an angry stalemate. Finally, one of the students turned to me and said "What do you think?" to which I responded: "I don't. I just want to know what Chuck D's argument is." The students moaned and grimaced and rolled their eyes, but they were teaching each other the most important lesson of the semester — that our opinions and values do count, but that we have to be prepared to analyze arguments that we do not agree with, or which agitate or anger us. Anger can be a useful emotion, of course, but a number of students concluded that if we let our anger cloud our understanding, then we run the risk of missing all of the points of an argument. "If we're so bugged that we don't get all the points down from some argument," one woman concluded, "then we can't counter it. It just gets to be like, I'm right, you're wrong, and then we don't go nowhere."

In the end, students could see Chuck D's rap song broken down into an IPSO — Issue, Position, Support, and Outcome. Through conversation we arrived at an understanding that anything, any text, whether it is a book, an article, a song, even a photograph or a movie, can make an argument, and that we can take the argument apart, analyze it, and figure out what the author is trying to say. IPSO, as seen on the board, was a good tool with which to do this—though I hastened to add that it is not the only tool for analyzing arguments. Moreover, since it is a tool, students should apply it as such. In other words, *IPSO is a tool for critical analysis, not critical analysis itself.* Once an argument is broken down, that is when the student can step in with counterargument or qualifications, either from his or her own thinking or from other sources.

After we had finished with the Public Enemy rap, I assigned a similar exercise—this time using the music that students had brought with them. Only three students had not brought a walkman or a boom box of some kind with them to Bloomington, and the three who did not have one on campus all lived with a roommate who did and were already in the habit of sharing the music source in their room. Music, then, was an integral part of their daily lives, something precious that they had brought from home to sustain them in new and unfamiliar surroundings. Our second IPSO exercise, then, involved students using the IPSO tool to break down arguments in their music and present these to the class. Students were invited to bring in their song on tape or CD, and I brought a CD/tape playing boom box to class for the occasion.

Needless to say, this exercise animated students. For many if not most of them, music was integral to identity—particularly in a multiethnic environment where identities had to be constantly reinforced and renegotiated. Fourteen students played snippets of songs, and everyone presented arguments (or at least story lines) extracted from their music using IPSO as a tool. Genres ranged from gangsta rap to R&B to heavy metal to Latin dance to country western. Students could not help occasionally mocking one another's music, but as a group we found positive and negative aspects in every kind of music. An African American woman, who had emerged as a class leader, scolded an African American man for ridiculing a white woman's choice of Tammy Wynette.

This exercise brought out interesting gender and ethnicity dynamics. Most males, African American and Latino, listened to gangsta rap—either primarily or at least occasionally—as did a few African American women. Most African American women, however, along with European American and Latina women, expressed a staunch dislike for the genre, particularly for its depiction of women and its glorification of violence. The only white male in the class happened to be a gangsta rap fan, but he was not as adamant in its defense as were the two African American men, who powerfully argued that Ice-T and NWA portrayed the reality of life for inner-city youth in America.

Although there was crossover between black and white musical preferences (several African American women liked bands such as the Beatles and certain country artists, and students of all ethnicities listened to one genre of African American music or another), no one outside of the Latino group listened to Latino music. Most of the Latino students listened to Mexican and Puerto Rican genres, but one Latino who preferred gangsta rap said, "I don't listen to that Spanish crap. I can't even understand it!" Regardless, the playing and discussion of Latino music in class was an important exposure for African and European Americans, whose musical forms predominate the air waves and the music industry. Moreover, the lengthy and often heated conversations about music were also conversations about the students' identity — both as youths, as women or men, and as members of a particular ethnic group.

This exercise brought home the difference between IPSO and critical analysis, in that students could see that what they had to say about one another's music went far beyond what they wrote on paper for their IPSO exercise. They were able to see that their level of interpretation and critical argument was enhanced with more evidence and forethought. Over the next several weeks we learned how to apply tools of critical analysis to different kinds of texts with different levels of complexity. Since the major theme for the course was "Racism and Prejudice," our course reader was replete with articles on racism, pluralism/multiculturalism, canon debates, discrimination, hate crimes, and student life culled from numerous newspapers, magazines, and scholarly publications. In order to sharpen their skills, I asked students to do an IPSO for every argument in every article that we read — keeping in mind that there might be more than one argument in any article, and that IPSO itself was a flexible tool. There might be no suggested outcome, for example, or the Issue and the Position might be difficult to disentangle or even identify.

I supplemented these articles with different kinds of materials. In one exercise, I familiarized students with the analysis of quantitative tables and reports. Using a set of numbers and percentages of soldiers that served in Viet Nam, broken down by ethnicity (white, black, Hispanic); a set of numbers of yearly combat fatalities in Viet Nam from 1964 to 1968, also broken down by ethnicity; and a racial/ethnic breakdown of the general population, I asked students to draw inferences. Working together in groups, they were to come up with an analysis of the society, to paint a general picture of the nature of social relationships, based on the three data tables. A fourth table, which I put on the board after the groups had finished, estimated the number of combat soldiers and combat deaths from a particular region in the Midwest broken down by social class — irrespective of race and ethnicity.[3] I then asked students to look at their original conclusions and either stand by them or modify and rework them as they saw fit. Final conclusions ranged from explanations based solely on racial/ethnic discrimination, to solely class discrimination, to class discrimination that hits racial/ethnic minorities the hardest. This exercise provided an excellent introduction to quantitative interpretation and provoked intense discussion about war and who fights and dies in war—a particularly poignant discussion, since most students in the class knew men and women who had served in the recent Gulf War.

Another excellent resource for sharpening analytical tools and provoking discussion is Philip S. Foner's *We the Other People,* a collection of alternative declarations of independence from a variety of American social movements, including labor organizations, farmers, blacks, women's rights advocates, and socialists, from 1829 to 1975.[4] Students were asked to read the original Declaration of Independence and to construct an IPSO analysis. Then they chose three alternative declarations and constructed IPSOs based on the arguments found there. Finally, I asked students to write a short paper on whether or not "American society has always provided freedom and equality to all groups," using evidence from the original and alternative declarations.

In the middle of the summer session, when I was satisfied that all students were adept at using various tools to take apart and analyze arguments, I introduced a strange and unfamiliar text. Up to that point, they had analyzed material that was either familiar to them (articles on racism and student life) or whose content was readily apprehensible (declarations of independence). Now, however, I was asking them to "read" a text whose messages and meanings were not so clearly stated and in fact were multiple. In this way I hoped to develop their interpretive abilities, since the text itself was beyond a recognizable point of reference in their lives. The text I used was Godfrey Reggio and Philip Glass's provocative film *Koyaanisqatsi.*[5] Students watched the film and wrote a paper in which they analyzed the movie's "message" or "argument." At this point in the course, it was up to them whether or not they used IPSO. For some, explicitly outlining the Issue, Position, Support, and Outcome was a helpful exercise that allowed them to construct a more coherent paper. Other students, however, had internalized IPSO in the writing of their papers and were able to skip the IPSO outline and move right into writing the paper.

Without exception, students were able to grasp most or all of *Koyaanisqatsi*'s principal arguments about environmental destruction, the pace of contemporary life, the tension between the natural and the human-made world, the myriad problems of urbanization, and the growing imbalance between people and their environments. Nearly all students added their own critical voices in appraisal of the movie's message. They debated each other's conclusions and were clearly uncomfortable at first with the possibility that a text could have multiple meanings. In the end, however, we decided that texts could indeed have different meanings and interpretations and that it is all right to feel perturbed and uneasy with this. I was able to make the point, and students generally agreed, that scholarship was really about choosing among multiple interpretations, various frames of reference, and numerous kinds of evidence. One student summed it up best when she said "I guess the best we can do is try to get as many of the arguments out of [the text] as we can, figure out what we think about it, and write about it in a way that's fair to the author's argument — whether we agree with it or not." Succeeding in this exercise, I felt, showed that they were ready to move on to the central assignment of the course: the research paper.

In the course of four or five weeks, we had rapidly built to a point where students could take on an issue, marshal evidence from multiple sources, assess multiple arguments, and draw critical conclusions. The writing of a final research paper would be the culmination of this process and the real test of learned critical capacities. In order to support students in this project, the Student Academic Center had arranged for two group visits to the Main Library at Indiana University: the first to take a tour and to familiarize everyone (including the instructor!) with the basic resources available, and the second to walk students through the process of finding books, journal articles, government publications information, and so on. Since by the fourth week students were expected to settle on a research topic, they spent their second group library visit locating two books, two journal articles, and two microfilm newspaper articles related to their research topics. If this sounds like a simple exercise, keep in mind that the Main Library at Indiana University is one of the larger research libraries in the United States. Faculty, let alone first-generation college students, are likely to get turned around trying to find materials in the cavernous stacks.

The Student Academic Center coordinated the visits with library personnel, while I provided research support to students in a number of ways. First, borrowing and expanding an idea from a colleague, I designed an eight-page research journal in which students could record their topic, their outline, their sources and citations (we had several exercises on proper citation), their attitudes and thoughts about the topic, and some of the main arguments from various sources. I took students through the construction of a useful and flexible outline, how to differentiate among kinds of sources (primary, secondary, scholarly, journalistic, editorial-opinion), how and when to cite sources, and how to construct clear sentences and paragraphs. Most importantly, drawing on students' experiences with IPSO and other short exercises, I facilitated a discussion about the importance of treating all sources critically, keeping in mind that no source or argument is flawless.

Over the course of two weeks, I met with students individually to discuss their papers, topics, and research approaches. Students were expected to hand in their outlines, bibliographies of at least five citations, and rough drafts of their papers one week prior to the deadline. In addition, the same week in which they were finishing their rough drafts, they gave oral presentations on their papers — relating the basic issue or argument as well as major findings, assessing the value of evidence collected to date, and listening to comments from fellow students. This peer review process, coupled with my feedback on their rough drafts, worked very well to put students on firm ground for producing good, coherent final papers.

The range of topics and the depth of engagement shown by students in their final projects testify to their diverse interests and intense curiosities. Given close and constant support, firm coaching, and a motivation grounded in empowering notions of self, identity, and background, students will nearly always find within themselves the ability to write interesting and provocative papers. Topics included "Is Farrakhan a Racist?" "Teaching Moral Character in Public Schools," "Exploitation of African-American Athletes," "Gang Violence in Hispanic East Chicago," "Japanese Education vs. American Education," "Prayer in Public Schools," "Racism in Rural Schools," "Date Rape on College Campuses," "Birth Control in High School," "Home Schooling," "Sexism in the College Classroom," and "Homosexual Lifestyles in the Public School Curriculum." Students went so far as to design surveys, conduct fieldwork, and write and interview prominent scholars in their topic's field. Of course the papers varied in quality of writing, sourcing, and argument construction; but more importantly, every student had grasped the basic *process* of critical writing and argument. Mastering basic approaches and becoming comfortable with doing research and making arguments are the crucial first steps toward college-level scholarship. Students can only improve with practice.

THE WORKING-CLASS CLASSROOM

Yet working-class students learned more in X152 than just how to write a college-level paper, and the lessons learned may carry them further in their lives than the nuts and bolts of research. First, they learned that they could do research, that each of them had the ability to think critically and put together complex arguments. Second, they learned that college need not be a radical break from their pasts. Students from working-class backgrounds go through enormous changes and challenges in the university, from financial distress in their families back home to the incongruous experience of classrooms that were not designed with them in mind. As instructors, we give as much comfort as we can when students have family crises that detract from their studies, but we cannot control these crises or will them away. What we *can* do is provide ways for students to build a bridge between the past and the present, to see college as a new but not discontinuous identity, so that when crises do arise in their lives they are better prepared to weather the demands of the classroom. Students must constantly navigate between family expectations and their own desires and aspirations, which often conflict with each other. Whether the student develops patterns of self-loathing, a troubled double consciousness, or an incomplete identity — or builds on the positive aspects of her background to meet the challenges of college is largely up to us, the teachers and administrators. We have the power to make or break the working-class student.

Perhaps the most important lessons we can teach such students are the ones that our class learned in the first few weeks of X152. Rather than launch straight into the topic of critical thinking and analysis, I took pains to foster among students both a learning community and a level of self-assurance and confidence necessary to move ahead in school. The time invested in discussing differences, becoming comfortable with everyone's styles and habits and codes, learning to disagree constructively, and building on one another's background as children of working people was time well spent. These lessons provided the building blocks upon which future lessons could be integrated more meaningfully into each student's worldview. Without the crucial, orienting catalysts of pride, confidence, and self-awareness, nontraditional students must enter the bewildering world of the research university at a severe disadvantage, with poor chances of competing successfully against the better preparation and generally higher self-esteem and expectations of their more affluent peers. A small amount of empowerment, facilitated at the beginning of nontraditional students' college careers, can provide each of them with lifelong skills — skills that grow out of abilities they have within them but which need a push-start and refinement in order to help them through academic life.

Perhaps working-class and nontraditional students will never fit well or completely within the classroom of the major research university. It would take a total reconsideration of the role of the university in public life to enable a good fit for such students, and this is only likely within the context of a broad, democratic transformation of American society. In the meantime, however, programs like Groups can empower working-class students with appropriate lenses to interpret their experience, lenses sensitive to their own backgrounds, their own interests, their own lives. This process, by which the sons and daughters of the working class come to see and account for their place in the university, by which they arrive at a position of strength and solidarity rather than weakness and isolation, is just as important as the process of scholarship itself. In programs aimed specifically at such students, empowerment should be the principal goal and should always precede or at least accompany the transmission of useful skills. Anything short of this dooms working-class students to failure.

"JUST AMERICAN"?
REVERSING ETHNIC AND CLASS
ASSIMILATION IN THE ACADEMY
CAROLINE PARI

FROM ITALIAN AMERICAN TO AMERICAN

When I began classes at John Adams High School, located in the predominantly working-class, Italian American community of Ozone Park, Queens, I decided to study Italian to fulfill my language requirement. I eagerly anticipated learning the language of my ancestors. But the language of my ancestors was Sicilian, not the Standard Italian I would be learning. Because my father's parents had refused to teach my father and his sister Italian at home, in their effort to Americanize them, Sicilian (and those strange hand gestures) was passed down through my mother. Sicilian was the mysterious language my mother's mother spoke with my aunts when they wanted to talk secretly. It was a language that I desperately wanted to know, but I had picked up only a few phrases and expressions, such as calling my aunt who lived with us "beda maggia."

My Italian teacher, Mr. Ippolito, one of the few gems in the New York City public school system, was a kind and gentle man in his fifties whose gray hair glistened under the fluorescent lights and whose warm smile welcomed students. He was a man fiercely devoted to transmitting the Italian language and culture to his Italian American students, who all adored him. I studied Italian for three years with Mr. Ippolito and completed some of my most meaningful schoolwork in his class. He told us about Italy's desperate need to unify its dialects into a standard language because people could not communicate with each other. For example, he explained, Italians from Rome do not understand Sicilians unless they both speak the standard form of Italian. I remember how confusing it was to learn that all those Sicilian expressions and words with which I was familiar at home were "wrong." I had to code-switch from this deficient regional dialect to a new language that was clearly more prestigious and more useful. I started to translate what I heard at home into "correct" Italian. I changed the Sicilian *b*'s into the Standard Italian *p*'s, the *g*'s into *c*'s, and the *r*'s into *d*'s: "Gabeesch?" was really "Capisce?" (Do you understand?), "Geesta ga?" was really "Questa che?" (What's that?), the expletive "Marrone mia" was "Madonna mia," "Beda maggia" was "bella madre" (beautiful mother), and so on. What I really learned, then, was that of the many dialects of a language, one is prestigious and becomes standard; other forms need correction. The former was learned at school and could be written or spoken, whereas the latter was my mother's discourse and could not even be represented orthographically. I also learned that in order to do well in school, I had to erase a dialect with which I was so familiar.

I encountered a similar conflict between a standard language and a dialect when I began graduate school. Entering the halls of academia at the City University of New York Graduate School on Forty-second Street and Fifth Avenue felt like entering (trespassing in) a new world. I heard the sounds of a new language — strange words, unheard-of theories — and wanted desperately to understand and speak it. The way I spoke was considered nonstandard, much like my Sicilian. Fellow students frequently said, "What?" when I spoke because of my nonelite dialect, which left *r*'s off the end of words. And although I spoke quite loudly, I spoke so fast that my words slurred. I mispronounced words often. I felt much more comfortable calling someone an "asshole" or asking my professor "what the fuck" he was talking about than I did speaking this sterile, unflavored language. But I sounded dumb. Feeling out of place because of my nonelite habits, speech, and writing, I soon realized that my working-class, Italian American background had not sufficiently prepared me for graduate work.

Since I didn't want to sound like a working-class woman from Queens anymore, I learned how to speak more clearly in graduate school, a shift that marks my assimilation process. Because the way I wrote was also considered nonstandard, like my Sicilian, I had to learn "correct" academic discourse, or Standard English. Like Emile Zola, who shocked his contemporaries by using working-class language, I seemed to offend my professors with usage errors, such as contractions, split infinitives, made-up words, and unclear referents. In addition, I had many rhetorical errors, such as weak thesis statements (I didn't like arguing only one point — and still don't), heavy reliance on plot summary (I didn't really know how to make my point), and unsophisticated theory (actually, I made few references to "others"); I had a preference for narrative, personal experience, and subjectivity. The words of literary critics would be sprinkled throughout my essays only for flavor. I consciously imitated "academic discourse" and struggled to find my own language. Because I was a good student and saw that I was expected to assimilate the language of the academy, I complied, as many of the working class do. Drawing on William Labov's work, Pat Belanoff claims that "working-class speakers are likely to adjust their language toward the formal more radically than other language users."[1]

In my search for a perfected and prestigious English, one that I did not have to be ashamed of, and one that did not reveal my ethnicity or class, I eventually forgot my Italian. Instead I studied German, the traditional language of "high" academics. I had even lived in Germany during an intensive summer program. I discovered there was little place for Italian in British literature, except for the Romantic poets' patronizing fascination with Italian culture and the pre-Raphaelite devotion to it. Italian was devalued in this part of the academy and of little use to my study of nineteenth-century British literature. As I studied German, and as my Italian was replaced, I was actually engaged in a process of academic assimilation, leaving my class and ethnicity behind to become an all-American scholar. But now I think it is sad that I was able to speak German fluently and Italian only in bits and pieces, and that I visited Germany twice in my life, for as long as six weeks one time, but have never been to Sicily. By studying for a Ph.D., I was continuing the assimilation process that began with my Italian grandparents who insisted that their children speak only English. But before the costs had become too high, before I lost too much of who I was, I set off on a backward journey to reclaim my class and ethnic roots and to find a way to develop a pedagogy that critically challenges assimilation.

FROM AMERICAN TO ITALIAN AMERICAN

Richard Gambino's *Blood of My Blood: The Dilemma of the Italian-Americans* is one of the texts responsible for halting my rapidly progressive assimilation in its tracks.[2] Gambino gracefully weaves his personal experience as a son of Italian immigrants with a sociological analysis of the conflicts of assimilation among second- and third-generation Italian Americans. I came across Gambino's book while doing a research project on ethnicity and race for a cultural studies course. My professor, during a conference about the project, had the audacity to suggest I study Italian Americans. I must have looked puzzled because he then told me I had the map of Italy on my face. Shocked and embarrassed, I thought, "He can tell?" I mean, no one had ever said such a thing to me. You see, while assimilating in graduate school I had become so distant from my Italian roots that they seemed invisible to me. But my professor suddenly reminded me that I could not erase the visible signs of my identity: thick, brown-black hair and eyebrows, olive skin, large, dark brown eyes, and the dark hairs above my lip that I bleach. I was now being implored not only to reveal my identity, but even to study it. I thought I had become what one English professor, Linda Brodkey, believed she could be: the "classless, genderless, raceless scholar," something we dangerously strive for in the academy.[3] In fact, I was close to becoming what Gambino warns against, the "transparent" American who has rejected her ethnic identity. I was experiencing what he terms "shame-born-of-confusion." In this condition, Italian American youngsters "resist being identified as Italian-American because [they are] only vaguely aware of [their] roots and ashamed of them in [their] confusion." They insist they are "just Americans."[4] At this crucial discovery, through Gambino's book, of how Southern Italian customs, rituals, and values had shaped me, I began the process of reclaiming my Italian American and working-class identities.

Gambino documents the confusion felt by Italian Americans that stems from the conflict between "la via vecchia" (old world ways) and "la via nuovo" (new world ways). I needed to read only as far as the first chapter, "The Family System," to realize that I experienced a conflict many third-generation Italian Americans have. For Italian Americans, Gambino tells us, "it is impossible to be untouched, if not determined, by 'la via vecchia.' "[5] These old-world customs place the family at the center of one's identity. I began to understand the conflicts in my life between my parents' traditional, Sicilian ways and restricted gender roles and my American desires for independence, intellectual fulfillment, and a stable middle-class identity.

This "tortured" compromise between the old and the new leaves many Italian Americans "permanently in lower-middle-class America." Indeed, one of the many conflicts second- and third-generation Italians face is between Italian and American work ethics. According to the Italian American viewpoint, Gambino tells us, "one labors for the positive well-being of those one loves on earth, one's family. To succeed in this is a source of great pride. And the closer the relation between the work and the family, the more assured of its success." Because many Southern Italians lost faith in their corrupt school system, work, especially work that is "personalized, concrete rather than anonymous, abstract team labor gained greater importance."[6] Gambino points out that Italians prefer to work with their hands. I see the short, stubby fingers and rough, callused hands of the working class as Italian hands. Because of this work ethic, Italians move out of the working class slowly.

The Southern Italians who immigrated to New York in large numbers in the early decades of this century were peasants (*contadino*): mostly unskilled, semiskilled, and farm laborers who worked as carpenters, masons, tailors, shoe-makers, seamstresses, barbers, gardeners. Most of their children entered the same occupations, with few entering professions or managerial positions. In contrast, Italian women of the first generation worked mostly in factories, whereas their daughters were employed mostly as secretaries, typists, and sales-girls. As a seamstress, my maternal grandmother was among the 77 percent of new immigrants who worked in factories, and my mother, before she married, was one of the 40 percent of the second generation who worked in offices.[7]

In my family, this work ethic explains why no one has entered the corpo-rate world, despite the B.A.'s in business that both my father and my brother earned. It explains why my father didn't make much money selling insurance and kept his office in our apartment. He struggled all his life with the stress of being the sole provider for a large, Italian American family while not feeling successful by American standards. This work ethic may explain why no one in my family seems to understand my academic "work," because they do not see what I produce or its connection and value to the family; yet somehow I have increased my family's status with my Ph.D. (Of course, I do work with my hands, as the calluses on my right index finger show: I type at my computer, and I write, grade student papers, and carry books.) To confess, the reasons I chose to be a college professor are connected to this Italian work ethic and to being a woman — I wanted to do work that was meaningful to me and that could give me a flexible schedule so that I could devote myself to my (future) children. Women of different ethnicities and races may find this reason familiar, but I think it is the primary reason for me. Obviously, other privileges of this profes-sion attracted me to it — gaining a public voice, the life of writing, intellectual activity, feminism, teaching, helping others, and becoming middle-class.

WHAT CLASS AM I?

But according to my parents, I have always been middle-class. Although it seems as if my mother's family is from the working class because of my grand-mother's and my mother's jobs, my mother has always argued that her family was middle-class. My mother's family is well educated and owned land in Sicily. Her father earned a law degree and her three sisters graduated from college — one even got a Ph.D. (in the 1940s and 1950s, no less) — but her brothers entered the trades of plumbing and tailoring. My mother's learning disabilities prevented her from finishing college, although she is impressively self-educated, even "expert" in business and investment ideas, medical diag-noses, and nutrition, knowledge she has gained from life experience and from magazines, TV, and radio. Two of her sisters worked as high school teachers, and the one with the Ph.D. was a school psychologist. They attracted and married professional men. The brothers also married well. Education, marriage, and hard work were the ways this side of my family assimilated into American culture and into the middle class securely.

My father's family, however, is working-class. My father's parents were not formally educated. His father was a shoemaker with his own shop on 125th Street in Harlem from 1920 until the late 1950s. His sister worked as a secretary, married at twenty-three, and worked later in life as a bank teller, whereas my father, encouraged by his mother to get educated (read that "assimilated") got a college degree and worked in retail for some time before becoming an insurance agent.

I have thus inherited an uncertainty about my class position, wondering if we have denied our working-class roots in our determination to be middle-class. There are so many class contradictions in my mother's family and in our own that make us part of both classes. My parents always rented an apartment, but they bought property later in life; our family income was always hovering around poverty level, qualifying us for free lunches, but my parents were able to save up quite a nest egg and invest in stocks; we do not speak proper English all the time, but we are educated.

However, my family's social position becomes much clearer to me when I look at it in terms of ethnic assimilation and Italian American values. According to Gambino, Italians live below their means, which would explain our shabby apartment and clothes and the hidden wealth. My parents' two families came to America to better themselves, and they did. As a result of this class-crossing union during a time of heightened pro-American assimilation values, we lost not only our mother tongue, but also our class identity in one generation. Some of those working-class traits still linger in our home, our speech, and our relationships with others. My Italian immigrant parents and grandparents, like all immigrants, were supposed to escape their class in their quest for economic stability, yet the later generations feel a sense of regret and loss when Italian is no longer spoken, Italian customs are no longer followed, and Italian foods are no longer served during a time when ethnic traditions are valued. Though I can attribute many of my beliefs, much of my behavior, and my speech to my class position, I learned from Gambino that much of what makes me tick can be explained by my ethnicity, by "la via vecchia." My own experience has taught me that we cannot ignore ethnicity in our analyses of class identity, nor should we examine ethnicity without looking at social class.

A CRITICAL PEDAGOGY FOR ASSIMILATION

This piecing together of my life, reuniting with my Italian heritage and disrupting an assimilation process that threatened to dilute my very sense of being, has profoundly influenced my pedagogy. I know that I would not have been so anxious to assimilate and dismiss my Italian American identity as irrelevant if I had been asked to write about it earlier. And I know that my students at the City University of New York (CUNY), who are predominantly immigrants and from the working class, have these same special needs. I taught basic writing, ESL, freshman comp, and literature courses for seven years as a part-timer at Bernard M. Baruch College, a four-year CUNY college, and for the past two years as a full-timer at the Borough of Manhattan Community College, or BMCC, also in CUNY, where approximately 45 percent of the students are African American, 23 percent are Hispanic, 7 percent are Asian, 18 percent are from other ethnic groups, and about 73 percent report having an income of less than fifteen thousand dollars.[8]

Over the past eight years I have been experimenting with a pedagogy that centers on students' cultural and class identities. My working-class and immigrant students reflect critically on their cultural conflict and examine their class and ethnic identities. In my class they use multiple discourses and participate actively, and they are not pressured to adopt a discourse that erases their class and ethnic identities. My students are not "initiated" into academic discourses but bring into the classroom languages and cultural knowledge that are valued.[9]

Because many of my students are recent immigrants and from the working class, they are currently engaged in assimilation processes, both that of Americanization and that of becoming middle-class. Immigrants "uproot" themselves from a familiar place and plant themselves in a new land; when they go to college they are again uprooted, this time from their class positions, languages, belief systems, and communities, as are working-class students. Assimilation takes many different forms, such as adopting the new culture's dress, food, cultural practices, religion, attitudes, and work ethic and acquiring Standard English. Students assimilate in varying degrees and at varying speeds. Some are so caught up with becoming American that they disassociate from their home cultures and languages. Others reject American culture and refuse to speak English. African Americans, on the other hand, experience what Tom Fox describes as "cultural conflict."[10] Thus, assimilation is key to understanding my students' cultural and class experiences.

I do not assume that assimilation is necessary for working-class and immigrant students' survival; in fact, I open up explorations of assimilation so that they can include resistance. Jane Nagle, who teaches twelfth-grade English, makes it clear that assuming that our working-class students want to assimilate into the middle class devalues their working-class culture: "If the price for school literacy, for most working-class students, is to deny or at least not express working-class values, then it would seem that educators need to examine closely their attitudes about social class. . . . I have always believed that the working class was something everyone needed and wanted to leave. My students . . . have awakened me to the fact that the working class is exactly where most of them want to be. My assumption that education was a way out of working-class status was elitist."[11] In her brave self-analysis of how her directives, her responses to her students' journals, and her class lectures revealed her bias against working-class values, Nagle claims that much of what goes on in our classrooms is shaped by our class values. Her students, thus, resisted a certain cultural or class assimilation.

Just as I chose to halt my assimilation process and reclaim my cultural identity, I want students to describe the extent to which they were compliant with, confused by, or resistant to assimilation into American culture. The concept of assimilation also enables students to examine the interactions between different ethnic and racial groups in America. Students are asked to look at their lives, much as I had looked at my own, to discover what values, beliefs, or traditions of their ethnicity or race have shaped or influenced them.

I will first describe my early experiments raising awareness of the benefits and costs of assimilation and show how students expressed and redefined their assimilation processes. Though students rarely addressed issues of class identity, primarily because I did not, I believe the processes of cultural assimilation have many important implications for class assimilation; in fact, the two cannot be separated at times, as my own experience shows. I will then describe my later experiments, which highlighted class identity.

JUST AMERICAN?

During my early experiments, I discovered that most students had difficulty writing about their ethnic or racial group precisely because of the degree of assimilation they had undergone. I was struck by their claim to be "just American" and searched for answers to this perplexity. Some students' families may have been living in America for as many as five generations and had lost touch with their roots; black students may have had roots that extended deeply into American history. But some children of immigrants also claimed this status, having assimilated at a rapid pace. I admitted it was not an easy assignment to sort out the pieces of one's identity and find their origins. I was surprised, then, that some students revealed a profound quest for identity, feeling a sense of loss that arose from their parents' failure to transmit traditions of their ethnicity but which led to the strange ability to identify with all cultures, as the case of Sarah showed.[12] Growing up with free-spirited parents greatly influenced by the sixties subculture, Sarah discovered that she had been left without a definitive ethnic identity. Her parents' divorce left her out of touch with her father's French culture and her mother's Jewish background. As a result, she wrote:

To this day I have difficulty with my specific cultural identity, I am an American, I love to visit the France of my father's birth, I want to be Jewish. The stress on our relationship with my maternal grandparents was on celebrating Hanukkah and Passover, but only in terms of Jewish food. We had Passover Seders with their friends, but many of the symbols were forgotten. . . . I remember visiting my maternal grandparents in Florida one Hanukkah. We played with the dreydahl and tried to win the little chocolate candies symbolic of the holiday. When we went to bed, however, I hung a stocking by my window for Santa Claus and his Christmas offerings. . . . I want to be more religious than my parents were and I want to bring up my children with a greater sense of cultural identity and roots.

Although Sarah was distinctly aware that she could participate in different cultures to her liking by choice, enjoying their symbols, she did not see this as empowering, but rather as a loss of identity, what Gambino identifies as the emptiness created by assimilation.

Some students who claimed they were "just American" identified themselves as overassimilated. Note how Dermot personalized this process:

Since the British had practically wiped out Gaelic before the Irish came to America and there is no Irish cuisine, I often wonder what it means to be Irish. Although I consider myself Catholic, I do not attend mass and disagree with several teachings of the Church. I keep abreast of the situation in Northern Ireland but I follow all world news closely. I've read Joyce and Yeats, but then I've read Tolstoy and Dostoyevsky too. I enjoy listening to traditional Irish music by the Chieftains and the Clancy Brothers, but I enjoy other ethnic music as well. I am proud of my Irish heritage but perhaps Andrew Greeley is right and we Irish are over-acculturated.

Dermot still identified himself as Irish, but other students claimed to have no cultural roots to write about, something we might expect with homogenous groups of students outside of multicultural New York City. These claims indicated the extent to which students felt assimilated enough to have disassociated from a specific cultural heritage, as I had. Those students seemed to be denying their ethnic ties, much the same as working-class students might, because of the lower prestige with which such groups were associated. In fact, as I discuss later, my working-class students tended to avoid identifying themselves as working class for these reasons.

Assimilation assumes a desire for the privileges and power that are accorded some whites. The history of the "whiteness" of Irish Americans is an interesting case in point, as historian David Roediger tells us in *The Wages of Whiteness*.[13]

The Irish Americans, who were once viewed as and closely tied to blacks because of the kind of unskilled, manual labor both groups secured, gradually distanced themselves from blacks as they moved toward a white identity when political groups sought to increase the "white" vote in the mid-1800s. Racism was the vehicle by which the Irish could eliminate job competition and gain social prestige and political power. Race in America is enormously complex and frequently finds its way into my New York City classroom. For these reasons, and many more, I think it is important to examine the issue of assimilation among my black students.

JUST BLACK AMERICAN

During my early experiments with the assimilation theme, I carefully studied how my black students identified themselves. Black Americans usually identified themselves as "just American" for different reasons, though a significant part of black experience is resistance and opposition to the dominant white culture. Of course, black students did not identify with an immigrant model of assimilation because their ancestry leads back to the period of slavery, or involuntary immigration. Some saw black culture as American and claimed a racial identity by using the terms *black* or *black American*. Others took a different approach by using the term *African American*. The difference corresponded to the students' conception of their cultural history. For example, the students who identified themselves as African Americans focused their research on Africa, whereas those who called themselves blacks traced their progress as a race from slavery up to the present, writing mostly about the civil rights movement. One student wrote, "As a black, my cultural history can be traced by the crisis of race relations." The identificational term *black* carries powerful political connotations. In contrast, the term *African American* represents the move toward embracing the ethnicity paradigm that began in the sixties as ethnic groups gained political visibility and government funds. Sociologists, such as Martin Kilson, have argued that the ethnicization of blacks is a form of legitimation in order for blacks to have access to a higher status.[14] The problem I find with the ethnicity paradigm for blacks is that it seems to devalue, if not completely erase, race.

Nonetheless, the majority of my black students were immigrants from Nigeria, Kenya, Jamaica, Haiti, Guyana, Cuba, Barbados, Trinidad, and Antigua, who followed the ethnicity paradigm and could discuss their cultural identity and assimilation in America. John, the son of black immigrants, described the complexities of black identity in America:

Even though I am American, my parents always told me that I am not no "Yankee Boy." This has always stayed in my head. I guess they don't want me to get Americanized. . . . Both of my parents immigrated from the Caribbean and speak English with a distinct accent. . . . My mother is from Grenada and my father was born in Grenada but moved to Trinidad at the age of ten. . . . My culture will stay with me because of the way I was raised and the way I live. The little things like the food I eat, the people I live with and the music I listen to will keep my culture going.

John was supported by his parents in his effort to cling to his Caribbean culture. He seemed to resist assimilation yet claimed to be "an American." Clearly, becoming American is fraught with conflict for black immigrants.

My students debate these terms all the time and have a very different understanding of them than I do. My theoretical knowledge is enriched by their experiential knowledge. The black immigrant students will tell American black students that they are "black," not "African American," because they are not from Africa. My black students tell me that black is a color and does not represent the color of their skin, which is brown or beige. Without even reading about theories of racial identity, these students clearly recognize the social construction of race. I have come to realize that race is very real in my students' lives, that racial tension dominates their lives, and that skin color matters in our society, and this is also why I prefer the term *black,* but I am still learning.

DECONSTRUCTING ASSIMILATION MODELS

Like the black immigrant students, some students struggled with their assimilation, feeling torn by their cultural affiliations. Tina, for example, explained that she felt "like a Puerto Rican in America because, among other things, I can read, write, and speak some Spanish and because my family eats Spanish food. But I don't feel like a Puerto Rican in Puerto Rico because again, among other things, I can't speak Spanish fluently. I don't know much about the country itself and I don't recognize half the foods they serve. So you see, I don't consider myself a true Puerto Rican but I don't consider myself a true 'American' either. To my surprise, however, according to Berle [her source], I am a Puerto Rican." Tina's confusion about her ethnic identity was typical. As she sorted out the markers for her separate American and Puerto Rican identities, she revealed the ways in which she saw herself and recognized how others saw her. Her reliance on a source to define her, however, was not typical. She surrounded the word *American* with quotation marks as if to distance herself from the culture, but then she was surprised she was defined by her source as a Puerto Rican. Although she did not explicitly contest her source's definition, which relies upon Census Bureau data, she subtly realized that the text did not necessarily represent her. As this example shows, students revealed little resistance to assimilation. However, in my recent teaching experience I have come across student writing more frequently that does, which makes me believe that my own pedagogy has become more politicized and more questioning.

Maria, one of my BMCC students, wrote parts of her essay on her cultural identity in Spanish and translated them for me. She described the "dos diferente mundos" that she comes from as a child of Dominican and Cuban parents. And she expressed resistance to being Americanized: "Pero la conciencia no me permitirá hacer gringa" (but my conscience wouldn't let me be an American). Not only did this student reveal the delicate complexities of cultural identity, but she also demonstrated how central language was to her identity: "The first language I learned was español (Spanish). While I was growing up my español started to fade away. After I got to High School, I made a decision that español was what I needed to relearn. Now I speak both español and English, but when I'm with my friends, I try to even eliminate English totally." As this student's writing illustrated, assimilation in American society can mean the loss of one's native language, but, more importantly, that loss can be consciously halted. Maria showed us that members of some oppressed groups carefully choose when to speak English and when not to. Some see Spanish-speakers as resistant to, or worse, incapable of learning English; yet, although this student spoke English beautifully, sometimes she did not want to speak the language of the dominant group. Recalling Nagle's discovery that her students were content with their working-class life, we can recognize the resistance in Maria's and other working-class students' refusal to speak "proper" English or adopt middle-class customs.

Clearly, Maria's resistance to assimilation and the other students' immigration or assimilation processes cannot fit into existing sociological models, such as Milton Gordon's "cultural pluralism," "Anglo-conformity," or the "melting pot" and the ideas of assimilation expressed in J. Hector St. John de Crèvecoeur's *Letters from an American Farmer* (1782), two texts I used in class.[15] As we have seen, when coming to America, students experience isolation, fear, confusion, and displacement. They also feel lucky and joyful at their newfound success. Some never consider themselves to be American, whereas others see themselves as overassimilated. American-born students may also feel some degree of identity crisis, especially if they are bilingual or biracial. Some students, such as Sephardic Jews, live in closed communities that minimize contact with the dominant American society. The established assimilation models are not true models for the immigrant's experience because, to paraphrase Glazer and Moynihan, to become simply American is inhibited by the social structure of the United States, by discrimination and prejudice, and by the "unavailability of a simple 'American' identity."[16]

"Melting pot" is the least accurate model and the least favorable one for students because they usually do not feel they have a new identity in America and because it is a model that devalues immigrants' languages, customs, traditions, beliefs, and behaviors by assuming they will erase their former culture. Gordon's attempt at establishing a precise description of the preservation and dissolution of certain components of ethnic groups is based on the assumption that some degree of assimilation is taking place; he does not question whether assimilation *should* occur. Even more problematic is Gordon's methodology: he bases his report of the degree to which certain groups have assimilated in certain areas (Cultural, Structural, Marital, Identificational, Attitude Receptional, Behavioral, and Civic) on hypothetical situations constructed from interviews with officials of agencies and organizations tied to ethnic concerns, instead of speaking with actual immigrants. In contrast, my conclusions were drawn from my students' writings and conversations. Their writings revealed a need to redefine how we describe assimilation and to question whether we should expect assimilation at all.

In class discussion and in their writings, students critiqued these assimilation models, often rejecting them in favor of others. Students created their own metaphors, symbols, or images for assimilation in American society. Carmen, one of BMCC's basic writers, wrote:

> "Melting Pot" the way I understood it doesn't make sense anymore. "Mosaic" and "Tossed Salad," to me, are just other phrases for separation and segregation. I don't agree with the terminology because of its unifying conclusion. Although America has become multi-cultural it does not . . . impose the American culture on its residents. As a result adverse segregation among people has taken place. . . . This unique separation is self imposed and has created what I call clusters. Clusters being people who only acknowledge their own personal realms and exclude our great countries one significant strength of unity. . . . To be an American, to me, means sharing the American dream. To do what is best for ones own family no matter what culture or heritage is followed, as well as, considering America our own country and give back what we have taken from her, instead of using her as an umbilical cord.

Carmen distinguished herself not only by her sophisticated writing talent, inventing a unique metaphor of America as birth mother, but by her unusual patriotism. Of Puerto Rican descent, Carmen argued with her predominantly African American and Hispanic classmates that America was too segregated and that the identity of "American" could establish some sort of unity. Her essay deeply explored the meaning of these terms. Though she expressed her confusion over her place in American society as a woman of Spanish descent, she confidently claims that she is American, "born, bred till buried." But was she just American? She was a beautiful, bilingual, dark-skinned Puerto Rican, and everyone recognized her as such. She dramatically challenged us to reconsider what an "American" was, expanding its meaning to include herself.

ASSIMILATION, CLASS IDENTITY, AND RACE (BMCC)

Assimilation in America implies that one becomes "middle-class." Yet studies of assimilation usually pay little attention to class identity. It is often assumed, in studies like Gordon's, that certain ethnic and racial groups want to adopt white, middle-class values and lifestyles and that this process will be rewarded. My recognition of the importance of class identity in my own life and in the lives of my students led me to experiment with emphasizing social class more prominently in my recent basic writing courses at BMCC.

Yet when I explicitly introduced social class issues in my courses, especially the idea that my students were working-class, I was (naively) surprised to encounter confusion, resistance, and hostility among the students. Their definitions of class also bewildered me. I saw in my students the same resistance that I had to my working-class background. Students mostly believed in the myth of the classless society and assumed that everyone, including themselves, was middle-class. But students in one of my basic writing classes threw me a curve ball when they introduced race into the equation.

I began our discussion by recording the students' definitions for each category of social class on the board. I did this so students could answer the social class questionnaire found in *Radical Teacher,* which was next on my agenda, and so that they would be prepared to analyze social class in upcoming readings and essays.[17] They would be revising a previous essay by including a discussion or an analysis of class identity. In my morning section, we used the traditional terms of social class, which appeared on the questionnaire and with which my students were familiar: working class; lower, middle, upper middle class; lower, middle, upper upper class; ruling class; and so on.

Because they lived in a society that made class invisible and "working class" shameful, students thought of the working class only as those who work and did not differentiate between the kinds of workers there are. In their eyes, doctors, secretaries, and meat packers were one homogenous group of workers. They seemed to have already begun a neat erasure of class identity. One student did suggest that the minimum wage, which he calculated to be a full-time salary of $10,000, was a defining characteristic of the working class. Another student said that such people live from check to check, having no savings or money for anything but necessities. Though on target, their discussion ended there.

Because the students were having difficulty defining the working class, I suggested we list some occupations we associate with working-class people and with the minimum wage. This wonderfully neat approach only introduced more complex problems because students began to recognize some contradictions. For example, some of the working-class jobs we listed earned high salaries, not a minimum wage, such as those in construction and those that had unions.

Thus, some students seemed confused about their class identity. Nicole actually asked me, "What am I?" Because she wrote that her parents had only high school diplomas and worked in low-paying manual labor jobs, I explained that this indicated she was working-class. She looked disappointed and said, "Oh, I thought I was middle-class." She did not embrace her working-class identity, which seemed to mean a lower status. During this awkward discussion, I sensed my students' shame and confusion as they discovered their working-class identities for the first time and confronted the American myth that everyone is middle-class.

Differentiating people by class seemed unfair or discriminatory to these students, whereas class denial seemed to promote equality and was needed for the upward mobility promised by college. For example, Delia wrote, "In my community [the Bronx] you have the working class, lower middle class and middle class. But I believe that no class in my community is superior than the other. Most of the people in the working class have just as much as the people in the middle class in terms of material possessions. . . . it really does not matter which class is higher because we all must work to purchase the things we need to survive in life." Delia insisted that class mattered less than the fact that all of us have to work.

Unlike their quiet attempts to define working class, students furiously clamored to describe the middle class, with which they were more familiar. Students associated the following with the middle class: suburban homes, cars, college degrees, professions, savings accounts, material possessions, and above-average incomes. Nevertheless, though most of them were the first in their families to attend college and lived "hand-to-mouth" in the inner city, they used the term *middle-class* most frequently to describe their own class status in their essays. They seemed to be denying class differences.

In contrast to Nagle's students who were proud of their working-class lives, the few students of mine who identified themselves as working-class expressed a desire to escape from their class, to better themselves. They saw education and work as the way to do this. Gene, one of the handful of students who used the term *working class*, explained that "everyone in the neighborhood belongs to the same class. We are all in the working class. Most of us live from check to check. I call it a working class because we as a whole strive for a better job, a better neighborhood. We want to own our own homes."

Although most of these students paid little attention to class distinctions, students in my other section of basic writing strongly denied the importance of class identity as they raised the issue of race. One student blurted out that "there are no classes, there's just black and white," and with his encouragement, the students in this section insisted on breaking down social class categories by race, arguing that the middle class is white and the poorer classes are made up of blacks and minorities. When I informed them that many of the poor in our country were white, they seemed surprised.

I thought these students would identify a working class, a middle class, and a ruling elite or wealthy class, as my morning section had. But they wanted to start with the poor. One student insisted there were some who were poorer than the poor, which he called "dirt poor." These students also felt it was significant that they had roofs over their heads and insisted on a category for the homeless. Eagerly waiting for the term "working class" to be called out, I asked for another term and got "welfare recipients," another group they felt should be represented. I obviously never got to focus on the traditional class categories I had in mind.

At first I thought these students were resisting my introduction to class identity every step of the way, but instead they were clearly developing their own "class" discourse. As Paulo Freire would tell us, they were "reading the world" in the language they brought to this problem. When we look closely, we see that they resisted the tripartite conception of class I preferred in favor of a much more experiential scheme that included underrepresented groups like the homeless and welfare recipients; their scheme was also complicated by race and worklessness. Given BMCC's student population, it should not have surprised me that class would be racialized. And given my student-centered teaching, I should not have been surprised that my students would take the opportunity to discuss class in their own terms. By frontloading my students' knowledge in this dialogic inquiry, I discovered the way they read "class." I was able to integrate my scheme into their foundation instead of merely "depositing" it into their brains. These students' reevaluations of social class led me to question the accuracy of my own class discourse and to explore further the ways in which my students were constructed by race and ethnicity, which I was able to do with their essays.

The relationship between cultural identity and class proved to be the basis of many of the students' essay revisions that now included discussions of class identity. A majority of the students in both classes chose to revise their essay on their cultural identity/assimilation to include a discussion of class. Since I gave little direction, allowing them to make their own choices, I am convinced that the students felt cultural assimilation and class identity were linked.

Moreover, my immigrant students, who made up approximately 38 percent of the total, seemed more aware of class differences because they had been more directly affected by them in their move to America. For example, Janine's move from a farm in Jamaica to America changed her class status. Her family was "poor working class" while in Jamaica but leaped into the middle class when they immigrated: "Now living in America, my family has progressed a great deal. They went to college and have graduated with many degrees, which has given them an opportunity to make a decent living. Many members of my family can now afford some of the luxury they once wished they had. They have bought many homes and cars, and have traveled all over the world. They are now considered to be living a middle-class lifestyle." Immigrant students usually raise their standard of living by coming here, but that is not always the case.

Immigrants and children of immigrants were also more aware of the role class plays in assimilation through language. For example, Julio, born in Puerto Rico, recognized that

> the dynamic mix between culture and class results in moral codes and be-havioral codes which create interesting interactions within the family. For ex-ample, when I speak to my parents, I speak in English or Spanish, depending on the mood I am in. Everyone in my family is bilingual. Being fluid in two or more languages can be one factor used to determine one's class and class assignments bestow privileges which are deeply respected within the family or in society. When I am at school or at work, I usually speak English. . . . But I am aware that the ability to speak two or more languages will ultimately help me in attaining a class status "superior" to most other Latinos.

Julio had a sophisticated sense of class and how it functioned in American society. He began his definition with reference to income and education levels but moved toward larger cultural symbols of prestige such as gender and beauty. Moreover, like the students in my second basic writing class, Julio racialized class identity. But most interesting was his belief not only that knowing standard English contributed to his class status, but also that his knowledge of Spanish had economic value on the job market.

Close family ties as a marker of one's ethnicity or race, which we saw in Julio's writing, also served as a class distinction in Dell's essay: "My heritage has taught me to work hard but have time for family. It also has showed me that even if you can't afford the material luxuries in life, you can afford luxuries of family and friends. This is what I call the middle class." In her redefinition of the middle class to include her family, Dell conflated class and cultural identity. She claimed a middle-class identity based on her notion of strong family ties.

Students tended to link their class identity with their ethnic or racial identity, even when I did not explicitly raise class issues. When students decided to compose letters of protest against the governor's proposed financial aid cutback and tuition hike, immigrant students showed how their immigrant identity and process of assimilation were related to their economic success in America. Liya told Governor Pataki:

> The reason I came to the United States is to achieve my goal and have a better opportunity for my future. Because of the difficulty in learning a new language, my father who I live with, had to work for a minimum wage in Chinatown where only Chinese is spoken. Not only does he have to support me, but also my mother who is still in China. Therefore, I am attending BMCC, a CUNY school where I can get Financial Aid. That is the only way for me to get the education I want, and when I graduate from college, I can get a good salary job to better our lives. But in the meanwhile, I have a part-time minimum wage job which I have to work twenty-five hours a week, just to help my father out.
>
> Life is not easy for my father and I from the first day that we stepped on this land. Because of our language and culture barriers, we have to struggle to survive. If you, Governor Pataki, keep on proposing tuition hikes and the cut backs on financial aid, [i]t is not going to be any easier for us. . . . Please take some consideration of us, the minority — new immigrants, do not let us become the losers in this society.

As this letter and the revised essays showed, students acknowledged the link between class identity, cultural identity or assimilation, and race/ethnicity. Hence, I am persuaded by my pedagogical experiments that issues of class identity are undoubtedly a part of the process of questioning assimilation ideologies, including those in the academy. I am still figuring out ways to raise awareness of the importance of class identity and its connection with ethnicity, race, and gender; to avoid essentializing these experiences; and to move students beyond critical reflection to collective action, a key part of critical pedagogy.

Working with mostly immigrant students, I found the issue of assimilation a topic about which students could produce lively and provocative essays and at the same time find a place to express their confusion, frustration, or delight in becoming "Americanized." Because CUNY was founded as a public institution to provide higher education to the city's immigrant and working-class population, its student population remains largely of those groups. Cultural, language, or class assimilation, however, can provoke fruitful discussion and writing at many other institutions and with many other kinds of student populations. An examination and critique of assimilation is more than appropriate for working-class students at elite institutions who struggle with feelings of displacement. And a pedagogy that places students' languages, cultures, and knowledge at the center of the writing classroom can enrich and improve the learning experiences of blacks, Latinos, and other marginalized groups.

Though my students may want or need to excel at academic discourse, just as I did, I want them to examine their choices and desires, what they gain or lose. My pedagogy, thus, can be placed in a recent tradition in composition studies that privileges our students' discourse and encourages students to retain their own language when faced with the overwhelming struggle with academic discourse. I do not believe that academic success depends upon breaking our students' ties with their communities or that the denial of a working-class background is the price to pay for academic success and upward mobility. My experience in complying with the silencing of my own culture makes me redouble my efforts in allowing my students the right to their own language. I believe, like Richard Gambino, that without a strong sense of our ethnic, racial or class identities, we lead empty lives.

WORKING-CLASS STUDIES

TO KNOW,
TO REMEMBER,
TO REALIZE:

ILLINOIS LABOR WORKS—
A HISTORY WORKERS CAN USE

ROBERT BRUNO AND LISA JORDAN

The People learn, unlearn, learn, a builder, a wrecker, a builder again . . .
Precisely who and what is the People?
— Carl Sandburg, *The People, Yes*

As members of a labor education faculty, we begin with a common creed: university-based labor education programs should respond to the needs of workers. Our mission is to take the best of what the university system has to offer into the community in order to educate working men and women. In the process we try to strengthen the institution of collective bargaining through a variety of training programs. The courses we teach include union administration, grievance handling, stewards' training, communications and media relations, women and the economy, labor and politics, union values, and labor history.

The scant academic literature on labor education focuses on skills training, but it is our contention that the broad contours of workers' history and their subjective meanings provide the worker-student the most fertile opportunity to link work-related knowledge with critical awareness of current labor-management relations. Labor history has too often been considered a "soft" item of study worthy of only modest, superficial coverage. For example, Brooke Broadbent, in discussing education needs assessment, argues that "the word 'needs' can be misleading. Sometimes what passes for needs are personal wishes or vain hopes. *Real education needs are practical.*"[1] As examples of "real" education needs he notes the legal rights and obligations of stewards, the union's structure and functions, and principles of financial management. Labor history, however, is not seen as "practical." Given the decline in union membership as a share of the total workforce since the mid-70s, as well as the vilification of union "bosses" by conservative politicians, it is not surprising that some in the labor movement focus on a narrowly conceived survival training. In this mind-set, current day-to-day issues become central. History is thus seen as sentimental, not empowering.

Although we agree that basic skills training is important, we believe that worker histories are not merely empty remembrances but vibrant portals to collective agency. Labor history, far from being a "soft" area of study, must (we contend) be defined and appropriated correctly if labor is to survive. For that reason we created the drama *Illinois Labor Works (ILW)*.

ILW is a three-act story structured around a fictitious organizing drive at a nondescript work site. The program is designed for an audience of worker-students who become the "workers" who are the subject of the United Workers of America's organizational efforts. Act 1 is a depiction of the reasons why workers formed unions. Act 2 focuses on militant struggles between capital and labor. Act 3 constructs a summary of worker achievements and contemporary challenges and closes with worker-students being asked to sign union cards. Throughout the presentation we assume different characters and read first-person accounts relevant to the story. We use modest props and costuming to thicken the "experiential" value of the story. Our narrative is supported by a thirty-one-minute video of photographs and moving sequences.

The program/script is flexible in that we regularly move characters in and out of the script in order to fit the needs of the group or union we are working with. For example, a presentation to the United Food and Commercial Workers (UFCW) incorporated a contemporary story of a food store worker; before the United Postal Workers of America (UPWA) we presented a mail-room sorter from the 1940s; and for the American Federation of State and County Employees (AFSCME) we dramatized a workday in the life of a government employee. By adjusting characters and stories, we can more effectively reduce the distance between the participants and their history.

Our commitment to *ILW* grows out of our concern that working people are not consciously connected to the history they created and consequently are handicapped in achieving practical change within their workplace and community. *ILW* was designed to reveal to workers their history-making potential. The program presents labor history to union members in a way that encourages them to connect with the history of working people and challenges them to use that history as a weapon of contemporary struggle.

Although we are currently focusing on a class created for nontraditional students, we believe the pedagogical approach used in *ILW* is also effective in traditional classroom settings. What is central is that students are seen as active creators of meaning and that students create that meaning in the context of their experiences. By providing working-class students with ways to connect their life experiences with the larger social, cultural, and political context, we validate the importance of personal stories. In our view, using the students' knowledge as a starting point significantly adds to the students' ability to understand complex theoretical material. This process is not neutral, politically or ideologically. As educators, we do not present or see ourselves as impartial observers. Furthermore, we believe that at its core good education challenges the student—disrupts a student's current attitudes. Disrupting people's accepted notions about the way the world works isn't easy and isn't always rewarded, but it is a crucial first step to critical thinking. We draw much of our thinking about education from Ira Shor, James Berlin, Kathleen McCormick, and others who challenge us to address the student as an individual who functions within society but also has the power to recreate that society.

This essay examines the creation and pedagogy of *ILW* and summarizes the early feedback offered by those worker-students who have participated in the program. We believe that our experience developing and teaching *ILW* and the program's overwhelming success have important implications for the teaching of nontraditional and other working-class students. Programs like *ILW* draw on the personal experience of students, challenge them to connect that experience with the larger context, and invite them to become active participants in their communities.

A HISTORY WORKERS CAN USE

ILW is grounded in a fundamental adult educational principle: to be effective with people who have real-world experiences requires narrowing the "distance" between student-as-object and student-as-subject. More precisely, labor education should remove the false consciousness that prevents workers from identifying themselves as authors of the world. In teaching labor history, however, the goal is more easily stated than accomplished. Consider some of the findings from Bruno's doctoral research, conducted on the classic case of postwar Youngstown, Ohio, steelworkers.[2]

From 1946 to the mid-1980s, steelworkers in Youngstown were responsible for making a lot of the steel that went into the country's car frames, skyscrapers, bridges, and army tanks. Many books have been written and numerous films have been produced about the meaning of working-class life, but most workers have not read any of the books, and, with the exception of *Hoffa* and *F.I.S.T.,* they probably have not seen much of themselves portrayed on the big screen.[3] Forget for the moment that neither of those films bore any honest resemblance to the state of working America or organized labor. The truth is that most Youngstown steelworkers have ignored working-class history. They did not read labor history books or labor journals, watch labor films, listen to labor songs or labor poems, visit labor landmarks or labor museums. It would appear, then, to borrow and revise a Marxist axiom, that "workers make history; but not always in a form they can use."

But why not? Why do workers not identify themselves as historical architects? Is it that workers do not see labor history as their story? Is it the discomfort of too often being addressed as either subjects of repression or secondary actors? Is the lack of formal education a deterrent to their historical appreciation? Or is it that the material is not presented in a way they can identify as authentic?

Maybe a clue to why workers do not cling to a remembered past lies in the monuments and public landmarks working-class people build. In Struthers (a neighboring town of Youngstown, Ohio) children play baseball at Mauthe Park. Mauthe Park was named after J. L. Mauthe, the long-standing chairman of the board of the Youngstown Sheet and Tube Company (YS&T). Mauthe and the corporate officers who preceded him had owned most of Youngstown and lorded over the property where steelworkers of all ethnic nationalities eventually built homes. Mauthe and his contemporaries were the same men who sold off the company in 1973 to a shipbuilding contractor who proceeded to milk the steel giant dry.[4] Eventually more than twenty thousand workers related to basic steelmaking lost their jobs in a devastating wave of mill closings. But Youngstown steelworkers did not blame YS&T for their misfortune, and the park continues to stand in Mauthe's honor.[5] Similarly, in Homestead, Pennsylvania, long after the steelworkers were gone, the Carnegie Library and Frick Park remain, both monuments to the owners of great wealth, not to the men and women who struggled to improve the conditions under which workers toiled.

According to Michael Frisch, workers often provide little support to preserve the sites of famous strikes or labor battles.[6] Of course, people do rally to save pieces of labor history, but not usually people nourished with the blood of their working-class ancestors. Typically it is historical society patrons and middle- and upper-class intellectuals who speak of the value of the sites' architectural aesthetics. Perhaps these physical markers are depressing reminders of faded dreams and lost opportunities for working men and women? John Russo, director of the Labor Studies Program at Youngstown State University, suggests that workers have revisited painful stories of community decay and family disjuncture many times and perhaps they have just grown tired of remembering.[7] It is true that much of labor's story is racked by corporate assault and government oppression. According to Patricia Sexton Cayo, America's labor history is the most violent in the world.[8] If labor wars were enough to leave a damaged spot on the collective memory wall, then certainly the modern implosion of industrial towns like Homestead and Youngstown should have been sufficient to blot out all recollection of a cherished past.

None of this should be surprising, given the power of myth in our society. The American myths of a consensual polity and individual self-making have been hallmarks of public education and political legitimization.[9] As James V. Catano points out, myth addresses a broad spectrum of needs: "In politics, the myth serves to enunciate ideals of democratic progress and individuality, while on a related economic level, the myth helps to mask the disturbing presence of corporate power."[10] Myth creates distance between the worker and his or her class history. Consider that the notion of a classless society conflicts in fundamental ways with actual working-class history. After all, labor history points to the separation of workers from owners, separations in the form of values, compensation, residency, career choices, and power. Then why do workers seem to accept uncritically the idea of a universal, "rugged individualist" American experience? Perhaps because it is the dominant cultural explanation for social mobility. Indeed, many "rags-to-riches" books were written about, and in some cases by, the owners of late-nineteenth- and twentieth-century capital.[11] Throughout the twentieth century, the school children of working-class parents have been brought up reading about the individual adventures of Tom Swift and the "boy inventors," not the class-oriented struggles of Albert Parsons, Samuel Gompers, Eugene Debs, and Mother Jones.[12]

Although some workers had access to local union newsletters, most always read local newspapers. They might have expected to find their stories popularized on the pages of a community paper, but even papers in union towns like Youngstown and Pittsburgh have historically covered labor as a necessary evil and effusively reported the success of free enterprise. Most important, schools raised generation after generation of working-class fodder without mentioning the labor movement or using the word *union* in a complete sentence. As Henry Giroux has pointed out, "schools . . . produce knowledge, and they provide students with a sense of place, worth and identity. In doing so, they offer students selected representations, skills, social relations, and values that presuppose particular histories and ways of being in the world. The moral and political dimension at work here is revealed in the question, 'Whose history, story, and experience prevails in the school setting?' In other words, who speaks for whom, under what conditions and for what purpose?"[13]

Is it any wonder that after more than two hundred years of working-class sacrifice and struggle, the names of workers rarely grace the facades of town libraries, city halls, and public parks? The point is that workers were denied, or have denied themselves, access to a labor history from *their perspective*. In its place they have accepted a constant diet of entrepreneurial heroism and rags-to-riches melodrama. It seems, then, that part of the problem in teaching labor history is that workers do not identify with the *collective* movement of workers against capital. Rather, they too easily see themselves as single workers in a struggle to get ahead, to improve their lot, to become capitalists, or at least to have their children do so.

Yet, if workers had completely bought into the myth of autonomous self-making, one would expect to find workers with little of an analytical nature to say about their experiences. However, this certainly does not seem to be the case. In our respective research on the steel industry and the role of women organizers in Appalachia, and in the oral histories done by others, workers are full of analytical stories rich in ideological perspective and material detail.[14] It appears that workers are eager to talk about their working lives. They just seem reluctant to witness or share in a public expression of working-class history. Telling *your* story is one thing; integrating it into the story of *the working class* is altogether different.

Given that workers are wonderful storytellers, anxious to numb the ears of a willing listener, it does not seem reasonable that it is simply content that prohibits them from hearing, reading, or witnessing labor history. Maybe the problem lies in the messenger. What might account for this apparent messenger problem? Consider the voluminous library of labor history books. With few exceptions, they are written by nonworkers. Most authors are academics — sensitive, intelligent academics, but still academics, writing mainly for an academic audience. Tenure and professional advancement being what they are in major universities, most labor texts are written with other academics in mind.

Books by nonacademics, such as William Serrin's *Homestead* and John Hoerr's *And the Wolf Finally Came*, though moving and insightful, were written by labor and business reporters.[15] Even labor lawyers such as Thomas Geohagen have written expressively about working-class experiences.[16] Rarer is the book written by a worker for other workers. America has had many educated and literate labor leaders, but few have written much outside of union publications. Three notable exceptions are United Electrical Workers' union organizer James Matles's *Them and Us*, the business journal writings of United

Textile Workers' secretary-treasurer, Solomon Barkin, and John Sweeney's *America Needs a Raise*.[17]

Undoubtedly, part of the problem has been a strain of mistrust that has infused the relationship between the academy and the labor movement. The question of labor's relationship with the labor education community is worth probing, but maybe a simpler reason exists for why workers do not read what academics write about them: workers lack the time and energy. Consider the stories told in Studs Terkel's *Working*.[18] If the workers had anything in common with one another, it was that they were *tired*. If you are tired you cannot read. Yet, even if workers could find the energy to read, few could decipher the jargon-filled texts required by intellectual disciplines.

Perhaps reading is too problematic. What about viewing movies? Certainly workers could have consumed labor history much more productively from honest labor films than from textual sources. Accounts of working-class movie-going reveal the potential of celluloid to communicate with America's workers.[19] Movies are affordable and entertaining ways to get away from the rigors of the workday. But though Hollywood has always been solicitous of the working-class's well-earned take-home pay, it has never been fond of organized workers. The labor movement in the studio and on the screen has been portrayed one-dimensionally at best and as plain evil at worst. With few exceptions (*Norma Rae*, 1979; *Matewan*, 1987) unionized workers were either missing from commercial releases (*Silkwood*, 1983) or treated as dishonest leaders (*On the Waterfront*, 1954; *Teamster Boss*, 1992), assassins and thugs (*Act of Vengeance*, 1985), or confused and alienated stiffs (*Blue Collar*, 1979).[20] Whether good or bad, most labor films focused on a central character; usually a union leader or organizer, or someone challenging the leadership. The problem is that most workers are not leaders, and few will ever aspire to leadership. The medium fails to direct its lens on the worker-subject.

If both the texts and the screen suffer from structural flaws, perhaps labor museums and landmarks can overcome what appears to restrain working people from appropriating their own history. Memorializing the site of a strike or the career of a labor notable overcomes the problems of a nonlegitimate messenger, an esoteric message, and the failure to emphasize the average worker. In Youngstown, steelworkers have access to a three-level "steel museum" dedicated to the nature and positive contributions of their work. Since 1992 Youngstown workers, past and present, have been able to visit the impressive exhibits at the Historical Center of Industry and Labor. Yet, despite the well-meaning efforts of the museum's directors, only a modest number of the area's retired steelworkers recall hearing anything of substance about the place.[21] Though much of the area's community history can be told from within the center's exhibits, barely a trickle of the community's working-class and sizable pensioner population has passed through the front door. Now, it's true that the "steel museum" is not strictly a *labor* facility. But a number of exhibits acknowledge the struggle for and the importance of unionization. In addition, the center has created a library of video interviews with retirees and is a repository for local union records and newspapers. In the summer of '95 it even hosted a retrospective on the Steel Worker Organizing Committee years (1935–42).

Exceptions to a total blackout of all working-class impressions do exist and are more memorable because of their scarcity. Thanks to people like Archie Green and Les Orear, director of the Illinois Labor History Society, and the cultural appreciation of unions such as the United Electrical, Radio, and Machine Workers (UE), the United Mine Workers (UMWA), and the United Automobile Workers (UAW), working-class stories get told in objects, words, songs, and pictures.[22] It is also worth noting that in Washington, D.C., the Labor Heritage Foundation sponsors the Great Labor Cultural Exchange. Unfortunately, in spite of all the creative efforts of organizers and performers, most workers cannot or do not want to go to Washington to experience a couple of days of labor culture. It would appear, then, that a dilemma challenges us as labor activists, writers, and educators: although workers are a dynamic source of working-class historical exposition, they are disinterested in their own subjectivity.

DISTANCE, DISTURBANCE, AND AGENCY

How then can labor education pull back the ideological shroud that hides the role of workers in creating the physical and social structures that define their identity? Consistent with ideas and approaches within the field of popular critical literacy, we "perceive the impossibility of a neutral education."[23]

We hold that a student's experiential knowledge functions as a base from which all subsequent critical analysis emerges. Paulo Freire's temporal observation that "human beings first changed the world, secondly proclaimed the world and then wrote the words" is a useful guide to how teaching should proceed.[24] Using the students' knowledge as a starting point significantly adds to their ability to understand complex theoretical material. That knowledge, however, must not be left undisturbed. In order to help worker-students understand their own historical objectivity and create previously unseen alternative futures, their knowing should be "disrupted."

We are keenly interested in helping worker-students find embedded in the meaning of labor struggles an appreciation of their own historical agency. But not just appreciation. Our objective is explicitly political in that we mean to mobilize workers for contemporary struggles. Our teaching is meant to negate the prevailing ways of knowing that have alienated worker-students from their own constitutive power. By admitting our political intent, we believe that we are doing what good educators have always done. As James Berlin has argued, "A way of teaching is never innocent. Every pedagogy is implicated in ideology, in a set of tactic assumptions about what is real, what is good, what is possible, and how power ought to be distributed." Teaching, as Berlin points out, should confront what is comfortable and settled about what workers know: "The material, the social, and the subjective are at once the producers and the products of ideology, and ideology must continually be challenged so as to reveal its economic and political consequences for individuals. In other words, what are the effects of our knowledge? Who benefits from a given version of truth? How are the material benefits of society distributed? What is the relation of this distribution to social relations? Do these relations encourage conflict? To whom does our knowledge designate power?"[25]

Much of the thinking about working-class education challenges educators to address the student not only as an individual who functions within society but also as a being with the power to recreate that society. Ideology, or what workers believe is true about their work structures and relationships, is central to this task. Again Berlin offers that "ideology . . . provides the subject with standards for making ethical and aesthetic decisions: what is good, right, just, beautiful, attractive, enjoyable, and its opposites. In this way our desires become structured and normalized."[26]

Doing this in the context of labor education presents a variety of challenges not typical in conventional on-campus classrooms. The first, and in some ways the most obvious, is the diversity of students we teach. In teaching labor education, our students range from those who are functionally illiterate to those who have master's degrees. Although typically this entire range is not present in a classroom at any one time, in developing an educational program the range must always be kept in mind. Second, labor education programs are typically short in duration. For example, *ILW* was developed to fill a two-hour slot. Third, many of our students spend much of their time actively engaged in the work they do, and more often than not, their work is physical. Therefore, they have difficulty being passive observers for long periods of time. Finally, many of our students initially feel distanced from us because of our respective educational backgrounds. Though knowledge is seen in a positive way, credentials from the academy often make for a less receptive student-worker audience.

ILW was designed to appeal to workers "where they are," while challenging them to think and act in the future upon different assumptions. In other words, we see the program as an effective way to convey historical content, but it also explicitly reflects our belief that student-workers are active agents in the learning process. In essence, they are agents who "read" the program from their own circumstances. It is that reading that makes *ILW* an effective teaching approach.

ILLINOIS LABOR WORKS: THE PROGRAM

In looking for a more effective way to bring labor history to workers, we concluded that the problem was both content and messenger and that what was needed was a medium that delivered a stimulating content from the voices of ordinary workers. We hypothesized that workers would enthusiastically embrace a history *of, by,* and *from* the workers that was not reliant on textual dexterity. In essence, what we needed was a "history the workers could hear." In many ways, we did what we are asking our students to do — take a lesson from the past. What in part distinguishes *ILW* from other educational programs is that it dramatizes labor history. It is in this sense a throwback to the "labor dramatics" of the CIO's pre–World War II and 1950s union theater.

ILW is a multimedia labor history program that utilizes the voices, photographs, and music of working-class people to tell the story of the American labor movement.[27] Although the focus is on Illinois labor history, the narrative themes are universal to a wage-earning working class. Among other resources, *ILW* makes use of untapped Works Progress Administration (WPA) archival worker narratives. The Illinois Writers Project — part of the WPA — was directed by John T. Frederick between 1936 and 1939 and provides a rich, multicultural account of labor throughout the state. A short list of project topics includes farm labor, urban minorities, organized labor, child labor in Illinois, compulsory education, immigration quotas, and the minimum hourly wage. Combined with contemporary images and stories, these personal narratives powerfully eclipse any separation between past and present labor struggles.

ILW was produced to remind worker-students of the struggles that have been won to get decent working conditions and to motivate them to continue the struggle to maintain hard-won protections. The underlying idea is that workers cannot fully comprehend their particular present condition without an understanding of how things have come to be as they are. Moreover, workers can best devise strategies to achieve their objectives by understanding how past victories were won and by incorporating their particular efforts within the wider context of workers' struggles everywhere. By demonstrating the relationship between the past and the present and between the present and the future, the program seeks to make each worker appreciate his or her *history-making potential.*

To that end the voices of working men and women are used to tell their own stories. This collective history and the connections that draw working people together are presented using a multimedia presentation. A narrative derived from oral histories weaves in and out of working-class poetry, videos, photographs, and music. Throughout the program, worker-students are actively involved in the dramatization. They participate as rank-and-file workers and witnesses at pivotal events. Since the program's focus is on working people, we call on the participants to share their own stories.

There are four reasons we feel that *ILW* bridges the gap between acting subject and passive observer. First, in *ILW,* the subject is a participant. The drama pulls worker-students into the action. They are not merely talked at or asked to watch a screen. *ILW* is interactive. On a number of occasions the "Organizer" (played by Lisa Jordan) ventures out into the audience and addresses the workers *as workers in need of a union.* She shakes hands, pats people on the back, and implores them to speak out for the union. When this happens, our worker-audience immediately feels a part of the story. They have, in fact, suffered poor working conditions, low pay, and employer indignities. The "Organizer" is a device to get them to bear witness to the truth they know so well. Once worker-students have given testimony to their own truths, they are no longer external to the story. *ILW* demands more from worker-students than does a good book or an entertaining movie, but it does not require "second order" reading or writing skills. All it asks is that students as workers speak truth to power.

Second, the script for *ILW* is inspired by the most comprehensive first-person accounts of working-class experiences ever collected — the Federal Writers Project (FWP). We culled through a large sample of oral histories and contemporary reports filed by writers hired to chronicle the condition of America's working class during the Depression. In addition, we read several labor plays produced under the administration of the Federal Theater Project.[28] These records were chock full of powerful testimony by workers from various occupational backgrounds about the nature of their working lives. As wonderful as these records were, an even bigger revelation was that few of the accounts had found their way to modern working-class audiences. We then began to draw character sketches from the FWP and other working-class narratives in order to construct a workers' story in workers' voices.

The result was a workers' narrative. As instructors, we never speak. Instead we perform as steelworkers, meat packers, store clerks, coal miners, and railroad workers. Using only worker voices eliminates the problem of authenticity and legitimacy. Now not only were the voices not second-party interpretations, but the workers speaking were all rank-and-filers. *ILW* is conspicuous as a labor history program in that, with one brief exception, it includes no national labor leaders.[29] There was no intent to defame union officers, but the point of

ILW was to demonstrate the history-making power of the working masses. When labor history focuses on the story of labor leaders it is inevitably more about their heroics than the sacrifice and struggle of the average worker, and it is this broader struggle that *ILW* is intended to convey.

Third, *ILW* is neither text, picture, nor site. But it does incorporate all of these communication media. Although worker-students hear a significant amount of dialogue, we are not lecturing as "experts." What is important here is that for a brief moment in time disbelief is suspended and worker-students come in contact with historical figures who mirror their own reality. We suspect that if someone had simply given the same information in a lecture, massive audience defection would be the norm.

Along with a considerable amount of listening, worker-students also see an array of visuals from photographs of workers on the job to archival footage of labor strikes and moving sequences of Labor Day parades. But *ILW* is not a film. Instead it utilizes visuals to texturize the narrative into a human form and place. The pictures are pieces of evidence that substantiate the story being told. For example, a first-person reading of the 1937 South Chicago Memorial Day Massacre is followed by a few minutes of newsreel footage shot on the grounds of Republic Steel that fateful day. After the participants have heard an account of the killings of innocent workers, they witness the butchery of police and company guards, gunfire and all. Workers have commented in postprogram evaluations that because of how this incident was dramatized they will never again think of the Memorial Day Massacre without feeling pain or hearing the gunfire.

The words presented and pictures shown are given further context through the use of simple props. The "stage" includes various hats, shirts, coats, and assorted items likely to be found at the scene. We change characters by putting on and taking off pieces of clothing and picking up objects relevant to the story being told. The point here is to transport worker-students to the places where all their rich labor history gets made: the workplace, the streets outside the plant, a town meeting room, a Senate hearing, a worker's home. These may not be landmarks, but they are places where workers can find their heritage and their power. With their history now embedded in setting, costume, and character, workers are doing much more than watching, listening, or in a conventional sense reading—they are experiencing. As one worker put it, "You're being educated and you don't know it."

Finally, *ILW* is a collective exercise. Unlike reading, passively listening, or watching a screen in the dark, workers participate in this history lesson with other workers. The program is built around shared experiences and attempts to evoke common feelings. Workers are given the chance to witness their past together as a class-developed history. They are called to remember and respond to the past by the "Organizer" and the cast of characters, *and they do so with their union brothers and sisters.* ILW unfolds at a meeting of workers in both dramatization and fact. The purpose of a public witnessing is to contrast the efforts of individual workers acting alone against the structural inequities of a free-enterprise economic system with the historical consequence of class action. To achieve this end realistically requires using a teaching methodology that forms a fictitious union out of a real, flesh and blood one.

REFLECTING ON *ILW*

Our fondest hope for *ILW* was that worker-students would "read" the program in a way that encouraged self-reflection, critical analysis of the labor movement, constructive dialogue about historical agency, and ultimately action. Postprogram evaluations suggest that *ILW* has for the most part been successful in reducing the distance between the worker-student and the history of the labor movement. Moreover, the students have made connections between past and present struggles. One member of the AFSCME described *ILW* in the following way: "This was very thought-provoking—I found myself swept into it—interesting, yes. *We need to know, to remember, to realize, to recapture the struggle and keep it alive and unyielding.* At some points, I felt sad. At some, the emotions were high and energizing. It touched my heart and my mind. The fight goes on."

Overall, the program has been extremely well received. In written evaluations, 84 percent of the worker-students have rated the program as "very good" to "excellent." More importantly, approximately 97 percent of the worker-students have endorsed the authenticity of the narratives, photos, and music selected to tell their stories. A robust 78 percent of student-workers "strongly agreed" that *ILW* was an "inspiring portrayal of working-class struggles," and 81 percent agreed that the program was "very effective" in making the connection between past and present struggle.

As encouraging as the above responses are, the most affirming evaluations are those relating to the spatial barriers separating subject from object and the need for collective action. Student-workers enthusiastically (82 percent) endorsed *ILW* as an expression of their own "feelings and experiences as a worker." It is important that 77 percent indicated that the program helped them to "recognize the importance of struggle" and "inspired [them] to protect union rights." Finally, 61 percent of participants said that *ILW* increased their knowledge of labor history, and another 57 percent saw their interest in the subject grow "a great deal."

It is important to consider these evaluations in the context of doing labor history for a union-labor audience. After all, labor's story is not without examples of racism, sexism, and factional violence. As we noted earlier, criticism is often seen as too risky and history lessons unnecessary and tedious. The conventional wisdom argues that labor has enough critics on the "outside" and cannot afford to be self-reflective. It is important then to present a unified front, and any challenge to that front is problematic.

Indeed, the program has not touched all worker-students. Some remain convinced that union training should be exclusively focused on skills. A worker-student from the UFCW epitomized that viewpoint when he said, referring to *ILW,* "This is a joke. I thought this was stewards' training." Fortunately, few of the over one thousand worker-students who have now seen *ILW* have expressed such a sentiment.

As successful as the program has been, we have learned important lessons. The program is presented in the voices of workers, but we chose the stories, the music, and the photos to be used. In part, the program's content reflects our understanding of labor history and *our expectations of people's reactions to the material.* However, during two years of doing the program, we have sometimes found our own assumptions and expectations challenged.

One such surprise occurred at our first presentation of *ILW* in January 1996, to members of the Laborer's International Union of North America (LIUNA). In developing the script, we had consciously taken a position against labor-management cooperation, but LIUNA is very much involved in joint programs. Thus, we reasoned that LIUNA would not be a friendly audience. We were wrong: the reaction was overwhelmingly positive. On the one hand, in post-program discussions, workers identified the benefits and problems of labor-management cooperation. On the other, opposition to the boss was enthusiastically cheered. Apparently, we disrupted conventional assumptions sufficiently to engage in a reflection on the conditions for genuine cooperation.

Another example of how our expectations diverged from worker-student responses dealt with the issue of intraclass cleavages. We firmly believe that solidarity cannot be built on a romanticized version of labor history. The ugliness of past (or current) racial, ethnic, or gender problems must not be sifted out of the story. Solidarity must be based on real tolerance that recognizes difference yet shares a unity of purpose. Thus, several times in the program we address the issue of racial, ethnic, and sexual discrimination within the labor movement.

In determining what characters to present, we decided to select the following narratives: an oral history of an African American meat packer who sees the union bring harmony to the "yards," the story of a German immigrant miner who was hung by native miners in Collinsville, Illinois, during World War I, and the transcript of a town meeting in East St. Louis discussing the increasing numbers of blacks coming from the South to work in meatpacking and railroads. The last choice was the most difficult. The transcript of the meeting was not only violent in tone but full of the term *nigger*. We had edited other narratives for time and aesthetic considerations, but we were unsure what to do with this piece.

After lengthy discussion, we decided to excise all but one use of the term. We wanted the scene not only to reflect the anger of the time, but also to address how destructive bigotry was and is to class solidarity. At the same time we were sensitive about offending the African Americans participating in the class. The result indicated that our concerns were overdrawn. Worker-students did react to the racism in the scene. But it was not African American workers we disturbed. In fact, at each of our presentations African American participants noted the authenticity of the dialogue, whereas some of the white worker-students were made uncomfortable by the scene and wanted to forget the ugliness. The African American participants said they could not forget because the behavior is still too much present.

Scripting and presenting *ILW* has been a path of discovery as we have integrated what we learn with each new presentation. The strength of this approach to teaching history is that the script is never final. After each presentation workers tell us what to add, what to take out, and what to try; consequently, *ILW* remains a history that is always relevant and worker-centered.

As educators we have an obligation to do more than participate in the telling of labor's story. Although our different audiences will include workers as well as nonworkers, we must always try to serve the universal needs of working men and women. One way we can do this is by using history as a powerful organizational and educational tool. *ILW* is a living history lesson that can inspire workers to take seriously their historical agency and in doing so confront those contemporary forces that would eviscerate a collective working-class voice. In the end, we are reminded of Karl Marx's admonition to philosophers that they "have only interpreted the world; the point, however, is to change it."[30] We see no reason why less should be expected of labor's storytellers.

STRIKING CLOSE TO HOME:

STUDENTS CONFRONT THE 1985 HORMEL STRIKE

COLETTE HYMAN

As a historian trained in social history in the 1970s and 1980s, I have always worked hard to make all my courses — but especially my introductory-level U.S. history survey course — as inclusive as possible. Through required readings, lectures, and discussions, my surveys address the changing social and economic conditions of women, of European (and, more recently, Asian) immigrants, of Latino migrants and immigrants, and of African American communities. We also study civil rights movements, left-wing movements, and feminism, as well as more conventional political narratives. I have also included discussions of major strikes, union organizing campaigns, and reform movements aimed at working people and the poor. Although I do not claim to have perfected the incorporation of gender and race into the U.S. survey, I have felt much more successful in introducing and exploring questions pertaining to race and gender than in discussing issues of class and working-class perspectives, even though, as a labor historian, this should be my stock in trade. Students' resistance to addressing such issues seems far greater than it is to discussing issues of race or gender; in contrast to these other two socially constructed categories, which, at the surface at least, seem "obvious," class is, both theoretically and empirically, a far more fluid and elusive category.

In the spring of 1995, in an effort to make labor and class issues more intelligible and accessible to students, I began to include discussions of the

1985 strike at the new plant of the Hormel Corporation based in Austin, Minnesota, one hundred miles away. The strike tore apart the community at the same time as it gained nationwide attention as one of the first militant rebuttals to the antilabor politics of the 1980s. The geographic and chronological proximity of this strike, I reasoned, would certainly strike familiar chords with students here at Winona State University, half of whom are from the region of southern Minnesota and western Wisconsin, and over half of whom are first-generation college students, which indicates working-class roots, if not identities.

The discussion of the strike, sparked by the assigned reading, Peter Rachleff's account *Hard-Pressed in the Heartland,* teased out the complexities of the strike, sorted out key players, and began making sense of this labor conflict in the context of de-industrialization and Reaganomics.[1] A subsequent written assignment asking students to compare the economic and political conditions of workers around the time of the 1909 garment strikes and those faced by Hormel strikers revealed, however, that students still failed to grasp a working-class perspective and could not see the female garment workers of 1909 and the mostly male meat packers of 1985 as having similar interests and concerns, much less class backgrounds. Students focused on differences between the female garment workers and the male meat packers, and noted how much better off working people were in the 1980s because of occupational health and safety regulations that had not existed in the early 1900s. Remarkably, they emphasized the improvements brought about by such regulation even though the deregulation of the meatpacking industry and the declining effectiveness of the Occupational Health and Safety Administration in maintaining a healthy workplace were emphasized in the book as central causes of the strike.

My efforts to make class and labor issues more accessible to students by discussing an event to which they could "relate" had been less than completely successful: despite earlier discussion of labor conflicts and emerging class consciousness among strikers, the notion of class eluded the students. They understood the meat packers' grievances without grasping the larger context of class relations. They made their way through the complexities of the immediate strike but were unable to connect it to broader structures of power and inequality grounded in class differences.

I tried the local/recent approach twice more, striving to develop both broader themes and more local issues in the discussion of the Hormel strike; this only convinced me that a more rigorous approach would be necessary in order for students to "get" class at a more fundamental level and to begin making connections over time and, eventually, between themselves and different parties engaged in strikes and class conflict more generally. What I realized in my early attempts to address class through a potential personal connection was that because class is a far more difficult social category to grasp than gender, race, ethnicity, or sexual orientation, among others, I could not integrate a discussion of class issues into a survey course without problematizing the nature of class, in particular as it has been experienced in the United States, over the course of the twentieth century. In order to address class issues in a way that was meaningful both in terms of how students understood U.S. history and in terms of how they see themselves within it, I would have to make class a central focus of the course.

In the fall of 1996, the U.S. history survey that I taught was organized around the concept and experiences of class. The course opened and closed with readings about class and class-related issues — the novel *Out of This Furnace,* by Thomas Bell, and, once more, Rachleff's *Hard-Pressed in the Heartland;* essay questions required students to address class from a variety of perspectives; and a new assignment, a family history paper, asked students to explore class status and identity among members of their own family or a family they knew well.[2] This focus on class was clearly stated in the syllabus, and discussion and essay questions asked students to think about class as one of many factors, among them gender, race, ethnicity, and region, that shaped individuals' experiences of historical events and developments.

The course was organized around discussion in large and small groups, with a few brief lectures interspersed. In addition to the book on the Hormel strike and the novel, required readings included a textbook and primary documents. The course was conceived and presented to students as a survey of twentieth-century U.S. history examined through the lens of class structure and class identity; the terms of discussion were set by *Out of This Furnace* and reexamined in the discussion of *Hard-Pressed in the Heartland* and the Hormel strike.

Out of This Furnace first appeared in 1941 and was reprinted in 1976. It has since been widely used, not only in survey courses, but in labor history and immigration history courses as well. The novel traces three generations of a Slovak family in the steel-mill towns surrounding Pittsburgh, from immigration in the 1880s to the successful CIO organizing drives of the 1930s. Along the way, members of the extended family marry, have children, start and lose businesses and homes, die of disease and industrial accidents, make new friends, take and lose jobs, and, eventually, organize unions. The novel focuses on the lives and experiences of the men in the family but presents sufficiently developed female characters to provide women's as well as men's perspectives on all these developments, and although it highlights the experiences of one particular European ethnic group, its main characters encounter enough Americans of other ethnic and racial backgrounds to provide useful insights into interethnic and interracial relations. Finally, descriptions of work environments, residential neighborhoods, local politics, and the innumerable interactions that make up community life make *Out of This Furnace* a good place to start a discussion of class identity.

The first significant discussion of class took place after students had read approximately half the book. Early discussions of the book followed George Kracha from his home in Hungary to the town of Whitehall, where he joins friends from back home, into the various jobs he takes and the home he makes with his wife, who has arrived from home. We addressed causes of migration, the process of chain migration, and the transition from rural peasant life to urban industrial life. With the entry of the second-generation men in the family into the steel mills, with their coming of age and the family's settling in the crowded, impoverished immigrant neighborhoods around the mills, discussion moved from the family itself to the milieu in which the men, women, and children in the Dobrecjak family lived. At this point I introduced the notion of class into the discussion and asked students to identify the class backgrounds of the different characters they had met so far.

Because the majority of the characters are the women and men encountered in daily life in the mills and surrounding communities, the class identities discussed were primarily those of working people and their families. Students sought to determine class identity by such factors as occupation, education, standard of living, and clothing. Issues raised by the class and discussed included the extent to which owning his own business, for instance, made the proprietor "middle-class"; the hierarchies that existed among ethnic groups in the mill and the surrounding communities; the impact of education on class status and identity; and the different identifying markers of class for women and for men. Specifically, we discussed whether the Irish American priest was working-class or middle-class, whether a penniless immigrant who can save enough to buy a butcher shop becomes middle-class when he becomes a business owner and what happens to his class identity when he loses the business, and whether women have their own class identities separate from those of their husbands. Ultimately, the discussion turned to the issue of power and autonomy: how much control do people have over their own lives? how much control do they have over the lives of others? This allowed for a discussion of characters who rarely appear in person but nevertheless shape the lives of the women and men portrayed in the novel: the mill owners, the bankers, the railroad magnates, and the politicians.

This discussion of *Out of This Furnace* clarified relations among the individuals and families in the novel; it also provided a touchstone for later discussions of class. I referred back to the lists of characters by class we had made on the blackboard when we later discussed the Great Depression and the New Deal, World War II, the Cold War and post–World War II affluence, and the Great

Society and the social movements of the 1960s. On each of these topics I directed students to consider how Americans' experiences of these events and developments differed according to gender, ethnicity, race, occupation, region, and, always, class.

By the time we reached the middle of the century, students had begun working on their family history assignment, which asked them to develop a portrait of two members of two different generations within one family, focusing on class background.[3] As a guide, they read the article "Class in America: Myths and Realities," by Gregory Mantsios, which demonstrates with very concrete examples how class distinctions operate in all aspects of life, despite the silence about them in mainstream American culture.[4]

Students proved remarkably candid in describing the lives of family members. Many wrote about grandparents who had lost livelihood and property, especially the family farm, during the Great Depression; fathers and uncles who "straightened out" while serving in the armed forces; mothers and grandmothers left to raise children on their own following a divorce or a husband's death; and their own ambitions as college students. The papers spoke fondly of family members and the difficulties they faced in their lives and quite assertively about their authors' expectations of a better life for themselves. Students from more comfortable backgrounds seemed equally confident that they would do as well as their parents.

Although the students appeared to place themselves outside of the functioning of class distinctions and of the real constraints imposed by class, they nevertheless made thoughtful choices in describing family members. In developing their portraits, students were to use "traits that, in your view, best reflect their class background." Jobs, homes, cars, boats, education, vacations, and leisure were described in detail, and students wrote most vividly about changes in family members' situations, both for better and for worse. Mantsios's article provided useful models for such portraits, but the detailed descriptions (absent from Mantsios's models) suggest an emerging understanding of the ways in which one's job or house or car — especially its age and condition! — reflect one's class status, and how class shapes many different aspects of life.

Students were finishing up their papers when we began discussing the Hormel strike; at this point, students had already discussed, thought about, and written about class in terms of characters in a novel, in terms of groups of Americans, and in terms of their own family members. We had discussed labor conflicts, strikes, and the meaning of collective bargaining. The stage was set for the Hormel strike.

Discussion was facilitated by the fact that *Hard-Pressed in the Heartland* provides an explicitly partisan perspective on the strike: the author states at the outset that he was an active participant in the strike, as chair of the strike support committee, and he refers to his own participation in the strike at various points in his account. Rachleff supplements his vivid prose with a timeline of events, including the information that between 1980 and 1990 "average take-home wages in the U.S. meatpacking industry fell by 44 percent. Meanwhile, Hormel Chief Executive Officer Richard Knowlton's annual salary, plus stock options, rose from $238,000 to $3,000,000."[5]

Because the author's point of view is so clearly stated, I asked students to discuss the strike in terms of the respective points of view of different parties in the conflict. Students were to prepare for a mock press conference with representatives from each of the parties involved: the Hormel Corporation, P-9 (the dissident packinghouse workers' local), the United Food and Commercial Workers' Union, the city of Austin. In small groups, students prepared a position statement for one of the parties; each small group selected a member to represent that position during the "press conference." Small groups were also assigned the task of developing questions to ask during the press conference.

What followed was a lively debate highlighted by a very arrogant Hormel representative, a very militant P-9er, an appropriately intransigent and bureaucratic UFCW representative, and a confused representative of the city of Austin. Within this role play, participants were able to articulate very clearly the positions of the different interests involved and, beyond that, to speak effectively from the perspective of a particular party in the conflict. The discussion ultimately moved beyond the specifics of the Hormel strike to the loss of well-paying industrial jobs, the weakness of working people vis-à-vis employers, the inadequacy of large unions in representing grassroots interests, and the control of large employers over small communities.

The discussion of the Hormel strike during the "press conference" made no direct references to steelworkers in western Pennsylvania, nor to students' own family members. Nevertheless, earlier discussion of the novel *Out of This Furnace* and students' own explorations of their families' class backgrounds laid the groundwork not only for figuring out a complex strike situation, but also for placing the strike in a broader context of class and power relations. In addition, the process of moving from discussion of class in the context of a novel set in an earlier historical period, to looking for class identity among family members, to connecting local experience to more abstract issues of class relations and national politics was one that fostered a gradual, almost developmental, understanding of class.

This incremental approach to discussing class is required, I believe, because of the taboo that surrounds the concept of class in the United States. Such discussions, in and of themselves, challenge the cherished notion that the United States is a classless society. Moreover, even though students were not required to talk about their own class status and identification in class, engaged students would make connections between their experiences and backgrounds and issues discussed in class. Broaching the topic of class in a university where more than half of the students are first-generation college students, I would speculate, strikes particularly close to home for many students who are already lacking confidence about their abilities and place at the university.

In *Out of This Furnace,* students encountered women and men living in circumstances sufficiently different from their own that they could discuss questions of money, power, and class without being personally implicated in the discussion. There was little risk to students in talking about the Irish priest and the Irish foreman, the saloon keeper, boarding house life, the doctor's family's summer-long vacations at the seashore, and the extraordinary power exerted by the steel-mill owners. Whatever their class and ethnic backgrounds, none of the students spoke of coming from families like those they came to know in the novel, and, indeed, I did not expect this of them.

Later in the quarter they did have the opportunity to examine their own families, and they did so in some of the same terms in which they discussed the Dobrejcaks and their neighbors in *Out of This Furnace.* They described working conditions, housing, and recreation. Few of the papers explicitly identified the families or their individual members by class, yet their descriptions bespoke a consciousness of class as a factor shaping the experiences of their family members. For many students, what they wrote about their families extended the story of *Out of This Furnace* to their own lives. Talking about the lives of fictional characters in a setting far removed from that of their own families allowed students to begin perceiving their own lives as part of the same story, as molded by some of the same opportunities and constraints.

Although it would have been gratifying to see students explicitly identify their families as middle-class or working-class, making such a leap would have been a great challenge for students surrounded by willful silence concerning class identity. This silence seems to have been reinforced by the individuals students interviewed. Several papers suggest that students encountered resistance to class identification when posing direct questions about it. One student noted at the opening of her paper that her research led her to realize that her paternal grandparents were not just "pretty comfortable," as she had always known, but were "very well off." When she asked her mother "what social class she considered herself to be in," the mother answered that "she thought of her family as being comfortable to well off." She was, however, able to challenge her mother's evasiveness and conclude that her mother's family was "upper class," especially in comparison to herself and her brothers, who are "definitely middle-class": "We have never been deprived of anything," she wrote, "but we have to work for what we get." (Unfortunately, she did not explain this change in status and condition from one generation to the next.)

The family history assignment was both an end in itself and a means to an end. It was designed to encourage students to reflect on their own background and place their family's experiences in the broader context of class relations and the history of the United States in the twentieth century. It was also designed to help students understand class as a personal, individual experience, as well as a collective experience with political implications. I am convinced that without the personal connection to notions of class fostered through discussions of *Out of This Furnace* and through the family history paper, students would have felt far less engagement with the issues surrounding the Hormel strike and therefore less capacity to grasp the broader implications of the strike, for the American working class and for themselves.

Making this kind of personal connection is essential for discussing class because of the many ways in which class is obscured in American culture and education. Most students graduating from high school in the 1990s would have encountered some teaching about women and people of color; all would be familiar with notions of sexism and racism. The same would not necessarily be true about materials pertaining to working-class people and classism. These terms might themselves be new to students socialized into the dominant culture's silence about class. Bringing up class is thus problematic in two ways: first, it opens up an area in which students have limited conceptual knowledge (though they might have considerable but unnamed experience with classism), and second, it challenges the norm of silence around class issues.

Because of this obscured nature of class in American culture, it must be addressed head-on if it is going to be addressed at all effectively. My course focused on class confirmed this for me and further persuaded me of the effectiveness of a process of teaching about class that begins outside of students' own experiences and identity. At the same time, in moving from a consideration of class in a foreign context to their own class background and identity, students developed an awareness of class — even a certain degree of "class consciousness" — that prepared them to understand more clearly class and class conflict beyond their own experience.

CRITICAL LITERACY AND THE ORGANIZING MODEL OF UNIONISM:
READING AND WRITING HISTORY AT A STEELWORKERS' UNION HALL

KELLY BELANGER, LINDA STROM, AND JOHN RUSSO

Historians have always understood that the past, the present, and the future are interconnected in ways that are not always predictable or well understood. Perhaps nowhere are these interconnections more evident than in Youngstown, Ohio, where attempts to prevent the closing of steel mills in the late seventies and early eighties led to landmark legislation regarding plant closing, eminent domain, and pension reform that could not have been anticipated. The reverberations of the massive mill closings can still be felt today, especially for unionized steelworkers who carry memories of the past upheaval into their present jobs. Remembering the swiftness with which most of the community's livelihood disappeared — seemingly overnight — the steelworkers of the 1990s have little faith that their present jobs will be there in the future. In part to prepare for and adapt to an uncertain tomorrow, members of the United Steelworkers of America negotiated in 1989 to put a career development program in their national contract. For the union and for the companies, such a program also holds the potential to develop workers' abilities to decipher, understand, and participate in the world where they live and work, ideally resulting in more skilled workers and more involved union members.

As a result of the national contract, in September of 1994 the Steelworkers' Local 1375 approached Youngstown State University about offering a program that would consist of on-site courses leading to an associate's degree in business or labor studies. University administrators responded positively to the idea, viewing it as a strategy to combat dwindling enrollment and as a means to serve adult learners in the surrounding working-class communities. The first courses offered included a labor history course and a writing course that would meet the university's general education requirements. The three of us were the first YSU faculty to teach at the site: Russo had taught labor studies courses at another off-campus site in the past; Strom became involved because of her interest in working-class studies; and Belanger brought to the program expertise in teaching writing to nontraditional and "at-risk" students. Because Russo's labor history students were simultaneously enrolled in Strom and Belanger's writing courses, this teaching experience gave us an exciting opportunity to collaborate across disciplines and create links between the courses. For all the classes, course content and teaching methodologies reflected and were in part informed by what is called the "organizing model" of unionism. This model emphasizes the importance of developing union members' problem-solving skills, commitment to ongoing education, effective communication strategies, and ability to work within an environment where authority is decentralized. After briefly outlining the structure and content of the writing and labor studies courses, we will discuss the extent to which the union hall courses contributed to creating a culture of organizing and education within Local 1375, while also encouraging students to set and realize individual goals for their own education.

All the parties involved in this program, including the university administration and the union leaders, shared a commitment to adapting the content and structure of the courses to students' needs and interests. Perhaps the most significant structural adaptation was necessary because steelworkers work on a system of twenty-one turns in which workers rotate weekly between day, afternoon, and night shifts. To accommodate their work schedules, we offered the same course twice each day at the union hall so that students could attend either a morning or an afternoon class depending on their shift that week. In an interview, Alan, a learning steward for the union who helps recruit steelworkers for the classes, explained that the "availability of the classes at the hall makes it easier. It's closer for me, it's a little more comfortable because you're with people your own age, not sitting where young students are. It felt more comfortable here."[1] Denise, a single mother and full-time steelworker, agreed and emphasized the importance of the classes being taught on shifts: "The fact that we could take [the classes] twice a day and we didn't miss [them] because we were on certain shifts [was important]. Having them here rather than traveling to the university made it much easier in fact. I don't know if I could've done it as well as I did had we not had them here." These adaptations, which all the students described as beneficial to them, represent one of the first steps in the university and the union's ongoing collaboration aimed at making the college courses accessible to working people.

Just as the course schedules were designed around students' work lives, the curricula for all the union hall courses were consciously "working-class student-centered"; that is, in every decision from text selection to assignment design, we put working-class history and experience at the center of the curriculum. In designing the writing courses, Strom and Belanger focused on the goals of building students' confidence in their ability to express their thoughts and feelings in writing, while challenging them to build upon their past literacy practices to develop a "critical literacy" that would enhance their ability to participate in the social and political processes of a democratic society. As Catherine Walsh puts it, critical literacy "should relate to the contexts of learners' lives, be interesting, purposeful, engaging, incite dialogue and struggle around meanings, interpretations, and identities and promote among learners a critical understanding of their relationship to a broader society, and of their and its political nature, and transformative possibilities."[2] Through focusing on variations of the general theme of work, the writing courses sought to segue with the labor studies courses: in both, students were encouraged to prepare working-class histories of their communities, thereby becoming active constructors of knowledge rather than passive recipients of experts' versions of history.

Although all three of the writing courses that have been offered to date have focused on developing critical literacies, a writing course in the fall of 1995 when their union was on strike gave students a real context for becoming active agents in a highly charged situation that not only affected them personally but also impacted on the community at large. The course's reading and writing assignments were developed around the "Little Steel Strike" of 1937, a strike against Republic Steel plants in Chicago, Youngstown, and Warren, Ohio (where our students' union hall is located). Since many of our students' fathers and other family members worked at Republic Steel as both rank and file and managers, they brought a collective memory of this violent conflict to the class. For our students and for the Warren community, the strike of 1995 became a kind of palimpsest of the 1937 strike, with rhetoric, key players, and artifacts of the earlier conflict resurfacing to imbue the current situation with the spirit of the past.

In the weeks preceding the 1995 strike, our students read accounts accompanied by original photographs of the 1937 strike in the *The Warren Steelworker*, the union's newsletter. In an issue featuring articles on the '37 strike, newsletter editor and union president Dennis Brubaker's editorial entreated the current union membership to prepare themselves for a possible lockout or strike if the upcoming negotiations broke down.[3] Just two months before the 1995 strike (and three months before our class began), the Ohio Historical

Society played host to a colloquium that brought together members of the Steelworkers' Organizing Committee (SWOC, the precursor of the United Steelworkers of America), a local journalist who had covered the action, and community members indirectly affected by the strike. The colloquium served to publicly create an oral history of the "climactic and often violent 'Little Steel' Strike of 1937."[4] Many of the organizers — including the strike captain and Communist leader Gus Hall (now eighty-five years old) — returned to the Youngstown-Warren area and, through their reminiscences, reawakened in community members and in many of Local 1375 steelworkers the legacy of activism that had galvanized the strikers in 1937. The public oral history they created was framed by an account of the strike presented by a labor history student and a labor historian. This event, by interweaving "expert" academic opinion with "history from below," reinscribed the pedagogical approach students experienced in the writing and labor studies classes, where students conducted original research based on interviews, analyses of original documents in the archives of the labor museum, and experts' conflicting representations of history.[5]

Just as the 1995 strike went into full swing, the fall quarter writing courses centered around the strike of 1937 began. Students sandwiched their course work between shifts on the picket line, and our classes were moved from room to room to make space for meetings, food distribution, and child care. The first assignment asked students to write on what they knew and felt about the current or past strikes. One purpose of the assignment was to gain insights into how the few students in the class who were not steelworkers felt about labor issues and what they knew about unionism. A second purpose was to encourage students to write about their prejudices, biases, assumptions, and emotional reactions. Students began to see writing as a means of self-expression, and through this assignment we were able to lay the groundwork for future exercises calling for students to engage in rhetorical analysis and critical thinking.

To give students tools for this type of analysis, the instructors had the class work through a series of applications from Vincent Ryan Ruggiero's text *Beyond Feelings: A Guide to Critical Thinking*.[6] The applications asked students to use their own experiences to examine the concepts of objectivity and subjectivity through exploring the questions of what constitutes truth, knowledge, and a "sound" opinion. As one student explained in his midterm self-evaluation, the applications led him to see that responses to issues are filtered through individuals' experiences and biases: "There are many factors that control the outcome of your response. Issues that may seem clear cut to you may be less black and white to others. Initial reaction to a topic may keep you from seeing both sides. You might only favor views that support yours, and discredit all others."

After practicing applying strategies for critical thinking to situations in their personal lives, students' next assignment moved them from examining personal experience to analyzing the public, published discourse surrounding the 1937 strike. First, the students read conflicting versions of the strike by David Brody, labor historian and author of a chapter in *Forging a Union of Steel;* Gus Hall, the strike captain and author of *Working Class U.S.A.: The Power and the Movement;* and Tom Girdler, the company president of Republic Steel and author of *Bootstraps.*[7] For each reading assignment, we asked students to use the critical thinking strategies developed in the first assignments to analyze and evaluate the truth value of the varying accounts. In journal entries recording their first readings of each text, students tended to summarize material and had difficulty doing the kind of careful analysis that would move them beyond their personal viewpoints, often shaped by the degree to which they felt allegiance to the union. Class discussions pushed students' thinking: they began to question Hall's self-representation as the hero of the strike as well as Girdler's assertion that his climb through the ranks of the steel industry made him an "insider" who could understand the concerns of working people better than "outside agitators" such as Hall. Students began to see how the Brody article could be read as intervening in this debate by putting Girdler's and Hall's accounts of the strike in a larger framework, one in which neither of the two men was even mentioned by name.

Along with giving students a framework in which to reread Hall and Girdler, the Brody piece challenged students to decipher its academic language and immerse themselves in a discourse community that students unfamiliar with the history of steelworkers' organizing efforts had difficulty entering into. In the morning "shift" of the class, which was often attended by traditional YSU students and workers in other industries, the students struggled to get even the literal meaning of the text. Whereas key terms and players in the historical events were unfamiliar to the morning students, steelworkers in the afternoon shift of the class took over the teaching of that text, explaining ideas such as the difference between an open and a closed shop and the significance of the Wagner Act. Through this experience, the steelworkers, teachers, and other class members collectively constructed a foundation of knowledge for rereading all three texts in order to prepare for the first major writing assignment.

The first multidraft essay assignment placed students in a fictitious rhetorical situation calling upon them to analyze the three sources we read as a class and then evaluate the texts' arguments for a specific audience. In one option, students wrote to a friend interested in researching the "SWOC years"; for the second option, students prepared the text of a talk for a colloquium on the SWOC years much like the one held at the Museum of Labor and Industry. Both options required that students draw upon the readings in *Beyond Feelings* as well as their own experiences in considering the kinds of evidence and arguments used by the authors. In addition, students reflected on how their own biases led them to "read" this moment in history in a particular way. This assignment, which asked students to generate criteria with which to evaluate their sources, apply the criteria, and then adapt and organize their analysis for an audience, proved challenging for the students.

In our experience, a multifaceted assignment like this one often meets with some confusion and resistance in first-year students, both on campus and at the union hall site. We find students often struggle when asked to "read against the grain" as David Bartholomae and Anthony Petrosky describe it: to question a writer's arguments, examples, or vision and to engage in a dialogue with the text.[8] In an interview, one student, Anna, laughingly reflects back upon her early naive readings of the opposing accounts of the '37 strike by Hall and Girdler: One text "was management and one was the workers. . . . First [we read] Gus Hall and we hated management, and after reading the CEO, my opinion changed completely and I hated Gus Hall." Another possible explanation for the difficulties students such as Anna experienced early in the course is that inexperienced college writers have not been exposed to the wide range of written discourse patterns required of academic writers. The complex reading and writing assignments in this course gave students experience with a variety of the discourse options available to writers, which, as Mike Rose notes, are "essential to the making and conveying of meaning in our culture."[9] Meanwhile, the applications in *Beyond Feelings* provided a kind of balance: they validated students' abilities as sophisticated thinkers by helping them discover ways in which they were already using these same interpretive and evaluative strategies to discover meanings in their everyday life.

In midterm analyses of their work, many students commented on what they had learned from the "SWOC" assignment. Dan, for example, wrote that "researching different sources was good to do because I usually try to rush my process and sometimes do not find the time to read different sources. The way this class is structured forced me to take the time to read different sources and see the biases that occur in writing." Although some students were never quite able successfully to organize and present their analyses, many students—as Dan's comment suggests—attained through this assignment a richer understanding of how critical analysis can make them more self-reflective and accepting of different points of view.

Perhaps the best example of this new awareness occurred when one of the students—a nonsteelworker in a management training position—wrote an essay that critiqued the union's actions during the 1937 strike. On the day Cheryl presented her draft to the class, she was nervous about her point of view not being well received or respected. The discussion that followed was lively but not hostile, focusing on the effectiveness of her argument; many of the students concluded that they found her ideas persuasive and challenging but disagreed with her conclusion. Significantly for Cheryl, this experience reinforced the idea that even potentially hostile audiences can be receptive to an opposing argument if the writer makes her case by fairly presenting opposing points of view and openly acknowledging her own biases. The draft she presented to the class gave a balanced view of her topic, conceding, on the one hand, that "the 1930s was a time in history [memorable because of] the contributions of the CIO, SWOC and the dedicated men and women who fought to shape the future environment for the working class people" while still asserting that "it is also important to take into account that the companies also had a valid position for their stand against the unions." In the end, though many of her classmates disagreed with her thesis, they appreciated that this balanced approach effectively supported her main claim that union organizers of the 1930s used objectionable means to achieve their goals.

In her mid-term self-evaluation, "Writing behind the Scenes," Cheryl wrote:

> Writing is more than having a pen and pencil in hand. It involves critical thinking, interpretation of the ideas of others, and being able to formulate a theory leaving some of our personal biases behind.
>
> Critical thinking is the topic that has hit me the hardest. Everyone is quick to say that they are a critical thinker. The [steel company] employees feel the union is a necessary stronghold and are quick to defend it, right or wrong. Yet, I found myself in my initial draft taking the other stand and jumping down the union's throat. A day or two later when I read it again, the bias of my writing was alarming. I too had fallen victim of my environment and beliefs.

This student's process of making an informed argument, presenting it to a knowledgeable audience, and then reevaluating her position in light of her own biases demonstrates well many of the strategies that empower students with the knowledge and critical tools necessary to be effective members of their union, their workplace, and their community.

Because the writing classes — like the organizing model of unionism — emphasize active rather than passive learning, nonauthoritarian leadership, and the importance of students' constructing their own knowledge rather than relying solely on experts, these courses complement the more direct focus on the organizing model that underpinned the labor studies courses. In his classes, Russo emphasizes that this model of unionism is grounded in a belief that the labor movement is in crisis and that only by adopting new methods that create a culture of organizing and education within unions will the labor movement survive. He explains that the organizing model differs from the traditional servicing models in that it is not limited to traditional approaches to union activities and education. Rather, the organizing model is proactive and structurally decentralized, and it stimulates and involves members/students in problem solving, group activities, and collective action. The model is based on a commitment to education, open communications, and information-sharing and participation within unions; therefore, without ongoing development of union members' skills and abilities, the model cannot succeed. As they learn about the organizing model, union leaders and students taking Russo's union hall class (some of whom may not be union members) are expected to imagine how they might answer the following questions: (1) How am I creating a culture of organizing and education within my local? (2) What elements in any situation can I use to mobilize membership support in order to achieve membership goals and gains? (3) Am I asking for membership participation or cooperation? (4) Do my words and/or actions mobilize or demobilize members? and (5) How have I gotten people to care and believe in their organization?

At the beginning of the course Russo uses a lecture-discussion model to introduce students to the philosophies behind the various models of unionism, but later shifts his pedagogy so as to get students to conduct their own research, thus putting into practice the organizing model's stress on active, participatory learning. Russo's commitment to students' and union members' participation in processes of constructing knowledge rather than passively receiving it is best reflected in his standard response when asked by union members to do research for their unions: "No! But I will teach you to do your own research." The notion of learning by doing is central to his classroom practices whether he is teaching labor law, union leadership skills, or labor history.

The story of how two labor history students' projects became interconnected best illustrates the benefits of this approach. The idea for the first student's project emerged when Rex found at his grandfather's house a book of 1920s photographs of Truscon Steel Corporation, the forerunner of Republic Steel. The photographs' visual power opened up for Rex a moment in which the past and the present coalesced, producing a sense of timelessness. He saw in the photographs evidence of both continuity and change: some machines looked the same as ones currently in use, whereas others had been replaced. When Rex brought the book to class, Russo encouraged him to consider the photographs as a critical primary source, one that might potentially help to fill in gaps in the written historical accounts of the steel industry. It was not, though, until some of the other students began examining the photos that some of their most significant contents came to light. Denise, through her project, had sought to discover the earliest presence of women in the mills; until she looked at the photographs, she had had no sources of information revealing their employment in steel mills during the 1920s. Interviews with nursing home residents had provided some information, but in looking at the photographs, she noticed women dressed in crisp uniforms and working in the tin mill, a finding that gave her the same personal sense of continuity with the past that Rex had experienced.

This sense of a real connection with the past often became the starting point for students' writing projects, all of which relied upon research techniques described in Jeremy Brecher's book, *History from Below,* rather than on more traditional library sources. These techniques include, for example, transcribing oral histories obtained through interviewing and analyzing videos or photographs documenting the building of local unions. This community-based research was particularly appropriate for the union hall classes because it allowed students — many of whom had had unsuccessful experiences with reading and writing in high school — to engage in academic projects that legitimated ideas and experiences from a familiar working-class culture. Such legitimization of students' working-class lives is valuable because it introduces them to new ways of reading, writing, and seeing the world without erasing their working-class identities.[10]

Almost unanimously, students' responses to the curricula in interviews and course evaluations indicate that through the classes they experienced significant individual growth. One student used a visual image to describe the experience of taking classes after being out of school for many years: "I was like an old rusty gate, just couldn't open up, but now that the gate is opened, the knowledge has flowed through. . . . It was closed for 25 years." For most students, the opening of the "gate" led to an attitude of confidence that they could imagine transferring to other endeavors: "Even if you never use the things you learn in these classes professionally, it gives you a mindset. You get a sense of accomplishment that makes you strive for more. . . . It does make you see the possibilities that weren't there before." Along with mentioning this shift in attitude, students also reported more confidence in their abilities to express themselves and use language to achieve practical goals such as writing strong cases for grievances within the union, composing letters to the editor, and writing articles for hobby and sports magazines. As this student quote suggests, there was also a sense that through taking these courses they had gained increased respect in the workplace: "I think they [coworkers and management] seem to respect you a little more if you're trying to expand your knowledge, wanting to learn instead of staying on a plateau and saying you're satisfied with yourself." For some students, however, that respect came at a price. One woman described "a little bit of antagonism" toward her from male coworkers who were not taking classes. She had to listen to comments such as "Oh, you're takin' college — what're you gonna be, the next Union President?"

The individual personal and academic development that all students experienced was complemented for some by a growth in commitment to union activity. Such growth was, for Russo and union president Denny Brubaker, a goal of the education program in general. For them, education provides steelworkers the opportunity to gain the critical tools and knowledge necessary to understand their role better and participate in the building and rebuilding of their own union. They see the education programs as key to getting union people to care about each other and believe in their organization. Their most hopeful vision for the program is illustrated in the words of the "rusty gate" steelworker: When asked how the classes affected the way he perceives or does his job, he responded, "I think we've tried to put our efforts into finding more ways of making our union strong." In response to another question about how the courses affected his perception of the union, he answered, "We studied unions and how they were formed, way in the 1800s and early 1900s, right up to the present—and we've seen how unions have been strong and have carried on. And I think our unions will always be there. There's no question about it. We have to continue." Through his enthusiastic participation in the classes, this student became part of a community already existing among many union members, but to which he had related only tangentially. Though his transformation was by no means typical of most students, it does suggest that classroom practices emphasizing cooperative learning and mutual support can carry over to other aspects of students' lives, in this case providing a steelworker with a new impetus to work in solidarity with other union members committed to a common cause.

Other students, though benefiting from the classes, saw less connection between their classroom experiences and possibilities for increased union activity. Their reactions to the organizing model, with its emphasis on union members' active participation, were negative or mixed. In one case, a student who belongs to a United Auto Workers local but took courses with the steelworkers, saw the organizing model as basically a ploy to get all the union members to do the work their representatives are getting paid to do. She interpreted the organizing model—or the "new theory"—as suggesting that "the union reps are too overworked." This interpretation led her to laughingly but emphatically offer the interviewer a series of questions and statements: "What am I paying my dues for? Get up there and DEAL WITH IT! If I don't have to pay dues, I'll do my own work." Her objections to the organizing model demonstrate her ability to think critically and offer legitimate reasons for her point of view.

Whereas this student's experience—although positive in terms of her growth as a critical thinker and writer—obviously did not draw her closer to her union, other students had more mixed reactions to the new models of unionism. One student described how the classes made him feel more a part of the union, but at the same time he admitted to "selfish motivations" to learn for his own self-improvement and career growth, which he saw as separate from growth as a union member. For another student, the classes did not significantly impact his ambivalence toward both the company and union: "I've always seen myself as an individual, and the union serves a purpose and the company serves a purpose. The union keeps the company at bay — back and forth — and I just try to eke out a living in between." The fact that this ambivalent attitude is expressed by one of the most academically successful students points to the limitations of an educational program that aims in part to stimulate union activism. Unlike students who had less knowledge of why and how unions were formed and the impact they have had on the steelmaking industry, this student brought to the courses an informed opinion about unions and an awareness of their history. This student's lack of enthusiasm for the benefits of unionism may reflect the general dissatisfaction or disinterest that many U.S. workers today have regarding unions.

In the end, what we see as most important about this union hall program is not how it affects students' thinking about unions, but the extent to which the classes contribute to creating among the workers a culture that values the kind of empowering education that critical literacy represents. Included in this culture is a heightened sense of how the events of history — which are constructed differently by the many voices that write it — echo and resound into the present and the future. Through the union hall classes, many students began to see themselves not just as passive inheritors of history, but as active agents who can reinterpret the events of the past and help shape the course of the future. In the words of a student who collaborated on a book the class wrote and dedicated to the Steel Museum in Youngstown, "we really have something to contribute to future generations."

TELLING TOIL:
ISSUES IN TEACHING LABOR LITERATURE
LAURA HAPKE

In a recent homage to Mike Gold, one of the best proletarian writers of the 1930s, Morris Dickstein remarks that the "poor may always be with us, but we seem to notice them [and their literary explicators] only at thirty-year intervals."[1] Commenting on the transience of labor writing, Nicholas Coles points out that "the tradition [of working-class literature] had to be regularly reinvented under the pressure of new historical circumstances and out of whatever formal materials [were] available."[2] Whether eternally unfashionable or ever new, labor fiction and the lived work history it both reflects and revises must prove themselves again and again.

As Pete Hamill reminds us, manual labor is not valued in this country. In view of the current antilabor climate, the traditional exclusion of labor studies subjects from literature curricula makes it all the more urgent to interest our students in texts about work. Given the way labor fiction is grounded in the social history of American proletarianism, such texts, moreover, need to be interdisciplinary in nature, selected as much from nonfiction narrative and a host of other reprinted sources as from fiction. This essay details the methods I have used with students nervously focused on competitive individualism and a pinched job world to interest them in the importance of a shared U.S. labor heritage and the literature that dramatizes it, clarifies the obstacles to and strategies involved in that enterprise, and argues for an interdisciplinary focus that joins class to the new multiculturalism.

THE SURROUND

Opportunities to give working-class studies courses are dependent on everything from successfully competing with "accessible" offerings to convincing administrators that business-oriented students will register. After fifteen years of teaching at an urban university with a business orientation but also with a sizable liberal arts college, I have gathered some anecdotal examples. A few years ago, at a university orientation for prospective students attended by faculty representing their disciplines, a colleague from another department inquired with a condescending tone, "Are you still writing about Ellis Island?" He knew of my interest in fiction's ostracized sexual workers and my broader concern with labor literature, and he also knew that I had published books and articles on what I loosely call the sweatshop canon. But he invoked, with a code phrase, my publications that use a labor-historical as well as a feminist framework to scrutinize immigrants and radicals. Last semester one of my students also used a highly charged word in describing his working-class father, although (unlike my colleague?) he thought he was being complimentary. After detailing the long workday his father spent on the construction site, he remarked that around the house at night his dad was "as normal as the business people who live next door." And this semester another student, less conversant with the blue-collar work world and disgusted with the hard-drinking tenement dwellers who people Stephen Crane's turn-of-the-century texts, quickly labeled them "white trash," with no protest from his classmates.

Anecdotes such as these suggest that working-class studies courses face resistance from both institutions, which doubt their appropriateness, and students, who question their utility. One of the chief institutional obstacles to developing such courses issues, ironically, from the myth of U.S. egalitarianism. Any university that draws a sizable number of students from Asian, Latino, and Russian Jewish homes, for instance, is like so many of the colleges that combine sophisticated vocational training with a liberal arts curriculum: the aim is to provide the opportunity to rise — my own teaching institution's logo is "Opportunitas." Acknowledging the myriad ways elites have structured and limited the upward mobility of the children of immigrants would add complexity to the mobility mission but would not enhance a school's marketability. The very issues central to labor studies, therefore, seem to fit uneasily with the self-scrutiny colleges must undertake to meet accreditation requirements.

In actuality, labor-related syllabi enable colleges to offer ways for students unfamiliar with American postsecondary education to negotiate its contradictions. Courses that uncover discriminatory attitudes toward disadvantaged economic groups can clarify students' own grievances and enable them to articulate reasoned criticisms of American culture. To develop such skills is neither to invalidate bourgeois ambitions nor idealize them. Nevertheless, it is crucial to cut through the premature cynicism implied by young people's fascination with acquisitiveness. In the current materialistic climate it is useful to review student assumptions about everything from the janitorial staff at the college to what "dignity of labor" and the "American working class" have meant historically — and mean now. Without propagandizing, such consciousness raising can enrich assignments using family history, crucial strikes, and the state (and plight) of unorganized labor. Moreover, to persuade other faculty to accept the idea of working-class studies, prolabor instructors should demonstrate that a "Masters of Literature" course can be replaced (or paralleled) by a "Masters of Working-Class Literature" course; that texts in "people's history" can supplement more elite readings; and that students' family histories, in which they survey the manual labor of their grandparents and parents, create new texts of the labor experience as well.

STRATEGIES FOR THE CLASSROOM ENVIRONMENT

A few winters back, in the bitter cold, during the first week of classes at my university, which is opposite New York's City Hall, the janitors of New York's private buildings went on strike. Locals 32B and 32J of the Service Employees International Union (SEIU) were represented by a small group of freezing workers. The workers in the picket line, holding placards and standing outside of the two university buildings, were well outnumbered by police officers.

In my literature/composition courses that semester, I scrapped the short story diagnostic and asked students to write essays responding to various topics related to the picket line they (and I) had just crossed. (As a salve to my conscience, I later apologized to the strikers and sent a check to their strike fund. I remain conflicted: one part of me is dedicated to my teaching job, the other disapproving of any "scab," myself included.)

The strike was a medium-bitter one and, characteristic of labor protest these days, was settled without significant gains. The students, many of whom are first-generation college students from working-class homes, were pursuing business degrees, and half of them opposed the strike actions. But when one student, whose uncle walked the line elsewhere in town, told the inside story of strike negotiations — and mentioned the four-hundred-thousand-dollar salary of Gus Bevona, president of SEIU Locals 32B and 32J — the class perked up and we had some good discussions.

The labor event suggested a good assignment to open with, but so do texts like Leonard Gardner's lower-rung-boxing novel *Fat City* (1969); Agnes Smedley's proletarian tale, *Daughter of Earth* (1929); Sandra Cisneros's reminiscent Latin novel *The House on Mango Street* (1984); Faye Ng's ode to San Francisco Chinatown familial strife, *Bone* (1993); and the oral-history nonfiction text *Working* (1972) by Studs Terkel. So, for that matter, do the two poetry collections *Working Classics: Poems of Industrial Life* (1990) and *For a Living: The Poetry of Work* (1995), both edited by Nicholas Coles and Peter Oresick. Other useful texts are discussed in essays by Janet Zandy (in her anthology *Calling Home: Working-Class Women's Writing* [1990] and Paul Lauter (who has a good essay on proletarian fiction in the recent *Columbia History of the American Novel* [1990]). But it is when students, whether with blue-collar backgrounds or not, relate such texts to their own family and work histories that they take hold more consistently of the learning process. I would like to describe how I employed *Working Classics* to that end.

As many instructors are all too aware, the traditional college course in literature or composition attempts to inspire reasoned opinions, competently developed in essay form, on social and literary-critical topics. But all too often students' end-of-term papers are at best a soulless composite of instructors' rules and at worst a muddle of ideas further weakened by errors of grammar, style, and organization. Efforts to inspire a sense of confidence and tap undergraduates' native eloquence and originality by assignments based on their life experiences have succeeded to a degree. Yet students have difficulty applying their newly won facility in expression to issues outside the realm of first-person narrative. My approach, developed this year through assignment of labor-class texts and student essays on them, relies on more challenging explorations into students' histories with an emphasis on interpreting the workplace lives of themselves and their families to establish meaningful connections between life and art. This new model synthesizes formal assignments and personal essays, encourages interdisciplinary study as well as expository prose of some originality, and infuses students with the voice of literate authority that only skill combined with knowledge can provide. Furthermore, such an approach has clear applications to courses in history, sociology, and social psychology, among others.

Early in the semester, I ask students to read a series of poems on the laboring life in the Oresick and Coles anthology (the authors' biographies are in the back of the book).[3] In the very fine "Steel Poem, 1912," Patricia Dobler enters the psyche of a steel man who curses the lard on his bread and dreams of succulent dinners. David Ignatow's "The Boss" contains the nice lines

it was his shop
and his machinery
and his steel cabinet
where the photos lay.

Lorna Dee Cervantes' "Cannery Town in August," a compassionate portrait of
Portuguese food-factory workingwomen, and Jim Daniels's "Factory Jungle"
are equally effective. Writes Daniels, for instance,

The parts are backing up
but I don't care
I rip open my overalls and pound my chest
trying to raise my voice above the roar of the machines
yelling louder than Tarzan ever had to.

Although the diction and structure, the sound and the sense, are superficially
simpler than those in poetry by John Donne or John Keats, some classes on the
interpretation of the poems are clearly in order. These lessons completed, students share reactions to the poems, including the occasional profanity (it is not
Shakespeare), the raw anger, and the fugue-like insistence on worker alienation
and the potential or actual dignity of labor.

At midsemester, or, if the instructor prefers, toward its end, students must
provide finished essays that make some link between the lives of workers in the
assigned text and the workers (or, if more applicable, professionals) they know
as family. In the weeks that follow, students share reactions to the assignment,
confer with me, and report on their problems and, I hope, revelations, as they
interview grandparents, parents, siblings, and coworkers, taping and transcribing the interviews (with the permission of the interviewee) and even using
background sources if the interview uncovers labor-historical events. In interviewing her mother, for instance, one student discovered that her grandmother,
though long gone, had participated in the Shirtwaist Strike of 1911 — and left
the sash she wore when she picketed the shops. I rushed to assign Malkiel's
Diary of a Shirtwaist Striker.

The assignment is no easy matter. Students who find it difficult to construct a
thesis wrestle with comparison form, feel defeated by the number of transitions
the essay requires, and sometimes simply misread the poems. But they rarely
misread their families or coworkers, and I'd like to share with you some examples of the written work students with varied writing strengths can produce.

One of the finest essays I ever received in twenty-five years of teaching was
from a transplanted coal miner's daughter, Rebecca. She chose a powerful Ed
Ochester poem from *Working Classics,* "Retired Miners," and wrote movingly

of her fifty-four-year-old father, the on-the-job victim of a heart attack, a shattered eye socket, a knee injury requiring surgery, and the worker compensation chicanery of a West Virginia coal company. Sounding like a poet herself, she wrote sadly and musically, "The company took his pride, his manhood, his dignity, and left him. . . . filled with shame because of all his hard work done in vain." She quoted her father elsewhere in the essay as well as Ochester, whose poem asks, "If any guy tells you he got rich through hard work ask him whose?"

Electricians, one male and one female, were the subjects of two essays by students who had less power over prose style but were alert to the underside of capitalism. Jennifer's essay on her family friend Pamela, like Rebecca's, implicitly pointed to the failure of OSHA and the perils of an underprotected workplace: "Pamela," she wrote, "is placed in life-threatening situations day after day. Throughout her eight years as an electrician she has broken two fingers, broken her right arm twice and has been knocked down ladders by high voltage cables." Contrasting Pamela with the worker in Gwen Hauser's poem "The Day after I Quit" (in which the health and safety inspector "couldn't believe that women's jobs were dangerous"), she analyzed the pressures on workers and drew a number of reasoned conclusions.

Richard wrote about his father, who was a prosperous electrician and kept his injuries to himself, so to speak, and Todd Jailer's poem "Time and a Half." Though the essay had many stylistic problems, the sentences had an eloquence born of life learning: "Men have to make many compromises to survive," Richard wrote in his own voice and his father's. And the laboring experiences that radicalized Rebecca and Jennifer made Richard more conservative. A finance major and the first of his family to graduate from a four-year college, he was the most conservative of my students and the most ardent in his defense of the upward mobility ethic. But his father's life of hard knocks had a home in his psyche too.

I have received comparison essays on a variety of occupations (the *Working Classics* anthology is a rich resource in that regard): on white-collar anomie; on housework as unpaid labor; and a few, a very few, on the satisfaction of working with one's hands. With the middle class billed as the newly hard pressed (and at risk for downsizing) working class, some papers have recognized that the salaries their parents were making did not measure up to the time-and-a-half lives they led. One student regaled the class with a hilarious anecdote about the Uriah Heapishness of her coworkers and their joy when they found she was quitting her Wall Street job to go to college — leaving more pickings for them.

Some students clearly found the work I asked for meaningful. Commented one, "Now I know which class I'm really in. Before I thought that how you dress is what makes you." "The worker endures pain so long as the loved one receives what he or she needs, I have discovered by doing this paper," remarked another. Other students were either angered by what they perceived as the difficulty of the essay or certain that manual labor was irrelevant to their lives. But they all did the work, and, as suggested by questionnaires on the assignment, all of them, I think, were in some way affected by the life-art connections they uncovered.

In his fine biography of the Amalgamated Clothing Workers tribune Sidney Hillman, Steven Fraser speaks of the "peculiar presentism of American culture."[4] At the very least, students who stayed with the assigned tasks entered a labor-historical past rich with meaning and its own passion: their own.

NAVIGATING THE INSTITUTION

For instructors who have neither the opportunity to teach working-class studies nor the prospect of doing so, I suggest two options. One is to take a laborist approach to classics of Western literature. Thus the "rude mechanicals" of Shakespeare's *A Midsummer Night's Dream* can be analyzed as disenfranchised workers rather than only the comic fools they appear to be. In the American literary canon, any novel by Henry James is obviously ripe for the revisionist's scrutiny. In *The Princess Casamassima,* why is the shopgirl Millicent Henning "vulgar"? In *The Ambassadors,* when a morally dubious woman of affluence is described as crying like a serving maid, the instructor might ask students what class bias is revealed.

A second option for instructors who have the leverage to do so is to add working-class literature to "standard" American literature courses. The old myths of Americanist literary critics, particularly the American Adam and the open road, were certainly disrupted by Robert Schenkkan's 1992 Pulitzer Prize–winning play *The Kentucky Cycle.* It provides a dramatic counternarrative to the injuries of class, racism, misogyny, and greed in the two hundred years of America's Indian policy. When his radical text is contrasted with one by literary folklorist Washington Irving or Puritan divine Cotton Mather, the trio of readings is invigorated and the subject of economic class inserted into the curriculum.

A final suggestion: interdisciplinary courses with instructors in literature joining those in the social sciences are a fine way to demonstrate the academic relevance of a labor studies approach to literature.

OTHER RESOURCES

Although the texts suggested thus far seem plentiful, it is almost a creative act to gather enough of them for a series of courses on working-class literature.

Whatever advances have been made in "recovering and reinserting the literary traditions of women and minority cultures have only tangentially extended to working-class literature, a tradition that, nevertheless, overlaps with those others and shares with them common preoccupations and themes."[5] Indeed, in the brilliant surge of revisionism that produced multicultural and feminist criticism and a host of literary rediscoveries in anthology and reprint form, texts by or about the worker (especially, as might be expected, about the white male) have received short shrift. Some blue-collar classics have been particularly neglected in the outrage over what, to use the title of a recent study, might be called the (male) texts' belief in "regeneration through violence," that "myth of the hunter as archetypal American."[6] Violence may indeed permeate such works as William Kennedy's 1979 homage to Depression riding-the-rails fiction, *Ironweed,* and, for that matter, a woman writer's text, *Them* (1969), Joyce Carol Oates's saga of the self-destructive Wendall clan of other-side-of-the-tracks post–World War II Detroit. But if these respective Pulitzer Prize and American Book Award winners and other texts are not reevaluated and reintroduced into a course on labor in American literature, they may languish in the now-unfashionable "masculine wilderness of [classic] American literature" that Carolyn Heilbrun found so suspect over twenty-five years ago.[7]

In terms of reprinted or new fiction that embraces a more feminist agenda, Agnes Smedley's *Daughter of Earth* (1929), a classic bildungsroman of the mining-camp girl turned international radical journalist; Tillie Olsen's *Yonnondio* (written 1934–37, published 1971); and their spiritual heir, the National Book Award nominee Dorothy Allison's *Bastard out of Carolina* (1992) can provide balance to the male proletarian novel. But I suggest applying another Coles insight, that "any reasonably complete course in working-class literature would . . . need to reach beyond . . . [what] we habitually treat as literary to include memoirs [and] work-place narratives."[8] In this regard, an excellent supplementary text is the collection of retrospective oral histories in Victoria Byerly's 1986 *Hard Times Cotton Mill Girls: Personal Histories of Womanhood and Poverty in the South.*[9] It is published by the ILR Press of the Cornell University/New York State School of Industrial and Labor Relations, a burgeoning source for labor novel reprints, including Theresa Serber Malkiel's *Diary of a Shirtwaist Striker* (1910), mentioned earlier, and Ruth McKenney's novel about the 1936 Akron Rubber Strike, *Industrial Valley* (1939). See also the catalog of International Publishers, which has reissued classic stories from the Communist Party organ *The New Masses,* if that journal can be said to have had classic stories.

Because *Hard Times* provides interviews with black and white southern textile mill hands and domestics who recall the 1930s through the 1950s, it contextualizes feminine labor sufferings in both a mill town and a familial setting, suggesting at once what Communist Party maverick Mary Inman in the 1940s termed the double burden of women under capitalism. Not that these women would have welcomed Inman's severe analysis: with names like Annie Viola Fries, Katie Geneva Cannon, and Ailene Walser, their collective resignation is best expressed by Walser, married at fourteen and a mill worker throughout the 1930s. Her summing up is softly regretful: "I was fifteen when I had my first baby and thirty-two when I had my eighth. I raised seven of them. No, I didn't know how not to have babies. If I had known, I don't think I would have had eight. No, I never heard tell of birth control pills. Lordy mercy, honey, them things come out since I quit having kids. I wish I had them back then, Maybe I wouldn't have been so tired."[10] The black worker Katie Cannon provides a further perspective by establishing Walser's work life, taxed as it was with child-rearing, as preferable to her own: "Black women were not allowed to work in the mill, then . . . [so they] clean[ed] people's houses."[11]

It might be argued, as Catherine Gallagher does in another labor literature context, that the simplicity of expression (language transcribed and strengthened stylistically by Byerly herself) in many of the anthologized workers' voices "is meaningful precisely because it ignores the issue of meaning."[12] That is, the simplicity is neither deceptive nor deliberate, but an expression of the unself-consciousness — and in some instances, lack of self-awareness — of the speakers. Those who theorize about working-class literature may find it important to settle that point, but for classroom purposes the very mirrorlike quality of the prose, far more connected to the students' lives and leisure talk than that of any proletarian author, is of great value in establishing a bond between undergraduate reader, whatever his or her economic class, and working-class source.

For more sophisticated work analyses from laboring sources, any instructor would do well to place on reserve a 1974 reprint of a collection of women's essays edited by Andria Taylor Hourwich and Gladys L. Palmer, *I Am a Woman Worker,*[13] which was first published in 1936 by the Affiliated Schools for Workers, an agency that coordinated the short-lived trade unionist worker colleges during the Depression. Because the authors of these essays were developing an oppositional awareness largely lacking in the reminiscing textile women of *Hard Times,* pieces such as the following raise tantalizing questions about the wage earner not only as impassioned eyewitness historian but as literary mythmaker. This briefest of the essays, "The President Visits the Mill," is a vignette of management policies in one of the most populous women-fueled trades:

One day at work, word was received that the President of our tobacco company was coming to visit the plant the next day. The boss sent me around to tell all the workers to get busy and start cleaning their machines. We had a half day to get everything ready for the President.

The next day, when the President came through he had several other men with him, some wearing diamond stick pins and rings which cost thousands of dollars. The President did not look at the cigarettes; he merely looked over the floor. When one of these very important looking men stopped at one of the cigarette machines that was making fourteen hundred cigarettes a minute, he found just one bad cigarette before the girl that was catching could get to it. (It is nothing unusual for a cigarette machine to run a bad cigarette in a short time.) This man showed the bad cigarette to the President. The President called the foreman and had the girl fired.

This girl had a mother and a little sister to take care of on $11 a week. The men went on their way to another floor, while the girl trudged home with the news that she had no job.[14]

Again, compared to an effort by Steinbeck, who himself adopted a deceptively Old Testament style, this selection is characterized by parataxis, understatement, and economy of language — Gallagher's descriptors of British working-class autobiography as well.[15] From another perspective, though, it is graced with the rude eloquence with which so many male proletarian writers, then and now, have tried to infuse their narratives. Without making grand claims for "high art," in any event an ambiguous term in a postmodern era, the instructor or even the critic can direct readers to see the very clarity of the language as a metaphor for working-class consciousness in search of itself. On a related matter, a text like *Woman Worker* can also provide closure to a course that keeps the economic and psychic costs, as well as the dignity and significance, of the labor-class work life as its central themes. But documentary collections of workers' essays from a time when union activity was rightly perceived as a good can only remind our students of how modern workers' spiritual dissatisfactions are in some way by-products of the demise of organized labor itself.

THE NEW CURRICULUM: CLASS, GENDER, RACE, ETHNICITY

To make the multicultural curriculum as inclusive as possible, it is essential to foreground class. The following suggested texts are useful in that direction. For example, as much workers as women, the anonymous authors of collections like *Woman Worker* fuel the ongoing debate over a truly feminist work allegiance. This is not the case in such new feminist classics as *Bastard out of Carolina* or the British Pat Barker's scathing slice of North England industrial life, *Union Street* (1982), both excellent and available in paperback, although such texts are not customarily thought of as studies of class relations.

Greg Sarris's beautifully realized novel-in-stories *Grand Avenue* (1994) is rightly linked to the newest Native American literary renaissance. It draws on old myths and new ethnic resentments. Yet Sarris's characters are undeniably members of a widening U.S. underclass plagued by alcohol, unemployment, an eroding kinship network, and poverty. His understanding of the plight of single mothers scraping a living from cannery work, rescuing their children from Juvenile Hall, and trying not to buy into cultural stereotypes of the Indian, is penetrating.

Narrative of the Life of Frederick Douglass, an American Slave (1845) is another particularly effective text when viewed from a work perspective. In my undergraduate course on the worker in American literature, I contextualize Douglass's forced-work narrative within this cultural debate on what soon became the black proletarian experience. (W. E. B. Du Bois charted the disenfranchisement of this black proletariat in his classic book, *Black Reconstruction*.) Though not customarily taught as a (pro)labor text, *Narrative* is a field-as-factory and skilled-mechanic tale of extraordinary richness. And it is an excellent introduction to other radical literature. Like many social protest texts that followed it, African American or not, *Narrative* strives to define a worker protagonist as he moves from economic oppression to self-definition. Douglass also grapples prophetically with what the dignity of labor means to a black man who, migrating to the "free" North, cannot secure a job worthy of his skills. Teaching the Douglass text from such a labor-literature perspective, I find it a precursor not only of African American proletarianism in novels such as Langston Hughes's *Not without Laughter* (1930) and William Attaway's *Blood on the Forge* (1941) but also of the white social protest writer's quest for self in texts such as Jack Conroy's *The Disinherited* (1933) and John Steinbeck's *The Grapes of Wrath* (1939). Douglass heralds all of these labor classics in his authorial struggle to balance Franklinesque individualism and worker solidarity, self-madeism and rising with one's class, a spirited defense of oppressed laboring people and wary hope for the fruits of the American Dream.

In a series of exercises linked to the above interpretations, I involve students in, for example, contrasting antebellum portrayals of manual labor with Douglass's meticulous descriptions of Colonel Lloyd's harsh "employment." In other essays students apply Douglass's famous remark, "Learn trades or starve!" to the modern African American (un)employment experience. I ask students to find *Narrative* passages prophetic of African American labor landmarks (including the Reconstruction South's work stoppages, the rise of the Brotherhood of Sleeping Car Porters, and the Harlem Food Boycott of 1934). And I assign papers comparing the iconography of enslavement in Douglass's *Narrative* to that in other important "slave" texts, such as Martin R. Delany's *Blake* (1859) and Harriet Wilson's indentured servant novel *Our Nig* (1859).

FURTHER RESOURCES: A BRIEF NOTE

There are myriad uses that instructors of literature can make of labor studies texts, particularly the valuable two-volume "new social history" *Who Built America?* which includes encapsulated narrative selections. Materials from *Building Hoover Dam: An Oral History of the Great Depression* (1993), Jacob A. Riis's *How the Other Half Lives* (1890), and the *IWW Songbook* all provide voices of or visual testimony to a people's history. Integrating a variety of sources like these into a labor-focused course widens the definition of working-class narrative and enables students to hear labor voices not represented in literary art.

CONCLUSION

Through texts not usually studied in literature classes, students can explore a body of protest fiction that gave ethnic, racial, and gender minorities a voice; questioned cherished American myths; and posed questions about personal and economic equality still not answered by American society. Of concern will be the value — and cost — of literature with a leftist or antiestablishment agenda. Does it demonstrate or fail to produce democratic eloquence? Instructors can alert their classes to the great labor conflicts of our time — in the 1930s period, for instance, the Gastonia Textile Strike, the Flint Auto Factory Sitdown Strike, and, most important, the battle for collective bargaining. Teachers of both history and literature can inspire discussions of the American Dream from a labor point of view. In our time, plagued again by joblessness and homelessness, our students, particularly those from working-class backgrounds, can use their responses not only to the success ethic but also to these labor texts to make connections between their family histories and the larger political histories of working-class people.

FILMS OF AND FOR A WORKING-CLASS WORLD

TOM ZANIELLO

Not long ago, at the end of a course for trade unionists on images of labor in film (in which we viewed and discussed mainly American and British films), I handed around reproductions of a number of Sebastiao Salgado's photographs of Third World labor. I asked the students whether anyone had seen any film that portrayed the kind of labor Salgado has photographed in such locales as the Serra Pelada, Brazil, gold mines. At first no one responded. Finally, one student suggested a film, specifically in regard to Salgado's justly famous photographs of those open-pit gold mines where thousands of workers, some semi-naked, others with poncholike garb, virtually all covered in mud, climb ladders in and out of what could only be described as a human ant hole at the edge of hell. The film suggested was *The Navigator: A Medieval Odyssey,* a fascinating 1988 New Zealand film about a band of time-travelers whose community accepts their cockamamy mission to burrow through the earth and top a church with a cross made of their own copper as a desperate means of escaping the approaching black plague. Their home base is full of mud and muck and molehills masquerading as hovels, all of them perched above some open-pit copper mines. In shots of the villagers rushing about the community and of our band of adventurers burrowing through the earth, one can indeed see in the filmmakers' mise-en-scène a remarkable similarity to some of Salgado's photographs.

Although *The Navigator* would never be considered a mainstream labor film by any stretch of most definitions, the student's suggestion was a revealing comment on the incredibly primitive conditions captured in Salgado's photographs *and* the often self-imposed limits we place on our discussions of labor films. We do not expect images of labor in our time-travel fantasies. And we certainly do not see enough of the Third World on First World screens.

In fact, unless we make a concerted effort to bring foreign films into our community halls and classrooms, our discussions of the impact of NAFTA on Mexican and American workers or the controversy about the manufacture of Gap jeans by Central Americans or the use of prison and child labor in Asian countries will take place in the vacuum of American politics where classlessness and the invisibility of labor are already too commonplace.

After I became sufficiently concerned about our tendencies, not only as teachers and students but also as members of various communities, to focus primarily on American and British films when we wished to see how Hollywood has represented such important issues as class and labor, I realized that still another screening of *Norma Rae* or *Matewan* would be insufficient to impart understanding of global trends in labor.

For university courses or community programs or labor education events, I proposed various films concentrating on Anglo-American images of labor by using these categories:

films about unions or labor organizations;
films about labor history;
films about working-class life where an economic factor is important;
films about political movements, if they are tied closely to organized labor;
films that focus on production or the struggle between labor and capital from a
    "top-down" — either entrepreneurial or managerial — perspective.

Many teachers and students have wrestled with the problem of access to the comprehensive range of images of working-class life and labor history in American culture available in videocassette form; the situation becomes even more acute if one wishes to internationalize the curriculum and expand film programming to include the working class of the world. Difficulties of distribution and ignorance of resources have prevented audiences from seeing — and understanding — the global variety of working-class lives and struggles.

When I began to explore the possibilities of offering courses with titles like "The World of Work in Film" or "Global Images of Work," it was reasonably common to include images of Soviet workers from the 1920s and 1930s and Italian working-class life in the 1940s and 1950s, since many of those films are classics of film history. But such use of Soviet silent films and Italian neorealistic films only began to address the problem of global access to images of class and labor in film.

All of the emphasis on Soviet and Italian filmmaking did have, however, one major advantage: film historians and critics had already isolated a number of classics of working-class life in those two national cinemas and had argued for their central importance in building a film aesthetic internationally and for other subjects in film. Why these two moments in cinematic history occurred when and where they did was still a matter of debate. A neglected but revealing book by George A. Huaco, *The Sociology of Film Art*, argued that the explosion of filmmaking in the Soviet era and in postwar Italy was the product of four social and economic factors: (1) "a cadre of trained film technicians, directors, editors, cameramen"; (2) "the industrial film plant, studios, laboratories, equipment"; (3) "a mode or organization of the film industry favorable or tolerant toward the ideology of the future film wave"; and (4) "a climate of political norms favorable or tolerant toward the ideology of the future film wave."[1]

Although Huaco's study could not possibly foresee the remarkable development of specifically national cinemas such as the enormous Hindu film industry or the curious merger of magic realism and economic analysis in contemporary West African films, and though it does not do justice to the intertextuality of world cinema (the effect of Soviet filmmaking or British social realism of the 1930s or the French New Wave on numerous other national cinemas), his schema will work for a number of the national "film waves" or national tendencies outlined below. And though it is outside the scope of this introduction to analyze all of these national cinemas along Huaco's lines, we might just briefly outline how his scheme would work with a significant number of the films released in the last fifteen years by the formerly French colonies of West Africa. There the French left behind the bare bones of an "industrial film plant" and some "trained film technicians" (although Senegal's prominent filmmaker Sembene Ousmane had been an apprentice to the Soviet filmmaker Mark Donskoi). Furthermore, the film industry in a number of West African countries was receptive to critiques of both the French colonial era and the lingering social, political, and economic repression typified by rising black bourgeois reactionaries. A number of the filmmakers in these countries fit comfortably in the American distributors' rubric categorizing their work as examples of "Africa's Second Independence," in part because their overall ideological tendency favored fiction films that merged traditional cultures and current economic problems.

Huaco's study as well as a broader sample of the films of the world will help us to understand why we have been too narrow in our presuppositions of what a *foreign* labor film is. We have tended to see a foreign film as an event of cinematic or cultural history and occasionally of political history but rarely as economic or working-class or labor history. I would like to broaden our definitions at this point and consider not only films from national traditions we have become accustomed to, but also those marked by emerging cinematic tendencies that we are only beginning to comprehend.

Soviet films and Italian neorealist films make up two well-known groups of films about labor; nonetheless, it is necessary to expand the list of available and worthy titles of even these national cinematic movements. Most experienced viewers know Vittorio De Sica's 1947 classic, *The Bicycle Thief,* whose anti-hero is a worker who loses the only means he has to hold on to his new job as a poster-hanger; less well-known is De Sica's 1956 *The Roof,* featuring a bricklayer who calls upon his fellow workers to help him and his wife build a one-room house in a single day (thereby satisfying a municipal regulation about legal squatting). Similarly, Luchino Visconti's late reprise of the neorealist tradition in *Rocco and His Brothers* in 1960 remains a standard of Italian working-class drama, but Visconti's virtually purely neorealist *La Terra Trema* (The earth shakes), released in 1947, used nonprofessionals, the fishermen of a Sicilian village, to portray themselves in an interpretation of a classic novel (*Under the Medlar Tree*) by Italian social realist Giovanni Verga.

Soviet classics such as Sergei Eisenstein's *Strike,* Vsevolod Pudovkin's *Mother,* and Alexander Dovzhenko's *Earth* have always been in the foreground of analysis of Soviet filmmaking and labor topics. *Strike* and *Mother* both feature pre-Bolshevik strikes and urban workers, whereas *Earth* points to the triumph of farm collectivization despite personal tragedies. But Pudovkin's 1927 silent, *The End of St. Petersburg,* which traces how a peasant boy is caught in the politics of an urban strike, and Dziga Vertov's 1931 *Enthusiasm* (also known as *Symphony of the Don Basin*), which celebrated the early completion of a five-year plan by the miners of the Don River coal basin, were both experimental films, somewhat less realistic and more symbolic interpretations of Soviet labor history.

Even with this cursory examination of two very well-known cinematic traditions, we find other titles worth exploring. How much more necessary is it, then, to approach other national cinemas and traditions? My third category, films about working-class life where an economic factor is important, was perhaps the most flexible of the lot and became the obvious point of entry for films from cultures not typically represented in our labor film surveys. Many national cinemas — especially non-European ones — do not have such a variety of genres and subgenres as we have grown accustomed to. No equivalent to our labor/Mafia films (*Hoffa*) or labor/terrorist films (*The Molly Maguires*) comes to mind; films with workers whose individual struggles mirror macroeconomic issues are more typical.

I have isolated five groups of films that are now available in videocassette but which, in my opinion, have not been sufficiently well-known to receive the attention they deserve as films about labor or issues of class:

1. African films, especially West African films, resist simple classification as labor films, but they often dramatize important economic questions under the rubric "Africa's Second Independence" publicized by an enthusiastic American distributor, California Newsreel. African nations' first independence was from European colonial control; its second is from neocolonial (and even totalitarian) control of an indigenous elite. The four films with special labor significance that I use are all from California Newsreel's impressive collection, The Library of African Cinema. Almost all of these films engage economic questions both large and small, whether it be a satiric vision of a street musician trying to win a lottery called "Devaluation" in Senegal's *Le Franc* or the supply of fish for the market women in Guinea-Bissau's *Udju Azul di Yonta* (The blue eyes of Yonta). The latter stresses the interrelationship of street markets and commercial fish sales; the former satirizes neocolonial monetary control. Mali's *Ta Dona* (Fire) involves agricultural or manual labor but also traces the effect of national policies on timber-cutting and health care as they often conflict with local traditions and mores. Tanzania's *These Hands* is an unrelenting documentary of Mozambican women refugees working in a stone quarry near Dar es Salaam. What seems to be only a record of numbing work is situated nonetheless in the context of their work: to provide, cheaply, the gravel for new buildings in the nearby city.

2. Any film about slavery is patently about an economic system, but most Hollywood films dramatize stories of individual freedom won or lost, psychosexual power relationships, and interracial love triangles. The films I use demonstrate slavery as a colonial and economic system instead and link Africa, the European powers, and the New World: the French *Tamango* (directed by the blacklisted American John Berry) loosely adapts an early-nineteenth-century story by Prosper Mérimée focusing almost exclusively on the Middle Passage, whereas the Brazilian films *Xica* and *Quilombo* dramatize both individual and collective struggles against slavery. Former slave Xica becomes mistress of a white government official and virtual queen of a diamond mining district; Quilombo is an "independent" runaway slave community fighting for its life. *Burn!* from the director of *The Battle of Algiers*, Gilo Pontecorvo, carefully dramatizes not only the transformation of slaves into wage earners but intramural competition among the colonizers as well. From Cuba, *The Last Supper* is a Bunuelian satire on a slaveholder who decides to stage a living tableau of the Last Supper using himself as Christ and twelve of his slaves as apostles.

3. Mexican cinema remains virtually unknown in "el Norte" despite the art house popularity of *Like Water for Chocolate*, but two native directors of

Mexican cinema, Emilio Fernandez and Roberto Gavaldon, and a "visiting" Spanish director, Luis Bunuel, have emphasized images of peasant and other working-class lives, as well as the urban *lumpenproletariat*. Three of the classics from the Fernandez-Gavaldon tradition come closest to the former's nickname — "el Indio" — in their portrayal of peasant lives: a woodcutter in *Macario*, a pearl fisherman in *The Pearl,* and a small-scale landowner in *The White Rose.* All three were photographed by Gabriel Figueroa, the cinematographer who pioneered a distinctly Mexican look: low-angle shots of peasants shot beneath cloud-filled skies with his trademark "curvilinear perspective." Spanish director Luis Bunuel spent two decades of his long career making more than twenty films in Mexico. His anarchistic visions often had a metaeconomic cast to their satire, such as his 1950 classic of street urchins (*Los Olvidados*), his 1953 comedy about tram workers (*Illusion Travels by Streetcar*), and his 1956 feature about a rebellious mining community (*Death of a Garden*).

4. European films from the political left, especially those about the Third World or those focusing on colonialism, have a revolutionary politics that has sometimes obscured their labor content. *Burn!* for example, involves the transition of sugar cane labor from slavery to wage status on a fictional Caribbean island, whereas *Ramparts of Clay,* with a critique of new national elites (like those of so many of the African films mentioned above) dramatizes the new controls over Tunisian quarry workers by the national government after liberation from France.

5. Other national cinemas have developed "new" or "parallel" film traditions that not only in some instances challenge the established conventions of their own national cinemas, but also confront neglected images of labor or economic questions of great importance to developing nations. The small number of noteworthy Asian films now available include the Indian (Hindi) *Spices* (1986), about a woman who takes refuge from a sadistic officer in a pepper factory, and two Chinese "Fifth Generation" films, *Red Sorghum* (1987), focusing in part on the struggles of the female owner and her workers at a winery as one indicator of historical change, and *Yellow Earth* (1986), in which a Red Army soldier visits a remote farming community to gather folk songs. The Filipino films of Kidlat Tahimuk are hard to classify: in *The Perfumed Nightmare* (1977), Tahimuk plays a version of himself as a naïf (like Michael Moore in *Roger and Me*) who tries to understand the immense appeal and contradictions of the Western economic system; in a similar way, his *Turumba* (1984) is a realistic but comic fable of the dangers of First World economic exploitation (and Third World self-delusion), as the artisans of a tiny village struggle to produce twenty-five thousand souvenir papier-mâché dachshunds for the 1972 Olympics in Germany.

Despite the proliferation of foreign titles of interest to us on videocassette, nobody should underestimate the difficulties of using foreign films in the classroom or as resources for organizations, because the resistance to subtitled films remains strong in the average viewer. Although foreign films represented less than 1 percent of the box office in American movie theaters in 1995, 10 percent or 5 of the top fifty rental titles in video stores during that same year were foreign films.[2] Two of the five were obviously very sexy films (*La Belle Epoque* and *The Lover*), but the other three were reasonably significant and challenging films (*Europa Europa*, *Red*, and *White*). From these figures we can assume that it is possible for foreign films with important subjects such as labor and class to make their way onto the home screen or into the classroom.

I handle potential resistance to such videos by organizing programs and lectures that develop both American and foreign images of the same or similar industries or issues. In the end it is more difficult but perhaps more useful to show *Harlan County USA* (American, 1977), *The Stars Look Down* (British, 1939), and *Germinal* (French, 1994), three films about miners; or *The Life and Times of Rosie the Riveter* (American, 1980) and *These Hands* (Tanzania, 1992), two documentary films about women workers. And though it might be ideal to show these films full-length, I find it no compromise of artistic integrity to show excerpts from a number of films, since what I am in part doing is attempting to direct students and others to films that they may rent or purchase on their own.

On other occasions I have mixed American and foreign films under the heading of "border crossings" or films about migration and immigration, in part to demonstrate the politicized implications of any discussion of working-class migration. I believe that a number of revealing films have demonstrated how fragile and political the concept of "national borders" is, especially when one considers films that deal with the Middle Passage of African slaves to the new world (*Tamango*, for example) or films that showed how colonial powers established national borders as an economic category (*Burn! Quilombo*, and *Walker*, for example). In a similar way other films have satirized the issue of border crossings in both comic (*Bread and Chocolate*) and tragic films (*The Emperor Jones*). It is inevitable in this context to use some American films, such as Tony Richardson's *The Border* (about illegal Mexican immigration) or *Nightsongs* (about legal Asian immigration to New York City) or even John Sayles's *Brother from Another Planet* (about the flight of an escaped slave from outer space).

Whatever the strategy of presentation or the choice of national cinemas, films of and for a working-class world are a natural but perhaps overdue component for teaching working class.[3]

APPENDIX 1:
FILM TITLES CLASSIFIED BY COUNTRY, REGION, OR TYPE

Those marked with a + are available in many large video rental chains; those unmarked would be available from such national vendors as Facets (1-800-331-6197) and Home Film Festival (1-800-258-3456) who both rent and sell, and Movies Unlimited (1-800-4-MOVIES), and Video Yesteryear (1-800-243-0987) who only sell. Public and university libraries sometimes have the African titles, which are also available for sale from California Newsreel (1-415-621-6196).

African Films:

Le Franc (in the videocassette *Three Tales from Senegal*)
Ta Dona (Fire)
These Hands
Udju Azul di Yonta (The blue eyes of Yonta)

Asian Films:

The Perfumed Nightmare
Red Sorghum +
Spices
Turumba
Yellow Earth

Films about Border-Crossings and Immigration:

The Border +
Bread and Chocolate
The Brother from Another Planet +
The Emperor Jones +
Nightsongs
These Hands

Latin American Films (other than Mexican):

The Last Supper
Quilombo
Xica

Mexican Films:

Death in the Garden
Illusion Travels by Streetcar
Los Olvidados +
Macario +
The Pearl
The White Rose

Italian Neorealist Films:

The Bicycle Thief +
La Terra Trema
Rocco and His Brothers +
The Roof

Films about Slavery:

Burn! +
The Last Supper
Quilombo
Tamango

Soviet Films:

Earth
The End of St. Petersburg
Enthusiasm
Mother

APPENDIX 2:
SELECTED AND ANNOTATED LIST OF PUBLISHED SOURCES ON FOREIGN FILMS WITH AN EMPHASIS ON WORK AND CLASS

African Films:

Givanni, June. "African Conversations." *Sight and Sound,* Sept. 1995, 30–31. An interview with Djibril Diop Mambety reviewing his career.

Library of African Cinema: 1993–94 and *Library of African Cinema: 1995–96.* San Francisco: California Newsreel, 1993, 1995. These guidebooks prepared by the distributor are very helpful for tracing themes in the series; the first has a brief "political and economic overview" of "Africa's Second Independence," i.e., the struggles against reactionary national elites, by Julius O. Ihonvbere.

Martin, Michael T., ed. *Cinemas of the Black Diaspora*. Detroit: Wayne State University, 1995. An extensive collection of informative essays about African cinema.

Asian Films:

Chow, Rey. *Primitive Passions: Visuality, Sexuality, Ethnography, and Contemporary Chinese Cinema*. New York: Columbia University Press, 1995. A jargony but intriguing study, with a long section on *Yellow Earth*, emphasizing (among many other things) how the identity of its tragic female heroine is linked to her music.

Dissanayake, Wimal, ed. *Cinema and Cultural Identity: Reflections on Films from Japan, India, and China*. Lanham, Md.: University Press of America, 1988. Includes a number of essays on Indian cinema, but Mira Reym Binford's "Innovation and Imitation in the Contemporary Indian Cinema" is an especially helpful overview, with a section on *Spices* and other films by Ketan Mehta.

McDougall, Bonnie S. *The Yellow Earth: A Film by Chen Kaige*. Hong Kong: Chinese University Press, 1991. An authoritative account of the genesis of the film and its reception in China and elsewhere, as well as the screenplay.

Films about Border-Crossings and Immigration:

Bogle, Donald. *Toms, Coons, Mulattoes, Mammies, and Bucks: An Interpretive History of Blacks in American Films*. New York: Continuum, 1994. 3d ed. Bogle devotes a section of his book to Paul Robeson, "the Black Colossus," who (Bogle suggests) had his "finest screen role" as The Emperor Jones.

Latin American Films (other than Mexican):

Burton, Julianne. *Cinema and Social Change in Latin America*. Austin: University of Texas Press, 1986. Includes an interview with the director of *Xica* and *Quilombo*.

Pick, Zuzanna M. *The New Latin American Cinema*. Austin: University of Texas Press, 1993. A good survey of Cuban film in general and of Alea's film *The Last Supper* in particular.

Mexican Films:

Berg, Charles Ramirez. *Cinema of Solitude: A Critical Study of Mexican Film, 1967–1983*. Austin: University of Texas Press, 1992. Includes a chapter on other films about the "unassimilated Indians," different because of skin color, geography, language, customs, and social status.

Feder, Elena. "A Reckoning: An Interview with Gabriel Figueroa." *Film Quarterly* (spring 1996): 2–14. An excellent overview of Figueroa, the cinematographer of *The Pearl*.

Traven, B. *The Night Visitor and Other Stories.* New York: Hill and Wang, 1966. Besides the novella that *Macario* adapts, this volume includes the neglected comic classic *The Assembly Line,* a short story of Indian handicraft versus American capitalism.

Turrent, Tomas Perez, and Jose de la Colina. *Objects of Desire: Conversations with Luis Bunuel.* Ed. and trans. Paul Lenti. New York: Marsilio Publishers, 1992. Excellent interviews in general, including Bunuel's amusing remarks about efforts to "reform" *Los Olvidados.*

Italian Neorealist Films:

Bazin, Andre. *What Is Cinema?* Vol. 2. Trans. Hugh Gray. Berkeley: University of California Press, 1971. Quirky but intriguing chapters on *The Bicycle Thief* and *La Terra Trema.*

Hainsworth, Peter. "The Human Reality of the Despised South." *Times Literary Supplement,* 19 July 1996, 10. Brief but revealing overview of Verga's career.

Huaco, George A. *The Sociology of Film Art.* New York: Basic Books, 1965. A neglected but revealing study that correlates the "ideology" of Italian neorealism with the social and political conditions of Italy's postwar film industry.

Hughes, Robert. *Film Book 1.* New York: Grove Press, 1959. Includes an essay by screenwriter Zavattini on the genesis of the ideas behind *The Roof.*

Nowell-Smith, Geoffrey. *Visconti.* Garden City, N.Y.: Doubleday, 1968. The first study of Visconti in English, but still good on *Rocco and His Brothers.*

Sitney, P. Adams. *Vital Crises in Italian Cinema.* Austin: University of Texas Press, 1995. Extensive discussion of *La Terra Trema* and its source novel by Verga; essential companion for the film.

Films about Slavery:

Burton, Julianne. *Cinema and Social Change in Latin America.* Austin: University of Texas Press, 1986. Includes interviews with a number of directors.

Georgakas, Dan, and Lenny Rubenstein, eds. *The Cineaste Interviews on the Art and Politics of the Cinema.* Chicago: Lake View Press, 1983. Two interviews with Pontecorvo, with the director's detailed commentary on *Burn!*

Johnson, Randal, and Robert Stam, eds. *Brazilian Cinema.* Expanded ed. New

York: Columbia University Press, 1995. Extensive discussions of Cinema Novo and the films of Diegues.

Pick, Zuzanna M. *The New Latin American Cinema*. Austin: University of Texas Press, 1993. Excellent section on *Quilombo*.

Price, Richard. *Maroon Societies: Rebel Slave Communities in the Americas*. 2d ed. Baltimore: Johns Hopkins University Press, 1979. Excellent history of four centuries of the pan-American "quilombos."

Soviet Films:

Kataev, Valentin. *Time, Forward!* (1932). Trans. Charles Malamuth. Bloomington: Indiana University Press, 1976. A literary cousin to *Enthusiasm,* as novelist Valentin celebrates the champion concrete-pourers of the Magnitogorsk metallurgical complex in the Ural Mountains.

Two Russian Film Classics. New York: Simon and Schuster, 1973. Zarkhy's screenplay for *Mother;* the second "classic" is Dovzkenko's *Earth.*

Youngblood, Denise J. *Soviet Cinema in the Silent Era, 1918–1935*. Austin: University of Texas Press, 1991. Especially good on the reception of Dovzhenko's *Earth* among the critics and censors.

TEACHING
WORKING-CLASS
LITERATURE TO
MIXED AUDIENCES

RENNY CHRISTOPHER

Jenny comes to my office door, obviously scared to talk to me but also, obviously, with something she really wants to get said. With a combination of shyness and aggressiveness, she says, "I have a comment on something you said in class today."

So I search for what I said that could have been offensive; that is what I expect, that I said something today that offended her in some way, probably religiously. During the years I have taught at this small, rural, regional university, I have been at loggerheads with my students most of the time. In my second semester of teaching here, in a class on multicultural literature, a student suggested that *multiculturalism* meant that one had to tolerate the views of racists (we had been discussing the existence of a local, and active, branch of the KKK). I said that although everyone has First Amendment rights, we certainly did not have to listen respectfully to the views of racists, because they are unconstitutional and morally wrong, and the student burst out angrily, "You're telling people what to think! You're a communist!" The point of calling me a communist, for these politically and socially conservative students, is to discredit anything I might say.

So now I'm searching for what terribly leftist thing I could have said today that Jenny is here to complain about. I invite her into my office, and she perches on the edge of a chair. "You know what you said about not fitting into school? I feel the same way here."

And suddenly I realize that I have mistaken the source of Jenny's nervousness. Today in class we had discussed a novel in which a son goes through higher education and abandons his family, leaving them bereft and bitter. We had talked about how education changes people, and in the course of the discussion I had told a story that has become central to my understanding of my own experience, one that I've told many times, to many different groups of students.

When I was in graduate school, I told my class, I felt that I did not belong, that I wasn't entitled to an education. I felt very out of place among my fellow students, most of whom came from much more privileged backgrounds than I did. Most of them had parents — and some even grandparents — who had B.A.'s or even advanced degrees. I, on the other hand, was the first in my family to get a college education, and being in a Ph.D. program really felt like being in another universe for me.

And, I told my students, I had often felt like dropping out. One of the things that had prevented me from doing it was something my (now ex-)husband told me over and over in my first two years of graduate school: my family had lived in California and paid state taxes for three generations and had never gotten anything back for all those taxes. Those generations of taxes had paid for my education, and therefore, no matter how out of place I felt, I was indeed entitled to that education.

The practicality of that advice cut through the near-hysteria I often felt in the rarefied air of the University of California, Santa Cruz. At the time I was there, UCSC students' median family incomes were the second highest of any university in the state (only the University of Southern California ranked higher). My undergraduate students were always telling me about their summer trips to Europe and giving me rides in their thirty- and forty-thousand-dollar cars. Nobody in my family has been to Europe since the immigrant generation came over in steerage. My affluent students always expressed surprise when they found out I had never been to Europe and invariably said, "You must go!" I always wanted to slap them and say, "Don't tell me what I *must* do!"

But of course the experience of working-class students in higher education is of constantly being told what they must do. They must master the vocabulary of the academy. They must not speak too loudly or take up too much physical space with their bodies. They must not object when the working class is referred to as a lesser category of being, when the term "white trash" is casually tossed out in a group that would never, never say "nigger" or "spic." They must disavow their ancestry in order to "fit in."

At least, that is what it was like for working-class students at an elite, prestigious, and rich university. At California State University, Stanislaus, the situation is very different. Not better, but different. There, 84 percent of undergraduates are the first in their families to go to college. The majority of students enter the university, either from high school or as community college transfers, terribly underprepared for academic work. The social atmosphere remains more working-class than middle-class (in terms of fashion style, quite visibly so). But there is also no real intellectual culture on the campus, and students are not given the best possible education. It is very easy to see the way the class system is enforced, even while individuals are allowed upward mobility. Students graduating from UCSC — both those with middle-class origins and those with working-class origins who manage to make it through — will go into graduate school, into the higher levels of the professions, and not only will carry with them more prestige from having graduated from the University of California system but will also have received a better education in terms of both the knowledge and the skill levels they will take with them. The students from the California State University, on the other hand, will go into the lower ranks of the professions — a very large percentage of our students go into teaching at the elementary and secondary levels — and will carry with them not only less prestige and earning power but also an inferior education in terms of both knowledge and skill levels.

Given the atmosphere at CSUS, I'm very surprised by Jenny's comment. As we talk, she tells me that she felt comfortable at the community college she transferred from, but that she has never felt comfortable at the university. She is afraid to speak in class, because she is afraid people will find what she has to say stupid and irrelevant. She's afraid everybody is smarter than she is. She tells me she gets no support from her friends and family. They routinely ask her why she isn't married yet and when she is going to have children. (I was luckier than Jenny in that way. My family, although they had a tendency to tease me about still being in school into my thirties — I didn't go straight through — did not oppose my education, as have the families of so many working-class students I have talked to.)

Even here, then, at a university whose main business is educating working-class students, a working-class student can feel marginalized, can feel as if she is not entitled to be here. This is why I believe it is vital to include social class in all discussions of multicultural issues and in all discussions of literature (the field in which I teach).

The class Jenny is in is not a class that is meant to be focused on such issues — it's a class called "The Contemporary Novel," defined in the university catalog as "the novel in English since 1970," and I am teaching a number of postcolonial novels from the English-speaking world. The novel we were discussing on the day Jenny came to see me was *The Joys of Motherhood,* by Nigerian novelist Buchi Emecheta. However, I have taught a course on U.S. working-class literature three times now, twice at UCSC and once at CSUS. The course has gone quite differently each time, partially because of the way I have designed it and partially because of the composition of the classes.

The first time I taught the course I was a teaching fellow at UCSC, a position that was awarded on a competitive basis to graduate students who submitted course proposals. Mine, called "White Working-Class Literature in the U.S." was chosen. I had developed an interest in working-class literature only belatedly while I was in graduate school at UCSC, for two reasons. First, class issues were thrust upon me as they had never been before. Although I had also gone to an elite undergraduate institution, Mills College, where I had encountered people from much more privileged backgrounds than mine, I had somehow managed not to really come to terms with what constituted my difference. When I first started at Mills, I lasted three semesters, then dropped out, all the time believing that I had simply been misled by my high school experience, where I was a whiz kid, and that I was, in fact, dumb. When I returned four years later to finish my B.A., I was a "resuming" student, and "resumers" were all the rage at Mills in the early 80s. Although most of the students who fit that category were about ten years older than I, I simply, happily, grouped myself with them, and so never had to think about social class. But when I got to UCSC, and "race, class, and gender" was the constant refrain, I suddenly realized what I had been so stolidly ignoring: that all my feelings of displacement came from having traveled from a class that is not supposed to enter higher education (or if they do, to enter it in a place like CSUS) right into what was for me a great heart of darkness, out of which eventually came the light of understanding but never any warmth or comfort.

Despite the reciting of "race, class, and gender" like a holy refrain, it has been pointed out many times that "class" is the term most often left out of substantive discussions. It certainly was at UCSC in all my graduate classes, except when the few of us who had come to understand our class difference brought it up over and over. (Here I would like to acknowledge my compatriots Carolyn Whitson and Ekua Omosupe). Although I was committed to writing a dissertation about representations of race in Viet Nam War literature, I had become thoroughly absorbed in working-class literature by the time I took my qualifying exams. For those exams graduate students constructed a reading list and developed four topics. My list included a good deal of work by working-class writers, and one of my topics focused on working-class literature. By then I had become known as the person who was interested in working-class literature, and I often felt that my interest was dealt with in a spirit of tolerant amusement. I often felt that faculty members were only pretending to take me seriously. Perhaps this is unjust; perhaps I was paranoid. One of the problems of being a working-class student in higher education (similar to being a woman or a student of color) is not having a basis to judge when you're just being paranoid and when they're really out to get you.

So when my fellowship proposal was accepted, I was very surprised. I thought at the time, and still believe, that it was a way for the board of studies in literature to offer a course defined primarily in terms of social class and therefore make themselves look as if they were on the cutting edge of "race, class, and gender" in literary studies, without devoting any real faculty resources to it.

The response to the course, however, startled everybody, including me. It was limited to thirty students, but on the first day the class was full and had a waiting list, and even more people showed up trying to add. The class could have been twice as large as it was scheduled to be. Where did all the interest come from?

For one thing, every undergraduate of working-class origin came out of the woodwork and tried to get into the course. As a result there was a disproportionate number of nontraditional students. The class was also disproportionately female. But, as it turned out, about half the students were of working-class origin and about half were of middle-class origin. I found that out as the quarter progressed and only by happenstance; I did nothing to have students identify themselves in relation to the literature we were reading, either privately, for their own use, or publicly, for class discussion. That turned out to be my first mistake.

I had never taken a course in working-class literature, nor taught one before, so I was really feeling my way. It was usual at UCSC for the most privileged groups to take up the most time in class discussions and to determine the direction of discussions; I had had many strategy sessions with friends who were teaching assistants in courses where they wanted to change that, particularly with friends who taught in "women of color" classes, where the white women in the class would always manage to make themselves the center of attention. And indeed, the middle-class students in my first working-class literature course made themselves and their concerns the center of attention. In that way the class was something of a disaster, because I spent a great deal of time simply defending the point of view represented in some of the novels we read — that of working people who were portrayed as wanting decent lives but not wanting to move into the middle class. Some of the middle-class students did not see how it was possible not to want to move into the middle class. And I spent a lot of time assuaging the guilt of the middle-class students.

Assuaging guilt is a problem I have encountered in other contexts, as well. When I have taught American studies courses and dealt with the uglier aspects of U.S. history, especially slavery and the genocide of Native Americans, I have found white students' reaction frequently to be guilt. Guilt is not a productive reaction, in my experience, because it allows people to feel that they have done enough — they have felt guilty, so their obligation is fulfilled. They don't need to carry their analysis any farther than that. For that reason I discourage students from feeling guilty over history. I tell them yes, feel bad, feel sad, feel outraged, but don't feel guilty if you're not responsible for what happened (a kind of hubris). Feel responsible for the future, not the past.

In a course on working-class literature, however, this issue of guilt was somewhat more complicated, because the difference in privilege was not historical; it was present, and it was very real. Middle-class students found themselves sitting next to students who came from backgrounds like those described in the novels we were reading, and both groups felt uncomfortable. The middle-class students felt guilty over their privilege, and the working-class students felt exposed.

But because the middle-class students were used to being the interpreters of the world, they *still* felt themselves to be the superior interpreters of the literature they were reading. Therefore, paradoxically, the working-class students still felt themselves marginalized to some degree by the discussions. Many of them came to my office to talk about how frustrated they were by what they characterized as the "ignorant" pronouncements of the middle-class students. This represented a reversal of the usual idea of "ignorance" and "knowledge." Since in most literature classes the literature being studied represents the world that middle-class students lay claim to, they are used to operating in a familiar realm.

I realized I had also made a mistake in my definition of working-class literature for the purposes of this course, because I had included literature by middle-class observers of working-class life, including Upton Sinclair's *The Jungle* and Harriette Arnow's *The Dollmaker,* both excellent works and extremely sympathetic representations of working-class lives but aligned with the viewpoint of the middle-class students, which gave them more leverage.[1]

Nonetheless, the experience of the working-class students in the class, despite their and my frustrations with some of the discussions dominated by the middle-class students, was an overwhelmingly positive one. In private conversations outside of class and in their essays, several of the working-class students said that they felt at home for the first time in their education. One student told me that she had always felt as if she had to talk about her own experiences in other classes, because her experience was so different from the books. In this class, she said, she could just talk about the books, because she understood the world they came from, and thus, paradoxically, could fulfill the expectations for participation governed by the norms of the university.

In the course evaluations, the positive comments focused on the value of discussing class issues. The following are representative of the majority of course evaluations (transcribed verbatim):

> This was an outstanding course, the best I have taken at UCSC. Renny has taken lit. out of the classroom and connected it with the world we live in.

> Everything seemed relevant. It was an unusual class — *talking* about *class issues* — something most people don't even whisper about on UCSC.

> These are issues that are extremely relevant. I learned alot about my class position and how it relates to America.

> When I look back over the last 4 years, I can honestly say that this class was the only one that spoke directly to me, without blurring issues with ancient terminology, antiquated concepts, and the stuffiness which sometimes accompanies "canonical" lit.

One of the most moving experiences I had as a teacher at that time was with Claire, a student whom I had taught in community college and who had transferred to the university. In my English 1A and 1B courses at the community college, Claire had struggled, getting a C average, not really grasping what was expected in college writing, either in terms of controlling standard written English or of understanding what an essay was supposed to consist of. At the university she had a sudden breakthrough (I had had exactly the same experience as an undergraduate writer), and one day in class I handed back a paper on which I had written "excellent." She laughed out loud, looked up at me, and said, "Education works!" At the time I was very pleased by that. Now, though, more cynically, I would say, "socialization works" — Claire had simply mastered another idiom, one granted more prestige in our society but not one that is inherently better. Claire's experience, coupled with the positive evaluation comments, represent what I think was vital about the course for working-class students.

However, in the evaluations, some of the middle-class students expressed their feelings of guilt and marginalization within the class. The most vehement and eloquent of these said, "The strengths of this course lay in the reading material and Renny's ability to get the class included in said books. *HOWEVER!!* one of the biggest problems with this class was the students very often felt a need to verbally whip themselves for having wealthy parents, being white, going to a university and my most un-favorite, being an American citizen. Too often this class turned into a bash fest during which certain elements in the class alienated others by voicing their beliefs w/out accepting dissenting opinions. Stop the middle class, white U.S. citizen bashing!" Despite the disagreements among students and between students and me, I never thought anything that had happened in the course could have been defined as "bashing." I believe this student was expressing his or her own discomfort at being displaced from the center of the discourse. Never in the class did anyone say to anyone else, "It's your fault I've suffered," as this student's comment implies. The student's most revealing phrase is "alienated others by voicing their beliefs w/out accepting dissenting opinions." Notice that she or he does not say without allowing "dissenting opinions" to be voiced, but rather, without "accepting dissenting opinions." What has happened to this middle-class student is that she or he has been moved into the position most often occupied by working-class students — his or her point of view has gone from the center to the margin, and he or she has been unable to get classmates or instructor to "accept" or validate that point of view.

The second time I taught the course, I approached it in such a way as to avoid the kind of conflict and difficulty expressed by that evaluation. I had been hired as a lecturer by UCSC after receiving my Ph.D. and was offered a senior seminar to teach on the topic of my choice. I chose "Working-Class Literature in the U.S.," and once again the course drew more students than it could take. This time, however, I began with a different strategy. First, I constructed the reading list differently, so that it contained only works by working-class writers focusing on class experience. Second, I started the first day of class by asking students to bring me their definitions of "working-class," which I then typed up and distributed to the class.

This exercise made students think about their own relationship to the material of the course and turned out to be the most productive way I could have started the course. Most of the definitions talked about type of work, money, social position. But the students spoke either from an insider or an outsider position, and the majority had a clear awareness of which position they spoke from.[2] Some of the middle-class students gave highly theoretical definitions; but even those whose definitions were more narrative than theoretical spoke in terms of "they":

What is "the working class"?
To what extent shall it be considered "the proletariat?"
— alternatives to Marxist interpretations?
— ie, advertising as the "commodification of desire"
Consider in terms of the dynamics of street life. . . .
The term "working class" has been codified in the US, it appears to connote differently according to which discourse it is invoked by/within. . . .
The extent to which work has become a reality for our existence has necessi-

tated (?) a hierarchical relation between peoples & corresponding sets of life "values": choices, sacrifices, exclusions.

Kevin

When I think of what characterizes the working class, images of struggle, hard work, and a lack of leisure time come to mind. Those in the working class are restricted to crappy jobs that provide them with only enough money to sub-sist — these jobs actually hold them back for because of lack of opportunity, education, etc. it is extremely difficult to rise above mere subsistence.

Morgan

When I think of "working class," I think of people who have nuclear families and 9-5 jobs. I think of people who work in jobs that don't pay low but don't pay excessive amounts of money, either. I think of people who will have to work until they retire and who will never be classified as wealthy — as defined by American culture. I think that the vast majority of advertising is directed at the "working class." . . . I also see a lot of the working class as oppressed and repressed both by the "working class" in which they exist and by other levels of the American class structure. The working class may pose either a struggle or a peaceful existence for people.

Dana

For some middle-class students, the theoretical definitions allowed them to distance themselves and, in the very theoretically inclined discourse community of literature majors at UCSC, acknowledge their difference from the object of study in the course. They were thus entitled to speak. For other middle-class students, such as Dana, the attempt to understand a working-class existence necessitated an imaginative act.

The most surprising response, however, was from middle-class students who willingly relinquished their own discursive authority, as in these examples:

I am uncomfortable defining "working class" for me, perhaps because my family has never had this label attached to it, so it seems like a classification very much removed from my own experience. I realize, though, that my posi-tion is connected to the positions of others within society, since we are operat-ing within a system where there can be no upper and middle classes without a working class and vice versa. What it means to be working class is oftentimes what it means to be marginalized, silenced, and oppressed. . . . These of course are generalizations, and I risk stereotyping what I don't know first hand. Where I grew up, in a wealthy suburb of LA, I do not remember going to school with anyone working class or interacting with anyone of working class, and this in itself should point out how segregated the country is.

Ronni

In a lot of ways, I don't feel qualified to define the working class. I don't come from a working class background, and I don't feel that I know enough about it to be able to contribute anything. I'm hoping to learn about what it is to be working class, and I don't feel that I can do that by categorizing now. So, rather than writing a well thought out and organized piece on what is the working class, I am going to give you some of my thoughts on what it might mean to be working class. It seems to mean working on something and for something that is not your own, giving your time and labor to someone else. . . . I don't know how much further I can go at this point. I already feel that I am making assumptions that I have no place to make. Am I being too sensitive? I don't know. It seems to me that part of what it means to be working class is that others often define who you are.

Monica

It is perhaps not coincidental that all of the students who expressed sentiments like Ronni's and Monica's were female; never fully possessing interpretive authority despite their class privilege, they were more willing to renounce it.

There was a significant difference in the way many of the working-class students shaped their definitions. They wrote from personal experience, speaking of "I" and "we," rather than "they," and many of them problematized their own relationship to the educational institution and the world in their definitions:

Working-class literature, in my mind, represents the working class from within the structure rather than the writer being an outsider looking in. The definition of working-class people is a bit harder for me to define and understand. . . . My father is an Electrician, heavy affiliated with labor unions. He embodies my idea of what working class means. However, he has pampered me, sheltered me, spent his life savings on me, therefore I am, to an extent, completely outside working class ideology, while at the same time, everything I have is a direct result of my father's working class life. I hope this class helps me to get a clearer idea of what working class is and where I fit in.

Stephanie

What is working class to me?

1. Being an adolescent in the 80s and having to wear my older cousins' hand-me-downs from the 70s. The other alternative, having Grandma sew my clothes.

2. Sometimes having to borrow money from Grandma for groceries; she gets aid from the state because she is old or something.

3. Being too embarrassed to bring friends home from school.

4. Not doing anything when you get home from work, because you're too tired to think or move.

5. Being a child and not being able to play or make any noise in the house because Dad will kill me. He sleeps all day and works graveyard.

6. Being a divorced woman with no job, having an asshole of an ex-husband, and having to take care of four kids.

7. Being a kid making different colored "cookies" by melting the caps of used up aerosol cans in Grandma's oven.

8. Being in college and waiting 2 hours in a financial aid line.

Alicia

How to Tell If You're Working Class

I guess you are working class if you use mainly your hands or strength in your job, rather than intellect. You're working class if you wear a uniform to work, you work long, hard, hours, and yet never seem to "make it" or break out of the cycle of near-poverty. You're working class if you don't read a lot of books and watch a lot of Oprah and Hard Copy — you might even seen yourself on Oprah and Hard Copy. But the key characteristic of the American working class, as far as white working class is concerned, is that America doesn't like you. We like to pretend you don't exist. We don't like your boorish behavior. We think that if you can't "make it" somehow it's your fault. The white working class make the white middle class very uncomfortable, somehow. It could possibly be because somewhere back in the annals of their (our?) family history, they (we?) were once like you.

But what if you're now in college? You're not supposed to be here. We will try to make you leave, because you do not belong. We will make you feel uncomfortable because you are not like us. We all know who you are, so don't bother trying to assimilate. Although in four years, you just might become one of us.

Jayme

Working class means being a piece of the machinery that runs the system that excludes you from its privilege. W/c means that as a workforce you are utterly required and as an individual worker you are utterly dispensable and replaceable. W/c means bootstrap rather than entitlement. It means Sears & Montgomery Wards. It means when you buy 501s & workshirts you intend to work in them. It does not mean paying $75 for jeans with a designer tear in the knee. W/c means constantly having to reinvent the myth and reality of "workers rights." It means believing in your country. It means being sent off to die for your country. It means pride & shame of canon fodder. It means resistance. It means going to work each day. It means kicking commie hippie asses. W/c means "getting a job" rather than "planning career moves." As a w/c student it means getting called stupid alot. And sometimes believing it. It means keeping quiet or paying the price. It means not knowing what AP English is. It means taking classes at the JC rather than "claiming an education." It means having teachers be surprised & delighted to "find out" you are intelligent. W/c means knowing you don't belong & feeling both shame & pride about it.

Deb

I also identified myself as having a working-class origin. Often in the course of class discussions, I told stories of my own and friends' experience, and I constantly (and deliberately) related the works we were reading to life experiences I could narrate. I also allowed students to do the same, rather than requiring the discussion to remain abstract and analytical. (Many of the discussions would probably have been seen as digressive by more traditional literature instructors.)[3] It is important that it was not only the working-class students who were able to make connections with the working-class literature. Many of the middle-class students were able to make other kinds of personal connections to the works, either through gender, or race, or family history (many of the middle-class students had grandparents who told stories of being working-class), or through more oblique connections. Once it became clear to the class that all such connections could be discussed and explored (something I had not done the first time I taught a working-class literature course), a true exchange took place, in which most of the students engaged in an honest attempt to learn not only from the works and from me but from one another.

This is not to say there was never friction — there was. Some discussions involved serious disagreements, and some students clearly (judging not from verbal comments, but from body language) disliked others. A couple of students, such as Kevin, quoted above, who were heavily invested in theoretical, impersonal approaches to literature, questioned the validity of our approach, but no one dropped the course; and I welcomed such questioning as an opportunity for us always to remain self-aware of what we were doing.

The difference in my approach to teaching the course this second time came out of the evolution of my critical approach to working-class literature. I believe that approaches that run against the grain of much contemporary theory are the best ways to approach working-class literature. The approach worked, at least in this course, where all of the students seemed to have a much better experience than did those in my first working-class literature course, and students cooperated across boundaries of difference in order to enhance each other's understandings. It remains to this day the best class I have ever taught.

The course evaluations agreed with my assessment of how successful the course had been. None of the students expressed serious dissatisfaction, and some saw it as revolutionary and necessary in the university's curriculum (comments transcribed verbatim):

This is the absolute best class I've taken @ UCSC. It is a down-to-earth no BS class dealing with real-life issues that affect all students and *citizens!* . . . Working class lit is an important subject that deserves more attention than one little seminar every other blue moon.

We were allowed to discuss any aspect of the readings, working class, and everything in general. . . . The interesting discussions about real life issues brought learning back into the classroom . . .

[strengths:] The social relevances of the texts being taught. We read voices that are usually not heard in the novel. It's great to read about issues that I can relate to. Also: defining class issues & that we are not all part of the middle class.

The greatest value of this course is that it breaks down the separation between the world of labor and that of academia. It brings the reality of working class life into the classroom. For once, we spent a lot of time looking @ *real* issues, rather than discussing more or less irrelevant critical/theoretical concepts.

This is the most important class I have taken at *any* institution. . . . Professor Christopher provided critical intervention into the lies of middle/upper class dominance & representation in life & literature. . . . Course was strong because it put w/c at the center of our study & perspective rather than marginalized. From that perspective, texts, life & politics were held vital & immediately relevant.

I particularly enjoyed our discussions connecting the ideas & experiences in the books w/the world around us. . . . I learned a lot as a literature student, but more than that I learned a lot as a human being (cheesy as that sounds). I wish the quarter was longer. [!]

What emerges, for me, from these comments (which are representative) is the emphasis students put on the holism of the educational experience in this class. Even the student who used the phrase "critical intervention," who clearly is one of those who favored a more theoretical approach, said basically the same thing as the student who said "I learned a lot as a human being." The students put emphasis on the "relevance" and "reality" of the experience in the class.

What they are suggesting, working-class and middle-class students alike, is that they found at least some of their university education to be irrelevant not only to their own lives, but also to the world outside the university. Thus, a course that insisted on connections between literature and the lives of actual persons gave them a way to put together their studies and the world.[4]

For example, in our discussion of Thomas Bell's 1941 novel about steel-workers and their families, *Out of This Furnace,* we had an excellent discussion of the nature of blue-collar work — of physical labor. Several working-class students spoke about their own or family members' experiences of labor, and several of the middle-class students who had worked summer jobs at manual labor could add their own experiences. We moved from those narratives to an analytic discussion of the ways that being a "hand," rather than a person, valued for the ability to reason, affects people, both as represented in the novel and in life.

The discussion then moved on to the domestic work of women, focusing first on the working-class labor of the women in the novel — cooking, cleaning, laundry (all without appliances to do the heaviest parts of the chores), then moving out to stories of students' experiences and those of their mothers and grandmothers. Here it was quite interesting to draw contrasts between the domestic labors of the middle-class and the working-class women in life and in the novel. The nature of the work performed was often similar; but in the middle-class experiences that were related, women's domestic labor was about maintaining class appearances and household comfort, never about economic survival for the family, as it was in the novel, where women always took boarders into their houses to supplement husbands' and fathers' inadequate wages. From there, we entered into an analytic discussion of gender roles and economics. Such movement of discussions from narrative to analysis was typical.

This style of discussion made the working-class students feel that they were not stupid. One of the students in the class, Deb Busman, wrote in an essay of definitions of intelligence,

> When intelligence is equated with class position a number of things must happen. . . . When "being smart" carries positive value for a society, and a privileged class *claims* that characteristic, then that class is further elevated in status and the non-privileged or working class becomes further degraded and 'lacking' in that trait; and third, the values and actions of the privileged class become equated with intelligence which is in turn rendered invisible in the values and actions of the poor.[5]

In this definition, Busman describes the experience of many working-class students at elite universities. They are made to feel stupid upon entrance, and throughout their careers, until they learn to "pass" for middle-class; only then can they become full-fledged members of the discourse community. The senior seminar privileged neither way of knowing; rather, it examined and evaluated diverse methods of seeing, experiencing, and explaining the world. Thus, working-class students could both claim their working-class identities in this course and feel entitled to speak, because their speech in this environment did not automatically label them "stupid."

This course happened to be the last one I taught at UCSC, where I was a lecturer for three years after finishing my Ph.D. and before finding a tenure-track position. So I left UCSC on a high, feeling that all my very difficult times in the Ph.D. program and teaching at such a snobbish place had been worthwhile, and feeling good about where I was going — California State University, Stanislaus, a university where I would have working-class students to whom I could bring the kind of educational experience that occurred in the senior seminar on working-class literature.

My rose-colored glasses soon came off. Within my first semester of teaching at CSUS, I realized to my surprise that I was as culturally different from my students here as I had been from the privileged student body of UCSC. CSUS is a regional university, a commuter campus that serves students from about a two-hundred-mile radius in a rural, agricultural area. The average age of our students is twenty-eight. Eighty-four percent are the first in their families to go to college. How, I wondered, could they be different from me? I was the first in my family to go to college; I had been a "reentry" student; I was from a rural, agricultural area. I had looked forward to teaching, for once, students who were more similar to me than different. I imagined a pure, unproblematic line of communication.

What I found was that I was not who I had been thinking I was during my years at UCSC. What I had forgotten about myself was how much, as a teenager and young adult, I had wanted out of the world I grew up in. I had longed for what I imagined I would find in the urban, educated world. I went to college literally to expand my horizons (I grew up in a valley four miles wide, a very bounded world). I wanted the new, the different. I wanted to explore.

My students want to stay put. That is why they are at CSUS, rather than somewhere else. They do not seek geographic or ideological mobility. They seek only a narrowly defined economic mobility. They are in college because they want better-paying jobs. The majority of students I have encountered are not interested in the content of their education, but only in its form. I immediately ran into what I considered to be horrors in terms of the university's lack of standards and the inability to teach students basic skills, critical thinking, or what I considered to be vitally contemporary course content. I found myself in the paradoxical position of being the UCSC snob.

In my second semester at CSUS, I taught a graduate course on U.S. working-class literature. The university offers an M.A., and most of the M.A. students in the English department are high school teachers seeking to increase their qualifications or students intending to teach at the community college level. When I talked about my course with the department's graduate coordinator, I told her I planned to revamp the senior seminar I had taught at UCSC and turn it into a graduate class. She told me the level of a UCSC senior seminar was probably about right for our graduate students. I was a little shocked, but I did not do the things I would have done for a UCSC graduate course — add in a great deal of criticism and theory on top of the primary works — although I did require the students to do some original research into criticism in writing their papers for the class. It turned out, as the graduate coordinator had predicted, that the course was pitched just right.

I had eight students in the course, six of whom had working-class or working-poor origins and two of whom had middle-class origins. There was no friction between the working-class and middle-class students. This may have been partly because all the graduate students in our small program know each other and are used to being in classes together. It was also, I believe, partially because working-class culture is the dominant culture at CSUS, and both the working-class students and their middle-class colleagues found themselves in a usual, rather than an unusual, context.

We followed the same style of discussion as in the UCSC senior seminar. We related the works to the real world, to ourselves, to our friends and families. But the discussions remained, for me, flat, and I constantly caught myself thinking they were "unsophisticated" or "uninspired." Every time I found myself thinking terms like that I went through a roller-coaster identity crisis. Weren't these the students I wanted to reach? Wasn't I reaching them? How could I think of them what my own instructors must have been thinking of me?

The evaluations of the course suggested I did reach them. These comments are typical:

This course has been the embodiment of what a college class ought to be. I not only learned about the material which was covered in class; I learned something about myself and the society in which we find ourselves. Students were encouraged to bring their ideas to the table and hash them out.

I enjoyed the course very much — the topic was something I had not been exposed to, & generally I had not thought a lot about class as a factor affecting life so definitively — the personal candor of the professor was appreciated — she made the discussion of the literature more meaningful by relating her own experience —

I really enjoyed the class because the instructor allowed each student to express his/her interpretation & opinion. Because of this fact, discussion was full & meaningful.

I enjoyed the concept of this class w/regards to the open-mindedness and student/instructor interaction. It's been a real opportunity to 'stretch out' and test myself —

Despite the positive tone of these comments, I wasn't satisfied with what had happened in the course. Part of the problem is revealed by the form of the comments. In the first one, note that the student conceptualizes a typical college course as consisting of "material" to be covered in class. He or she sees learning as mastering a "body of material." This is for me a very old-fashioned, authoritarian, and intellectually impoverished notion of what higher education is supposed to do. It completely undervalues the role of the learner and discourages active engagement and participation in forming one's own intellectual universe. The student notes that this class did something different, but one course is not enough to counteract his or her preexisting concept of higher education. Note also the phrasing in the third quote, in which the student says the instructor "allowed" expression by students. This student is clearly operating in a disciplinary model of education, as authoritarian as the first student's. And note also the prevalence of the passive voice in these comments. It is clear to me (not just from these comments, but I think they are a good illustration) that these students have not learned to be autonomous thinkers with a sense of their intellectual worth. Paradoxically, the working-class students at UCSC seemed, despite their feelings of oppression, to have gained that sense of themselves that these students had not.

It took me a year after the course, another year of teaching at CSUS, feeling torn in two, before I finally was able to identify what I perceived as a problem. In the graduate class, the discussion had indeed been one-note. It remained at the level of personal narrative. Whenever I tried to move out of that mode into discussions of literary form, technique, literary history, symbolism, narrativity, or any sort of metalevel discussion, it fell flat. I realized, in retrospect, that the UCSC senior seminar discussions had moved among narrative and analytic levels; that had occurred so smoothly that I had not even really identified the pattern until I was presented with a contrast. Those discussions were what I had identified (and still do) as ideal, *because they contained both elements.*

The discussions in the CSUS graduate course did not contain nearly as much of a mix of both elements, for two reasons. The first is that I did not have a clear analysis of what had worked so well at UCSC and therefore did not clearly see, at the time, what was missing in the CSUS graduate class. Second, the CSUS graduate students, many of them B.A. graduates of CSUS or similar institutions, had simply never been socialized/educated into the abstract, theoretical level of discussions that all the UCSC seniors had been extensively exposed to. (None of them could claim Claire's revelation: "Education works!" because it had not worked in that way for them.) Many of the working-class UCSC students found that form of education oppressive, but only, I now believe, because it was unmixed with educational elements that they would have identified as "relevant" or "real." The CSUS students, not having been exposed to abstract, theoretical discourse, are, *in my view,* missing an important element, a tool with which to think about literature and the world. (In their own view they are probably not missing anything; I remember myself before my extensive education in abstraction. I did not think I was missing anything, and while I was gaining the ability to deal extensively in theoretical abstraction, I felt oppressed. Specifically, I felt I was being told that my way of being was wrong, inadequate. That, I never want to pass on to anyone.)[6]

And so, through the process of personal experience (still the only way I ever really learn anything) and using the combined practices of narration (I have told versions of these stories many times, to myself and others) and analysis (asking why the stories go the way they do), I have come to see how working-class students are oppressed and cheated in both elite and nonelite educational arenas.

At the elite university, working-class students are oppressed because their ways of knowing are not valued in the discourse community. Their life experiences rarely form the content of study. They are asked to re-form themselves without being told what that reformation entails. They are cheated because they are asked to conform or leave, rather than being invited to synthesize elements they find of value from their world and the elite university world.

At the nonelite university, working-class students are oppressed by the very nature of the university, in that they are *not* asked to re-form themselves; they are not invited into the realm that the true holders of power in our society inhabit, that of theoretical abstraction. And they are cheated because their second-class status (particularly in terms of economic power) is enforced by the two-tiered higher education system. Universities such as CSUS graduate them without giving them basic skills (particularly the ability to write standard English and to do mathematics beyond prealgebra); this lack of skills will restrict their employment opportunities.

What, then, would be the solution, the way to give working-class students the most useful education? Put the two levels of education together. Draw what is good from both. From the elite university take the introduction to theoretical discourse and offer it to all students — working- and middle-class — nonexclusively. That is, do not make it the only discursive mode of value. From the nonelite university, take the cultural atmosphere in which working-class students can feel themselves to be of value. Relate the realms of abstraction and concreteness (which my students refer to as "reality"). Create, in entire educational institutions, rather than in single classrooms, the holism of the experience my UCSC senior seminar students encountered.

The most radical version of this bringing together of the different levels of education, the one I most favor, would require structural change that would be institutionally revolutionary. I would like to see the two-tiered structure of state higher education systems collapsed. In California, that would mean putting the state university system and the University of California system on the same footing in terms of budgetary allocations, teaching load, resources devoted to each student, and, most importantly, academic standards, admissions policies, and tuition. That would mean bringing admissions standards "down" at the UC system, and "up" at the CSU system; any student would still be able to enter the community college system and then transfer after receiving sufficient preparation.

Since that would, however, require a revolution in social and educational thought and policy, what can we actually do now? Those of us with social class awareness can work to educate our colleagues at both elite research institutions and regional universities in the different ways they may need to be educated about class issues. We can insist that the discussion of pedagogy is as important at department meetings or colloquia as administrative issues or research, and we can bring these class-based issues into the discussion. We can make available and ask our colleagues to read works like this anthology. We can talk to administrators about the needs of our students, at whichever kind of institution we find ourselves. At elite institutions, that might mean insisting on the availability of free tutoring programs and on presenting those programs in such a way that using them does not carry a stigma. At regional universities that might mean talking about the necessity of ensuring that our students leave our campuses with both basic skills and critical thinking skills.

And most importantly, we can bring discussions of social class issues, as they affect our own lives, the lives of our students and their families, and the fabric of our society, into every course in the humanities and social sciences, not as marginal, "if this is Wednesday it must be social class" tourist modes, but as central, along with issues of race and gender. We must consider the efficacy for *all* classes of modes of pedagogy that have long been explored in women's studies and ethnic studies classrooms and stand up for those modes of pedagogy as legitimate, productive, humane, and rigorous.

If we do so, that will be a beginning. If we do so, we will be giving something to Jenny and to Claire that we can say beyond any doubt is of value, something that gives our struggles meaning.

CLASS, RACE, AND CULTURE:

TEACHING INTERCULTURAL COMMUNICATION

ANTHONY ESPOSITO

Perhaps the most crucial task for those who are concerned with teaching working-class students is to comprehend the rhetorics of individual students or groups who represent different races, genders, classes, and other demographic variables. These differing voices are a rich resource for disciplines and individual instructors attempting to link together courses that involve a pluralistic focus on, for example, class. But in order to grasp what these suppressed voices are attempting to say, we must recognize the inherent qualities of each group through discussing and understanding the various groups represented in our classrooms. According to K. Anthony Appiah, "Crossculturally it matters to people that their lives have a certain narrative unity, they want to be able to tell a story of their lives that makes sense. The story — my story — should cohere in the way appropriate by the standards made available in my culture to a person of my identity."[1] Appiah articulates what some academicians are attempting to implement in their classes and disciplines: they are encouraging multipolarity rather than bipolarity, with respect to race, class, gender, and culture and enabling a greater respect for others' perspectives.[2] The discipline of communication in particular tries to establish an environment different from that usually encountered in mainstream society — one where students can use their communication skills, cultural heritage, and social class to explain their individual voices.

In a course that deals with culture, rhetoric, class, and communication, the task of understanding all kinds of student "stories," as they vary by race, class, gender, must become paramount. With the thought that the description of a course so constrained may be useful to teachers in other disciplines, I offer in this essay a framework for use by anyone attempting to implement a course that deals with these important variables. To this end I will (1) briefly describe my students, (2) point out that class is not generally reflected in our journals and textbooks, (3) describe the course, discussing its objectives and defining key terms, and (4) highlight the studies, movies, and music that I use to consider functions of class in those media. Finally, I will consider the sense of community and atmosphere that are established in the class.

DEMOGRAPHICS OF THE STUDENT POPULATION

Coming from a blue-collar background and growing up in Youngstown, Ohio, I always felt a little out of place in an academic environment. For example, my incorrect blue-collar speaking patterns were a hindrance as I began to break through the boundaries into the academic arena. But when I taught at a historically black university, Fayetteville State University in North Carolina, I found that my own earlier struggles helped me understand the difficult transition that many of my African American students had to make as first-generation college students. This experience at different times was enlightening, difficult, and satisfying for a new assistant professor attempting to teach and understand variations in communication, culture, race, and class.

Fayetteville is a military town, home to Fort Bragg. African Americans account for 40 percent of the city's diverse population. The student population is 64 percent black and 30 percent white; the faculty is 55 percent black and 29 percent white. The students, many of them first-generation college students, come mostly from lower-working-class backgrounds. The Cumberland County School System in Fayetteville ranks below state and national median SAT scores, and many of my students came to college less prepared than those from more affluent regions.

As an instructor, I had to acknowledge these facts about my students. Understanding that language is symbolic is important in understanding their unique and pluralistic voices. As James B. White explains, rhetoric "is contiguous to a ground that is common to all of us. Rhetoric must deal with ordinary language because it is the art of speaking to people who already have a language, and it is their language you must speak to reach and persuade them. This is the sense, as I suggested above, rhetoric is always culture specific. You must take the language you are given and work with that."[3] So I tried to understand the multicultural voices that are part of Fayetteville State University.

CLASS IN THE COMMUNICATION LITERATURE

The study of class has been essentially ignored in the communication literature. Elsewhere, class is subordinate to culture and communication, but it is not even mentioned in our research endeavors. Constance Coiner explains, "Despite its place in the now familiar list—race, gender, class, ethnicity, and disability— class is often the least addressed of these issues."[4] How can a discipline that is supposed to be solving societal problems diminish the role of class? Fred Jandt escalates this negative ideology when he states, "While the United States does have social classes and while these social classes have been shown to have different values, many black people in the United States believe that these barriers of social class are easier to transcend in the United States than in other countries."[5] The indifference indicated by Jandt's view is only escalating class conflict and alienating the different classes and their distinctive ways of speaking that are overtly present in our multicultural community. In my view, the interdependence among communication, culture, and class should be primary rather than subordinate in our journals and research endeavors. There are excellent books dealing with *culture* and communication, which make one recognize the importance of the discipline in promoting different voices and unique cultural entities. The omission of class, however, needs to be remedied.

COURSE DESCRIPTION AND OBJECTIVES

The primary objective of the course "Intercultural Communication" was to provide an overview of the study of American cultures with a special emphasis on class and how culture, class, and socioeconomic and environmental influences affect our communication interactions. The student learned how to understand and communicate with people from other cultures and ethnic groups. The course also sought to increase students' understanding of the relationship between rhetoric, culture, communication, and class; how culture interacts with social, psychological, and environmental factors to influence communication; ethical issues in communicating with someone from another culture or class; and the role of communication in adapting to others. The student was expected to learn, furthermore, how to transcend cultural, ethnic, and class differences in an attempt to build community and how to explain cultural and class similarities and differences in communication.

This list is not exhaustive, but it indicates some of the issues and concepts that can be discussed. Another goal of the course was to show the class similarities between different racial groups in America. It was not intended to be a race relations course; but because of the unique symbol systems of many of my students, it was important to discuss the role of race in communication encounters. In courses like this at predominantly black universities or schools with diverse populations, we must not negate the significance of race in attempting to understand what students, individually or in groups, are attempting to communicate.

DEFINITIONS OF TERMS

First of all, because students must understand how the concepts of race, class, culture, and rhetoric are interdependent, they must have clear definitions of these terms. I will define rhetoric and culture and then show how both of these terms can be used to highlight the importance of class.

Rhetoric

Rhetoric can be a difficult term for students to understand, so I define it as communication. I follow that with a historical explanation of the concept as defined by Aristotle: "the faculty of observing in any given case the available means of persuasion."[6] Sonja K. Foss, Karen A. Foss, and Robert Trapp's definition of rhetoric as "an action humans perform when they use symbols for the purpose of communicating with one another" is also helpful.[7] These definitions of rhetoric contribute to the study of communication, but we need to look further to show how cultural or class communities use symbols in ways that distinguish them from members of other communities, to help students see how language is symbolic as learned from their cultural communities or class positions. For example, I would ask the class, What does success mean to you? The various responses, including money, family, and marriage, enabled students to see how their class backgrounds influenced their thoughts and actions. This in-class assignment helped students think critically about how they construct their own individual realities. Some of the answers might suggest class differences. Specifically, for some of my lower-class students (in terms of economic background), money seemed to be an important goal: they hoped that through education they could improve their economic status. I am not generalizing that students from lower-working-class backgrounds strive only for monetary rewards, but my students showed this tendency. The same type of exercise could be used to see whether the students' class backgrounds influence their individual or group identities.

To further enlighten students on the concept of language as symbolic, I referred to Sonja K. Foss's definition of rhetoric as "the use of symbols to influence thought and action"[8] and asked the students, Does your class or cultural standing affect how you use language to influence others who are similar to or different from your own frame of reference? For example, when we discussed Ebonics in class, some stated that speaking "white" was important when a person was attempting to cross a new boundary in mainstream society. Others felt that speaking "white" was selling out and buying into mainstream ideologies that had oppressed African Americans throughout time. Many, but not all, of my students felt that acting "smart" would cause them to be labeled by others in the African American community as deviating from their cultural surroundings. One student argued that speaking "white" meant using Standard English. Another stated that all white people use that form of English. Numerous students agreed with his inference.

This was a difficult area for me as a white instructor. I had to attempt to provide a context in which students felt comfortable discussing issues of culture, class, and race, but I often wondered how successful I was. Did they say only what they thought I wanted to hear, or did they reveal only part of the real story? I found that I had to rely on all of my training in communication to interpret and respond to the signals I received—my own difficulty demonstrates that language is symbolic.

After students understood that rhetoric is basic to human interaction, we could begin to analyze the various ways in which the study of rhetoric through different cultures and class systems could enhance our understanding. Defining rhetoric from this perspective emphasizes the importance of rhetoric as the art of knowing and discovering the world around us; it enables students to see how culture and class are interdependent as they examine the values, norms, and traditions of a particular culture or class system.

Rhetoric, as stated by Foss, "functions as an invitation for us to change our lives in some way."[9] Throughout the semester, I showed films of speeches by both black and white rhetors, such as Martin Luther King Jr., John F. Kennedy, Jesse Jackson, and Congressman James Traficant from Ohio. I asked, How do they employ rhetoric to change or transform the members of their audiences? Such an exercise stimulated critical thinking from the entire class. Specifically, it showed how both black and white rhetors from different generations, representing different classes and different races, use rhetoric to respond to the needs of their audiences. From a pedagogical standpoint, this type of exercise invites us as teachers also to respond to different cultures and classes; as we do so, our students are enabled either to change ideologies or to become more accepting of voices that they usually deem inappropriate. An exercise that emphasizes the different cultural or class standpoints can highlight language, values, or mores that are often neglected by members of mainstream ideologies. After spending some time during the semester defining rhetoric, I moved on to show the interdependence between rhetoric and culture.

Culture

I was often enlightened when I asked my students to give their own definitions of culture. Specifically, because it was sometimes difficult for them to understand culture from the standardized dictionary definition, the subjectivity of their individual viewpoints came through and enabled me to hear their pluralistic voices. Most of the students defined culture as equivalent to race. I began to show them that class can at times transcend racial barriers. Teaching in the South, and specifically at Fayetteville State University, provided me with both an urban and a rural element not usually found in midwestern or northern universities. Since North Carolina is partly in the Appalachian Mountains, I began to highlight the speaking patterns of that pluralistic community. Employing studies on the rhetoric of American farmers and on the speech patterns in an Appalachian community, I tried to show the differing communication patterns and class systems outside the traditional middle-class white community.[10] To stimulate discussion, I posed the following questions: Are there different cultures in North Carolina? Are there different cultures within the black community? within the white community? Do cultures differ depending on the regional area of the country? Can fraternities and sororities be considered cultures? Such questions prompted the students to think critically about the topic.

After clearing up any uncertainty in this area, I focused on defining culture. According to Bradford J. Hall, it is "the concept that describes the situated meanings that community members create, recognize, share and enact that identify them as members of that community."[11] Others feel that communication is subordinate to culture, but such a view negates the interdependence of the two terms. The notion of interdependence, which insists that culture is communication and communication is culture, asserts the mutual influence and dynamics between culture and communication. Such a definition is the most accessible for the beginning student of culture and communication.

Another reflective view, that "speech is not merely a medium of or an accompaniment to the social interaction but also shapes and constitutes social life," also illuminates communication and rhetoric from a class perspective.[12] By enabling the students to understand the culture, class, and communication practices of members of a community, I could help them gain a deeper understanding of how communication functions in diverse situations. Within this framework, the instructor can emancipate the voices of different groups that have been suppressed by a majority system or other influences that attempt to negate their cultural or class identities.

Class

Class influences profoundly the ways in which we view and communicate with others. Social class is a position in society's hierarchy based on income, education, occupation, or neighborhood.[13] This definition seems to work for students who at times find the term *class* both confusing and ambiguous. I asked my students to define class from an African American perspective and felt the unusualness of my situation as a white professor at a mostly black institution. Specifically, from a race perspective, they defined themselves as African Americans. But when class was the focus, they began to distinguish themselves from others who they felt were lower on the status chart. Even though a majority of my students came from lower-working-class backgrounds, they used education to distinguish themselves from inner-city blacks and uneducated blacks. Although they appeared to view themselves as still part of the African American community, they acknowledged that within that pluralistic community, class was now an overt component of their total persona. Because of that understanding, I could — rather than negating race — show how race could be seen as a catalyst in constructing the students' reality through their social and class systems.

Such perspectives allow an instructor to explore the concepts of culture and class and how they influence communication in ways that enable students to transcend boundaries. They begin to see the advantages of being pluralistic speakers when speaking in different class systems in both the black and the white community.

Class, Race, and Culture

If we can show how class, race, culture, and communication are interdependent, our students can better understand the commonalities between different cultural communities. Students need to see, for example, that different races can have similar class systems and speaking patterns. For this purpose my "Intercultural Communication" class spent over two weeks analyzing class differences and similarities between African American street-corner culture and white street-corner culture.

At first the students were hesitant to accept that the speaking patterns of poor whites could be compared to those of blacks. Many students believed that all white people spoke Standard English. After dispelling that notion, I highlighted the commonalities between different cultures and their modes of rhetoric. Using readings and my own frame of reference, I began to show them narratives or speaking patterns from blue-collar culture that contained nonstandard usages. For example, using clips from *All in the Family,* I highlighted the speaking patterns that were familiar to me from my own cultural frame of reference in Youngstown, Ohio, and related some personal narratives as well. In my effort to show that there are similarities in the ways blacks and whites construct their individual symbolic reality, I also used *Tally's Corner: A Study of Negro Streetcorner Men,* by Elliot Liebow, and Gerry Philipsen's germinal 1975 study entitled "Speaking like a Man in Teamsterville: Cultural Patterns of Role Enactment in an Urban Environment."[14] The importance of race must not be negated. Rather, I used race as a frame to display how class plays a major role in the construction of speaking patterns.

A consideration of class is important to understanding the communication patterns of the communities portrayed in these works. Liebow's study focuses on a group of African Americans who live in a blighted section of Washington's inner city during the early 1960s; Philipsen's Teamsterville analysis concerns a white, blue-collar neighborhood located on the near south side of Chicago. Both authors show how class setting can have a major impact on how people communicate with outsiders, those who are not part of their class or cultural communities. Such explorations demonstrate the similarities between black and white class systems. Again, I pointed out that race is a factor that may determine differences between communities. It is also helpful to discuss the class commonalities between the two cultures described by Liebow and Philipsen.

Both Philipsen's and Liebow's research treats the values, norms, language, and roles of the cultures. In both cultures there is a strong male-oriented system in which males especially, sensitive to their low position in the class hierarchy, distrust outsiders. Furthermore, because males in those groups are not formally educated, and because they may be intimidated by contact with more highly educated people, they hold positions that require little verbal interaction with their employers. Of course, not all individuals with low education levels feel inferior to those who are better educated. For the purpose of class discussion, however, it is imperative to call attention to such possibilities.

Place was the next topic discussed in relation to the two cultural communities. In both studies, the neighborhood was a place where residents felt comfortable communicating with one another: place as a physical setting enabled people to share information and ideas. According to Philipsen, place is a "position in a social hierarchy, a physical setting, or the niche properly occupied by a thing, person, or idea."[15] Neighborhood as a comfortable place is in part responsible for Liebow's observation that "the socio-spatial boundaries that residents perceive as the neighborhood make up the largest region within which it is considered most appropriate and in which it is most natural to engage in talk."[16] Exposing students to that thought enables them to see how the two cultures are alike in acting out specific rituals that become norms for their communities. Specifically, place refers to the street corner, the porch, and other locations that are the settings for communication encounters. Face-to-face communication is emphasized to show how place provides a context for members of lower socioeconomic status. The consideration of how place functions in the two communities also helps students to see the class similarities between white and black cultures.

I attempted to show my students that although race and culture play a significant role in the communication patterns of individuals, class is also basic to the enactment of an individual. In a sense, according to Philipsen, "every cultural way of speaking is a distinctive answer to the questions (1) What is a person? (2) What is a society? and (3) How are persons and society linked through communication?"[17] These are the questions that I encouraged my students to think about when analyzing the cultural and class patterns of communities differing from their own. I also discussed the authenticity and strength of the social bonds that unite the people of these neighborhoods, which must be seen as real communities with real values and real politics. Such analysis brought out cultural variables, but it also enabled me to discuss how important class is in the communication patterns between individuals.

Instructors employing this pedagogical approach can make use of the ritual view of communication, which stresses sharing, participation, association, and fellowship.[18] From a communication standpoint, the ritual view of the lived experiences of different cultural and class groups helps students to understand how they may share a class perception or reality with individuals outside their own frame of reference. Though it attempts to show the drama or unfolding narrative of groups, the ritual view focuses primarily neither on the individual nor on the group but on the individuals' sharing symbolically their distinctive and pluralistic culture and class identities.

Making use of the ritual perspective, I highlighted the conflictual view of class and culture, which also stresses difference but is sometimes negated in our academic journals and mainstream media. John Fiske shows the weakness of a consensual viewpoint when he posits that it requires that "language must mean the same to everyone, words must have commonly agreed meanings, or at least, an agreed area of polysemy whose internal differences work harmoniously and pluralistically within the common framework." Fiske adds, "Such a denial of class and race conflict serves the interests of those with power — the disadvantaged and disempowered can improve their lot only by engaging in social conflict, not by denying it."[19] That assertion is consistent with the theoretical and teaching approach that I incorporated in the course.

These various classroom exercises and discussions were then transformed into a paper in which students compared and contrasted the class, communication, and cultural differences of cultural communities. Students gained other-awareness along with specific knowledge of groups such as farmers, African American communities, blue-collar workers, and Mexican Americans, which students had learned about from written materials discussed throughout the semester. The assignment asked students to show how class, race, or cultural differences were integral to the communication patterns of the individual or group. It also asked them to compare their own class situations with the reading or readings they had chosen for their individual papers. Thus students had the opportunity to apply culture, race, or class principles and components to case studies of cultural interaction and to synthesize knowledge of "other" cultures with knowledge of their own as they predicted areas of shared meaning and areas of communication challenge. Students also presented informative speeches that described predicted interaction challenges between two different cultures. This project allowed students to understand the value or class differences of a group in the hope of using communication skills to bring about constructive intercultural interaction.

CLASS AND CULTURE IN FEATURE FILMS

As part of my attempt to implement unique and exciting learning tools for my students, I use films in my courses. How does this medium fit in a class that focuses on culture, class, and communication? Probably one of the clearest arguments for linking communication with film is offered by Don C. Shields and Vince V. Kidd: "Speech-communication theory attempts to explain communication in society, and film attempts artistically to reproduce communication on the screen. From this perspective, communication theory ideally underlies both practice and the depiction of that practice in film. Such a convergence of art and theory provides a mandate for using art forms to explicate communication theory."[20] This concept can be applied to any discipline that stresses the importance of critical thinking.

Specifically, I asked my students to look at films as a means of communicating class, cultural, and racial values to a diverse audience. This caused the students to think of films that depict their cultural variables through the medium of popular culture. Interestingly, many of my African American students felt that blacks were usually portrayed negatively by Hollywood. They felt that too many black and white producers wanted to show — for white audiences — the negative side of the black culture, including rap music, gangs, and sports in which blacks are acting in a deviant way. Consequently, I asked the students to either dispel or accept these myths. The students noted that class variables within the black community were not shown by the movie industry, and I tend to agree with them. Discussing the importance of stereotypes in film was an important part of this section of the course to show how racial, ethnic, or class stereotypes shape mainstream ideologies.

I used films to illustrate both class and cultural aspects of groups or individuals, such as *The Breakfast Club, Breaking Away, Children of a Lesser God, Do the Right Thing, Jungle Fever, Gung Ho, The Joy Luck Club, The Deer Hunter,* and *Grapes of Wrath.* This list is not exhaustive, but it is indicative of films that can help students to think about the importance of cultural and class variables through the medium of popular culture.

For example, *The Breakfast Club* demonstrates overtly how a person's class determines how he or she interacts with people from a different class background. Even though this movie has only white characters, it seemed to work well with my predominantly African American students. *The Breakfast Club* takes place at an Illinois high school, where five dissimilar students, from different class backgrounds, are sentenced to spend a Saturday detention session together: the princess, the jock, the brain, the criminal, and the basket case. One aspect in particular stands out: the stereotypical or class role that has been assigned to each character by his or her peers or society. The princess, who comes from an upper-middle-class background, must learn to communicate with others from lower-class backgrounds. The convict comes from a lower-class background and is perceived to be a criminal. As the individuals become acquainted, they begin to shed the "wall" or class system that has inhibited them from communicating with one another. The class system becomes minimized as they see that it only hinders them from actually experiencing a different culture. This is an excellent movie to use to show the importance of class, culture, and communication and how those elements affect perceptions of class and culture. Though the relationships in *The Breakfast Club* are transient (at the end of the movie the day of detention ends, too), class differences are obvious in each of them.

This is a fine movie to show to college audiences because it reveals the role of class differences in both teens and adults. It was received in a positive light by my students. First, it showed them the class differences that are part of the many facets of the white population. Because of that I asked whether this movie could have been made about a predominantly black high school, portraying differing classes within the African American community. All of my students responded "yes" to this question. They felt that more movies needed to be made that show African Americans living in positive situations, movies that deal more with class than with race.

Other movies that depict working-class culture (*The Deer Hunter*), African American culture (*Do the Right Thing* and *Jungle Fever*), and many others show that not only does culture play a significant role in communication, but that class is also an important indicator of how one is treated by members of one's own racial group. Spike Lee's *Jungle Fever* is an exemplary movie that reveals the class differences within the African American community. It portrays two brothers, one a successful businessman and the other a drug addict. Differing characters show the class system that is often negated by mainstream movies, in which African Americans are usually living in housing projects and dealing drugs. My students seemed to like the portrayal of the differing characters and the filmmaker's view that there are some class differences in the African American community.

USING MUSIC TO PORTRAY CULTURE AND CLASS

The various themes articulated through popular music can also show how culture, class, and communication are integrated. Even though this class did not focus on popular culture, I found music helpful as a pedagogical tool. When students see that music contains cultural and class codes of communication, their knowledge of other cultures is enhanced.

I discussed various songwriters who employ music to inform and persuade the members of their audience. We talked about how their lyrics may have been written about political, personal, and worldwide issues and how cultural or class variables influence the artist. I provided a wide range of artists who focus on class and culture, from singer-songwriters (Bob Dylan, Bruce Springsteen, Marvin Gaye) to country musicians (Woody Guthrie and other modern artists) to rappers.

One of the most effective musicians whose work I employed in this class is Bruce Springsteen. It may seem strange to play a blue-collar white singer to a mostly black audience, but the results were beneficial. Even though the students may not have liked his voice or his musical arrangements, they seemed to resonate to his lyrics of despair, loss of community, and the corruption of the American government. In such songs as "Badlands," "Born in the USA," and "Trapped," Springsteen displays the despair of the individuals he is attempting to represent. After playing Springsteen to the class, I asked whether they could relate to his message. Since many of my students were of the same class as many of Springsteen's characters, they found aspects of their own situations in his lyrics. Realizing that they could not identify with the race of these fictional characters, they found nonetheless that as African Americans they could empathize with Springsteen's message of government deceit and oppression.

I then asked, Can white Americans or African Americans from affluent backgrounds understand the importance and cultural narratives couched within rap music? The students answered "no." We then spent some time listening to the overt messages of race and class in this genre of music. Again, this experience would be enlightening to anyone who had never experienced this frame of reference. To some of my students, rap music was a form of rhetoric or communication that only an insider could understand. That type of critical thinking makes it obvious that race is still a paramount factor that should not be neglected as we move forward to understanding how class does or does not affect our understanding of the rhetoric of oppressed groups.

I used both film and music to help students to understand terms and concepts I discussed throughout the semester; both media serve as a "cutting edge" approach to illustrate the importance of class, race, and communication in popular culture. I have found these materials invaluable in trying to reach students who have not had the same opportunities as many of their privileged counterparts at other universities. Instructors at any college or university, though, should consider showing movies or playing music that represents perspectives different from those of the students.

ESTABLISHING A SENSE OF COMMUNITY IN THE CLASSROOM

In my teaching, it is important for me to celebrate the uniqueness and diversity of my students and the pluralistic cultures from which they come. Therefore, I use language that is nonsexist, nonracist, and not otherwise harmful to even one student. As William B. Gudyskunst, Stella Ting-Toomey, and Richard L. Wiseman suggest, I am also careful about using stereotypes in lectures.[21] I followed both of these practices quite stringently in order to create a positive environment devoid of self-fulfilling negative prophecies.

Contemporary rhetoric, as defined by Douglass Ehninger, is "an instrument for understanding and improving human relations."[22] I provided an open environment where the "public sphere" was open to all individuals and their unique cultural and class ideas.[23] Open communication, empathy, class and race consciousness, and the absence of dogmatism are a few of the factors that created an open and honest environment between the students and myself. Enhancing the sense of open communication should be a goal for any instructor in the twenty-first century because it enables students to feel more comfortable about embarking on a difficult and foreign subject.

As I worked for open communication, I tried to create a sense of community for the students — even to form the class into a community — as they attempted to cross boundaries into the academic forum. The term *community* has become commonplace for politicians in the 1990s. In my case, however, community truly was my goal for my students. Eugene J. Dionne explains it best when he argues for the collaboration of races and those with different ethnic backgrounds: "Separatism, with its implication that 'white values' and 'black' values are fundamentally different, has proven an abysmal failure. We need to reassert that our goal as a nation is the integration of races. This does not mean denying the distinct riches of black, Native American, Asian, or Hispanic cultures. It does mean asserting that Americans, black and white, Hispanic and Asian, in fact share goals and values and are willing to work together to promote them."[24] Dionne's comments emphasize what one should highlight in a course that deals with culture, communication, and class. I pointed out to my students that we must complement awareness of our own culture or class with understanding and appreciation of others' culture or class. Pride in our own heritage and traditions, though justified, is no excuse for ignorance or arrogance about those of others. In a sense, I am pushing my students to expand, not to disband, the public sphere. Through building this sense of community, I could understand better and negate some of the stereotypes that have become a redundant theme of numerous members of society. Showing two sides or unique readings of a story or a group will create a sense of community within a group. Although it may seem logically inconsistent, it is rhetorically feasible to have it both ways.

IMMIGRANT FICTION, WORKING- AND MIDDLE-CLASS WHITE STUDENTS, AND MULTICULTURAL EMPATHY:

A PEDAGOGICAL BALANCING ACT

CHARLES JOHANNINGSMEIER

The situation is familiar to many college instructors of multicultural American literature: all prepared for a semester filled with diverse readings, you find yourself on the first day of class looking at a classroom full of white students. Certainly, a number of these students are eager to learn about Americans who are different from them, but you know that many share the apprehension, indifference, or hostility toward racial and ethnic minorities that the majority of white Americans feel. Those feelings are often especially strong among working- and middle-class whites who believe themselves most threatened by immigrants and people of color. Reaching such students is an enormous challenge, and successfully meeting that challenge requires more than simply assigning texts by African Americans, Latino/Latina Americans, Asian Americans, Native Americans, and others and hoping for attitudinal change through simple contact. Instead, one needs to experiment with various strategies of teaching multicultural literature that will better engage these students and possibly breach the hard shell they have constructed over the years against the onslaught of "liberal" teachers and professors, members of the professional class. The approach I adopted last year — which proved quite successful — was to focus all the course readings, discussions, assignments, and exams on the theme of "The Immigrant Experience in American Fiction."

Begun as a normal school in the nineteenth century, the institution I teach at is now part of the State University of New York system, constructed after World War II to serve the thousands of returning soldiers (many of them ethnic whites) going to college under the GI Bill. In some respects it has retained its identity as a normal school: a large number of its students major in elementary and secondary education or in such professional studies programs as health science, physical education, and recreation. Only 1,364 of the total 6,278 students enrolled at the college in the fall of 1996 were liberal arts majors, which in itself is a reflection of the working- and middle-class backgrounds of most of these students; the idea of getting an education simply to "better one-self" or to prepare for graduate school sounds like a luxury to many, an option available only to those who already possess financial security.[1] For the most part my students' aspirations are quite modest, limited by their class positions and their secondary schooling; few dream of becoming doctors, lawyers, or veterinarians, but a large majority hope to become school teachers, speech pathologists, physical therapists, or health aides. For these students such oc-cupations would allow them either to attain membership in the middle class or to solidify the middle-class status recently achieved by their parents. Many students tell me that they are the first in the family to attend college, and typical occupations of their parents include "medical assistant," "garage door re-pairman," "real estate broker," "store owners," "registered nurse," "gas me-chanic for a utility company," "occupational therapist," "seamstress," and "manager in a clothing factory." Not surprisingly, all of my students regard themselves as middle-class, even those whose parents academics would regard as working-class.

As befits a state university, too, almost all of the students at SUNY Cortland come from New York state; however, despite the diversity of the state's popula-tion, Cortland's students are overwhelmingly white and of European ancestry. In the fall of 1995, out of the total 6,278 students enrolled, there were only 27 Native American students, 117 African American students, 44 Asian/Pacific Islander students, and 133 Latino/Latina students; combined, those minorities made up only 5.1 percent of the total student population. There are even fewer foreign students, twenty-eight in all, and these are mostly European exchange students.[2] As a result, students have little opportunity to learn from people of cultures substantially different from their own. In the past four years I have taught approximately seven hundred students, but I have had fewer than fifteen African American, Latino/Latina, Asian American, and Native American stu-dents. Unfortunately, some of my students have come to associate American racial minorities with "foreigners." On the final day of one "Introduction to Fiction" course a few years ago, in which all the works we had discussed were by African American, Native American, and Latino/Latina American authors, one student raised his hand to complain, "Why did we have to read all those books about foreigners?" Slightly puzzled, I asked him what he meant exactly; after conferring briefly with the student sitting next to him he pronounced, "You know, minorities." I do not wish to imply that all my students wholly share that sentiment, but judging from classroom discussions, most agree at least in part with it.

There are other factors that also help create an unreceptive environment for multicultural literature. For instance, my students and their parents often represent the disaffected working- and lower-middle-class whites who feel threatened, both economically and culturally, by those they perceive as benefiting most from Affirmative Action programs or more liberal immigration policies. Many of my students, for whom a three-hundred-dollar yearly increase in tuition would force them to leave school, do not support government programs that assist people on the basis of race rather than of class. Not surprisingly, the attitude toward immigrants, the focus of this course, is generally conservative. Among my students there is strong agreement with Hector St. Jean de Crèvecoeur's desire that in America "individuals of all nations [be] melted into a new race of men," as well as with the belief that anyone, no matter what race, gender, ethnicity, class, or religion, can be "successful" in America if he or she only works hard enough.[3] Viewing prejudice against the cultural values or skin color of some immigrant groups (and racial minorities) as the reason for their lack of "success" is often dismissed as bleeding-heart liberalism (espoused by those wealthy enough not to be economically threatened by such groups) or, worse yet, the fabrications of those groups in order to obtain special treatment. Because of their class backgrounds, my students also accept the view that in order to "succeed" in America, one must transform oneself and give up something of who one is. Because of this belief, such students have little or no empathy for minority group members who decry losing their ethnic or racial identities via assimilation. Their favorite texts, quite naturally, are about immigrants who are willing to shed their former identities and who succeed as a result. They are generally skeptical, too, of separate college courses on the literature of various minority groups and women, for these represent to many of my students how people from these groups do not really want to be "American" and play by the same rules (roughly those set out by Crèvecoeur and Benjamin Franklin) that they and their immigrant ancestors were expected to follow, instead using political pressure to retain their cultures and get special curricular and social consideration. Because the college offers such courses (and indeed there is a general education category titled "Prejudice and Discrimination"), the institution itself — and its agents, such as professors — is often distrusted as overly liberal and out of touch with the economic and social realities of students' working- and middle-class lives. As a result of all these factors, my students' attitudes toward multicultural literature closely resemble those of the students at Youngstown State University in Ohio, who, as Sherry Linkon and Bill Mullen have recently written, "often perceive such readings as 'token' representatives of an alien culture to be endured, treated with suspicion, or blown off. They also may judge them as politically charged attempts by the instructor to force curricular integration of the classroom — the equivalent for many in closed white ethnic working-class communities of 'busing' ideas."[4]

I.

In response to the challenge this environment represents, I developed a theme of "The Immigrant Experience in American Fiction" for my "Introduction to Fiction" course for nonmajors. This course had many goals besides teaching students about how authors use literary devices and helping them to become better writers. My primary goal was for students to gain some understanding of the diverse cultures present in the United States and to learn to empathize with people from those groups instead of dismissing them as "alien." I was fully aware that with such a motive I was a complicit agent of the college's "liberal," professional-class agenda.

I chose the subject of immigrant fiction because I believed it was a theme that would help break down my students' resistance to learning about people from cultures other than their own (including American racial minorities) and would encourage them to see similarities between their experiences and those of people from these other cultures rather than seeing only the differences. Almost all immigrants and their descendants, including the unwilling African American immigrants, have experienced at one time or another the hope of achieving some type of "success" in America, as well as the pain of dislocation and discrimination at the hands of those who had already gained the status of "Americans." Because few students perceive themselves as "ethnic," one of my first goals was to spur them into recognizing and exploring their own ethnicity or lack thereof. I wanted students to realize, too, that the process of assimilation, which is sometimes liberating and joyful, can also be debilitating and painful. To encourage empathy for those whose skin color and language often make assimilation difficult, I drew parallels not only with their ancestors' immigrant experiences but also with their own experiences of "assimilating" into the educated middle class, which usually involves learning a new language and new customs, leaving their old ways behind, and distancing themselves from the family and friends still living in the working- and lower-middle-class worlds from which they come. Further, we brought to the fore the subtle forms of discrimination they had experienced as a result of their class position and compared this discrimination to that which people of color experience.

Along the way I also wished to deconstruct the ways my students (and

American society as a whole, generally) categorize by race. They of course have come to accept their own inclusion in the category of "white." However, by highlighting the quite diverse mix of *ethnicities* at Cortland (Irish, Italian, Polish, Greek, Ukrainian, and so forth), I demonstrated that not all whites are alike and that immigrants (and their descendants) from certain European countries and regions have had advantages over others. The texts I used also indicated that there is great variation among individual members of ethnic groups. Furthermore, students were encouraged to look past race and ethnicity as categories and to explore the possibilities of class affinity across these boundaries. It was my hope that what students learned would help transform their attitudes toward racial minorities and immigrants today, whom they should see as deserving the same consideration that their ancestors did and that they do now. I also wanted students to understand by the end of the course that the degree of personal initiative and work one exhibits is not the only factor affecting one's chances of "success" in this country; certain other factors — including discrimination — related to ethnicity, class, race, gender, and religion also exert a powerful influence.

II.

The course began with an exercise in definition. Students read "What Is an American?" from Hector St. Jean de Crèvecoeur's *Letters from an American Farmer* and were asked to make a list of those qualities they felt a person must have today to be considered an "American." We interrogated Crèvecoeur's text and noted that he includes only northern European immigrants, implicitly excludes women and Native Americans, and expects that an American will leave "behind him all his ancient prejudices and manners."[5] On the board we then listed the qualities they came up with and used these as a springboard for discussion. Can one *really* practice any religion one wants and be free from discrimination? Do you have to speak English? We then discussed how the "melting pot" theory applied to their lives, specifically to their class positions, and we examined what adjustments they had to make in habits, language, and ways of thinking in order to assimilate into the educated middle class.

Another nonfiction piece I used to advantage at the beginning of this course was an article by Billie Wright Dziech of the University of Cincinnati that had recently appeared in the *Chronicle of Higher Education:* "Coping with the Alienation of White Male Students." One of the key passages we discussed was this: "They have heard exhortations and sermons about the white-male, racist, Eurocentric hold on American history, but they have not always responded as we hoped they would. Outside of class, when they talk to parents, peers, and faculty members whom they trust, many of them say they are being forced to pay for history they had no part in and that they feel weary, angry, and alienated."[6] Discussion of this article sent a number of important signals to my students. First, it showed them that I was aware of the excesses multiculturalist education could be guilty of, and it allowed us to talk about how no one, including white males, likes to be stereotyped. Second, the article brought out into the open their feeling that professors sometimes try to ideologically influence students and inflict punishment (either through low grades or through other means) on those students who do not toe the liberal ideological line. Given the working-class and tenuously middle-class status of most of the students, it was not surprising that many felt professors and college administrators — whom they view as solidly middle-class — did not appreciate how affirmative action and other programs were threatening their dreams of middle-class status. Instead of belittling these feelings as white "whining," I seized the opportunity to stress that mine was a classroom where all viewpoints and concerns could be voiced freely without condemnation, either from the professor or from other students. Although I am sure that despite such assurances a number of students continued to conceal their true feelings, this discussion almost certainly helped preempt some of the apprehension students might have felt toward multicultural literature and toward me as a member of the professional class, thus making discussions more open and honest.

Selecting the proper fiction texts for this course was a difficult task. There are many works of fiction by or about first- or second-generation immigrants (my first criterion for inclusion), but it is essential to create a proper mix. First, one must have a balance of texts that are positive about the immigrant experience in America and those that present a more critical view. Choosing only texts that lambaste white Americans, I felt, would have sent my students running to hide behind their impermeable shields once again, possibly silently mouthing "Love it or leave it," with no understanding that one could love America even while pointing out where it needs improvement. Furthermore, it is necessary to choose texts that involve characters' transitions from working-class to middle-class status, because that allows students to see how, even when they are not of the same race or gender as the main characters, they might still have much in common with them because of their similar class situations. For these reasons I included not only texts that are parables of the steep price one must pay for trying to assimilate into middle-class America but also works that present the virtues of breaking away from one's class heritage.

In addition, I tried to select texts that demonstrated a wide range of individual experiences *within* particular ethnic and class groups. In Mary Doyle Curran's *The Parish and the Hill* (1948) and Claude McKay's *Home to Harlem* (1928) there are open interethnic conflicts; in the former these are among Irish immigrants, and in the latter they are between native-born African Americans and West Indian immigrants. Mario Puzo's *The Fortunate Pilgrim* (1965), too, portrays a great diversity of experience among Italian immigrants and their children. These works also indicate how working-class people are not all the same but instead possess a variety of individual characteristics. Such texts serve well my purpose of helping students to view members of different ethnic and class groups as individuals rather than as stereotypes. Finally, when it came to the particular ethnic groups represented in the texts, I made sure to mix those that were more familiar to them, such as the Irish and Italians, with those about which they knew almost nothing, such as the Chinese, West Indians, Jews, and Indians.

Probably the most important texts to include are those that deal with the immigrant experiences of the majority of one's students. At Cortland a great number of my students have an Irish and/or an Italian heritage, although few have much knowledge about their heritages. I presented *The Parish and the Hill* first, not only because the Irish were the first major immigrant group to challenge America to live up to its ideals and promises, but also because it is highly readable and I hoped it would engage the interest of students who would be surprised to find their own ancestors included in a "multicultural" course.

The Parish and the Hill, narrated by Mary O'Connor, a second-generation American of Irish descent, chronicles the experiences of the O'Sullivan and O'Connor families in an industrial New England city in the late nineteenth and early twentieth centuries. My students are fascinated by this tale, and many tell me they have recommended it to their parents or grandparents to read. In it they learn that even against these "white" people there was housing segregation (the "Parish" section for "Shanty Irish," as opposed to the "Hill," where "Lace Curtain" Irish mixed with established, Yankee Protestant families), language discrimination (those with brogues had difficulty getting jobs), and most of all, religious discrimination. Students are especially surprised to learn that the Irish did not all band together but instead fractured into groupings based on class, and that Lace Curtain Irish often sided with the Yankees in order to gain favor. In an attempt to counter the prevalent sentiment of, "My ancestors assimilated and succeeded with no problems" (and thus, by implication, so should today's immigrants and racial minorities), I draw attention to how some characters in the book — most notably James O'Connor and Mary's Aunt Hannah — try to assimilate into the Yankee, Protestant, middle-class world but are either rejected or suffer a painful loss of identity. Many of my students, who long for the "Lace Curtain" middle-class respectability of today's suburbia, readily identify with those who wish to move to the "Hill" and enter that world, but this novel forces them to consider whether that is as desirable or easily accomplished as they imagine it will be. The most positive character is the narrator's grandfather, John O'Sullivan, who is a paradigm of working-class solidarity and tolerance for others. At one point when some Irish complain about how the Poles are threatening to take their jobs, John declares that "it will do no good to be fighting with them. It's what the Yankees may be looking for. They're great dividers of the opposition, as you well know, setting one half of a country against another. You've all seen the waste in that."[7] One long class discussion focused on this quotation and the question of whether in the United States today the upper-class people in power are still trying to maintain their privilege by turning white working- and middle-class people against immigrants and persons of color.

Most important to my purposes, *The Parish and the Hill* introduced the idea that even white people are not all the same, for they can have both class and ethnic loyalties that distinguish them from one another, and thus that "whiteness" itself is a socially constructed category. What one student wrote in a paper on this topic was representative: "Coming from a middle-class, Christian community and being male caucasian I have grown up believing the term 'ethnic' does not apply to my family or myself. The term 'ethnic' as I understand it has come to mean being a member of a minority within a larger group in a society based on either race, religion, or in some cases, even gender. By this definition I find it difficult to refer to myself as being 'ethnic' in any way." We discussed at length why neither they nor American society in general now regarded whites as "ethnic," using *The Parish and the Hill* to see how many Irish immigrants, widely regarded as members of an inferior race, were initially proud of their ethnicity but then usually found it more expedient to submerge it in order to blend in. Admittance to the middle class, I pointed out, was in large part the "carrot" offered to the Irish not only to get them to assimilate but also to turn them against darker-skinned white ethnics and African Americans (a subject explored in depth by Noel Ignatiev in his recent *How the Irish Became White*).[8] Only when their place among whites was secure, I noted, could the Irish afford to display their ethnicity publicly with St. Patrick's Day parades, green beer, and "Kiss Me, I'm Irish" bumper stickers. However, such security came with a price tag: breaking their class solidarity with other immigrants and African Americans.

In the classroom it was very helpful to have students recognize that their ancestors were once quite poor and that they, too, despite being white, are still sometimes influenced by their ethnicity and the class positions often associated with it; for this opened up possible avenues of empathy with members of various minority groups. They began to see that their ancestors were discriminated against because of their ethnicity and working-class behaviors and treated in some of the same ways many immigrants and "others" are treated today; the only difference is that today they, unlike their ancestors, are members of the more privileged group that holds power. The idea that whites have not always been seen as similar to one another was an idea quite new and striking to them, in part because, as Harvard educator Sara Stotsky writes, so few high school literature anthologies include works about European immigrants. As a result, she argues, students often mistakenly believe that those Americans "who are not members of [the] four [affirmative action] categories [African American, Latino/Latina, Asian, Native American] — those who supposedly belong to the 'mainstream' — are all of Anglo-Saxon stock and are all alike with respect to values, beliefs, and customs."[9] I would further posit that the exclusion of European immigrant texts from most students' education both in high school and college misleads them to believe that their ancestors smoothly integrated into American society and that today's immigrants and racial minorities should be able to do the same without causing so much "trouble."

I also highlighted the ethnicity of some of my white students with works of fiction about the experiences of Italian Americans. I used such Italian American short stories as John Fante's "Odyssey of a Wop" and Pietro di Donato's "Christ in Concrete" to introduce students to the painful discrimination encountered by working-class southern Italians and Sicilians, who in their minds were today part of the middle-class "white" race. The best work I have found to teach about Italian immigrants is Mario Puzo's *The Fortunate Pilgrim* (1965). Although much less well-known than his Mafia fiction (we discussed why such portrayals are more popular), this novel is a masterpiece of autobiographical insight into the diversity of Italian American experience in New York City's Hell's Kitchen during the 1920s and 1930s. Some of the working-class characters view formal, school-based education positively, whereas others do not; one drifts into organized crime; one family fraudulently obtains social relief checks; some wish to escape this world and do, while others fail; some women wish to assume traditional southern Italian roles, and others wish to carve a more independent identity for themselves. Many of these behaviors, we noted, derive from their class backgrounds and insecure economic situations. Discrimination is not blatant but it is always there as an undercurrent; these "swarthy" people with poor English language skills, dirty houses, and too many children are seen as very different from the "true" Americans and are scorned by the assimilated middle-class Italians in the book, Dr. Barbato and La Fortezza the social worker. Many students were quick to identify the Italians as the Latino/Latina immigrants of today: European and "white," yet viewed as different and discriminated against as a result. Such insights helped inform later discussion of such Latino short stories as Virgil Suarez's "Miami during the Reagan Years" and Nash Candelaria's "El Patròn."

The Fortunate Pilgrim was generally well liked by my students, not only because they recognized many of the Italian American "types" from their own lives, but also because it illustrates the hardships one encounters when trying to break away from a close-knit working-class family and community. The daughter Octavia, for example, tries to use education as her means of escape but is drawn back by the sense of family responsibility. La Fortezza and Dr. Barbato gain more education than Octavia, earning a law degree and a medical degree, respectively; thus, they would appear to have attained the middle-class status the other characters so eagerly work for. Yet La Fortezza's law degree gets him nothing more than a social work job where he has to rely on kickbacks to make a living, and Dr. Barbato suffers in a no-man's-land, accepted neither by the Italian working-class community nor by the powerful Anglo world. Many of the working-class characters, indeed, resent these middle-class professionals' telling them what to do. The son Gino — the figure of Puzo — successfully escapes via military service, but it is implied that he will eventually feel nostalgic for the world he leaves behind. Many of my students could identify with such characters who lack a sense of "belonging" because they themselves were in between class and sometimes ethnic worlds. By bringing these feelings to the surface, I believe that I helped them feel greater affinity with those many upwardly mobile members of minority groups today who also feel torn between two worlds. In many ways, too, the various trajectories of these characters also problematized my students' faith that hard work and education would always — and easily — lead to happiness, making them realize that it is often quite difficult to escape the attitudes toward education, obligation to family networks, gender roles, and so forth that characterize not only Italian American life but also working- and lower-middle-class life.

By far the most popular text in the course, Anzia Yezierska's *Bread Givers,* also concerns white ethnics, but ones who are non-Christians. It does not surprise me that students rave about this story of how Sara Smolinsky overcomes her poverty-stricken life on Hester Street and her strict Jewish Orthodox father to achieve her dream of becoming a schoolteacher. Even though almost all of my students come from either Protestant or Catholic backgrounds, they strongly identify with Sara because like many of them, in her quest for education, self-fulfillment, and middle-class "respectability," she suffers abuse from her friends and family for trying to make herself "better" than they are. One student unhappily concluded in an essay, "I have, like Sara, devoted much of my time to going to school, and because of that, I have had to face many difficulties in my personal relationships and have become emotionally distant from members of my family." As will be seen later, this student was not alone in looking past Sara's ethnicity and identifying with her on the basis of class and family similarities.

Between *The Parish and the Hill* and *The Fortunate Pilgrim* we read and discussed Maxine Hong Kingston's *China Men.* I had high hopes for this novel, especially for the way in which it weaves together history and fiction and shows how hard work is not always sufficient for working-class people to overcome racism. This is pointedly shown in one scene where BaBa, the narrator's father and the operator of a small laundry, feels impotent in the face of a white gypsy woman's charges of fraudulent practices. Confined by his lack of English skills and his desperate desire to hold onto his tenuous middle-class status as the owner of a small store, BaBa is forced to pay "damages" to the woman because she can speak English and enlists the aid of a policeman, the enforcer of white, middle-class regulations. Unfortunately, *China Men* met with hearty disapproval from almost all of my students. To some extent that is probably because it deals with a group more "alien" to them; in their lifetimes they have encountered many fewer Chinese Americans than Italian, Irish, or Jewish Americans. However, I ascribe its unpopularity primarily to its complex narrative structure, which provoked numerous bewildered, negative comments.

For one of the semesters during which I taught this course, I used Jamaican-born Claude McKay's *Home to Harlem* (1928), because it challenges stereotypes not only of African Americans and West Indians but also of men and women. Students are exposed to a wide variety of individual "black" experiences. The book focuses on the relationship between Jake, a native-born African American who served in World War I and deserted because of the racism he experienced at the hands of fellow soldiers, and Ray, an educated Haitian immigrant. Jake is initially concerned primarily with sensual pleasures of various types, whereas Ray is more interested in intellectual pursuits; this contrast does not remain static throughout the novel, however, with each realizing that the ideal is to blend an appreciation for each lifestyle and set of values. *Home to Harlem* also allowed me to make the link between the difficulties Ray as an immigrant encounters in trying to assimilate into "American" society and those Jake experiences as a native-born black person trying to make his way in a white-controlled culture that is equally foreign and hostile to him. As with *The Fortunate Pilgrim,* students see that for some people, education is not sufficient to gain happy entrance and acceptance into the white middle class. In fact Ray, with all his education, eventually leaves the United States because he realizes that whites will always judge him by the color of his skin, not by his intelligence. Finally, I used this book because, despite its extensive portrayal of the differences and antagonisms among blacks in America, it embodies a positive message of the desirability of a racial unity that transcends class distinctions. John O'Connor's warning about the Irish playing into the hands of the Yankees by fighting among themselves or against the Poles is very relevant here, and thus I connected the Irish experience to the African American. Students thereby began to understand that white prejudice is in large part responsible for prompting many people of color to band together along racial lines for security, whether it be in political organizations or in groups of students at certain tables in the dining hall. Unfortunately, of course, this usually discourages whites who share their socioeconomic class conditions from mixing with these people of color.

Somewhat surprising to me was my students' positive reception of *Jasmine* by Bharati Mukherjee, which I substituted one semester for *Home to Harlem*, because their reaction in general to texts about people of color was not as enthusiastic as for works about white ethnics. One might argue that the response to *Jasmine* can be partially explained by the fact that Indians occupy an ambivalent racial position and are not numerous enough in America to represent an economic or cultural threat. More likely, though, students like *Jasmine* so much because, like *Bread Givers,* it emphasizes the necessity of severing one's ties to an ethnic past and an inherited class position in order to achieve American success. This coincides with my students' generally conservative outlook that "you can't expect to get something without losing something of who you are." They see Jyoti (a.k.a. Jasmine) as positively, not negatively, transformed by America. Moreover, she undergoes that transformation willingly, because she comes to view America as a great opportunity to shed what she believes are the oppressive practices and stifling beliefs of her home country (India) and the Hindu religion. In class terms, she is a successful "climber," starting as a penniless immigrant left on a Florida beach, who subsequently becomes a housekeeper and nanny for a yuppie family on New York's upper west side, a bank teller in Iowa, a prosperous banker's wife, and finally the future wife of a Berkeley physics professor. Along the way Jasmine makes a number of criticisms about America and its people, but because she ultimately does embrace America, my students, instead of dismissing her for her lack of patriotism, tended to be willing to at least consider the accuracy of her criticisms. My students liked this book also, I believe, because Jasmine does not dwell on what she has lost through her class-climbing and assimilation. Interestingly enough, when students read *Bread Givers* early in the semester, they were unwilling to acknowledge the "negatives" of Sara Smolinsky's assimilation that Yezierska highlights; however, by the time they read *Jasmine* they were much more willing and able to identify the "negatives" of Jasmine's assimilation, even though neither she nor Mukherjee fully acknowledges them.

III.

In addition to our class discussions of the fiction texts themselves, for one class period before we began consideration of each immigrant/ethnic group, I asked students to engage in an exercise designed to establish what they believed about the groups and also to educate them about these ethnic cultures. I put two questions on the board: "What do you know about this group of immigrants?"

and "What are the prevalent ideas in American culture about these immigrants and their descendants?" I deliberately phrased the second question so that students did not feel they were being asked for *their* stereotypes, for they have been trained quite well to avoid being seen, especially by professors, as politically incorrect. Instead, they could make comments anonymously, as if these were just things they had heard or seen somewhere. Students then broke into groups of four or five to construct lists of responses. These small groups are essential, because students participate more actively in them than in the larger class setting, and also because they are more willing to "test the waters" with a certain stereotype or received impression in a small group than in a large group. I made it clear to students before they started that stereotypes, personal experiences, epithets, movie and television portrayals, and so forth could be included in the latter list. After fifteen to twenty minutes of brainstorming and constructing these lists, students were invited to remake the large circle for class discussion.

Not surprisingly, the amount of real "knowledge" about various ethnic groups was quite small, whereas the number of "impressions" and stereotypes was quite large. Despite one's own feelings about what students say, however, it is essential that one list these stereotypes and impressions and discuss them in a nonjudgmental way. To do otherwise is to invite distrust and to end all frank discussion later in the course. In response to the lack of solid knowledge about any group, I often used the occasion to deliver a minilecture on the immigration of a particular group to the United States, including why they came, where they settled, what occupations they assumed, how American society reacted to them, and what their status is today. Even though discrimination is often evident in the fiction texts, I used these informational classes to preview how all immigrant groups have suffered discrimination against their members for the ways in which they were different from or represented a "threat" to established Americans.

IV.

Some of the writing assignments for this course explicitly dealt with how authors use certain literary tools such as narrative voice, metaphor, and so forth. Others, though, sought to lead students to understand their own ethnicity or lack thereof, how they might relate to people from cultures different from their own, and the similarities and differences between characters from different ethnic groups. Fortunately, most students were willing to share the thoughts from their own papers during class discussion; even when they were reluctant to do so, though, at least three other members of the class had the chance to read an individual's paper during a required editing session.

For the first paper of the semester I asked students to write on the topic "Why my ethnic/religious/racial heritage does or doesn't play a significant role in my life." As an option, students who did not identify with any particular heritage(s) could write about why they felt American. Using Crèvecoeur's essay as a base, these latter students were invited to define a new American ethnicity by telling what attitudes that they possessed and practices that they followed made them American. Thus, students who were so completely assimilated that they had no idea of their ethnicity or heritage (many described themselves as "mongrels" or "mutts"), or who resisted acknowledging their ethnicity, still had the opportunity for self-analysis.

About 80 percent of students did end up writing about how their various heritages did or did not play a role in their lives. For many students, this was the first time they had been asked to examine such questions. Typical of their age, many had never looked into their family history. One of the things I hoped they would learn from this assignment was how despite the American myth of self-creation, who they were—their attitudes, customs, and so forth—to some extent depended on their ethnic heritage and the socioeconomic class positions often predicted by that heritage. This, then, should give them an idea of how members of some ethnic and class groups might be unwilling to, or find it difficult to, change practices that do not coincide with those the mainstream middle-class culture dictates are necessary for "success." Furthermore, students began to understand that when their family members became "American" (and possibly middle-class), they usually lost something, whether it was the family name, the language, long-held customs, or even a sense of rootedness in the world. In the same way, they saw that their personal goals involving class mobility would probably have a similar cost.

At times, students found recognition of their ethnic ties unsettling. One student wrote about how, unfortunately, her younger brother had become a skinhead white supremacist by embracing one part of their German heritage. For most, though, the assignment led to a more positive attitude toward their own ethnicity. It pleased me greatly to hear from students that they had had long talks with their parents or grandparents in preparation for writing the paper. One student, over six months after completing the course, wrote to me, "After taking the course my attitude towards my own personal ethnicity has changed in . . . that I feel a stronger affiliation. Writing essays about my ethnicity [Italian] gave me a sense of pride that I don't think I would have had otherwise. In the process of gathering information for my essays, I created a closer bond with my family because we shared stories and I learned more about my past." Most striking was what one student found out after the death of her great-grandmother. Up until just a few months before, this student had "always

[been] under the impression that my family was largely of German descent, with some Scottish thrown in," but her paternal great-grandmother, whose maiden name the family had always thought was Adams, had then died. Among her personal effects the student's great-aunt had found immigration papers from 1907, showing that in fact her great-grandmother was an Irish immigrant. The student wrote, "I find that learning about my background after so much mystery to be quite settling. I feel like I belong and I am accepted for who I am and what I've come from." Fortunately for the class, this student shared her discovery and sentiments during discussion of *The Parish and the Hill,* and it was wonderful to have a real-life example to reinforce how so many Irish suppressed their ethnicity and working-class background to "fit in."

Just as I had hoped, too, some students began to realize that some of their traits could be traced to their ethnic roots, and that despite the American mythology on the subject, one is rarely able to completely construct one's own identity and behavior free from inherited tendencies, not only of one's ethnicity but also of one's class. One student wrote, "Before I began analyzing which aspects of my personality were Italian and which were Irish I didn't fully grasp the impact my ethnic heritage has had on who I am today. . . . I realize now that the characteristics that make up the person I am are pieces of my Nana, my Papa and my mother. Each time from now on when I look in the mirror, I will not just see myself, but a piece of each person who has made me who I am today." Students who make such connections, I hope, will be less likely to argue that more recent immigrants and people of color should be forced to disassociate themselves from their ethnic and class heritages in order to achieve "success," or that such a change can be accomplished easily.

Another writing assignment asked students to compare their personal or family experiences with those of one character or family portrayed in the literary works. This assignment was designed to help students explore possible affinities with people who on the surface appear to have nothing in common with them. I did not wish to have students ignore how race, gender, class, religion, and ethnicity can affect one's experiences in America, but at the same time I did not want students to feel as if they were writing about characters so completely different from them that they could not identify with them.

As noted previously, the character with whom most students closely identified was Sara Smolinsky, from *Bread Givers*. This identification often cut across boundaries of religion and class, for only a handful of my students are Jewish, and very few have experienced the oppressive poverty Sarah grows up with. Students generally ignored how Sara wished to distance herself from her father's orthodox Judaism and instead identified with her simply because she wished to escape a tyrannical father. One male student wrote, "The situation in my family was very similar to Sara's. My father always ran my life and my siblings' lives." This student recalled that when he decided to go away to college, his father, like Reb, "was not happy with my decision, but just as Sara did, I did what I thought was right for me." This parental resistance is not surprising, because many of my students have working-class parents who never attended college and are possibly of two minds about their children's college education. After all, though this education will probably help their children achieve middle-class security, it will also most likely change the beliefs, values, and practices that the parents taught them. Students are generally less ambivalent about the value of education; one wrote, "Education is important to me because it also allows me [like Sara] to break away from my parents and my responsibilities at home." The pain involved in Sara's climb to middle-class respectability also struck a chord with these students. One child of a single parent living in a wealthy Long Island suburb (ironically, a suburb that is predominantly Jewish) told of how bad she felt being surrounded by wealthier people and wrote, "I help my mom with the bills when she does not have quite enough money to cover them. I can really understand Sara and her sisters' lifestyle. While they were far worse off than I, the principles and feelings involved are the same. You make the best with what you have, and are thankful you have something."

The third writing assignment was more open-ended, asking students to compare two characters from different books in terms of their dreams, ambitions, achievements, regrets, and so forth—as well as the obstacles they encountered—in America. This assignment reinforced what we often did in classroom discussions, which was to ask what types of continuities they saw between, say, the American reaction to the Irish and to the Chinese, the role education plays in Jewish, Italian, and African American life, the treatment of working-class people, whatever their ethnicity, the prevalent gender expectations among various ethnic groups, and so forth. One student compared the fathers BaBa from *China Men* and Frank Corbo from *The Fortunate Pilgrim,* arguing that although "they seem to be very different men on the surface . . . when one looks deeper into these characters one can see that both came to America because they were unhappy in their countries, and while attempting to take on family responsibilities, suffered depression that they could not handle." Another compared Mary O'Connor, narrator of *The Parish and the Hill,* with the unnamed narrator of *China Men,* for both consider "assimilation to be distressful." A third student contrasted the ways in which Hannah O'Sullivan of *The Parish and the Hill* and Octavia Angeluzzi of *The Fortunate Pilgrim* try to Americanize themselves, detailing how Octavia finds a way to do so without losing her sense of self, whereas Hannah cannot.

V.

Gauging the "success" of this course is extremely difficult. As educators we well know that seeds planted during one semester may not bear fruit until many years or even decades later. I believe that the effectiveness of the immigrant fiction approach is quite evident in many of the quotations from student essays cited above. But in an attempt to ascertain some students' recalled reactions to this course, I E-mailed those former students whose addresses I could find and gave hard-copy questionnaires to other former students whom I ran into on campus. The questions included "factual" ones as well as "evaluative" ones, such as: "Did this course in any way change your attitude toward your own personal ethnicity?" and "Did your definition and/or attitude toward any specific ethnic group change as a result of taking this class?" The answers to these questions are sketchy and incomplete at best, though, for although I emphasized in the questionnaire that I wanted to hear all viewpoints, I assume that students who strongly disliked the course or whose attitudes toward ethnic minorities had not changed at all simply did not respond.

Corroborating what I have recounted earlier, many students responded that they had indeed changed their attitudes toward their own ethnicity. I was also pleased by the response to the question whether the course had changed their attitudes toward people of other cultures within the United States. Some offered only a terse "The course did broaden my views on other ethnicities" or "The course didn't change my views any, it just opened me up to different aspects of other people's ethnicities"; others elaborated a bit more. One wrote, "I think I gained a lot more respect for ethnic groups, overall, who chose to come to America and start a new life. They knew the struggles involved and came anyway." Another stated, "I think that I have just become more understanding overall of different ethnic groups. The knowledge that your class helped me acquire has let me become more understanding about what different ethnic groups have gone through here in the U.S." Finally, one respondent from a rural upstate village acknowledged that "Jewish people are portrayed in the media as being wealthy and in comfortable occupations, and [our study of] *Bread Givers* made me realize that this is not always true now and especially during this period of history."

Possibly most pleasing to me was a lengthy response by one female student that indicated that the connections I attempted to make between ethnicity and class had struck home with some students. She wrote that she had begun "to feel much less distinction between people of different cultures and more of a connection to others as human beings above all else," and that she had started "to change [her] opinion on the poor." Elaborating, she stated, "I always tended to look at the poor and feel sorry for their condition but wonder why they didn't try to change it. . . . Now I see there is a reason for this . . . [and] I am embarrassed that I ever felt this way when I have never had to go without anything that I have needed in my life."

Such a response is extremely gratifying to any instructor, and I would like to believe that a majority of my students would pen such sentiments if they only took the time. My suspicion, though, is that such is not the case. I found it extremely difficult myself to juggle the issues of race, ethnicity, and class simultaneously, and students probably found it equally difficult to make the connections between their experiences with class definition, discrimination, and assimilation and those of immigrants who had difficulty assimilating and who experienced discrimination because of language, religion, and race. However, using the immigrant fiction approach definitely had some positive results. Many students, for example, began to acknowledge the diversity among white Americans and see ways in which their own or their ancestors' experiences relate to those of immigrants and minorities today. At the end of the course, too, discussions indicated that a good number of students were more flexible in their requirements for "American" status, were more interested in discovering commonalities with people of "other" ethnic and class cultures, and were more likely to empathize with those going through the difficult process of assimilation. For these reasons, I will continue to use immigrant fiction as a theme, because I have found that overall, the "common ground" it represents is quite effective in building bridges between my students and people from cultures they know little or nothing about.

TEACHING THE CONVERGENCE OF RACE AND CLASS IN INTRODUCTORY ASIAN AMERICAN STUDIES

JOHN STREAMAS

Utter the phrase "model minority" before an Asian American and expect to see a frown or a sneer. Those words have stigmatized us for more than three decades now, trapping us in a double bind: they permit white Americans not only to laud our apparent success but also to prod us to keep achieving, and they can provoke resentment among other nonwhite Americans for our "playing a white man's game" and thus further marginalizing them. We would banish the phrase and its entrapments from our lexicons and our lives.

Yet a course in introductory Asian American studies must grapple with the phrase. For, like "manifest destiny" and "melting pot," it names an important idea that announces expansiveness and inclusiveness but that exacts the costs of marginalization and provisional assimilation. And, like those phrases, it is meant by whites to celebrate an inclusiveness that helps define an "American Dream" come true. For what could be more gloriously American than a whole community's "pulling itself up by its own bootstraps," as Japanese Americans apparently did after World War II? This was the message of sociologist William Petersen, who, though he might not have invented the term *model minority* and its idea, certainly expressed it most openly and influentially in a 1966 article for the *New York Times Magazine*.[1] To be sure, Petersen fully understood the enormous injustice of the wartime internment of Japanese Americans. He even applied the proper but—by 1966 standards—controversial term *concentra-*

tion camps to name the sites of imprisonment.² But it was this knowledge, contrasted so radically with what he perceived as unparalleled success, that prompted his astonishment. "Japanese Americans are better than any other group in our society, including native-born whites," he wrote; and then he explained the significance of this achievement: "They have established this remarkable record, moreover, by their own almost totally unaided effort. Every attempt to hamper their progress resulted only in enhancing their determination to succeed. Even in a country whose patron saint is the Horatio Alger hero, there is no parallel to this success story."³

By 1982 the term *model minority* applied more generally to all Asian Americans, and it was popular enough to name us in the title of a *Newsweek* article. To be fair, the article does enclose the term in quotation marks, and it acknowledges problems such as underemployment, Chinatown sweatshops, the hardships of Hmong refugees, and violence aimed at Vietnamese immigrants. Yet it opens with a profile of Connie Chung's fortunes and closes with a Koreatown realtor's exulting, "The future's so bright."⁴ In this way the irony of framing "model minority" in quotation marks is reversed: *Newsweek* would have us believe that—a few problems notwithstanding—we really *are* a model minority. Like Petersen, then, *Newsweek* invokes familiar but still impressive statistics on comparative incomes and educational achievement; and, like Petersen, it ascribes to us old mythical virtues of a pre-Asian whiteness: "Asians believe they are contributing a needed shot of some vanishing American values: thrift, strong family ties, sacrifice for the children."⁵

The "model minority" stereotype is everywhere. For several years, when I taught freshman English and casually mentioned on the first day of class my Japanese American ethnicity, students of non-Asian ethnicities expressed admiration of Asian Americans. Today, even conservative white students express disgust over the internment of Japanese Americans with a glibness made possible by their admiration of model minority success.

This is what confronts us in Asian American studies. Our students see people named Wang, Tanaka, Kapur, and Kim living in "good" neighborhoods, working as engineers and surgeons, sending their children to prestigious schools. Some of these children are graduate assistants teaching freshman-level math and science classes. Our students thus see the stereotype in the flesh. Then perhaps they see statistics suggesting that Japanese Americans, Chinese Americans, and South Asian Americans generally prosper not only more than other nonwhite groups but also more than whites. Surely they know that the stereotype is not a perfect fit to reality. A few may know about the hardships of Southeast Asian immigrants, particularly the Hmong. A few may connect Japan-bashing to anti-Asian hostilities, seeing a link between, on one hand, Senator Hollings's atomic-bomb "joke" and, on the other, the murders of Vincent Chin and a Japanese exchange student.[6] More are likely to know the tensions surrounding immigrant Vietnamese fishermen or immigrant Korean shopkeepers, or the exploitation of immigrant Asians in urban sweatshops. Many of our students, especially those from cities, have actually *seen* Asian Americans who are not prospering. Yet all these qualifications must seem like deviations from a norm to many students entering our introductory Asian American studies course, students who have never been asked to analyze critically the model minority stereotype. When they see a Benetton ad or another promoter's exploitative multicultural fantasy, surely they believe that the most comfortable-looking "minorities" are those with Asian faces. And they are less surprised by success in an "upper-class" sport of an Asian American such as Michael Chang or Kristi Yamaguchi than by the success of an African American such as Zina Garrison or Arthur Ashe.[7] They may even be unsurprised by an apparently conservative cast in Asian American politics: the conservative vote in the 1992 presidential election, for example, or an ambivalence over affirmative action, or involvement in soliciting large sums of money toward political campaigns.[8] Our students are thus unlikely to view Asian Americans as active participants in a class struggle, unless perhaps as defenders of — and aspirants to — a ruling elite. Before we can help them deflate the model minority thesis, we must construct a credible critique of the racialized class structure.

Racism is less a manifestation of hate than it is an exercise of power. This is a difficult lesson to learn and, once learned, an easy lesson to forget as we still see police officers beating black motorists and crazed veterans entering schoolyards to murder immigrant Asian children. Less sensational but more pervasive issues of unequal funding for schools, the "glass ceiling," and the curtailment of social programs in the name of budget-cutting. The cruel irony of these issues is that, though they permeate the institutional structures with which we daily interact, they resist efforts to understand them in recognizable, palpable terms of race and class. Moreover, the dominant group co-opts the language of racial justice to de-racialize the issues. Thus Proposition 209 in California, meant to end the state's affirmative action programs, was named the "California Civil Rights Initiative," and it stated in its main clause that California "should not discriminate against, or grant preferential treatment to, any individual or group on the basis of race, sex, color, ethnicity, or national origin."[9] Such language in the 1960s would have aimed at equality on the assumption that whites (and males) discriminate to gain unfair advantage; such language in the 1990s can only assume that nonwhites (and women) now discriminate to gain unfair advantage. But such advantage translates into power — in a capitalist culture, into *economic* power. Yet, as we see, not even the "model minority" realizes such power. A study by the organization Leadership Education for

Asian Pacifics reveals that white men "are 85 percent of tenured professors, 85 percent of partners in major law firms, . . . 95 percent of the Fortune 500 CEOs."[10] Only when we understand—and teach—racism as a function of power can we begin to rebut "white backlash." Where is the "model minority" when 95 percent of Fortune 500 CEOs are white men?

Not coincidentally, it was white men who invented the *model minority* label and attached it to us. In so naming us, they have claimed the right to tell our story—to recast it in the mold of European immigration. Hardships in the homeland brought us here, the story goes, just as they brought Europeans. The immigrant generation struggled and sacrificed in various ways—the white mythmakers consider the internment of Japanese Americans as a variant on economic hardships endured by, say, Irish and Italian immigrants—but left a better America for their children, who would enter college, graduate into business, and enjoy middle-class comfort. By telling our story as a mere variant on the European immigration story, these white men de-racialize us. Whereas in the real America the phrase *model minority* is a cruel oxymoron, white mythmakers de-racialize it and reconstruct us as virtual Europeans. In this way they foreclose the possibility of our complaints of glass ceilings and other economic injustices. Therefore, like the novelists and memoirists named below, we must take back our stories. We must discard old Eurocentrist immigration myths and construct our own immigration histories.

Such new construction constitutes much of the project of Lisa Lowe's important book *Immigrant Acts: On Asian American Cultural Politics*. One of Lowe's purposes is to note that, unlike European Americans, Asian Americans live with a sense that their lives and cultures are circumscribed by the state "through the apparatus of immigration laws and policies, through the enfranchisements denied or extended to immigrant individuals and communities, and through the processes of naturalization and citizenship." Another is to stress that "immigration has been a crucial *locus* through which U.S. interests have recruited and regulated both labor and capital from Asia."[11]

One of Lowe's considerable achievements is the integrating of many valuable studies of Asian American labor. A claim underlying her work is the inseparability of concerns of race, class, and gender. For example, she argues that "the concentration of women of color in domestic service or reproductive labor (child care, home care, nursing) in the contemporary United States is not adequately explained by a nation-based model of analysis," as she refers readers to the studies by Evelyn Nakano Glenn of Japanese American women in domestic service.[12] Glenn's discovery is notable: "I realized that the case of Japanese American women could be used to address broad issues related to the labor systems of capitalist economics, the role of immigrant and racial-ethnic women in those systems, and the consequences of race- and gender-stratified labor systems for the family and cultural systems of minority groups."[13] The original "model minority" is therefore no model at all but simply another minority. That Glenn could study domestic labor across three generations of Japanese American women testifies further to the broader implications of her study. Another book cited by Lowe is the collection of essays titled *The New Asian Immigration in Los Angeles and Global Restructuring*, one of whose editors, Edna Bonacich, contributes an examination of the garment industry. Bonacich notes that some Asian immigrants in the industry are contractors, "small business owners who contract from manufacturers to do the cutting and sewing" and who "directly employ labor."[14] Although some critics praise this "triumph" of "entrepreneurship," Bonacich more properly regards it as a second tier of exploitation, in which manufacturers entice a few "lucky" nonwhite contractors to do the "dirty work" of managing the truly oppressed laborers. Bonacich concludes, "The garment industry reveals starkly some of the problems of capitalism and how it helps construct racial and ethnic antagonisms."[15]

We can begin our course with stories.

Those of us who have taught ethnic studies surveys or similar courses in a university whose white students have, for reasons of geography or class, had little or no contact with nonwhites must surely be impressed by the impact on our classes of nonwhite or non-mainstream guest speakers. Even allowing for the fact that guest speakers represent a break in routine or even for the possibility that our guests may be better teachers than we are, still we must heed our students' observations that our guests provide a helpful — and necessary — new perspective. One of my students wrote, "It helps to see and talk to someone that experiences discrimination on a daily basis," and another noted that "when we had guest speakers talking about their ethnicity and their personal experiences, that helped me understand more." Although alternative perspectives are helpful in any course, they are particularly valuable in a course on race and ethnicity. Any such semester-long course is vastly improved by two or three guests. My ethnic studies survey students were treated to a presentation on Appalachian peoples by my friend Judy Gussler, who spoke both professionally as an anthropologist and personally as a "hill person." Students were impressed by her stories: she has escaped rural poverty and its attendant suffering, but she made clear that many good people in Appalachia still struggle to survive poverty and despair. Students would never get this from our textbook, not just because it ignores Appalachian peoples but also because it covers various ethnic histories with demographics and with sweeping historical overviews. Whether by choice or expediency or perceived necessity, our book, like many others, tells no individual or family stories. Perhaps its author assumes that such storytelling risks exceptionalism, valorizing the individual over the group, and thus inadvertently validating mainstream myths of the triumph of rugged individualism. The assumption is understandable, given the mainstream "white bread" versions of the lives of such nonwhite figures as Jim Thorpe, Pocahantas, and Martin Luther King Jr. But we foreclose the possibility of such mainstreaming when we allow marginalized peoples to speak for themselves, to tell their own stories. In his memoir *Angela's Ashes*, the Irish writer Frank McCourt remembers thinking as a child, "I wonder what kind of world is it where anyone can sing anyone else's song."[16] And so our guest speakers sing their own songs, tell their own stories. Even if their stories bring them a triumph that is uncommon among their communities, still their struggles differ radically from the struggles of mainstream Horatio Alger–like heroes. Theirs is a struggle against a white middle-class culture whose institutions are constructed to oppress their people. Therefore the achievement of a Zora Neale Hurston may be individual and unique, but her struggle is representative and familiar. Perhaps our textbooks, if we read them charitably, aim for a solidarity in generalizations; but still we need the flesh and blood and song of stories. In stories our students will confront the convergence of race and class.

These stories take different forms: oral histories, memoirs, fiction. The first story my students hear is my own. I immigrated as an infant. My mother is a war bride. The Second World War ended her education when she was a young girl, and so years later, in the United States, when she and my American soldier-father divorced, having little English and little schooling, she came to depend on public assistance. This is not a Japanese American model minority success story of the sort William Petersen wrote about. But she was no anomaly. One of her friends was another young Japanese American single mother on welfare. Other Japanese American friends lived at the low end of the working class. As a child growing up in the 1960s in Hamilton, Ohio, I knew these Japanese Americans and no others—certainly none of Petersen's thriving model minority overachievers. My mother, my brother, and I lived in a welfare neighborhood, grateful for low-cost school lunches and for a Christmas ham given us by the Salvation Army. My mother, when she remarried, found work in a school cafeteria. Her nine-month job never paid much better than minimum wage, though she was grateful for its benefits. My white grandparents drew on their savings to send me to college. My brother could not afford college. A friend from another welfare household, a Japanese American whose grades were at the top of his class, feared the real debt of loans and the moral debt of scholarships, and so he too passed up college. This was *my* Japanese American community. This is my story.

Other stories are coming into print. Joann Faung Jean Lee gathers brief oral histories in her book *Asian Americans*. Her interviewees range widely across ethnic, generational, and socioeconomic backgrounds; and her principal concerns are individual experiences, Americanization, and interracial relationships. The stories are helpful for our introductory Asian American studies students, who may register surprise when they read a biracial Japanese American lawyer's concession that, having a gold card, "I would say I don't experience prejudice, but I think that's because of my economic status."[17] Two other useful collections include *Hmong Means Free,* historian Sucheng Chan's gathering of the stories of Hmong refugees, and *East to America,* a gathering by Elaine Kim and Eui-Young Yu of the stories of Korean immigrants: these are important books because their subjects, Hmong Americans and Korean Americans, have been victims of cruel stereotyping and racial and economic oppression.[18] While these books provide useful supplements, an essential book for this introductory course is the anthology *The State of Asian America,* edited by Karin Aguilar–San Juan.[19] Here we find both personal stories and many essays whose oppositional perspective — which may startle some students — builds a prescriptive platform for activism.

Asian American memoirs and autobiographies are accumulating, too. Most of the recent ones — by such writers as Lydia Minatoya, Garrett Hongo, and David Mura — are the work of Chinese Americans or Japanese Americans who are professional middle-class writers.[20] Older books by former internees may also be written from a middle-class perspective, but the internment story argues loudly that class warfare is a powerful tool of a capitalist racism. Regardless of wealth or income, Japanese Americans living on the West Coast in early 1942 were given little time to prepare for departure and still less opportunity to secure their belongings. In her memoir *Desert Exile,* Yoshiko Uchida recalls her exasperated mother's asking, "How can we clear out in ten days a house we've lived in for fifteen years?"[21] And in a memoir first published in 1953, Monica Sone remembers that her mother "distributed sheets, pillowcases, and blankets, which we stuffed into seabags. . . . The one seabag and two suitcases apiece were going to be the backbone of our future home."[22] In effect, evacuees could take no more than they could carry. Many of them lost everything they left behind. But of course they all lost more than just property: they lost time and jobs and opportunities. And they lost their culture. The recovery that by 1966 so profoundly impressed William Petersen was made possible by the extent of what was lost. Thus a government policy impelled by "military necessity" and "national security" achieved instead the ends of class and cultural warfare. Almost literally overnight many Japanese Americans were expelled from the middle class. Their children might have rebounded to become Petersen's "model minority," but surely without blind faith in "American values," as memories of internment reminded them that all can vanish at the whim of a ruling class and race. This is why memoirs of camp, though usually written from a middle-class perspective, are rooted in a wariness and distrust of the mainstream master class. These memoirs may therefore be taught not only as critiques of institutional racism but also as warnings that race and class can converge in oppression.

We must not neglect the usefulness of fiction. As with memoirs, Japanese Americans' short stories of internment provide a useful starting point toward a critique of class. Among the best are Hisaye Yamamoto's stories, collected in *"Seventeen Syllables" and Other Stories,* which often depict prewar and postwar Japanese Americans as farmers, domestics, shopkeepers, and even gamblers, often in relationships with Latinos and African Americans, and which implicitly depict internees' enforced "de-classing" as a sign of class oppression.[23] Filipino American writers have also published indictments of the American class system. Most impressive is Carlos Bulosan, whose stories and essays and whose powerful book *America Is in the Heart*— "a popular-front allegory that articulates class, race, nation (ethnicity), and gender in a protean configuration"—reconstruct the sobering lessons of immigrant labor.[24] Though a literature of garment-industry sweatshops waits to be established, still Jean Fong Kwok's recent short story "Disguises" takes a promising step. In it an immigrant Chinese woman, knowing little English and still unfamiliar with New York's subway system, panics when she misses her stop and yet—late that night, finally returned home—calmly and gratefully stays up to repair a garment torn at the factory, "joining again the severed parts with thread."[25] Young Southeast Asian American writers are coming into print in literary magazines, and their stories too should undermine the model minority thesis.

A point must be made about recent popular and trendy books by such writers as Maxine Hong Kingston, Chang-rae Lee, Amy Tan, and Gish Jen. Some of these books expose oppression in Asian homelands but, written from a present middle-class perspective, do not sufficiently match this to exposures of class oppression in America. They tell important stories about racial politics, but their very popularity in a country that ignores class issues warns us that they do not readily lend themselves to studies of class.

The stories we do teach—oral histories, memoirs, and fictions—should be brief and diverse. And we should scatter them throughout the course. For, as this is an introductory course, we anchor our teaching to a central text, one of the popular and accessible histories of Asian Americans such as Ronald Takaki's *Strangers from a Different Shore* or Sucheng Chan's *Asian Americans: An Interpretive History.*[26] In the nature of such texts, these books are organized by chronology and ethnicity. This organizing principle complicates our study of class issues; for, after an opening chapter examines early Chinese and Japanese immigration, subsequent chapters observe *both* the hardships of new immigrant groups *and* the rising fortunes of settled groups. The brief oral histories and fictions can supplement and subvert the chronological survey. For example, I teach Kwok's sweatshop story "Disguises" early in the course, so that we may compare the economic oppressions of both contemporary immigrants and first immigrants. Late in the term, when chronology brings us to the exploitation of Korean Americans and new Southeast Asian immigrants, not only do we read Edna Bonacich's examination of the garment industry but we also review nineteenth-century laws that restricted immigrant Chinese labor. In this issue-centered course, knowing details of exclusion laws and affirmative action policies matters less than grasping patterns of class oppression. Personal stories raise this awareness to the level of flesh and blood.

We offer stories, and we analyze. For we must at last confront the model minority perception with the very kind of information that constructs it. To be sure, some statistics released in the early 1990s by the Census Bureau would make William Petersen gloat. For example, among Asian and Pacific Americans (APAs) twenty-five years old and older, 39 percent had attended four or more years of college, compared to 22 percent among whites.[27] Furthermore, median family income for APAs was $42,245, compared to $36,915 for whites.[28] Is Petersen then correct? Surely somewhere a cynical capitalist suggests that a healthy income offsets unhealthy discrimination. A less cynical observer suggests that these statistics corroborate the stereotype.

In rebuttal we begin with a few offsetting and contextualizing statistics. For example, while in 1990 nearly 66 percent of Asian Indian Americans had achieved at least an undergraduate degree, among Hmong and other Laotian Americans the figure was only 7 percent.[29] Furthermore, household income had to provide for larger families: among all U.S. groups the average family had 3.2 persons, but the average Asian American family contained 3.8 persons, and more particularly the average Hmong family had 6.6 persons. Not surprisingly, then, the average Asian American family had more members in the workforce: 13 percent of all U.S. families but 20 percent of Asian American families had three or more workers; in Filipino American families the figure was 30 percent.[30] A stunning comparison of two Asian American groups in 1990 bears making: Japanese American families were less than half the size of Hmong American families, yet while Japanese Americans, with a poverty rate of 7 percent, earned $19,373 per capita, Hmong Americans earned only $2,692 per capita with a 64 percent rate of poverty.[31] Although Hmong immigrants occupy a small portion of Asian America, Southeast Asian immigrants generally are among the nation's fastest-growing ethnic groups. Overall, despite the above-cited and much-publicized figures on median incomes, APAs' per capita income of $13,420 was significantly below whites' $15,270. And, still more significantly, while 8 percent of white families lived in poverty in 1990, the figure for APAs was 11 percent.[32] These numbers tell us, if nothing else, to guard against applying the stereotype to all Asian American ethnic groups. Southeast Asian Americans are, for example, enjoying little model minority success even as their populations grow much faster than most established Asian Americans' numbers. By the end of the 1990s Vietnamese Americans will be the third-largest APA group — Filipino Americans will be the largest — and Japanese Americans, who were the largest APA group up to 1970, will be only sixth-largest.[33] Numbers alone can therefore usefully remind us of the vast differences among Asian American groups. Model minority accounts such as *Newsweek*'s, which have cursorily acknowledged such differences, cannot continue to ignore changing demographics. When well-off Japanese Americans are vastly outnumbered by struggling Vietnamese Americans, whites will have to amend their assumptions.

And yet, however unrepresentative they may be, at least Japanese Americans and Asian Indian Americans prosper — do they not? Again the numbers show that to a certain extent they do. But then they hit a glass ceiling. For all their greater education and greater per capita income, Japanese Americans are less than half as likely as whites to enter management.[34] And with four or more years of college Asian Americans are generally likely to out-earn whites in income categories up to forty thousand dollars — above which level whites significantly out-earn Asian Americans.[35] Finally, among full-time college faculty, whites have the highest rate of tenure at 53 percent, while Asian Americans (along with African Americans) have the lowest at 41 percent.[36]

Numbers do not lie, though they can be applied deceptively. Here they go far toward unraveling the model minority myth. Aside from reminding us of vast differences among Asian American groups, they indicate that even the relatively prosperous groups feel the economic sting of racism. For all their differences, these groups — and, by extension, all other nonwhite groups — have more in common with each other than any of them have with the dominant group.

Must we teach all these numbers? Surely we need ready access to them. But in the classroom we can cite briefly only enough of them to show that they exist and that they credibly contextualize and refute the impressive though incomplete statistics invoked by model minority advocates. And though they derive from recent studies, they are appropriate in any part of the course.

This last point bears elaborating. For while the course is anchored to the chronology in the central historical text, our focus on class issues encourages comparisons across time periods. One goal of this introductory course should be to determine not only the progression of economic oppression but also the patterns of oppression. This is why the ordering of the stories is unimportant. Past and present illuminate each other. The central text helps us contextualize the stories, the statistics, and the guest speakers. Students often embrace the contextualizing. One student wrote and presented to the class an argument that the 1992 multiethnic uprising in Los Angeles was, for the Korean American community, a decisive breach of the "American Dream." Another examined intersections of language and class issues affecting native Hawai'ians. Contextualization is thus the exercise by which we highlight class. In the discussions that fill most of our meetings we are forever comparing — say, implications of the Chinese Exclusion Act to current immigration "reform," or the gendering of immigrant farm labor and the garment industry — not to compare two phenomena but to contextualize all. This is, I believe, the best way in an introductory course to learn about institutional racism and its expression in the class structure. Moreover, students are remarkably good contextualizers.

Finally we return to stories. For one danger of Asian American studies — or, generally, of the study of any nondominant group — is that our subverting of myths can be reduced to whining, to a litany of victimizations. Critics carefully exhort us to avoid this construction of nonwhites as mere punching bags awaiting the blow of the next fist. Lisa Lowe alerts us, for example, to "the *agency* of Asian immigrants and Asian Americans: the *acts* of labor, resistance, memory, and survival."[37] These acts form the plots of our new, affirming stories. Some of these stories involve labor activism. For example, an electronic open letter urges APA students to join a Students Stop Sweatshop campaign, arguing, "We have to make retailers and manufacturers take responsibility for conditions in Los Angeles and in Indonesia, in New York and in New Delhi."[38] Other stories involve cross-ethnic solidarities. A statement from a group called Concerned Asian Pacific Students for Action argues, "Despite all the hype about Asian Pacific Islander (API) success, API wage-earners continue to earn significantly less than whites with similar levels of education. . . . Asian Pacific Islanders must support affirmative action alongside other people of color."[39] One observer charges that California governor "Pete Wilson's attempt to foment hostility between Asian American and African American communities has already backfired" because of "an awakened sense that an injury to one is an injury to all."[40] And in an ongoing, interactive story many Asian Americans, like many Native Americans, subvert stereotypes and advance their interests through electronic channels while these new media remain relatively inexpensive and publicly accessible — that is, before the dominant group finds a way to racialize and capitalize these media out of their reach. Wataru Ebihara has compiled and written an Asian American Internet guide, and he maintains the Asian American Cybernauts Page with links not only to a variety of APA resources but also to African American, Arab American, Native American, and Chicano-Latino resources. Surely we can expect students to explore these resources.

The "moral" of these new stories then is not only that Asian Americans are denouncing damaging stereotypes but also that they are recognizing their connectedness both to other nonwhite groups in the United States and to oppressed peoples elsewhere. The international story of the garment industry alerts us to this benefit of our interweaving race and class in our research and in our teaching.

A final caution bears sounding to those of us who, Asian Americans ourselves, would teach Asian American studies: It is a lesson gleaned from Rey Chow's book *Writing Diaspora,* and it concerns "third world" critics teaching in "first world" universities.

> While their cultures once existed for Western historians and anthropologists as objects of inquiry within well-defined geographical domains, the growing presence of these intellectuals in "first world" intellectual circles fundamentally disrupts the production of knowledge — what Edward Said calls Orientalism — that has hitherto proceeded by hiding the agenda of the inquirers and naturalizing the "objects" as givens. To paraphrase Hegel, "first world" inquirers must now cope with the fact that their "objects" no longer correspond to their "consciousness." "Third world" intellectuals, on their part, acquire and affirm their own "consciousness" only to find, continually, that it is a "consciousness" laden with the history of their objecthood.[41]

The "third world" critic who teaches in a "first world" university risks compromising what liberal white critics call "authenticity." Such compromise results from the critic's failing to acknowledge the relationship between an oppressed (or potentially oppressed) past in the "third world" homeland and a privileged present in a cozy university neighborhood. To acknowledge the relationship is to disclose, to narrate — to tell one's own story. The lesson for us is that, if we mean to teach the convergence of race and class, we have not only the model minority stereotype to denounce but also the charge that, as college teachers, we are brilliant embodiments of the model minority.

DIFFICULT DIALOGUES:
WORKING-CLASS STUDIES IN A MULTICULTURAL LITERATURE CLASSROOM

TERRY EASTON AND
JENNIFER LUTZENBERGER

In the 1996 spring semester, we were teaching assistants for four sections of Constance Coiner's "Multicultural Women Writers of the United States" (English/Women's Studies 383A) at the State University of New York at Binghamton. Coiner designed the course as a site where students' critical engagement of class could provide a foundation for thinking about and working toward multicultural unity; she had designed and was teaching 383A as part of a larger commitment to progressive social change through collective struggle. As she explained in *Radical Teacher*, "Canon reformation has legitimized the study of literary texts by women and people of color, but multicultural educational reform will defeat its egalitarian purpose if gender and racial identities are allowed to suppress class identities."[1] In the early stages of the course, we shared her vision. But we learned over the course of the semester that class analysis, though certainly an important site for critical inquiry, does not necessarily unify a divided and highly racially aware student body, nor does it necessarily change preconceived notions about identity, difference, and political action. Instead, class analysis became a crucible where some of the most vocal students contested our continued attempts to bring class studies into discussion sections, lectures, and student presentations.

Student responses to our attempts at foregrounding class were neither uniform nor easily categorized: Some students were interested in our ideas and responded enthusiastically to the course. Many others resisted the course, in various ways and for diverse reasons. And despite our political and pedagogical similarities, the three of us found ourselves misunderstanding, inadvertently working against, or overtly disagreeing with each other. In order to make sense of these responses, we had to give voice to our own complex histories and multiple identities (our "subject positions") and consider the relationship between our own subject positions and the diverse and often conflicting subject positions of the other people involved in the classroom. As Emma Goldman explains in a statement that Coiner chose as an epigraph for the syllabus, "It requires something more than personal experience to gain a philosophy or point of view from any specific event. It is the quality of our response to the event and our capacity to enter into the lives of others that help us to make their lives and experiences our own."[2] We are all multicultural. To teach multiculturalism requires that we begin difficult dialogues with our teaching partners, our students, and ourselves to better understand what these cultures *do* and *mean* in our current sociohistorical moment.

Our dialogue in this essay is in many ways incomplete; most significantly, it lacks Coiner's strong-willed, determined, impassioned voice. Constance Coiner and her daughter Ana Duarte-Coiner died on TWA flight 800 in July 1996, two months after we finished teaching English 383A. We had not yet finished discussing our teaching experiences, and we see our work here as a way to continue our conversation in the face of tremendous loss. On another level, multicultural pedagogy is always incomplete: our job is not to determine, through observation, what culture "is" or to find and teach "true" representations of different cultures as a way to promote tolerance and understanding. Instead, we see the multicultural literature classroom as a place to confront and articulate the ways we each fit and do not fit the categories assigned to us and to begin to consider different kinds of categories. We present our experiences to encourage other teachers to engage their own difficult dialogues, knowing that, as Paulo Freire and Myles Horton (reading Antonio Macado) explained in a book of the same title, we make the road by walking.[3]

TEACHING GOALS AND CLASS POSITIONALITY

Easton:

I divided my goals for the course into three general categories: I aimed to interrogate the ways that working-class literary texts demonstrate to working-class students that their histories are valid subjects of study in academia; I hoped to offer students not of the working class complex visions of working-class lives; and I wanted students to investigate the multiple ways that concepts such as work, career, and labor inform our lives, telling us who and what we are. Historically, colleges and universities have been places where middle-class and upper-class lives are idealized as the norm; the result has been that most students leave college with little or no understanding about the working class beyond the stereotypes and myths they learn through television, films, magazines, books, and other ideological apparatuses. I wanted students in this course to view working-class lives in a way that neither demeaned nor romanticized the working class. My interest in working-class studies stems from the material conditions of my own life: my immediate and extended family has always been working-class; for the first twenty years of my life I lived in housing projects in southern Illinois, and for the last eighteen years I have held various blue-collar jobs. I am daily reminded of class stratification, and I hoped that this course would encourage students to think through the ways that class (though often rendered invisible) informs all of our lives.

Lutzenberger:

I came to English 383A without a commitment to, or even knowledge of, working-class studies. I had grown up comfortably middle-class in a working-class Wisconsin suburb and was extremely conscious of the difference between my family's income and the incomes of most of our working-class neighbors and relatives. I had been trained to politely disregard these differences by considering myself "fortunate" and others less so, as though class had been assigned randomly among people and the ensuing injustice had to be quietly borne as inevitable. I had been an activist throughout my high school and college years for a variety of causes that tended to be attractive to people of my background: feminism (especially abortion rights), environmentalism, and human rights. I applied for and was accepted into a position in the Peace Corps, but I declined and decided instead to teach in the States.

My pedagogical interests were therefore political but also idealistic and related to my class position. Coiner foregrounded class not only in her construction of the course topic and materials, but also in our collaboration. The first time we all met together was at a syllabus-revision working lunch. Coiner explained joyfully that she had chosen the restaurant because it was where "the workers" ate. Throughout the semester, she and Easton often talked with each other and to students about their working-class backgrounds; it was obvious they felt a real sense of camaraderie from their shared histories. I was aware of my difference at these meetings and was not sure how to make this difference "not matter"; at the same time I realized it was my job not to erase but to understand these differences.

THE STUDENTS

Easton:

Lutzenberger and I each led two weekly discussion sections. Of the twenty-six students enrolled in my two sections, twenty-five were women. Approximately one-half of the students in my sections grew up in or around New York City; the remaining students arrived at Binghamton from a variety of locations within the state of New York. Students came from a range of class backgrounds. A few students described how their families had moved from working-class to middle-class economic status within their lifetimes. Racial categories in my sections varied, with about one-third of the students identifying themselves as Asian American, Caribbean American, or Latina; the remainder considered themselves white or Jewish. The students in my sections were dispersed quite evenly along class, race, and sexual categories of difference.

Lutzenberger:

Both of Easton's sections were organized as "traditional" lecture discussions, but one of my two sections was coordinated through the Educational Opportunity Program (EOP) as a link (meaning, among other requirements, that students took English 383A simultaneously with a rhetoric course).[4] Out of eighteen students, only one (a white, middle-class woman) was not admitted through EOP. Many students in this section were politically active on campus, especially in the fight to save EOP from budget cuts and the continued attempt to institute a campus-wide diversity requirement. Most students identified themselves as African American, Latina, or Latino, and two students identified themselves as white. In the other, more traditional section, three groups of students were housemates taking all or most of their classes together, and the other "single" students did not know each other or the groups. I recognized my own family and class history in the most vocal students and also felt allied to their liberal politics. This section was entirely female and was racially diverse (students identified themselves as Latina, African American, Asian American, Jewish, and white). There was enormous class disparity among students in this section. Pre-class chatter often centered around spring break vacations to tropical locations, weekend boating trips, or expensive credit-card purchases, but I knew from student writing and discussions during office hours that an equal number of students needed to work during spring break simply to remain at the university.

STRATEGIES/METHODS

Lutzenberger and Easton:

Coiner designed English 383A as part of a larger commitment to progressive social change and educational reform. Absolutely essential to the thrust of the course was the idea that Formalist analysis and the methods employed by New Criticism (both descriptive of the "text for text's sake" analysis that has served as the standard form of literary criticism in American English departments for the last fifty years) do not go far enough in enabling students to think through relationships between cultural texts, class studies, and multiculturalism both within and beyond the university. Troubled by Formalist critical practices that assert the autonomy of a literary text, we found that materialist-feminist and ideological analysis offered our students alternative frames for viewing literary texts and literary production. Judith Newton and Deborah Rosenfelt explain that materialist-feminist criticism "emphasizes the way in which a text is produced by its readers, and [is] reproduced differently in changing historical conditions."[5] This "contextual" reading contrasts the objectivity sought by Formalist and New Critical readers and offers students a framework for understanding how cultural histories and class positionalities inform readers' interpretations of texts. Because we wanted students to examine the ways that in any given society each citizen is invested in class stratification, we believed that they needed to understand how the "institutional and/or textual apparatuses . . . work on the reader's or spectator's imaginary conceptions of self and social order in order to call or *solicit* (or 'interpellate,' as Althusser puts it, using a quasi-legal term that combines the senses of 'summons' and 'hail') him/her into a specific form of social 'reality' and social subjectivity."[6] Coiner attempted to delineate the history of "traditional" literary analysis in the academy and challenged students to explore the limits of this critical paradigm; in lecture and discussion sections, we encouraged students to describe how we each were and were not contained in the categories we were "called" to inhabit.

We wanted students to read texts in a way that taught them to become "decoders" rather than passive readers of literary texts and other cultural representations. Toward this goal, we required students to write a number of one-page response essays focused on their "subject position" in relation to a text. Not merely an experiential reading or initial reaction to texts, subject position analysis asks students to examine the assumptions they make when reading texts and to reflect on the ways their responses are shaped by the multiple cultural identities and social histories that they bring to texts. We hoped the texts would then become not just an "object" of study, but a "means" by which students could learn more about their own complex identities.[7] Our intent was to encourage students to "unlearn" their identities as natural and self-determined and to begin to understand their identities as constructed and relational. As Bish Sen explains, "This unlearning leads to multiculturalism in a very different way. The white subject does not study Africa to know more about himself but rather studies himself to find the Africa-in-him; the heterosexual does not study gays and lesbians to understand others, she studies the construction of her own sexuality to conceptualize the differences in sexuality."[8] Most students struggled to turn their critical eyes toward their own experiences. Some found it difficult to understand why their social histories and analysis of their own class positionality in relation to the texts should be included in a "formal" paper, and others resisted our attempts to push their responses beyond repetition of static identity categories. These students felt as though their "authentic" cultural voices or experiences ought to be beyond critical scrutiny.

WRITING, DISCUSSING, AND RESISTING SUBJECT POSITION

Lutzenberger:

Students were caught off guard by our emphasis on materialist-feminist critique within the larger context of a multicultural women writer's course. Though I was aware (from my own experiences as an undergraduate) that our course was not "the norm," I did not predict how alien our critical approach would be to many students. Newton and Rosenfelt's introductory essay to *Feminist Criticism and Social Change* proved a useful introduction to the basic concept of materialist-feminist criticism. The authors provide a historical context for the development of materialist-feminist analysis, within larger frameworks of feminism, Marxism, multiculturalism, and critical literary studies. Before I had a chance to discuss Newton and Rosenfelt's essay in my sections, one of Easton's students had visited our shared office during office hours to talk to us about Coiner's lecture on Formalism and New Criticism. Coiner had suggested that no response to literature is "natural" or nonpolitical, despite Formalist claims toward universality. This student (a middle-class, married, conservative white female who wrote Formalist close readings of course texts with considerable skill and insight) wondered what was so "bad" about reading and interpreting texts "the old way." Easton and I tried to bring in Newton and Rosenfelt's argument that "traditional" literary critique "has divorced the study of ideas and language from the study of social conditions and has fostered a view of intellectual activity as a solitary individual enterprise rather than as a project with social origins and political consequences."[9] The student was reluctant to accept this argument and was even more reluctant to write about her own cultural experiences; she felt very strongly that English class was not a place for confessing or sharing personal stories, and she could not see what any of this had to do with multiculturalism. Despite our continued attempt to explain how important we felt the writing assignments were to the goals of the course and that we were asking for a critical, rather than a confessional, reading of her experiences, we decided finally that we could not force this student to accept a perspective she had such trouble with.

Though we did end up coming to an agreement that worked for the student, I was troubled by our conversation and decided to bring it up in both my discussion sections (without, of course, naming the student). I then asked students the same question Newton and Rosenfelt ask of their readers: "So what?"[10] I was hoping to prompt discussion on the relationship between the writing we were doing in the course (which most students were struggling to understand) and Newton and Rosenfelt's critical perspective. Students were eager to discuss the article but were more confused than enthusiastic, especially regarding the authors' assertion that traditional feminism erases differences among women in order to provide a ground for coalition based on gender. Students in both sections had trouble understanding what a feminist coalition (or, for that matter, any coalition) would be like without a "common ground." One student wrote in a response paper, "It is important to acknowledge differences, yet I am confused about what the consequences of specifying these differences will be, and if they could lead to further prejudice." She went on to explain, "As a white middle class woman, I feel less oppressed than a minority woman of another class may. I fear overlooking these further identities will lead to overcoming my own feeling of domination, while leaving other women at a disadvantage. Perhaps by just acknowledging that we are not only 'woman' without specifying our exact identities, it is possible to overcome inequality." Reading this paper now, I can see that this young woman was unsure about the relationship between "difference" and "inequality" except that pretending not to notice difference could lead her to unintentionally discriminate against other women. She believes difference equals inequality, rather than that difference comes from (or is representative of) material and historical inequality. She is therefore reluctant to challenge the identity category "woman" by adding to it the "exact" differences of "other" women, because to her understanding, equality comes from unity, not difference, and spending time thinking and talking about our differences is therefore against a goal of equality.

Her position was similar to that of most students in both sections, though the two sections voiced this understanding differently; in both cases, they seemed to believe that inequality comes from personal ignorance and prejudice and that education about "others" can change the ways individuals are treated in society.[11] I could understand this perspective but felt it was individualistic and ahistorical and that it conflicted with the kind of coalition politics the class was built to explore. I tried to explain these ideas to both classes but was unable to use experiences, either from my own life or from the lives of others, to illustrate the way I was thinking about difference. As an activist, I had always been involved in coalitions of mostly similar people — or, if not similar, people who at least did not foreground their differences — working toward a unified goal. Though I agreed with Newton and Rosenfelt's critique, I had not yet lived it. Some students had similar activist experiences to my own, some were devoted to their grades and graduation rather than social change, and others were involved in political groups where issues of identity, culture, history, and voice took center stage. I was not sure where to place myself into this mix, nor did I know how to facilitate student dialogue so that the differences of the people present in the classroom became as open to discussion, analysis, and critical thought as were the course texts.

Easton:

In addition to mining their own subject positions as they read the literary texts, students tested their newly acquired skills in subject position analysis when they critiqued student presentations. The student Lutzenberger described above, the middle-class white female resistant to reading texts the "new way," was forced to examine her "objective" reading of texts after her classmates questioned the way that her (all-white) group handled their presentation on Sandra Cisneros's *The House on Mango Street.* A concept that weaved its way through the presentation was the idea that women who live in places like Mango Street can "get out" of "oppressive" situations. The presenters never claimed that it would be easy to get out or that it was always possible, but they clearly suggested that if one tried hard enough, freedom from economic, gender, and racial discrimination could generally be gained as an individual enterprise. Latina students and students aware of the complex intersections between class, race, and hegemony resisted the presenters' claims to individual power and authority. Immediately following the presentation, students provoked the presenters into subject position analysis when they asked whether they had considered how their interpretations of the text and their concept of "getting out" were based on their own rather than the characters' class and racial identities.

Subject position analysis proved an integral part of the course when students investigated their own lives in relation to the literary texts. Responding, for example, to Tillie Olsen's delineation of circumstanced motherhood in "I Stand Here Ironing" and Maxine Hong Kingston's portrayal of a working mother in *The Woman Warrior,* two students (an Asian American student responding to Olsen and a white student responding to Kingston) described in their response papers how their relationship to their mothers had been clipped by the demands of single motherhood. Three students saw portraits of their own lives in *Mango Street:* two Latina students recognized their own childhood in Esperanza's neighborhood, and a white student compared the shame she felt growing up in a mobile home trailer park with the shame some characters feel because they live on Mango Street. Not all students saw their own lives in the texts, but they still engaged in materialist analysis. A few students investigated the concept of home and examined the connections between Dorothy Allison's rendering of home in *Bastard out of Carolina* and Cisneros's delineation of home in *Mango Street*. Several students also questioned how "opportunity" might be different (or the same) for characters in *Bastard* and *Mango Street*. The connections these students made between the texts would be useful pathways for interrogation in any literature course that seeks to situate working-class studies in the larger framework of multiculturalism.[12]

CONSTRUCTED IDENTITIES

Lutzenberger:

Our discussions on *Bastard out of Carolina,* in discussion section and in lecture, were some of the most important for me as a teacher and learner, because they brought into focus the racial tensions that animated many students' resistance to or critique of class as a unifying discourse. Students in the linked section were furious with Anney and her decision to remain with an abusive man—more furious than they were with Glen, the abuser. Several students shared stories about how their own mothers had struggled to get away from abusive husbands and boyfriends, thereby proving Anney a bad mother in comparison with their own good mothers. Many response papers focused on the same theme. In both formats, I asked whether Bone (the abused little girl who narrates the story) felt as though her mother loved her and whether Bone's opinion complicated their reading. I also asked whether the students saw links between the social and financial hardships these characters endured (such as Glen's inability to keep a low-wage job and Anney's inability to raise her daughters on a waitress's salary) and the abusive situations depicted in the novel. Students reminded me that they had grown up without much money, but their mothers had kept them safe. One student asked whether I was suggesting that only poor men abused and raped their children. Though I was continually asking students to investigate "socioeconomic conditions," I had only a vague idea what was meant by this (chiefly "class injustice"), and I did not know how to account for the differences between Bone's and the students' experiences in a way that encouraged these larger connections. Furthermore, students were extremely resistant to discussing Bone's lesbian Aunt Raylene or Dorothy Allison as a lesbian writer. Unsure how to elicit responses to the novel, I broke students into groups and asked them to focus on the theme of forgiveness in *Bastard* and in another Allison work we'd read, *Trash,* essentially asking them to do the kind of Formalist analysis we had been working against all semester — but I felt stuck and simply didn't know another way to make the class "productive."

In contrast, students in the traditional section were sympathetic to Anney's plight. They believed that the nebulous socioeconomic conditions I was so fond of mentioning had forced Anney to stay with Glen and that she had been the best mother she could be given her situation. This analysis took up the first few minutes of class, and then students were eager to investigate the meaning behind repeated symbols in the novel to demonstrate how Bone "transcended" poverty and abuse to become (in their interpretation) the "real" Dorothy Allison — successful writer and lesbian activist. Where I had fallen into Formalism in the linked class out of exasperation, I resisted it in the traditional section and attempted to elicit analysis based on subject position. Students in both classes read this task as a three-step process: identification of one's class, race, and gender (students conspicuously avoided naming their own sexualities); identification of the "other" presented by the text — or, if the text was presenting an experience like the students' own, identification of this similarity; and suggestion of synthesis between one's own identity and the identity of the "other" toward understanding and tolerance — or, if the student felt aligned with the text, a suggestion about how "others" could learn from the experiences presented. Several students in this class were English majors and loved to conduct close readings of symbols and characters, and since they could not figure out how to plug such work into the subject position formula, they hoped to be able to demonstrate their analytic prowess during discussion.

Both groups were struggling to recognize ideology, defined by Newton and Rosenfelt as "a complex and contradictory system of representations (discourses, images, myths) through which we experience ourselves in relation to each other and to the social structures in which we live," while still protecting the sanctity of their own opinions and experiences as beyond ideology.[13] When we read Toni Morrison's *Beloved,* for example, students in both sections were willing to accept Sethe as a "good" mother despite the fact that she murders her baby daughter, because they could see how slavery constructed and constrained her individual choices. *Bastard* presented a different problem to students because the characters are white. Students were forced to confront what for them was an ahistorical oppression. Having come from schools at least nominally invested in alternative race and ethnicity-based American histories, they were unable to determine why a white family might lead lives burdened by economic oppression and job discrimination.

This posed a greater "threat" to students in the linked section than in the traditional section, I think because students of color had found so much power and authority — were developing their "voices" — in the race and ethnic affinity groups most belonged to on campus. Though most of these same students had been a part of the summer bridge program for incoming EOP students and so were already familiar with class analysis, their strongest personal alliances were still with people who shared their histories — and in America today, history is dole out in racially limited "mainstream" (dominant) and "alternative" (other) categories. Classed, gendered, and sexed histories had not been made available to students in the same resonant way, and students' minds were apparently not going to be changed in one semester-long course on multiculturalism that focused on class and, to a lesser extent, on gender, sexuality, and race.

Easton:

The difficulty of foregrounding subject position and class was made clear in a student presentation on *Bastard out of Carolina*. When the students met with Lutzenberger and me for a rehearsal, they were still developing their idea: a mock talk show, complete with a show host who would ask characters to explain and defend their actions. The students had begun to write the dialogue, and Lutzenberger was excited about their ideas. I was more apprehensive about the format, wondering whether it would allow them to effectively analyze the text. As I watched the students formulate and rehearse their lines, the things they were saying seemed to me parodies of the working poor and the working class. I wondered silently whether or not my objections to what they were doing and saying were based simply on my sensitivity to the ways that middle-class students from New York City were portraying working poor, southern whites; after all, the events in the text reminded me of many of my own experiences growing up in southern Illinois and the characters seemed so real to me, reminding me (in some ways at least) of my own aunts, uncles, brothers, and grandparents. As the rehearsal progressed, I realized that the presentation lacked critical analysis of the characters' historical circumstances and material conditions. The students moved in what I believed was the right direction when they discussed the ideological assumptions of the ways that families are "supposed" to function, investigating the differences between "ideal" and "real" families. I wanted the students to continue this kind of analysis, so I asked them to think through the ways Allison delineates the economic realities of the working poor. I also encouraged the students to think about Allison's urgency in writing *Bastard* and to explore what it means for a working-class author to publish a novel, especially one that so closely resembles the author's own life.

During the presentation the students strained toward materialist analysis when they used the phrase "socioeconomic conditions" to explain conflict between characters and to think through tension in the text. The student who portrayed Bone, for example, exclaimed that she realized her mother had to be away from home because "she had bigger things in mind for us kids, she had to get food on the table and clothes on our backs." The student who played Anney agreed with Bone, telling the talk show host and the audience that she often "had no choice" when trying to decide whether to go to work or to stay at home with Bone and Reese. Throughout the presentation the students demonstrated that Anney is highly aware of the necessity for (some) mothers to work outside of the home. The students also showed that Anney, unlike Glen, has no illusions about the difficulties of raising children within the limited parameters of low-wage employment. Her history, of course, differs from Glen's in that she was raised working poor, whereas Glen's childhood was comfortably middle-class.

Coiner's handwritten notes taken during the presentation reveal a concern that she voiced at our meeting shortly after the presentation: she felt that rather than analyzing the text, the students had merely reenacted it. She explained in our meeting that the talk show format had been popular in her courses for the last few years and that students seldom used the form in a way that enabled the audience to learn anything new about the text at hand. She admitted that the presenters did a fine job of recreating specific scenes and characters and that the heteroglossic ending deployed was an effective device in interrogating the talk show format, but she believed that the presentation would have been more interesting (and perhaps more useful to the audience) had the presenters more fully contextualized the characters' historical and economic circumstances.[14] One thing that she really liked, for example, was the way that the student portraying Shannon Pearl used the term *rape* to describe how Glen was a victim of material circumstance. Coiner's enthusiasm for this reading, I think, is grounded in the notion that Glen's position in the market economy is a precarious one. Glen believes individuals can "pull themselves up by their bootstraps," so he fails to see that his means of "self-sufficiency" (a phrase suggestive of bourgeois individualism) is inextricably linked to fluctuations in the labor market. The presenters revealed Glen's unquestioning belief in self-sufficiency and the spoils of the "American Dream" — material accumulation, leisure time, and a family unit supported through a single-wage income — when the student who played Glen stated that Anney should not work because his own mother never did and that his function was to be the sole breadwinner in the family. In light of this, Glen's violent acts stem, at least to some degree, from his inability to accept that he, Anney, Bone, and Reese cannot survive on his single-wage income.

Following my instructions to interrogate the material circumstances of the characters in the text, the presenters frequently invoked the phrase "socioeconomic conditions" as a way to engage in materialist analysis. But as it turned out, the phrase was invoked so often and for such disparate purposes that it became a mere cliché, empty of any critical significance. Moreover, as I later found out in students' weekly comments and questions, some students found the presenters' frequent use of the phrase offensive, especially when the student portraying Shannon Pearl suggested that all of the Boatwrights had been victims of "socioeconomic conditions" and therefore had been (figuratively) raped. Students protested this particular interpretation of the text, believing that the presenters diminished Bone's (literal) rape and emotional abuse.

During my presentation on the relationship between literary texts and ideology (several weeks after the *Bastard* presentation), I voiced my critique of the way that the student portraying Anney stated that she had to deal with "repulsive truck drivers" when waiting tables at the White Horse Cafe. I pointed out that one of the problems with the student's interpretation is that Anney never says that truck drivers are repulsive. Wondering if the student failed to examine her own subject position when interpreting the text, I suggested to the class that perhaps the student's class-biased reading was informed by stereotypes of truck drivers, images popularized in television, film, and other media. I explained that the literary texts we were studying in the course reclaim particular class-based versions of history, and consequently they offer us a chance to look at ourselves and our collective histories in a different way. I then closed the presentation by urging students to consider the ways that working-class writers ask readers to place an inquisitive gaze not only on the characters in the text but also on themselves.

In the context of the course goals and the kinds of learning we were aiming for in the class, the *Bastard* presentation provided a valuable lesson in subject position analysis. Even though at the beginning of my presentation I had revealed my subject position through discussing the ways that my working-class origins and class consciousness influence the ways that I interpret texts, I did not reveal that my brother is a truck driver. In hindsight I realize that my response to the student's comment about truck drivers stems as much from what I believed to be a misreading of the text as what I perceived to be a naive (and offensive) perception about working-class lives. I understand now that in addition to using the student's comment as a way to demonstrate how class positionality influences the way we read cultural texts, I also used the event to assuage my own frustrations with the class-bias that is common to (some forms of) cultural discourse.

CONFLICT

Lutzenberger:
Near the end of the semester, students in the linked section turned their class-reluctance into a critique about the way the course positioned race. They

agreed with Coiner's decision to include Allison, Olsen, and Carolyn Forché (all white women) in a multicultural syllabus but wondered why the same class-complicated investigation of monolithic racial identity did not take place in any of the other represented cultures. Students felt as though only "canonized" multicultural texts (like Morrison's *Beloved,* which many students had already read in two or three other classes) had been included in the syllabus, except for the texts written by white women. They also wondered if Coiner felt as though class erased or was more important than race. Students decided that they would ask Coiner these questions in discussion the following week, since she, Easton, Diane Allen (the graduate student who taught the rhetoric course linked to my section), and my other section were going to sit in. Though I had prepared Coiner for this question, she was upset by it (I learned later that other graduate students had expressed the same critique and were met with a similar response). She suggested that the students did not understand what the course was all about and that the foundational premises of this criticism prevented other-than-identity-based coalition formation and effective political action. She obviously felt attacked, as did the students, and tension escalated.

When the section was over, I attended Allen's section with the students and continued the discussion; some students (and later both Allen and I) burst into tears. I was overwhelmed and frustrated by the fact that I could not articulate in a "professional" way the multitude of half-formed theories I was trying to understand while being required to teach them. I felt pulled in several directions, all of which were beyond my ability to explain. First, I felt that I had let down my students by not anticipating Coiner's reaction. Second, I felt that I had let Coiner down by placing her in an unreasonably difficult situation. Third, I felt that I had not fully understood the goal of the class and had realized this too late to fix it. Finally, I was growing deeply unsure of my own class, scholastic, pedagogical, and political identifications, all of which seemed secure and well-developed before the course began. I left the session feeling desperately shaken and not at all confident in my abilities—I felt like a failure.

Easton:

Coiner exclaimed during the first week of the semester that "real learning" involves "taking a stand, articulating, and challenging." In light of this, I expected students to provoke a lively discussion in Lutzenberger's section as they voiced their complaints about the form and content of the course. And yet I also expected (based on discussions with Coiner and Lutzenberger about students' complaints) that Coiner would be reluctant to defend the thrust of the course, the literary texts, and the secondary readings. As Lutzenberger mentioned earlier, Coiner believed that students' complaints were based on a mis-understanding of the basic premise of the course — that class consciousness and its subsequent cultural formation, a class-based alliance for social change, could provide a unified coalition politics that moves across and beyond individual categories of difference. A central tenet of the course was the idea that identity politics (and its associated cultural formation, political correctness) stalls effective coalitions across multiple sites of identity. Barbara Epstein perhaps best outlines Coiner's frustration with identity politics and political correctness when she suggests that these social formations arise from a political atmosphere that is "more oriented toward moral than strategic thinking . . . more concerned with what language is used than with what changes are made in the social structure."[15] Coiner believed (as did I) that coalitions based on class could allow students to interrogate the social structure of American society while moving beyond the essentialism common to identity politics. Midway through the semester Coiner hinted at what a class-based coalition might look like when she explained how workers at a 1912 Lawrence, Massachusetts, mill strike organized women and men from a wide range of racial identities, ethnicities, and nationalities into a collective effort to create better working conditions for all workers.

In an effort to provoke discussion on Forché's poetry, Lutzenberger divided us into groups of four or five students. After only a few minutes of relatively unproductive discussion on Forché's poetry, my group turned from analysis of the poetry to a critique of the course. An African American student asked why we were studying "just one more white woman traveling around the globe." I tried to move the conversation toward an investigation of the ways that Forché, as a writer of working-class origins with specific democratic and humane political commitments, moves against dominant ideological, cultural, and poetic paradigms. Many students had been wondering throughout the semester how literary texts might be read as "gestures toward history and gestures with political effect" and I believed that Forché's poetry, with its summons for readers to leave "the safety of self-contemplation to imagine and address the larger world" could provide a foundation for understanding the ways that cultural texts inform class consciousness and provoke political action.[16] This notion of "addressing the larger world" (identified by Coiner's use of the phrase *transindividualism*) asks readers to go beyond the individualism inherent in identity politics while moving toward a collective consciousness.[17] Ironically, at the moment when we attempted to explore the possibilities of transindividualism, student coalitions fragmented into racial and ethnic identity groups, thus stalling alliances based on class solidarity.

When it was time to report to the class, the students from my group voiced their criticisms of the form and content of the course. Tension heightened as students formed alliances against each other and against Coiner. As students teamed up based on racial and ethnic identity, it became quite clear that a coalition based on class would not occur in this particular version of "Multicultural Women Writers." Pressured by students to explain her course goals and clarify her definition of multiculturalism, Coiner (interpreting students' criticisms as products of identity politics) responded with a suggestion that I photocopy and hand out to students for the next class session an article that she and I had recently read, Michael Lind's "To Have and Have Not: Notes on the Progress of the American Class War."[18] She believed that it would be best for students to reconsider their responses to the form and content of the course after having read Lind's (convincing) articulation of the ways that an erasure of class-based coalitions for social change leads, in most cases, to political stasis.[19]

During this discussion section I felt caught between polarized interpretive communities. Although I agreed with Coiner's effort to foreground class studies as a way to promote class consciousness and class-based coalitions for social change that move across many sites of identity and difference, I also understood students' criticisms of the course. One of the goals of the course that was never explicitly addressed in lecture was Coiner's desire to examine the construction of whiteness as a racial identity. As I understood now, studying three texts by white working-class authors was an attempt to move beyond monolithic identity categories and to demonstrate that, in Coco Fusco's words, "racial identities are not only Black, Latino, Asian, Native American and so on; they are also white and to ignore white ethnicity is to redouble its hegemony by naturalizing it."[20] But as Lutzenberger stated earlier, some students had become suspicious of the ways that the course did not treat minority-authored texts with the same intensity and complexity allotted to the white-authored texts. At this late stage in the semester, these and other students did not seem interested in listening to our attempts to defend the form and content of the course. In retrospect, I realize that I could have pointed out to students how two of the secondary readings for the course, Hazel Carby's "The Multicultural Wars" and a chapter from bell hooks's *Outlaw Culture: Resisting Representations,* interrogate the complexities of black cultural texts and address intersections between class and race.[21] Because these and other essays were not discussed in the large lecture format with Coiner, and because they were only briefly covered in discussion sections (as part of a rather large chunk of material on multiculturalism, identity politics, and political correctness), I believe that the students' criticisms of the form and content of the course were perceptive and justified.

AN OPEN-ENDED CONCLUSION

Lutzenberger:

The "traditional" and "linked" students tended to view my role as TA, Coiner's role as lecture professor, the course material, and the underlying principles of the course very differently. Students in the traditional section, for example, remained uncomfortable bringing their own experiences of class into discussion-time "proper," though students did identify and discuss class status within the margins of our public space (such as before and after class, in "private" student papers and responses, or occasionally in the more anonymous and teacher-centered large-group lecture hall). I believe the discomfort we all felt throughout the semester (a discomfort that reached its peak when I brought both sections together to speak with Coiner) came from a fear of saying "the wrong thing" in such a diverse classroom, rather than indicating a refusal to think about the meaning of class status. This was a fear I shared, though I have reached this conclusion in retrospect. In comparison, students in the linked section were eager to discuss class inequity, as long as class did not supersede race. Students in this section were extremely reluctant to accept arguments made in several readings (and by Coiner in lecture) that class could present a "unifying" force in coalition politics because, as one African American male student explained, "A poor white man will always be better off in America than a poor black man."

If I were to teach this course again, I would pay more attention to the contradictions present in students' written and spoken responses to the course texts as a starting point for further dialogue. For example, when the Latina students criticized the presentation on *House on Mango Street,* they prefaced their comments with the phrase "As a Latina, I . . . ," believing (correctly) that this phrase would protect their comments from attack from those who could not claim experiential authority as Latinos. Non–Latin American students were willing to accept the Latina students' criticisms as "the final word" on the *Mango Street* presentation. This same identity-as-authority determination was not extended to Easton's working-class reading of *Bastard out of Carolina* and to the *Bastard* presentation. Students were reluctant or unwilling to accept Coiner's, Allen's, and Easton's criticisms of the presentation and felt that because they hadn't "meant anything" by their comment about the truck driver, Easton's critique was unfair. This contradiction presented us with an opportunity to ask students why they believe race and class are different, who is served by "privileging" racial categories over class categories, and what specific fears, desires, senses of community, and sense of self encourage this privileging. I would then use these discussions as a foundation to imagine with the students whether there are ways to form new coalitions that do not require us to give up or "trash" our current support systems.

Multicultural pedagogy requires teachers and students to listen to the subject positions of others and to speak our own subject positions. Listening and speaking are extremely complex, risky, and potentially painful, especially when speaking within institutional settings (such as universities) structurally hostile to many of the subject positions expressed. I had no idea what I was taking on when I agreed to teach this course and to explore multicultural pedagogy; I, like students, required a great deal of tolerance, understanding, and principled critique from my teaching colleagues as I mucked my way through the semester. Such stumbling is inherent to coalition politics in every setting. At a minimum it requires that all participants be committed to viewing and supporting the others as unfinished, struggling, "works in progress."

Easton:

As a teaching assistant in this course, I learned that a pedagogy interested in class studies is certainly much easier to handle in the abstract sense than in actual praxis. Before teaching this course, I entertained ideas of how all of the students would be enthusiastic participants in class-based literary and cultural critique. Although it is true that many students engaged in at least some form of materialist analysis during the semester, and a few students became quite adept at class analysis, as a teacher and a student in this course I would have liked to experience more sustained and rigorous attempts at class-based literary and cultural critique. Perhaps I set my goals too high for the semester. Ideologically, of course, the deep structure of American society is highly invested in masking, discrediting, or otherwise preventing class analysis. When Lutzenberger writes about the "uncomfortable" feeling that she and her students experienced when discussing class, she highlights the "hidden" ways that ideology silences class analysis.

The "silencing" of class analysis in my sections can be attributed (in some ways at least) to my own reluctance to push students beyond their initial responses and toward more complicated readings of the literary texts and secondary materials. In hindsight I realize that because I wanted to use class analysis as a unifying discourse, I inadvertently foregrounded and interrogated class as if it were an autonomous identity not connected to other culturally constructed identities such as race, gender, and sexuality. I recall distinctly, for example, how a Latina student breathed a sigh of anger when I stated that I wanted to "push aside for a moment" racial differences between the authors we studied in the course. In this particular discussion, I aimed to demonstrate how all of the writers we studied in the course share a cultural history based on class origin rather than racial or ethnic identity. Bish Sen speaks of multiculturalism as a location where a range of cultural identities are studied in relation to one another, where no one identity is given precedence over another.[22] It is only now, one year after teaching the course, that I understand Sen's model of multiculturalism and recognize its (unrealized) potential in integrating class studies into our course on multicultural women writers.

Lutzenberger and Easton:

Through this experience, Coiner provided us an opportunity to teach the intersections between working-class studies and multiculturalism. At the time, we sometimes felt that our inexperience prevented us from "living up" to her political and pedagogical vision, but we have come to believe that teaching multiculturalism is a necessarily imperfect and difficult endeavor because it reflects and challenges imperfect and difficult social relations. The intensity of our class discussions can be taken as a measure of our success in engaging rather than changing minds; real social change takes much longer than a semester to enact. We write from our experience as a way of thinking about our own teaching, but we hope to provoke readers of this essay to begin their own investigations into teaching working-class studies in a multicultural context.

NOTES

INTRODUCTION

1. Some of the best of these stories appear in three anthologies that provide valuable insight into the experiences of working-class academics: Jake Ryan and Charles Sackrey, *Strangers in Paradise: Academics from the Working Class* (Boston: South End Press, 1984), which was reprinted by the University Press of America in 1996; Michelle Tokarczyk and Elizabeth A. Fay, eds., *Working-Class Women in the Academy: Laborers in the Knowledge Factory* (Amherst: University of Massachusetts Press, 1993); C. L. Barney Dews and Carolyn Leste Law, *This Fine Place So Far from Home: Voices of Academics from the Working Class* (Philadelphia: Temple University Press, 1995).

2. See Richard Hoggart, *The Uses of Literacy: Changing Patterns in English Mass Culture* (Fair Lawn, N.J.: Essential Books, 1957).

3. Ira Shor, *Critical Teaching and Everyday Life* (1980; reprint, Chicago: University of Chicago Press, 1987).

4. Carolyn Kay Steedman, *Landscape for a Good Woman: A Story of Two Lives* (1986; reprint, New Brunswick, N.J.: Rutgers University Press, 1987), 9.

5. "Codebook Variable: CLASS, 185," *General Social Survey* WWW Index, http:// www.icpsr.umich.edu/GSS/codebook/class.htmi; Linda Feldmann, "Campaign Quest: To Define the Middle Class," *Christian Science Monitor* 84, no. 55 (13 Feb. 1992): 1–2; Elia Kacapyr, "Are You Middle Class?" *American Demographics* 18, no. 10 (Oct. 1996): 31–32.

6. Larry Smith, "Some General Values of Working Class Culture," Web site, current address http://members.aol.com/lsmithdog/bottomdog/WCValuespost.htm. The chart also appears in Smith's article, "Working Class Matters: Myths and Values," *The Heartlands Today:* 6 (1996): 35–44.

7. Shor, *Critical Teaching and Everyday Life,* 36–37, 86–87.

8. Ibid., 81.

9. Irvin Peckham, "Complicity in Class Codes," in Dews and Law, *This Fine Place,* 272.

10. Ibid., 273.

11. Larry Smith, "Reaching and Welcoming Working Class Students into the College," handout, Department of English, Firelands College of Bowling Green State University, photocopy.

12. Janet Zandy, *Liberating Memory: Our Work and Our Working-Class Consciousness* (New Brunswick, N.J.: Rutgers University Press, 1995); Nicholas Coles and Peter Oresick, *Working Classics: Poems on Industrial Life* (Urbana: University of Illinois Press, 1990); Kurt Vonnegut, *Player Piano* (1952; reprint, New York: Dell Publishing, 1980).

13. Zandy, *Liberating Memory,* 1.

14. See Gerda Lerner, "Rethinking the Paradigm," in her *Why History Matters: Life and Thought* (New York: Oxford University Press, 1997), 146–98.

15. Benjamin DeMott, *Created Equal: Reading and Writing about Class in America* (New York: HarperCollins, 1996); Tom Zaniello, *Working Stiffs, Union Maids, Reds, and Riffraff: An Organized Guide to Films about Labor* (Ithaca, N.Y.: ILR Press, 1996); George Lipsitz, *Time Passages: Collective Memory and American Popular Culture* (Minneapolis: University of Minnesota Press, 1990); George Lipsitz, *A Rainbow at Midnight: Labor and Culture in the 1940s* (Urbana: University of Illinois Press, 1994).

16. Shor, *Critical Teaching and Everyday Life,* xi.

17. I was disappointed that I did not receive any proposals for teaching-focused essays that carefully examined issues of sexuality in conjunction with class. There is good work being done on the links between class and sexuality, though. For a useful overview, see Donald Morton, "Review: The Class Politics of Queer Theory," *College English* 58 (April 1996): 471–82.

WRITING THE PERSONAL

A version of this paper was originally presented at the 1996 Conference on College Composition and Communication, and another version of part of this paper was presented at the State University of New York at Albany Nexus of Discourse Conference, fall 1995. I would like to thank Jeffrey Berman, Stephen M. North, Chris W. Gallagher, and Edward C. Fristrom for their perceptive readings of earlier drafts of this essay, and Robert P. Yagelski for the talks about social class and pedagogy. I also thank the students in "Introduction to Women Writers" at the State University of New York, during the summer of 1995 for thinking with me about issues of class, race, sexuality, and gender.

1. Janet Zandy, introduction to *Liberating Memory: Our Work and Our Working-Class Consciousness* (New Brunswick, N.J.: Rutgers University Press, 1995).

2. Nancy Mack and James Thomas Zebroski, "Transforming Composition: A Question of Privilege," in *Composition and Resistance,* ed. C. Mark Hurlbert and Michael Blitz (Portsmouth, N.H.: Boynton/Cook Publishers, 1991), 160.

3. bell hooks, *Teaching to Transgress: Education as the Practice of Freedom* (New York: Routledge, 1994), 183.

4. Dorothy Allison, *Skin: Talking about Sex, Class, and Literature* (Ithaca, N.Y.: Firebrand Books, 1994), 35.

5. Lillian Bridwell-Bowles, "Discourse and Diversity: Experimental Writing within the Academy," *College Composition and Communication* 43 (Oct. 1992): 349–68.

6. Zandy, *Liberating Memory,* 5.

7. hooks, *Teaching to Transgress,* 186.

8. Hephzibah Roskelly, "Telling Tales in School: A Redneck Daughter in the Academy," in *Working-Class Women in the Academy: Laborers in the Knowledge Factory,* ed. Michelle M. Tokarczyk and Elizabeth A. Fay (Amherst: University of Massachusetts Press, 1993), 295.

9. J. Elspeth Stuckey, *The Violence of Literacy* (Portsmouth, N.H.: Boynton/Cook, 1991), 95.

10. The personal created an important part of what bell hooks calls "community." She further describes community as "creat[ing] a climate of openness and intellectual rigor. Rather than focusing on issues of safety, I think that a feeling of community creates a sense that there is shared commitment and a common good that binds us." hooks, *Teaching to Transgress,* 40.

11. I am using "diverse discourse" here as Bridwell-Bowles does in her groundbreaking text, "Discourse and Diversity." I find Bridwell-Bowles's insights to be crucial in my conceptualization of the autobiographical and the experimental.

12. Dorothy Allison, "Mama" from *Trash* (Ithaca, N.Y.: Firebrand Books, 1988).

13. Michelle Cliff, "If I Could Write This in Fire, I Would Write This in Fire," in *The Land of Look Behind* (Ithaca, N.Y.: Firebrand Books, 1985), 57–76.

14. Allison, *Trash.*

15. Linda Brodkey, "On the Subjects of Class and Gender in 'The Literacy Letters,'" *College English* 51 (Feb. 1989): 140.

16. Zandy, *Liberating Memory,* 8.

17. Valerie Miner, "Writing and Teaching with Class," in *Working-Class Women in the Academy,* 74.

18. Elizabeth Ellsworth, "Why Doesn't This Feel Empowering? Working through the Repressive Myths of Critical Pedagogy," in *Feminisms and Critical Pedagogy,* ed. Carmen Luke and Jennifer Gore (New York: Routledge, 1992), 108.

19. bell hooks, *Talking Back: Thinking Feminist, Thinking Black* (Boston, Mass.: South End Press, 1989), 77.

20. Brodkey, "'The Literacy Letters,'" 140.

21. Michael Lind, "To Have and Have Not: Notes on the Progress of the American Class War," *Harper's Magazine,* June 1995, 35–47.

22. Madeleine R. Grumet, "The Politics of Personal Knowledge," in *The Stories Lives*

Tell: Narrative and Dialogue in Education, ed. Nel Noddings and Carol Witherall (New York: Teachers College, 1991), 72.

23. Gregory Jay, "Taking Multiculturalism Personally: Ethnos and Ethos in the Classroom," *American Literary History* 6 (1994): 626.

24. I had similar results to Jay's, and I hope to further explore the implications of this topic in another paper.

BORDER CROSSINGS

1. Jake Ryan and Charles Sackrey, *Strangers in Paradise: Academics from the Working Class* (Boston: South End Press, 1984). This work profoundly influenced Greenwald, who first encountered the book in 1989.

2. Cornel West discusses this in *Race Matters* (Boston: Beacon Press, 1993).

3. bell hooks, *Teaching to Transgress: Education as the Practice of Freedom* (New York: Routledge, 1994), 12.

4. See Paulo Freire's masterful and influential work, *Pedagogy of the Oppressed* (New York: Continuum Press, 1990).

5. Lest it be forgotten or misunderstood, working-class students still today pinch pennies and sacrifice personal comfort in order to "get an education."

6. One problem we have encountered on our campus is a rural-urban split. Most students focus on the differences rather than the similarities. And each kind of student sees the other as "the other." So urban students define working-class in rural stereotypes, and rural students defined it in terms of urban poverty.

REVERSALS OF FORTUNE

Special thanks to Betsy Wehrwein for assistance in gathering information about current economic conditions and to Michael Dickel for his generous assistance with this project.

1. See Karen Uehling, "Older and Younger Students Writing Together: A Rich Learning Community," *Writing Instructor* 15 (summer 1996): 61–69.

2. Howard Risher, "Behind the Big Picture: Employment Trends in the 1990s," *Compensation and Benefits Review* 29, no. 1 (Jan.–Feb. 1997): 8.

3. Ibid.

4. "Productivity Up 0.7% in '96," *Minneapolis Star Tribune,* 12 Mar. 1997, Minneapolis edition.

5. Katherine S. Newman, *Declining Fortunes: The Withering of the American Dream* (New York: Basic Books, 1993), 40.

6. Ibid., 18.

7. Jean Bethke Elshtain, "Lost City," *New Republic* 215, no. 19 (4 Nov. 1996): 25.

8. Patricia Hill Collins, "Learning from the Outsider Within: The Sociological Significance of Black Feminist Thought," *Social Problems* 33, no. 6 (Dec. 1986): 14–32.

9. Richard Hoggart, *The Uses of Literacy* (London: Chatto and Windus, 1957);

Richard Sennett and Jonathan Cobb, *The Hidden Injuries of Class* (New York: Knopf, 1972); Richard Rodriguez, *Hunger of Memory* (Boston: Godine, 1983).

10. Nancy LaPaglia, "Working-Class Women as Academics: Seeing in Two Directions, Awkwardly," in *This Fine Place So Far from Home: Voices of Academics from the Working Class,* ed. C. L. Barney Dews and Carolyn Leste Law (Philadelphia: Temple University Press, 1995), 178.

11. Dwight Lang, "The Social Construction of a Working-Class Academic," in Dews and Law, *This Fine Place,* 161.

12. The focus on class was not advertised for this section of "Intermediate Writing." In other words, students taking this class did not self-select.

13. Benjamin DeMott, *Created Equal: Reading and Writing about Class in America* (New York: HarperCollins, 1996); Ben Hamper, *Rivethead: Tales from the Assembly Line* (New York: Warner Books, 1991).

14. Nicholas Coles and Susan V. Wall, "Conflict and Power in the Reader-Responses of Adult Basic Writers," *College English* 49 (Mar. 1987): 311.

15. See Patricia K. Smith, "Downward Mobility: Is It a Growing Problem?" *American Journal of Economics and Sociology* 53 (Jan. 1994): 57–72. In her study of downward mobility patterns in the 1970s and the 1980s, Smith found the risk of losing 50 percent or more in family income among young people leaving the nest doubled in the '80s compared to the '70s. See also Neil Howe and William Stares, *13th Generation: Abort, Retry, Ignore, Fail* (New York: Vintage, 1993).

16. According to the Congressional Budget Office, over one-quarter of displaced workers in the 1980s were not working one to three years after they lost their jobs. "Displaced Workers: Trends in the 1980s and Implications for the Future," Washington D.C., Feb. 1993. See also Risher, "Behind the Big Picture," 5.

17. Lynn Z. Bloom, "Freshman Composition as a Middle-Class Enterprise," *College English* 58 (Oct. 1996), 668.

18. Shirley Brice Heath, "Work, Class, and Categories: Dilemmas of Identity," in *Composition in the 21st Century: Crisis and Change,* ed. Lynn Z. Bloom, Donald A. Daiker, and Edward M. White (Carbondale: Southern Illinois University Press, 1996), 236.

19. Linda Brodkey, "On the Subjects of Class and Gender in 'The Literacy Letters,'" *College English* 51 (Feb. 1989): 125–41.

20. James A. Berlin, "English Studies, Work, and Politics in the New Economy," in Bloom, Daiker, and White, *Composition in the 21st Century,* 224.

THE (DIS)LOCATION OF CULTURE

1. The formal teaching of English literature began with colonial projects in India. British schools of the nineteenth century trained their students in the classics of Greek and Latin; colonial schools converted Indian peoples into British citizens by acculturating them through the study of English literature. See Gauri Viswanathan, "The Beginnings of English Literary Study in British India," in *Language and Literacy in Social Practice,* ed. Janet Maybin (Clevedon, U.K.: Open University Press, 1990), 215–32.

2. See Joseph Oran Aimona, "Teaching Literature in the Academy Today: A Round-table," *PMLA* 112.1 (Jan. 1997), 101–12.

3. See Manuel Castells, *The Informational City: Information Technology, Economic Restructuring, and the Urban-Regional Process* (Oxford, U.K.: Blackwell, 1989).

4. A few examples: Trinh T. Minh-ha's *Woman Native Other* (Bloomington: Indiana University Press, 1989) and Homi Bhabha's *Location of Culture* (New York: Routledge, 1994) are pioneering "theory" texts. Scholars of African American culture have long documented the phenomena of double-coding or "signifyin(g)"; see Henry Louis Gates Jr.'s *The Signifying Monkey* (Oxford: Oxford University Press, 1988). Gloria Anzaldua's *Borderlands/La Frontera* (San Francisco: Aunt Lute, 1988) and Coco Fusco's *English Is Broken Here* (New York City: New Press, 1995) address the textual and performative construction of mestizo/a consciousness in the Americas. Dick Hebdige's *Subculture and the Meaning of Style* (London: Methuen, 1979) broke ground for (sub)cultural studies; in a Hebdige-like style, George Lipsitz's *Time Passages* (Minneapolis: University of Minnesota Press, 1990) and *Dangerous Crossroads: Popular Music, Postmodernism, and the Poetics of Place* (London: Verso, 1994) testify to the power of political resistance through cultural memory and collaboration.

5. I borrow the word "depositing" from Paulo Freire's critique of the "banking model" of education in *Pedagogy of the Oppressed* (New York: Seabury Press, 1970).

6. Iain Chambers, *Migrancy, Culture, Identity* (New York: Routledge, 1994), 5.

7. See Peter McLaren and Tomasz Tadeu da Silva, "Decentering Pedagogy: Critical Literacy, Resistance, and the Politics of Memory," in *Paulo Freire: A Critical Encounter,* ed. Peter McClaren and Peter Leonard (New York: Routledge, 1993), 47–89.

8. Henry Giroux, introduction to *Literacy: Reading the Word and the World,* by Paulo Freire and Donald Macedo (South Hadley, Mass.: Bergin and Garvey, 1987), 3.

9. Giroux, introduction to Freire and Macedo, *Literacy,* 5.

10. Richard Hoggart, *The Uses of Literacy: Changing Patterns in English Mass Culture* (Boston: Beacon Press, 1961), 238.

11. Magda Gere Lewis, *Without a Word: Teaching beyond Women's Silence* (New York: Routledge, 1993), 49.

12. Peter McLaren, *Critical Pedagogy and Predatory Culture: Oppositional Politics in a Postmodern Era* (New York: Routledge, 1995), 45.

13. Elizabeth Ellsworth, "Why Doesn't This Feel Empowering? Working through the Repressive Myths of Critical Pedagogy," in *The Education Feminism Reader,* ed. Lynda Stone (New York: Routledge, 1994), 313.

14. See Raymond Williams, *Culture and Society: 1780–1950* (New York: Columbia University Press, 1983); Raymond Williams, *Marxism and Literature* (Oxford: Oxford University Press, 1977).

15. Eric Bogosian, *Suburbia* (New York: Theater Communications Group, 1995), 116.

BETWEEN DIRTY DISHES AND POLISHED DISCOURSE

1. In *Empowering Education* (Chicago: University of Chicago Press, 1992), Ira Shor defines critical pedagogy as "a democratic curriculum examining all subjects and learn-

ing processes with systematic depth, to connect student individuality to larger historical and social issues, to encourage students to examine how their experience relates to academic knowledge, to power, and to inequality in society, and to approach received wisdom and the status quo with questions" (16–17). See also James Banks, "A Curriculum for Empowerment, Action, and Change," in *Empowerment through Multicultural Education,* ed. Christine Sleeter (Boston: Allyn and Bacon, 1991); Peter McLaren, *Life in Schools: An Introduction to Critical Pedagogy in the Foundations of Education* (New York: Longman, 1989); Stephen D. Brookfield, *Developing Critical Thinkers: Challenging Adults to Explore Alternative Ways of Thinking and Acting* (San Francisco: Jossey-Bass, 1987); and John Dewey, *Democracy and Education* (1916; reprint, New York: Free Press, 1966).

2. After ninety credits, paras can apply for a title change (from Education Associate to Auxiliary Trainer) at a slightly higher salary, but these positions are limited to one or two per school site and vacancies are rare.

3. I have taught freshman and basic writing in the paraprofessional program at Kingsborough over ten consecutive semesters. The student writing I include and the classroom descriptions and dialogue come from the fall 1992 semester, when I also kept a teaching journal to document the way I developed the first course for the paras. All the students gave me permission to use their narratives in this essay. Other than omitting repetitive texts (indicated by ellipses), I did not alter their writing.

4. See Linda Brodkey, "Writing on the Bias," *College English* 56 (Sept. 1994): 527–47; Linda Brodkey, "On the Subjects of Class and Gender in 'The Literacy Letters,'" *College English* 51 (Feb. 1989): 129–41; Lorene Cary, *Black Ice* (New York: Vintage, 1991); Keith Gilyard, *Voices of the Self* (Wayne State University Press: Detroit, 1991); Victor Villanueva, *Bootstraps: From an American Academic of Color* (Urbana, Ill.: NCTE, 1993); Mike Rose, *Lives on the Boundary* (New York: Penguin, 1990).

5. In his seminal cultural studies text, *The Uses of Literacy* (1957; reprint, New Brunswick, N.J.: Transaction Books, 1992), Richard Hoggart devoted a chapter to "The Uprooted and Anxious Scholarship Boy" of England. Hoggart's model was used by Richard Rodriguez in *Hunger of Memory* (New York: Bantam, 1982) to identify himself as a working-class student who underwent a process of cultural separation from his working-class origins as he assimilated into academic culture. Other authors in the genre include writers whose narratives appear in anthologies such as Michelle M. Tokarczyk and Elizabeth A. Fay, eds., *Working-Class Women in the Academy: Laborers in the Knowledge Factory* (Amherst: University of Massachusetts Press, 1993); C. L. Barney Dews and Carolyn Leste Law, eds., *This Fine Place So Far from Home* (Philadelphia: Temple University Press, 1995); and Janet Zandy, ed., *Liberating Memory* (New Brunswick, N.J.: Rutgers University Press, 1995).

6. See Joseph Harris, "The Idea of Community in the Study of Writing," *College Composition and Communication* 40 (1989): 19.

7. Although the demographics of this first group are largely representative of subsequent sections of freshman composition, there were many more African Americans, Haitians, and Hispanic women in my basic writing classes. Age and gender complicate the literacy narratives of the paras, but race and ethnic background complicate class and

gender. More women of color and members of other minority groups found it harder to assimilate into academic discourse than did white ethnic paras.

8. I use pseudonyms to protect the women's identities. The names attached to particular excerpts are pseudonyms students selected for themselves.

9. Generative themes grow out of student culture and express problematic conditions in daily life that are useful for generating critical discussion. Freire discusses generative themes in *Pedagogy of the Oppressed* (1970; reprint, New York: Continuum, 1990) and in *Education for Critical Consciousness* (New York: Seabury, 1973). Ira Shor also discusses the generative theme method in *Empowering Education*. For a report on the use of generative themes in a writing curriculum designed for adult women in the Bahamas, see Kyle Fiore and Nan Elsasser's "Strangers No More: A Liberatory Literacy Curriculum," *College English* 44 (Feb. 1982): 115–28. The subject of "external threats" in the narratives of working-class women writers is explored by Linda Brodkey, who reports on a study she set up ("Literacy Letters") in which teachers and working-class students corresponded. The working women wrote narratives about external threats, as opposed to the internal conflicts expressed in the narratives of middle-class women. She also found that when teachers avoided making reference to the scenes of violence in their replies, letters between the two became increasingly unsuccessful as communications.

10. Richard Hoggart observed in *The Uses of Literacy* that the core of working-class life is a sense of "the personal, the concrete, and the local . . . embodied in the idea of first, the family, and second, the neighborhood" (18). His findings are evident in the paras' narratives on family life, which are the source of their most compelling, intense, and complex writing.

11. I use a slash to link "gendered" and "classed" to emphasize the close interconnection between these two elements in constructing the paras' experiences and roles within their homes, their jobs, and the college. The gender patterns and ideologies that influence them are deeply marked by class, since gender expectations differ according to social class, just as experiences of class are deeply marked by gender. I want to be clear that the two cannot be separated, that class and gender are implicated in each other.

12. Mary Soliday, "Translating Self and Difference through Literacy Narratives," *College English* 56 (Sept. 1994): 512. Soliday considers the relevance of literacy narratives to writing pedagogy for nontraditional students: "If writers construct their interpretations of past events from the vantage point of a particular present, the life story becomes a dialogical account of one's experience rather than a chronological report of verifiable events" (514).

13. See Alice Walker, *The Color Purple* (Orlando, Fla.: Harcourt, Brace, 1982).

14. See Brodkey, "Writing on the Bias," 536. See Rodriguez, *Hunger of Memory,* 45.

15. In *Pedagogy of the Oppressed,* Freire defines the banking concept of education as "an act of depositing, in which the students are the depositories and the teacher is the depositor" (58).

16. See Rose, *Lives on the Boundary,* 188.

17. See Shor, *Empowering Education,* 20.

18. See Rose Zimbardo, "Teaching the Working Woman," in Tokarczyk and Fay,

Working-Class Women in the Academy, 209. Zimbardo discusses the dilemma she faces in adult education teaching to uncover "hidden ideologies." She says, "The paradox I encounter in assuming this approach is that while they (adult students) are often more sophisticated and aware of their history . . . they are, at the same time, unaware of the ways in which social forces that operate upon us have affected their own lives" (210). She also addresses the gendered/classed position of her adult women students, who, she says, "almost without exception come from homes where boys are thought to be more valuable than girls and in which intelligence in a woman is thought to be a social defect which should be disguised at all costs" (209).

19. See Judy Syfers, "I Want a Wife," in *The Gender Reader* (Needham Heights, Mass.: Allyn and Bacon, 1991), 341–43.

20. bell hooks, *Feminist Theory: From Margin to Center* (Boston: South End, 1984), 18.

21. Audre Lorde, "Age, Race, Class, and Sex: Women Redefining Difference," in *Sister/Outsider,* 10th ed. (Freedom, Calif.: Crossing Press, 1996), 114.

22. Ibid., 116.

23. See Carol Tarlen, "Sisters in the Flames," *Women's Studies Quarterly* 23, nos. 1 and 2 (1984): 171–72; Mary Fell, *The Persistence of Memory* (New York: Random House, 1984); Sofiya Henderson Holmes, "Rituals of Spring," *Women's Studies Quarterly* 23, nos. 1 and 2 (1994): 173–77; and Chris Llewellyn, *Fragments from the Fire: The Triangle Shirtwaist Company Fire of March 25, 1911* (Huron, Ohio: Bottom Dog Press, 1987).

24. J. Todd Erkel, "The Mighty Wedge of Class," *Utne Reader* (Nov.-Dec. 1994): 100–103. Erkel concludes that "embracing the promise of higher education requires working-class students to construct an inner sense of themselves that is radically different from their parents, siblings and friends, to betray their allegiance to the only source of identity and support they have ever known" (103).

25. David Bleich, *The Double Perspective: Language, Literacy, and Social Relations* (New York: Oxford University Press, 1988), 183–84.

26. Adrienne Rich, "Taking Women Students Seriously," in *The Gender Reader* (Needham Heights, Mass.: Allyn and Bacon, 1991), 328–36.

27. In *Women's Ways of Knowing: The Development of Self, Voice, and Mind,* ed. Mary Belenky, Blythe Clinchy, Nancy Golderburger, and Jill Tarule (New York: Basic, 1986), the authors found that "for many women, the real and valued lessons learned do not necessarily grow out of their academic work but in relationships with friends and teachers, life crises, and community involvement. . . . They conclude that women's ways of knowing conflict with what schools value and that education and clinical services, as traditionally defined and practiced, do not adequately serve the needs of women" (4).

28. See Jean Anyon, "Social Class and the Hidden Curriculum of Work," in *Rereading America: Cultural Contexts for Critical Teaching and Writing,* ed. Gary Colombo, Robert Cullen, and Bonnie Lisle (Boston: St. Martin's Press, 1992), 524–40, originally published in the *Journal of Education,* 1980, for a discussion of the characteristics of working-class school curricula.

THE SHAPE OF THE FORM

1. All students in these classes, including those whose work I cite here, signed consent forms allowing me to study their writing and use it in research. The names used here are pseudonyms.

2. Mina Shaughnessy, *Errors and Expectations* (New York: Oxford University Press, 1977), 14.

3. For example, see Sondra Perl, "The Composing Processes of Unskilled College Writers," *Research in the Teaching of English* 13 (Dec. 1979): 317–36, and her later "A Look at Basic Writers in the Process of Composing," in *Basic Writing: Essays for Teachers, Researchers, and Administrators,* ed. Lawrence Kasden and Daniel Hoeber (Urbana, Ill.: National Council of Teachers of English, 1980), 13–32; Mike Rose, *When a Writer Can't Write: Studies in Writer's Block and Other Composing Problems* (New York: Guilford, 1985), as well as numerous essays; and David Bartholomae and Anthony Petrosky, *Facts, Artifacts, and Counterfacts* (Portsmouth, N.H.: Boynton/Cook, 1986).

4. The idea that language (and, in this essay, form as well) reflects and refracts values and ideologies of cultural groups comes from the work of V. N. Voloshinov, *Marxism and the Philosophy of Language* (Cambridge, Mass.: Harvard University Press, 1986).

5. This idea incorporates theory from several sources. See, for example, James Carey, "A Cultural Approach to Communication," in his *Communication as Culture: Essays on Media and Society* (Boston: Unwin Hyman, 1989), and Benedict Anderson, *Imagined Communities,* 2d ed. (New York: Verso, 1991).

6. Lynn Z. Bloom, "Freshman Composition as a Middle-Class Enterprise," *College English* 58 (Oct. 1996): 654–75.

7. Syl Jones, "At Center of Ebonics Debate: Children's Futures," *Minneapolis Star-Tribune,* 3 Jan. 1997, A19.

8. The arrangement of these components might look different in some disciplines (for example, some social and hard science research begins with a hypothesis, discusses evidence, and concludes with results). However, since the essay employs essentially the same conventions, this difference is primarily a matter of rearranging the proverbial deck chairs. Further, the kind of expository essay described in the text is taught in most first-year composition classes.

9. Jasper Neel, *Aristotle's Voice: Rhetoric, Theory, and Writing in America* (Carbondale: Southern Illinois University Press, 1994), 6.

10. To distinguish between progressive compositionists (those working within a particular paradigm) and the Progressive Era (a period in American history), I use the lower-case *p* when referring to the compositionists.

11. Donald Stewart, "Rediscovering Fred Newton Scott," *College English* 40 (Jan. 1979): 539–47.

12. Progressive compositionists shared with other progressive educators the belief that education was vital if cultural values were to be transmitted from one generation to the next. Early in *Democracy and Education,* John Dewey made this position clear when he wrote that "society exists through a process of transmission quite as much as

biological life," but that unless all members of the society participated in this transmission [of values from one generation to the next], the society would "be permanently done for." To ensure the community's survival, therefore, members must first share the same values [passed through communication generally, and education, as a form of communication, specifically] and then act to maintain their shared agreement. For more on Progressive education and cultural survival, see Dewey, *Democracy and Education* (New York: Macmillan, 1916), 4.

13. Fred Newton Scott, "A Substitute for the Classics," in his *The Standard of American Speech and Other Papers* (Boston: Allyn and Bacon, 1926), 96.

14. Scott, "Two Ideals in Composition Teaching," ibid., 44.

15. Scott, "A Substitute for the Classics," 96.

16. This definition draws on one found in Russell Hanson, *The Democratic Imagination* (Princeton, N.J.: Princeton University Press, 1985), 60, 62–63.

17. See, for example, Robert Crunden, *Ministers of Reform* (New York: Basic Books, 1982); Eldon Eisenach, *The Lost Promise of Progressivism* (Lawrence: University of Kansas Press, 1994); Richard Hofstadter, *The Age of Reform: From Bryant to F.D.R.* (New York: Alfred A. Knopf, 1968); Jackson Lears, *No Place of Grace: Antimodernism and the Transformation of American Culture, 1880–1920* (New York: Pantheon Books, 1981); or Warren Susman, *Culture as History* (New York: Pantheon Books, 1984).

18. For more on the connections between Progressive and expressivist compositionists, see Linda Adler-Kassner, "Ownership Revisited: An Exploration in Progressive Era and Expressivist Composition Scholarship," *College Composition and Communication* 49, no. 2 (May 1998): 208–33.

19. Donald C. Stewart, "Prose with Integrity: A Primary Objective," *College Composition and Communication* 20 (Oct. 1969): 225.

20. The "students' right" resolution (as it is known) was completed in 1972 and adopted in 1974. A special issue of *College Composition and Communication* (fall 1974, 1–19) includes the resolution and a fifteen-section rationale explaining the logic behind it. Quotation from p. 1.

21. David Bartholomae, "Inventing the University," in Rose, *When a Writer Can't Write*, 135.

22. Excerpts from student essays here are abridged. *** indicates that I have omitted paragraphs from the excerpt, although the sequence of the essay has not been altered.

23. The class in which the essays discussed here were written met for five hours weekly in a room where each student had access to a computer for writing. Of the five hours of class time, about two to three hours per week were devoted to working one-on-one with other students and me. One of the aspects of composition that I emphasize most with students like this is organization—helping the readers to follow the writer's argument by pointing them through the essay with things like topic sentences. As I tell students, readers are not inside their heads—what seems really obvious to them is likely so insightful and based on their own individual processes that the readers will need to be guided through those processes in order to understand the extremely astute point the writer is making.

24. For example, in "The Tidy House: Basic Writing in the American Curriculum"

(*Journal of Basic Writing* 12, no. 1 [1993]: 4–21), Bartholomae draws on the work of Mary Louise Pratt to "imagine" a classroom different from the one he portrayed in "Inventing the University." Here, he sees "a curricular program designed not to hide differences . . . but to highlight them, to make them not only the subject of the writing curriculum, but the source of its goals and values (at least one of the versions of writing one can learn at the university)" (13). Although Bartholomae does not fully explicate this vision, it nonetheless seems more confrontationally collaborative than the one implicit in "Inventing the University."

25. Basil Bernstein, *Class, Codes, and Control,* vol. 3 (London: Routledge and Kegan Paul, 1975), 89. This does not mean that students will not or should not learn Standard English in a composition course. However, it does mean that there is room within composition courses for them to use other dialects along the way and in addition to Standard English.

26. Mina Shaughnessy, "Diving In: An Introduction to Basic Writing," *College Composition and Communication* 27 (Oct. 1976): 234–39.

WHAT KIND OF TOOLS?

1. This essay was pieced together from course notes, assignment guides, one-page instructor responses to students' final projects, brief interviews with Groups personnel, student portfolios, and course-instructor evaluations completed by students. I alone am responsible for the content of the essay.

2. In addition to Howard Zinn's excellent chapter "The Coming Revolt of the Guards," in his *A People's History of the United States* (New York: Harper Colophon, 1980), and *The Politics of History* (Boston: Beacon Press, 1970), see an interview with Zinn by Barbara Miner, "Why Should Students Study History?" in *Rethinking Our Classrooms: Teaching for Equity and Justice,* ed. Bill Bigelow et al. (Milwaukee: Rethinking Schools, Ltd., 1994). Of course, I am also indebted to the pedagogical theories and practice of Paulo Freire.

3. Though the U.S. military did not keep official statistics regarding the social class of soldiers in Viet Nam, numerous studies since the war have compiled figures from demographic samples. Many of these studies make up the statistical base of Christian Appy's *Working-Class War: American Combat Soldiers and Vietnam* (Chapel Hill: University of North Carolina Press, 1993).

4. Philip S. Foner, ed. *We, the Other People: Alternative Declarations of Independence by Labor Groups, Farmers, Woman's Rights Advocates, Socialists, and Blacks, 1829–1975* (Urbana: University of Illinois Press, 1976).

5. Godfrey Reggio, director, and Philip Glass, music, *Koyaanisqatsi: Life out of Balance* (Carmel, Calif.: Pacific Arts Video Records, 1983), videorecording, 87 min.

"JUST AMERICAN"?

1. Pat Belanoff, "The Generalized Other and Me: Working Women's Language and the Academy," *Pretext* 11, nos. 1–2 (1990): 67.

2. Richard Gambino, *Blood of My Blood: The Dilemma of the Italian-Americans* (Garden City, N.Y.: Anchor Press/Doubleday, 1974).

3. Linda Brodkey, "Writing on the Bias," *College English* 56 (Sept. 1994): 543.

4. Gambino, *Blood of My Blood,* 363.

5. Ibid., 5.

6. Ibid., 37, 92, 91.

7. Ibid., 90–91.

8. Figures are from Office of Institutional Research and Academic Affairs, *Fact Book: 1995–1996* (Borough of Manhattan Community College, City University of New York, n.d.), and one of BMCC's NSF grant applications.

9. The "initiation" theories expressed in David Bartholomae's "Inventing the University," in *Perspectives on Literacy,* ed. Eugene R. Kintgen, Barry M. Kroll, and Mike Rose (Carbondale: Southern Illinois University Press, 1988), and in Patricia Bizzell's "What Happens When Basic Writers Come to College," *College Composition and Communication* 37 (Oct. 1986): 294–301, have been challenged in recent years, although they continue to dominate policies and curricula in higher education, as my own experience shows. See Belanoff, "The Generalized Other and Me"; Peter Elbow, "Reflections on Academic Discourse," *College English* 53 (Feb. 1991): 135–55; and Keith Gilyard, *Voices of the Self: A Study of Language Competence* (Detroit, Mich.: Wayne State University Press, 1991).

10. Tom Fox, "Basic Writing as Cultural Conflict," *Journal of Education* 172, no. 1 (1990): 65–83.

11. Jane Nagle, "Social Class and School Literacy," *Radical Teacher* 44 (winter 1993): 21–23.

12. The names I use are not my students' real names.

13. David Roediger, *The Wages of Whiteness* (London: Verso, 1991), 133–63.

14. Martin Kilson, "Blacks and Neo-Ethnicity in American Political Life," in *Ethnicity: Theory and Experience,* ed. Nathan Glazer and Daniel P. Moynihan (Cambridge, Mass.: Harvard University Press, 1975), 236–66.

15. Milton Gordon, *Assimilation in American Life* (New York: Oxford University Press, 1964); J. Hector St. John de Crèvecoeur, *Letters from an American Farmer* (1782; reprint, New York: Penguin, 1981).

16. Nathan Glazer and Daniel P. Moynihan, *Beyond the Melting Pot,* 2d ed. (Cambridge, Mass.: Harvard University Press, 1975), xxxiii.

17. Susan Smulyan, "Social Class Questionnaire," *Radical Teacher* 46 (1995): 19.

TO KNOW, TO REMEMBER, TO REALIZE

1. Brooke Broadbent, "Education Needs Assessment," *Labour Education* 91, no. 2 (1993): 21; emphasis added.

2. Robert Bruno, *From Mill Gate to Front Porch: The Working-Class Life of Youngstown Steelworkers* (Ithaca, N.Y.: Cornell University Press, forthcoming).

3. *Hoffa,* directed by Danny DeVito, Twentieth Century Fox, 1992; *F.I.S.T.,* directed by Norman Jewison, United Artists, 1978.

4. Staughton Lynd, *The Fight against Shutdowns: Youngstown's Steel Mill Closings* (San Pedro, Calif.: Singlejack Books, 1983); Thomas Fuechtman, *Steeples and Stacks* (Cambridge: Cambridge University Press, 1989).

5. Oral interviews with retired steelworkers conducted by Bruno from June to August 1993 in and around Youngstown for a doctoral dissertation (to be published by Cornell University Press).

6. Notes taken from the commentator's address at the Milton Plesur History Conference, State University at Buffalo, New York, 30 Apr. 1994.

7. Conversation with John Russo at the conference "Working-Class Culture/Working-Class Lives" June 1995, sponsored by the Center for Working-Class Studies, Youngstown State University.

8. Patricia Sexton Cayo, *The War on Labor and the Left: Understanding America's Unique Conservatism* (Boulder, Colo.: Westview Press, 1991).

9. Louis Hartz, *The Liberal Tradition in America* (New York: Harcourt, Brace, 1955).

10. James V. Catano, "The Rhetoric of Masculinity: Origins, Institutions, and the Myth of the Self Made Man," *College English* 52 (Apr. 1990): 421.

11. Andrew Carnegie, *The Gospel of Wealth and Other Timely Essays* (Cambridge, Mass.: Belknap Press of Harvard University Press, 1962); Tom Girdler, *Bootstraps* (New York: Scribner's, 1943); Lee Iacocca, *Iacocca: An Autobiography* (New York: Bantam Books, 1984); William Gates, *The Road Ahead* (New York: Viking, 1995).

12. For a good survey of this kind of writing, see Francis Molson's essay "The Boy Inventor in American Series Fiction: 1900–1930," *Journal of Popular Culture* 24, no. 1 (summer 1994): 31–48.

13. Henry A. Giroux, "Literacy, Pedagogy, and the Politics of Difference," *College Literature* 19 (Feb. 1992): 7.

14. A few of our favorites are Jacquelyn Dowd Hall, James Leloudis, Robert Korstad, Mary Murphy, Lou Ann Jones, and Christopher Dail, *Like a Family: The Making of a Southern Cotton Mill World* (Chapel Hill: University of North Carolina Press, 1987); John Bodnar, *Workers' World* (Baltimore: Johns Hopkins University Press, 1982); and David Halle, *America's Working Man* (Chicago: University of Chicago Press, 1984).

15. William Serrin, *Homestead: Glory and Tragedy of an American Steel Town* (New York: New York Times Books, 1992); and John Hoerr, *And the Wolf Finally Came: The Decline of the American Steel Industry* (Pittsburgh: Pittsburgh University Press, 1988).

16. Thomas Geohagen, *Which Side Are You On?* (New York: Plume Book, 1991).

17. James Matles and James Higgins, *Them and Us: Struggles of a Rank-and-File Union* (Englewood Cliffs, N.J.: Prentice Hall, 1974); Solomon Barkin, "A Trade Unionist Appraises Management Personnel Philosophy," *Harvard Business Review* (Sept. 1950): 59–64; John Sweeney, *America Needs a Raise* (Boston: Houghton Mifflin, 1996).

18. Studs Terkel, *Working* (New York: Ballantine Books, 1974).

19. Lizabeth Cohen, *Making a New Deal: Industrial Workers in Chicago, 1919–1939* (Cambridge: Cambridge University Press, 1990).

20. *Norma Rae,* directed by Martin Ritt, CBS/FOX, 1979; *Matewan,* directed by John Sayles, Cinecom Pictures, 1987; *Silkwood,* directed by Mike Nichols, ABC Pictures, 1983; *On the Waterfront,* directed by Elia Kazan, Columbia Pictures, 1954; *Teamster Boss: The Jackie Presser Story,* directed by Alistair Reids, HBO Pictures, 1992; *Act of Vengeance,* directed by John Mckenzie, HBO Pictures, 1985; *Blue Collar,* directed by Paul Schrader, Universal Studios, 1979. Also see Peter Roffman and Jim Purdy, "The Worker and Hollywood," *Cineaste* 9, no. 1 (1995): 48–49.

21. Remarkably, out of the workers interviewed, only two had even visited the Historical Center. Bruno's father worked for thirty-seven years in the mill and after retirement did not visit the center until his son took him.

22. Archie Green has published numerous works on labor folklore and culture. His most recent is *Wobblies, Pile Butts, and Other Heroes: Laborlore Explorations* (Urbana: University of Illinois Press, 1995).

23. Paulo Freire and Donaldo Macedo, *Literacy: Reading the Word and the World* (South Hadley, Mass.: Bergin and Garvey, 1987), 39.

24. Ibid.

25. James Berlin, "Rhetoric and Ideology in the Writing Class," *College English* 50, no. 5 (Sept. 1988): 492, 479.

26. Ibid., 479.

27. It is called *Illinois Labor Works* because the events depicted and the stories told are of Illinois history. In addition, with minor exceptions all the worker voices are from Illinois.

28. See Paul Spors, *Against Itself: The Federal Theater Project and Writers' Project in the Midwest* (Detroit: Wayne State University Press, 1995).

29. AFL-CIO secretary-treasurer Richard Trumka is shown addressing a massive rally of Illinois union members in April 1996.

30. Karl Marx, "Theses on Feuerbach," in *The Marx-Engels Reader,* ed. Robert Tucker (New York: W. W. Norton, 1972), 145.

STRIKING CLOSE TO HOME

1. Peter Rachleff, *Hard-Pressed in the Heartland: The Hormel Strike and the Future of the Labor Movement* (Boston: South End Press, 1993).

2. Thomas Bell, *Out of This Furnace* (1941; reprint, Pittsburgh: University of Pittsburgh Press, 1976).

3. In recognition of the difficulty that students might face in talking about their family's money, power, and lack thereof, I gave them the option of discussing a family other than their own. All but one focused on their own family; several reported some resistance on the part of relatives to talking about their own class status.

4. Published in Paula S. Rothenberg, ed., *Racism and Sexism: An Integrated Study* (New York: St. Martin's Press, 1988).

5. Rachleff, *Hard-Pressed in the Heartland,* 125.

CRITICAL LITERACY AND THE ORGANIZING MODEL
OF UNIONISM

This article originally appeared in *Radical Teacher* 51 (summer 1997): 16–21 and is reprinted with permission.

1. Interviews ranging from twenty to forty-five minutes were conducted and transcribed over a period of one academic year (September 1995–June 1996) by two research assistants, who also observed several class sessions. All interviews were tape recorded, and most took place at the union hall, sometimes with two or three students meeting to be interviewed as a group. Additional insights about the course and the students come from our own teaching logs, observations of each other's classes, photocopies of students' work (we copied all the work produced by the classes), and our extensive, ongoing discussions about the courses with each other and with the union hall learning coordinator.

2. Catherine Walsh, ed. *Literacy as Praxis: Culture, Language, and Pedagogy* (Norwood, N.J.: Ablex, 1991), 17.

3. Dennis Brubaker, "From the President's Desk," *Warren Steelworker* 2, no. 1 (June 1995): 2.

4. See "Steel Museum to Host 'SWOC Years 1937–42,'" *Warren Steelworker* 2, no. 1 (June 1995): 1.

5. Of course, we remind students that participants' testimony in oral histories can be just as conflicting (or even as inaccurate) as traditional approaches to labor history and business unionism. Nevertheless, Brecher's *History from Below: How to Uncover and Tell the Story of Your Community, Association, or Union* (New Haven, Conn.: Advocate, 1988) provides a methodological framework that promotes the development of basic and historical research skills and the strengthening of participatory and community unionism.

6. Vincent Ryan Ruggiero, *Beyond Feelings: A Guide to Critical Thinking* (Mountain View, Calif.: Mayfield Publishing, 1995).

7. See David Brody, "The Origins of Modern Steel Unionism," in *Forging a Union of Steel: Philip Murray, SWOC, and the United Steelworkers,* ed. Paul F. Clark, Peter Gottlieb, and Donald Kennedy (Ithaca, N.Y.: ILR Press, 1987), 13–29; Gus Hall, *Working Class USA: The Power and the Movement* (New York: International Publishers, 1987); and Tom Girdler, *Bootstraps* (New York: Scribner's, 1943).

8. David Bartholomae and Anthony Petrosky, eds. *Ways of Reading: An Anthology for Writers* (Boston: Bedford, 1996), 11.

9. Mike Rose, "Remedial Writing Courses: A Critique and a Proposal," in *A Sourcebook for Basic Writing Teachers,* ed. Theresa Enos (New York: Random House, 1987), 331.

10. For further discussion of the gains and losses education often brings to working-class and minority students, see, for example, Mike Rose's *Lives on the Boundary: A Moving Account of Achievements of America's Educational Underclass* (New York: Penguin, 1990); Richard Rodriguez's *Hunger of Memory: The Education of Richard*

Rodriguez: An Autobiography (Boston: Godine, 1981); Janet Zandy's *Liberating Memory: Our Work and Our Working-Class Consciousness* (New Brunswick, N.J.: University Press, 1995).

TELLING TOIL

I would like to thank my colleague Mark Hussey for his suggestions regarding this essay.

1. Morris Dickstein, "Hallucinating the Past: *Jews without Money* Revisited," *Grand Street* 9 (winter 1989): 155.
2. See Nicholas Coles, "Democratizing Literature: Issues in Teaching Working-Class Literature," *College English* 48 (Nov. 1986): 664.
3. Patricia Dobler, "Steel Poem, 1912," 59; David Ignatow, "The Boss," 110; Lorna Dee Cervantes, "Cannery Town in August," 37; and Jim Daniels, "Factory Jungle," 47; all in *Working Classics: Poems on Industrial Life,* ed. Peter Oresick and Nicholas Coles (Urbana: University of Illinois Press, 1990).
4. See Steven Fraser, *Labor Will Rule: Sidney Hillman and the Rise of American Labor* (Ithaca, N.Y.: Cornell University Press, 1991), xiii.
5. Coles, "Democratizing Literature," 668.
6. Richard Slotkin, *Regeneration through Violence: The Mythology of the American Frontier, 1600–1860* (Middletown, Conn.: Wesleyan University Press, 1973), 23.
7. Carolyn Heilbrun, "The Masculine Wilderness of the American Novel," *Saturday Review,* 29 Jan. 1972, 41.
8. Coles, "Democratizing Literature," 672.
9. Victoria Byerly, ed., *Hard Times Cotton Mill Girls: Personal Histories of Womanhood and Poverty in the South* (Ithaca, N.Y.: ILR Press of Cornell University, 1986).
10. Ibid., 81.
11. Ibid., 35.
12. Catherine Gallagher, "Workers," *University Publishing* 1 (summer 1978): 1, 5.
13. Andria Taylor Hourwich and Gladys L. Palmer, eds., *I Am a Woman Worker: A Scrapbook of Autobiographies* (1936; reprint, New York: Arno Press/New York Times, 1974).
14. Ibid., unpaginated.
15. Gallagher, "Workers," 5.

FILMS OF AND FOR A WORKING-CLASS WORLD

1. George A. Huaco, *The Sociology of Film Art* (New York: Basic Books, 1965), 157, 159, 161–62.
2. *New York Times,* 9 Dec. 1996.
3. I am always interested in expanding the selection of films beyond those included in this essay or in Tom Zaniello, *Working Stiffs, Union Maids, Reds, and Riffraff: An Organized Guide to Films about Labor* (Ithaca: ILR/Cornell University Press, 1996). Please contact me at tzaniello@nku.edu if you have suggestions of films that should be added.

TEACHING WORKING-CLASS LITERATURE

1. The definition of working-class literature, one of the major critical issues in the emerging field of working-class literary studies, is beyond the scope of what I am addressing here; the issue here is simply what would have worked best in this particular course.

2. I identified the class positions of the writers of these definitions not only through the definitions themselves, but through subsequent information revealed in class discussions, essays, and private conversations.

3. A couple of years before I taught my first working-class literature course, I was present at a literature board party where two graduate students were discussing a women's studies course in which students were encouraged to discuss their own experience in relation to the course texts. A senior professor of classics declared that he never wanted to hear students discuss their experience in his classroom, because it was simply never relevant to literary analysis.

4. I do not believe courses in working-class literature are the only way to provide this sort of holistic learning experience. I believe many courses in ethnic literatures, women's studies, or any sort of multicultural issues also frequently do so.

5. Deb Busman, "Representations of 'Intelligence': A Look at the Workings of Bias in Life and Literature," *Women's Studies Quarterly* 26 (spring 1998): 1–2.

6. I do not mean to suggest that working-class students are incapable of abstraction. What I am really referring to is a discourse community (represented here by UCSC) that deals extensively, practically exclusively, in theoretical abstraction and privileges analysis over narration.

CLASS, RACE, AND CULTURE

1. K. Anthony Appiah, "Identity, Authenticity, Survival: Multiculturalism, Societies and Social Reproduction," in *Multiculturalism: Examining the Politics of Recognition,* ed. Charles Taylor and Amy Gutman (Princeton, N.J.: Princeton University Press, 1994), 160.

2. Grace L. Boggs, "Beyond Eurocentrism," *Monthly Review* 41 (1990): 12–18.

3. James B. White, *Hercules' Bow: Essays on the Rhetoric of Poetics and Law* (Madison: University of Wisconsin Press, 1985), 45.

4. Constance Coiner, "Introduction," *Radical Teacher* 46 (1995): 2.

5. Fred E. Jandt, *Intercultural Communication: An Introduction* (Thousand Oaks, Calif.: Sage Publications, 1995), 11.

6. Richard McKeon, *Introduction to Aristotle* (New York: Modern Library, 1947), 621.

7. Sonja K. Foss, Karen A. Foss, and Robert Trapp, *Contemporary Perspectives on Rhetoric* (Prospect Heights, Ill.: Waveland Press, 1991), 14.

8. Sonja K. Foss, *Rhetorical Criticism: Exploration and Practice* (Prospect Heights, Ill.: Waveland Press, 1989), 4.

9. Ibid.

10. Tarla R. Peterson, "Telling the Farmers' Story: Competing Responses to Soil Conservation Rhetoric," *Quarterly Journal of Speech* 77 (1991): 298–308; George B. Ray, "Sex Roles in Speech Events in an Appalachian Community," in *Communication, Gender, and Sex Roles in Diverse Interaction,* ed. Lea Stewart and Stella Ting-Toomey (Norwood, N.J.: Alex, 1987), 161–78.

11. Bradford J. Hall, "Theories of Culture and Communication," *Communication Theory* 11 (1992): 52.

12. Gerry Philipsen, *Speaking Culturally: Explorations in Social Communication* (Albany: State University of New York Press, 1992), 248.

13. Jandt, *Intercultural Communication,* 13.

14. Elliot Liebow, *Tally's Corner: A Study of Negro Streetcorner Men* (New York: Little, Brown, 1967); Gerry Philipsen, "Speaking Like a Man in Teamsterville: Cultural Patterns of Role Enactment in an Urban Environment," *Quarterly Journal of Speech* 61 (1975): 16.

15. Philipsen, "Teamsterville," 16.

16. Liebow, *Tally's Corner,* 24.

17. Philipsen, "Teamsterville," 23.

18. James W. Carey, *Communication as Culture: Essays on Media and Society* (Boston: Unpin Amman, 1988).

19. John Fiske, "For Cultural Interpretation: A Study of the Culture of the Homelessness," *Critical Studies in Mass Communication* 8 (1991): 322, 323.

20. Don C. Shields and Vince V. Kidd, "Teaching through Popular Film: A Small Group Analysis of the *Poseidon Adventure*," *Speech Teacher* 22 (1973): 203.

21. William B. Gudyskunst, Stella Ting-Toomey, and Richard L. Wiseman, "Taming the Beast: Designing a Course in Intercultural Communication," *Communication Theory* 40 (1991): 247–72.

22. Douglass Ehninger, "On Systems of Rhetoric," *Philosophy and Rhetoric* 1 (1968): 137.

23. Kendall R. Philips, "The Spaces of Public Dissension: Reconsidering the Public Sphere," *Communication Monographs* 63 (1996): 233. Philips defines the public sphere as "an open space in which impartial citizens come to intersubjective understanding through reasoned discussions of public issues and attempt to compel authorities to action. The spheres emphasis on openness, common issues, impartiality, intersubjectivity, and rationality are procedural manifestations of the underlying centrality of consensus in social rhetoric" (233).

24. Eugene J. Dionne, *Why Americans Hate Politics* (New York: Simon and Schuster, 1991), 53.

IMMIGRANT FICTION, WHITE STUDENTS, AND MULTICULTURAL EMPATHY

I would like to thank the members of my immigrant literature courses during the academic year 1995–96, not only for their participation in the classes but also for their generous help in providing important information and for giving their permission to use quotations from their papers.

1. *Enrollment and Degrees Granted Report* (Cortland, N.Y.: State University of New York, Cortland, 1996), table 2.

2. See *Enrollment and Degrees Granted,* tables 15 and 11.

3. Hector St. Jean de Crèvecoeur, "What Is an American," in *American Literature,* ed. Emory Elliott, Linda K. Kerber, A. Walton Litz, and Terence Martin, vol. 1 (Englewood Cliffs, N.J.: Prentice Hall, 1991), 499.

4. Sherry Linkon and Bill Mullen, "Gender, Race, and Place: Teaching Working-Class Students in Youngstown," *Radical Teacher* 46 (1995): 28.

5. Crèvecoeur, "What Is an American," 499.

6. Billie Wright Dziech, "Coping with the Alienation of White Male Students," *Chronicle of Higher Education* 13 (Jan. 1995): B2.

7. Mary Doyle Curran, *The Parish and the Hill* (1948; reprint, New York: Feminist Press, 1986), 26–27.

8. Noel Ignatiev, *How the Irish Became White* (New York: Routledge, 1995).

9. Sandra Stotsky, "All of Us Have Come to America: Broadening Student Understanding of the American Ethnic Experience," *American Educator* 19, no. 3 (fall 1995): 36.

TEACHING THE CONVERGENCE OF RACE AND CLASS

1. Actually, most critics do attribute the idea's origin to William Petersen; but Glenn Omatsu writes that "the model minority stereotype first arose in the late 1950s." "The 'Four Prisons' and the Movements of Liberation: Asian American Activism from the 1960s to the 1990s," in *The State of Asian America: Activism and Resistance in the 1990s,* ed. Karin Aguilar–San Juan (Boston: South End Press, 1994), 65.

2. Roger Daniels briefly and helpfully explains the appropriateness of the term *concentration camps* — and of President Roosevelt's own application of the term to Japanese Americans. See "The Conference Keynote Address: Relocation, Redress, and the Report — A Historical Appraisal," in *Japanese Americans: From Relocation to Redress,* ed. Roger Daniels, Sandra C. Taylor, and Harry H. L. Kitano, 2d ed. (Seattle: University of Washington Press, 1991), 6.

3. William Petersen, "Success Story, Japanese-American Style," *New York Times Magazine,* 9 Jan. 1966, 21.

4. Martin Kasindorf, "Asian-Americans: A 'Model Minority,'" *Newsweek,* 6 Dec. 1982, 51.

5. Ibid., 39.

6. The senator exhorted a group of workers to "draw a mushroom cloud and put underneath it: 'Made in America by lazy and illiterate Americans and tested in Japan.'" *New York Times,* 4 Mar. 1992, A12.

7. Is it any wonder that golfer Tiger Woods is better known for his African lineage

than for his Asian (Thai) lineage? Mainstream culture perceives an African American golf star as more "exotic," more anomalous.

8. As for the 1992 presidential election, Lane Ryo Hirabayashi and Marilyn Alquizola report that "the vast majority (almost 70 percent) of the Asian American electorate supported either Bush or Perot." "Asian American Studies: Reevaluating for the 1990s," in Aguilar–San Juan, *The State of Asian America,* 359. As for affirmative action, the *New York Times* dedicated the cover story of a special Education Life supplement to the issues splitting Asian American students between those who support it for political and moral reasons and those who openly declare that they would fare better without it. Norimitsu Onishi, "Affirmative Action: Choosing Sides," *New York Times* Education Life Supplement, 31 Mar. 1996, 26–29, 32–35.

9. Wataru Ebihara, "Aftermath of 209," E-mail to Asian American Graduate and Professional Students Organization, 21 Nov. 1996.

10. Quoted in ibid.

11. Lisa Lowe, *Immigrant Acts: On Asian American Cultural Politics* (Durham, N.C.: Duke University Press, 1996), 7.

12. Ibid., 73.

13. Evelyn Nakano Glenn, *Issei, Nisei, War Bride: Three Generations of Japanese American Women in Domestic Service* (Philadelphia: Temple University Press, 1986), xiv–xv.

14. Edna Bonacich, "Asians in the Los Angeles Garment Industry," in *The New Asian Immigration in Los Angeles and Global Restructuring,* ed. Paul Ong, Edna Bonacich, and Lucie Cheng (Philadelphia: Temple University Press, 1994), 138.

15. Ibid., 158.

16. Frank McCourt, *Angela's Ashes* (New York: Scribner's, 1996), 29.

17. Joann Faung Jean Lee, *Asian Americans: Oral Histories of First to Fourth Generation Americans from China, the Philippines, Japan, India, the Pacific Islands, Vietnam, and Cambodia* (New York: New Press, 1992), xii, 217.

18. Sucheng Chan, ed., *Hmong Means Free: Life in Laos and America* (Philadelphia: Temple University Press, 1994); and Elaine H. Kim and Eui-Young Yu, *East to America: Korean American Life Stories* (New York: New Press, 1996).

19. Aguilar–San Juan, *The State of Asian America.*

20. See Minatoya's *Talking to High Monks in the Snow: An Asian American Odyssey* (New York: HarperCollins, 1992); Hongo's *Volcano: A Memoir of Hawaii* (New York: Knopf, 1995); and Mura's *Turning Japanese: Memoirs of a Sansei* (New York: Atlantic Monthly, 1991).

21. Yoshiko Uchida, *Desert Exile: The Uprooting of a Japanese-American Family* (Seattle: University of Washington Press, 1982), 59.

22. Monica Sone, *Nisei Daughter,* 2d ed. (Seattle: University of Washington Press, 1973), 166.

23. Hisaye Yamamoto, *"Seventeen Syllables" and Other Stories* (Latham, N.Y.: Kitchen Table: Women of Color Press, 1988).

24. Carlos Bulosan, *America Is in the Heart* (New York: Harcourt, Brace, 1946;

reprint, Seattle: University of Washington Press, 1973). E. San Juan Jr., introduction to *On Becoming Filipino: Selected Writings of Carlos Bulosan,* ed. E. San Juan Jr. (Philadelphia: Temple University Press, 1995), 12.

25. Jean Fong Kwok, "Disguises," *Story* (winter 1997), 106.

26. Ronald Takaki, *Strangers from a Different Shore: A History of Asian Americans* (Boston: Little, Brown, 1989); and Sucheng Chan, *Asian Americans: An Interpretive History* (Boston: Twayne, 1991).

27. U.S. Bureau of the Census, Statistical Brief, *Asian and Pacific Islander Americans: A Profile* (Washington, D.C.: GPO, 1993).

28. U.S. Bureau of the Census, Current Population Reports, P20-459, *The Asian and Pacific Islander Population in the United States: March 1991 and 1990,* by Claudette E. Bennett (Washington, D.C.: GPO, 1992), 41.

29. U.S. Bureau of the Census, *We the American Asians* (Washington, D.C.: GPO, 1993), 4.

30. Ibid., 4, 6.

31. Ibid., 4, 6, 7.

32. Census, Current Population Reports, 2.

33. Lee, *Asian Americans,* 55.

34. Susan B. Gall and Timothy L. Gall, eds., *Statistical Record of Asian Americans* (Detroit: Gale Research, 1993), 282.

35. Census, Current Population Reports, 27, 30.

36. Gall and Gall, *Statistical Record,* 297.

37. Lowe, *Immigrant Acts,* 9.

38. Anji Malhotra, "Asian American Labor Activism," E-mail to Oliver Wang, forwarded, 19 Dec. 1996.

39. Quoted in Paul Rockwell, "Asian American Voices for Affirmative Action," 1996. Current address, http://www.cts.com/browse/publish/rockasn.html.

40. Ibid.

41. Rey Chow, *Writing Diaspora: Tactics of Intervention in Contemporary Cultural Studies* (Bloomington, Ind.: Indiana University Press, 1993), 115.

DIFFICULT DIALOGUES

Special thanks to Sherry Linkon for her revision and editing suggestions during all phases of the writing of this essay. Without her assistance and incredible patience, this essay would never have seen the light of day.

1. Constance Coiner, "Introduction," *Radical Teacher* 46 (spring 1995): 2.

2. Constance Coiner, "Course Syllabus: Multicultural Women Writers of the United States," Department of English, General Literature, and Rhetoric. State University of New York, Binghamton, 1996, 1.

3. See *Radical Teacher* 46 (spring 1995) for two additional perspectives on Constance's course on multicultural women writers. In "A Response to Pam Annas: Using Undergraduate Teaching Assistants," Marjorie Feld writes about her experience as an

undergraduate teaching assistant for Constance (17–19). In "Class in the Classroom: Transcription of an American Studies Workshop," Constance illuminates a pivotal teaching experience in one of her courses on multicultural women writers (46–48).

4. SUNY Binghamton linked courses are organized through the Educational Opportunity Program (EOP) and are open to all students regardless of EOP status. Students enroll in two writing-emphasis courses "linked" through a pedagogical commitment made by the instructors, who then discuss the course with EOP directors Steve Duarte and Susie Williams in weekly curriculum coordination meetings.

The Educational Opportunity Program provides counseling, tutorial assistance, financial aid, and other services to students from educationally and financially disadvantaged backgrounds who, despite these disadvantages, demonstrate the potential to complete college. The cut-off income for a family of four (according to the Program's financial guidelines) is $23,000 a year.

5. Judith Newton and Deborah Rosenfelt, "Introduction: Toward a Materialist-Feminist Criticism," in *Feminist Criticism and Social Change: Sex, Class, and Race in Literature and Culture,* ed. Newton and Rosenfelt (New York: Methuen, 1985), xxiii.

6. James H. Kavanagh, "Ideology," in *Critical Terms for Literary Study,* ed. Frank Letricchia and Thomas McLaughlin (Chicago: University of Chicago Press, 1990, 1995), 310.

7. This idea is perhaps best explained in the work of adult educator Paulo Freire. Freire explains that to make connections between individual lived experience and the systems of oppression within which these experiences occur, a reader must connect the word of the text to the lived world: "Reading is not exhausted merely by decoding the written world or written language, but rather anticipated by and extending into knowledge of the world. Reading the world precedes reading the word, and the subsequent reading of the word cannot dispense with continually reading the world. Language and reality are dynamically intertwined. The understanding attained by critical reading of a text implies perceiving the relationship between text and context." "The Importance of the Act of Reading," in *Rewriting Literacy: Culture and the Discourse of the Other,* ed. Candace Mitchell and Kathleen Weiler (New York: Bergin and Garvey, 1991), 139.

8. Bish Sen, "Identity and Difference," *Forum* (a SUNY Binghamton publication) 4, no. 4 (Mar. 1991): 9.

9. Newton and Rosenfelt, "Introduction," xvi.

10. Newton and Rosenfelt explain this as follows: "Lillian Robinson once said that the most important question we can ask ourselves as feminist critics is 'So what?' Implied in that question is a view most of us share — that the point of our work is to change the world. But to begin with the question 'So what?' is to take on the task of asking other questions as well — like what is the relation of literature and therefore of literary criticism to the social and economic conditions of our lives?" "Introduction," xv.

11. Students in the linked section tended to think that they were studying literature of their own cultures to "celebrate" their difference and were reading literature of other people of color to learn more about that particular culture. These students were not sure what to do with literature about the white working class, as will be shown in subsequent

sections, because there was not anything to "celebrate." Students in the traditional section believed they were reading texts of "other" cultures to learn to be more tolerant of difference. The middle-class and upper-middle-class students especially tended not to see their own cultures as cultures and certainly did not believe they had anything to "celebrate."

12. An excellent resource for thinking through the concept of home and its relationship to working-class studies and women's writings is Janet Zandy's *Calling Home: Working-Class Women's Writings* (New Brunswick, N.J.: Rutgers University Press, 1993).

13. Newton and Rosenfelt, "Introduction," xix.

14. In an effort to manipulate, parody, and "expose" the talk show format, the students decided to develop a "heteroglossic" ending, one that would "resis[t] the dominance of monologism by fragmenting and disrupting it." Constance Coiner, " 'No One's Private Ground': A Bakhtinian Reading of Tillie Olsen's *Tell Me a Riddle,*" in *Listening to Silences,* ed. Elaine Hedges and Shelley Fisher Fishkin (New York: Oxford University Press, 1994), 72, reprinted from *Feminist Studies* 18, no. 2 (summer 1992): 257–81.

15. Barbara Epstein, "Political Correctness and Identity Politics," in *Beyond PC: Toward a Politics of Understanding,* ed. Patricia Aufderheide (Saint Paul, Minn.: Graywolf Press, 1992), 152.

16. Newton and Rosenfelt, "Introduction," xv.

17. Carolyn Forché, "A Lesson in Commitment," *Tri-Quarterly* (winter, 1986): 30–38.

18. Michael Lind, "To Have and Have Not: Notes on the Progress of the American Class War," *Harper's,* June 1995: 35–47.

19. In a final paper for the course, Constance asked students to write an essay on at least two texts we had read during the semester and to think through some ways that class analysis might be a unifying element among diverse cultural groups. She prefaced the essay question with a summary of her thoughts on class studies: "While many university students of color proudly identify themselves with their particular cultural group, few students of working-class origin readily announce — or, in some cases, even recognize — themselves as such. This obfuscation of class has consequences within the academy, forestalling alliances across identities of race, culture, gender, and sexuality among scholars and among our students. We do not recognize our shared interests as 'ordinary' Americans." "Course Take-Home Paper: Multicultural Women Writers of the United States," Department of English, General Literature, and Rhetoric. State University of New York, Binghamton, 1996, 3.

20. Fusco is quoted in David R. Roediger, *Towards the Abolition of Whiteness: Essays on Race, Politics, and Working Class History* (New York: Verso, 1994), 12.

21. Hazel V. Carby, "The Multicultural Wars," in *Black Popular Culture,* ed. Gina Dent (Seattle: Bay Press, 1992), 187–99; bell hooks, *Outlaw Culture: Resisting Representations* (New York: Routledge, 1994).

22. Sen, "Identity and Difference," 9.

CONTRIBUTORS

LINDA ADLER-KASSNER is an assistant professor of composition at the University of Michigan, Dearborn, where her teaching and research focus on the relationship between student and academic literacies, past and present, including the relationship between Progressive Era composition textbooks and the culture of that period. She is coeditor of *Writing the Community: Concepts and Models for Service-Learning in Composition* (AAHE/NCTE, 1997) and author of numerous articles on composition and literacy.

ANNE ARONSON is an associate professor in the writing department at Metropolitan State University, Saint Paul, Minnesota. She teaches composition, professional writing, and women's studies. Her research interests include feminist approaches to composition, basic writing, adult development, and the material conditions for composing. Her articles have appeared in *Women's Studies Quarterly, Frontiers, Research and Teaching in Developmental Education,* and other journals.

KELLY BELANGER is an associate professor of English at the University of Wyoming and teaches courses in composition and rhetoric. She has published articles on basic writing, gender and writing, business communication, and critical literacy. She is currently working with Linda Strom on a book entitled *Crafting Resistance: Teaching Writing to Working Adults.*

JOANNA BROOKS is a Charlotte W. Newcombe fellow and a doctoral candidate in

English at the University of California, Los Angeles. Her dissertation focuses on the relationship between early American religious culture and the advent of literary production by African Americans, Native Americans, and working-class women. Her poetry, short fiction, and critical essays have appeared in a number of literary journals.

ROBERT BRUNO, who holds a Ph.D. in political science from New York University and a Labor Studies Certificate from Cornell University, is an assistant professor of labor and industrial relations at the University of Illinois. His book, *From Mill Gate to Front Porch: The Working-Class Life of Youngstown Steelworkers,* is forthcoming from Cornell University Press; he has also published numerous articles on labor history and labor studies.

FERN CAYETANO is a senior at the University of California, Los Angeles. She has also completed the Woodrow Wilson Program in Public Policy in Washington, D.C. Her research and activism center around urban education.

RENNY CHRISTOPHER teaches American literature at California State University, Stanislaus, and works as a horse wrangler in national parks during the summer. Her book *The Viet Nam War/The American War* was published by the University of Massachusetts Press in 1995, and her poetry collection, *Longing Fervently for Revolution,* by Slipstream Press in 1998.

TERRY EASTON is pursuing a Ph.D. in American studies in the Graduate Institute of the Liberal Arts at Emory University. His teaching and research interests include working-class culture and history, disability studies, and the novel as a literary form.

ANTHONY ESPOSITO is an assistant professor in the speech and communication studies department at Edinboro University of Pennsylvania, where he teaches interpersonal and small-group communication, public speaking, and argumentation and debate. His research interests include political communication and the intersection of culture, class, and communication.

EILEEN FERRETTI earned a doctorate at the Graduate School and University Center of the City of New York in 1998. Her dissertation, "Not Scholarship Girls: Recomposing the Lives of Adult Working-Class Women through Literacy Narratives," examines the impact of domestic and work identities on the education process of a group of adult working-class women. She is an assistant professor of English at Kingsborough Community College of the City University of New York.

ELIZABETH A. GRANT has been teaching on the college level for twenty-three years. She earned her Doctor of Arts in English from St. John's University in 1996 and is an assistant professor of English at the State University of New York, Morrisville. Her reviews and essays have appeared in *Central New York Environment* and *Studies in American Indian Literature.*

Contributors

ANN E. GREEN earned a Ph.D. from the State University of New York, Albany. Her dissertation examined the rhetoric of the personal, social class, and the teaching of writing. Her essay "Selling Out: Reflections of a Farm Daughter" appears in *Calyx's* special anniversary issue on young women writers, and another essay is forthcoming in *Concerns*, the publication of the Women's Caucus of the Modern Language Association. She is an assistant professor of English and director of the writing center at St. Joseph's University.

RICHARD GREENWALD, an assistant professor of history at the State University of New York, Morrisville, received his Ph.D. in American history from New York University in 1998. His reviews and essays have appeared in the *Journal of Policy History,* the *Journal of Social History, Labor History,* the *Radical History Review,* and *Labor's Heritage.*

LAURA HAPKE is professor of English at Pace University in New York and the author of three books and numerous articles on labor fiction and its historical context, including *Daughters of the Great Depression: Women, Work, and Fiction in the American 1930s* (University of Georgia Press, 1995). She is currently writing a book about workers in American literature.

JOSEPH HEATHCOTT, who grew up on the southern edge of the rustbelt, in Evansville, Indiana, holds a B.A. in history from Washington University in St. Louis and an M.A. in history from Indiana University, Bloomington. He has taught skills-linked courses in a variety of institutional and geographic settings. Currently he is a writer, a community activist, and a doctoral student at Indiana University. His primary research interests are in labor and urban history, particularly in the formation of working-class cultures and communities, both in the United States and internationally.

COLETTE A. HYMAN teaches history and women's studies at Winona State University in Winona, Minnesota. Her book, *Staging Strikes: Workers' Theatre and the American Labor Movement in the Twentieth Century* (Temple University Press), appeared in 1997. She is coeditor of a special issue of *Women's Studies Quarterly* on women's studies and activism, and she is currently at work on a project on divorce and domestic violence from 1890 to 1930.

CHARLES JOHANNINGSMEIER is the author of *Fiction and the American Literary Marketplace: The Rule of Newspaper Syndicates, 1860–1900* (Cambridge University Press, 1997). He is an assistant professor of English at the University of Nebraska, Omaha.

LISA JORDAN received her Ph.D. in labor economics at the University of Notre Dame. Currently the director of Gender and Diversity Programming in the Labor Education Service at the University of Minnesota, she does research in the areas of contingent employment, lean production, and feminist pedagogy.

Contributors

SHERRY LEE LINKON is a professor of English and coordinator of the American studies program at Youngstown State University. She is also a founding member of the university's Center for Working-Class Studies. She has edited books on 1930s culture and nineteenth-century American women essayists and is currently working with John Russo on *My Sweet Jenny: Work, Representation, and Erasure in a Working-Class Community,* a study of ideas about work and the loss of work focusing on Youngstown's steel industry.

JENNIFER LUTZENBERGER is a Ph.D. candidate and an instructor in literature and rhetoric at the State University of New York, Binghamton. Her dissertation explores the role of multicultural literature and pedagogy in resistant political practice. She is the coauthor of the instructor's guide to *Against the Current* (Prentice Hall, 1998).

CAROLINE PARI is an assistant professor of English at the Borough of Manhattan Community College, part of the City University of New York system. She specializes in composition and rhetoric and has edited with Ira Shor three volumes of essays on critical pedagogy: *Critical Literacy in Action* and volumes one and two of *Education and Politics* (Heinemann/Boynton-Cook, forthcoming).

JOHN RUSSO is director of the Center for Working-Class Studies and Coordinator of the Labor Studies Program at Youngstown State University. He has published widely on labor and social issues.

JOHN STREAMAS has published critical and journalistic essays on Japanese American literature and culture in *A Gathering of Voices on the Asian American Experience* and *Ethnicity and the American Short Story.* A doctoral student in American culture studies at Bowling Green State University, a teacher in ethnic studies, and a fiction writer, his main research interest is the politics of narrativizing Japanese American internment.

LINDA STROM is an associate professor of English at Youngstown State University where she specializes in working-class studies and serves as coordinator of workforce education. With Kelly Belanger, she is currently completing *Crafting Resistance: Teaching Writing to Working Adults.*

TOM ZANIELLO has published *Working Stiffs, Union Maids, Reds, and Riffraff: An Organized Guide to Films about Labor* with ILR/Cornell University Press. He is a professor of English and director of the Honors Program at Northern Kentucky University and a visiting professor at the National Labor College of the AFL-CIO, specializing in film studies.

INDEX